The Complete
VALLEY OF THE KINGS

Tombs and Treasures of Egypt's Greatest Pharaohs

532 illustrations, 76 in colour

NICHOLAS REEVES • RICHARD H. WILKINSON

BCA

LONDON NEW YORK SYDNEY TORONTO

Half-title: *Osiris, Foremost of the Westerners. Seen here in a depiction in the tomb of Tuthmosis IV, the chief netherworld deity played a leading role in royal afterlife ideology in New Kingdom times.* Title pages: *View of the main, eastern branch of the Valley of the Kings.* Contents pages: *Tuthmosis IV rides in his chariots: details, after drawings by Howard Carter, of the plaster-relief decoration on the king's chariot, found in his tomb.*

A note on spellings

Because the hieroglyphs preserve no more than the consonantal skeleton of the Egyptian language, the ancient pronunciation cannot usually be established. For this reason, Egyptian names exhibit a variety of modern spellings, and are often based upon the Greek form rather than the Egyptian. For example, Amenophis I and Sethos I are here employed as the preferred spellings, but other versions of these kings' names exist – such as Amenhotep I and Seti I; these variants have been retained where appropriate in book titles and quotations.

The Egyptian seasons: *akhet* – inundation; *peret* – winter; *shemu* – summer.

This edition published 1996
by BCA by arrangement with
Thames and Hudson Ltd

Reprinted 1997

© 1996 Thames and Hudson Ltd, London
Text © 1996 Nicholas Reeves and Richard H. Wilkinson
The right of Nicholas Reeves and Richard H. Wilkinson to be identified as authors of this work has been asserted by them in accordance with the Copyright, Designs and Patents Act 1988

CN 9796

Printed and bound in Slovenia by Mladinska Knjiga

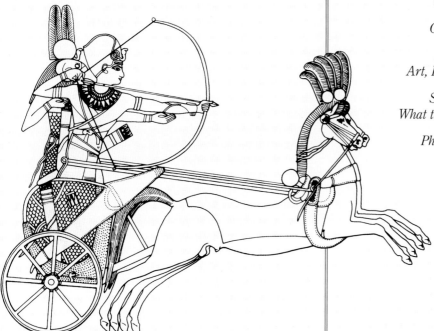

I
PREPARATIONS FOR THE AFTERLIFE

*'Osiris ... Great is the awe of him
in the hearts of men, spirits and
the dead ... and many are his
shapes in the Pure Place.'*

Book of the Dead, Spell 185

II
AGENTS OF DISCOVERY

III
TOMBS OF THE KINGS

IV
DECLINE OF A ROYAL
NECROPOLIS

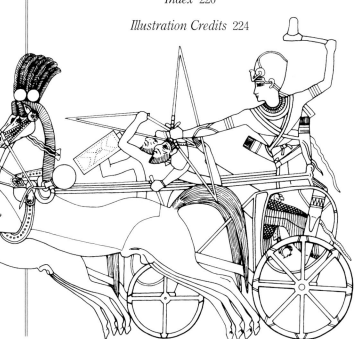

Introduction

Tutankhamun's gold mask, the icon of valley studies – 10.23 kg of thick sheet gold, inlaid with glass, faience and semi-precious stones.

(Opposite) Ramesses I makes an offering to Nefertum: a detail from the king's painted burial chamber in KV16.

Wadi Biban el-Muluk – better known today as the Valley of the Kings – has excited the interest and imagination of countless visitors over thousands of years, and for one reason: it stands without equal as the most magnificent burial ground the world has ever seen. Here, during the second half of the 2nd millennium BC, in a dried-up river valley dominated by a natural, pyramid-shaped peak sacred to the goddess Hathor, Egyptian workers toiled in the desert heat to quarry a series of tombs of extraordinary beauty and awesome scale. The walls of these sepulchres were decorated from top to bottom with mysterious guides to the underworld, and their chambers filled to overflowing with treasures of ritual and daily life. This valley was to be a repository for the mortal remains of the New Kingdom's greatest rulers; and as the cemetery of Pharaoh, intercessor between gods and humankind, it was among Egypt's most sacred sites.

The massive red granite lid of the sarcophagus of Ramesses III, showing the mummified figure of the king supported by the two 'kites', Isis and Nephthys.

Fortune favours, it possesses an extraordinary capacity to surprise. In the decades following 1898, when excavation began in earnest, the valley was rarely out of the news, spotlit by a whole series of breathtaking discoveries of kings and courtiers. The madness culminated one late afternoon in November 1922 with those 'wonderful things' which were caught in the glow of Lord Carnarvon and Howard Carter's flickering candle.

Carnarvon and Carter's prize was the burial of a minor boy-king, Tutankhamun (p. 122), the all-but-forgotten son of the heretic pharaoh Akhenaten: a burial stuffed to bursting with 'gold – everywhere the glint of gold'. Because of this vast show of wealth, 70 years after the discovery Tutankhamun remains the valley's most famous son. Yet his burial was but one among many; some 80 and more tombs and pits are currently known in the royal wadi, and it is no exaggeration to say that the tombs of any of the *truly* great kings of Egypt – Tuthmosis III (p. 97), Amenophis III (p. 110), Sethos I (p. 137), Ramesses II, 'the Great' (p. 140) – would have put the child-pharaoh to shame.

After three millennia of plunder, exploration and tourism, the bullion-riches of the larger sepulchres are long-gone. But a mass of evocative evidence remains: the beautifully painted chambers themselves; a thousand-score vivid remnants of the spectacular treasures the tombs once contained; countless illuminating references in the ostraca and papyri; and, of course, the wonderfully preserved mummies of the kings themselves, gathered together and hidden at the time the cemetery was dismantled around 1000 BC. For years, these materials were sorely neglected because of their complexity and their fragmentary nature. Now, as the evidence is reexamined in ever closer detail, and as ongoing fieldwork adds still further to the store, our understanding of the royal wadi in all its aspects begins to clarify. Step by step, as more and more of its scattered pieces drop into place, the design of the archaeological jigsaw puzzle becomes ever easier to read.

Many questions remain to be answered and, with continuing study and exploration, new lines of enquiry will inevitably arise. Who, 20 years ago, could have imagined the extraordinary potential of the long-known tomb KV5 – now revealed by Kent Weeks as the burial place of Ramesses the Great's enormous progeny (p. 144)? And who, today, can say what treasures await discovery in those parts of the valley which have not yet been disturbed by the archaeologist's trowel (p. 126)?

This is the story to date – but be certain that there are further surprises to come.

Today, 3,000 years after it was abandoned, the Valley of the Kings remains a solemn and holy place, its emptied sepulchres reflecting still the might of Pharaoh's rule and allowing a brief, tantalizing glimpse into the ancient Egyptian soul. Harsh and unyielding, the royal wadi is a picture of changelessness, emptiness, death; and yet, when

The precise dates of the Egyptian dynasties and of individual reigns are still the subject of much scholarly debate. The dates employed here are based on the chronology developed by Professor John Baines and Dr Jaromír Málek and put forward in their *Atlas of Ancient Egypt*. Details of the rulers of the 18th–21st dynasties, the period covered by this book, have been given in full; the approximate positions of the principal High Priests of Amun during the late 20th and 21st dynasties have also been indicated.

Chronology

Late Predynastic	*c.* 3000 BC

Early Dynastic Period	
1st–3rd dynasties	2920–2575

Old Kingdom	
4th–8th dynasties	2575–2134

First Intermediate Period	
9th–11th dynasties	2134–2040

Middle Kingdom	
11th–14th dynasties	2040–1640

Second Intermediate Period	
15th–17th dynasties	1640–1532

New Kingdom

18th dynasty	**1550–1319**
Amosis	1550–1525
Amenophis I	1525–1504
Tuthmosis I	1504–1492
Tuthmosis II	1492–1479
Tuthmosis III	1479–1425
Hatshepsut	1473–1458
Amenophis II	1427–1401
Tuthmosis IV	1401–1391
Amenophis III	1391–1353
Amenophis IV/Akhenaten	
	1353–1333
Smenkhkare (Nefertiti?)	1335–1333
Tutankhamun	1333–1323
Ay	1323–1319
19th dynasty	**1319–1196**
Horemheb	1319–1307
Ramesses I	1307–1306
Sethos I	1306–1290
Ramesses II	1290–1224
Merenptah	1224–1214

Amenmesse	1214–1210
Sethos II	1210–1204
Siptah	1204–1198
Tawosret	1198–1196
20th dynasty	**1196–1070**
Sethnakhte	1196–1194
Ramesses III	1194–1163
Ramesses IV	1163–1156
Ramesses V	1156–1151
Ramesses VI	1151–1143
Ramesses VII	1143–1136
Ramesses VIII	1136–1131
Ramesses IX	1131–1112
Ramesses X	1112–1100
Ramesses XI	1100–1070
(High Priests of Amun Piankh, Herihor)	

Third Intermediate Period

21st dynasty	**1070–945**
Smendes	1070–1044
(High Priests of Amun Pinudjem I, Masaharta)	
Amenemnisu	1044–1040
Psusennes I	1040–992
(High Priest of Amun Menkheperre)	
Amenemopet	993–984
Osorkon I	984–978
Siamun	978–959
(High Priest of Amun Pinudjem II)	
Psusennes II	959–945
22nd dynasty	**945–712**
23rd dynasty	***c.* 828–712**
24th dynasty (Sais)	**724–712**
25th dynasty	
(Nubia and Theban area)	**770–712**

Late Period	
25th dynasty–2nd Persian Period	
	712–332

Greco-Roman Period	
Macedonian dynasty–Roman emperors	
	332 BC–AD 395

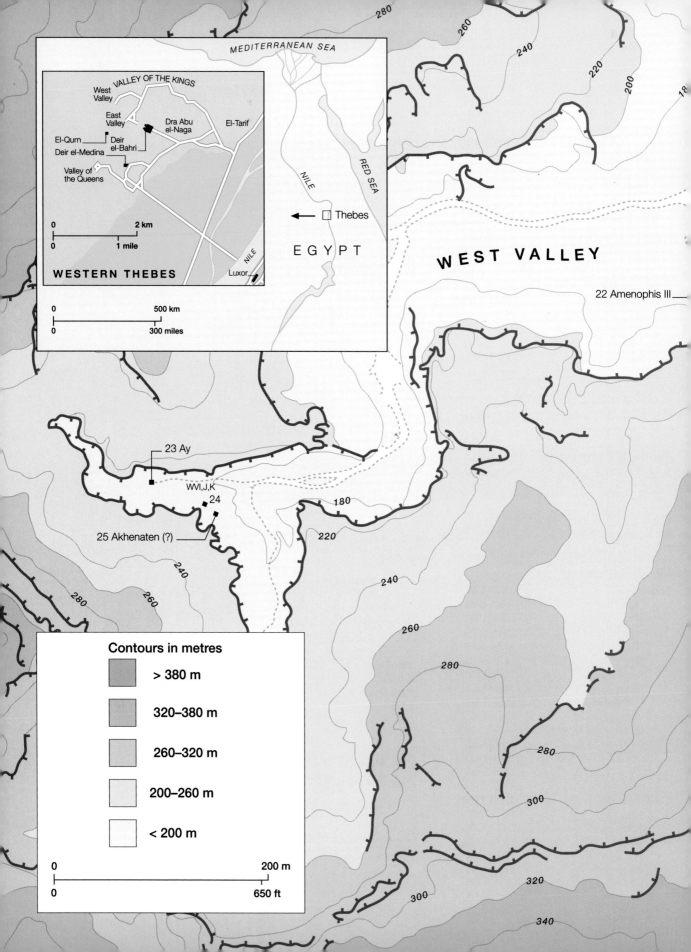

MEDITERRANEAN SEA

VALLEY OF THE KINGS

West
Valley

East
Valley

Dra Abu
el-Naga

El-Tarif

El-Qurn

Deir
el-Bahri

Deir el-Medina

Valley of
the Queens

0   2 km

0   1 mile

WESTERN THEBES

NILE

RED SEA

⟵   □ Thebes

EGYPT

NILE

Luxor

0   500 km

0   300 miles

WEST VALLEY

22 Amenophis III

23 Ay

WVI,J,K

24

25 Akhenaten (?)

Contours in metres

> 380 m

320–380 m

260–320 m

200–260 m

< 200 m

0   200 m

0   650 ft

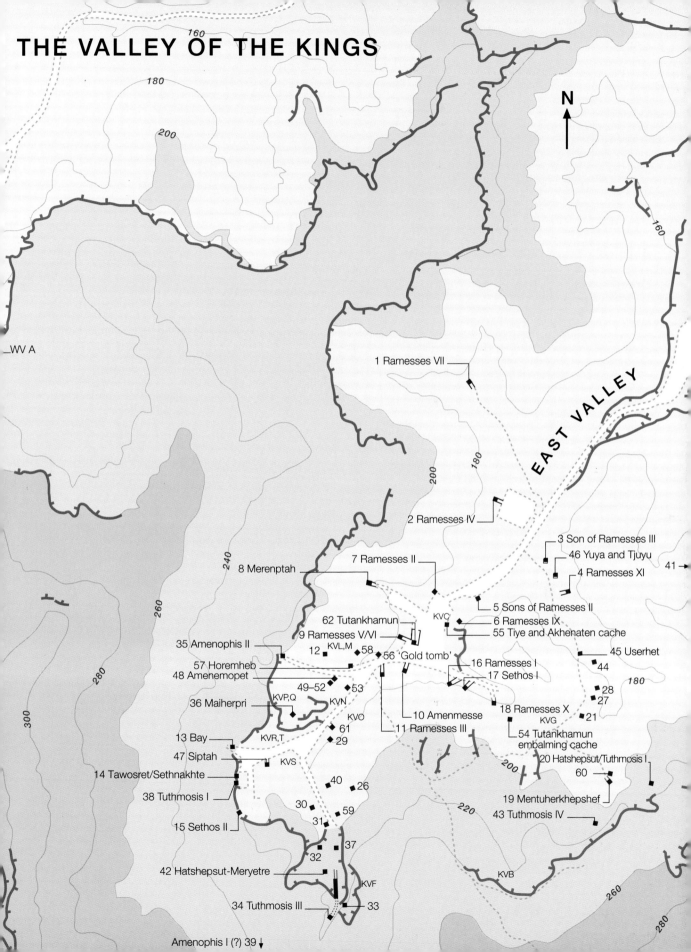

THE VALLEY OF THE KINGS

N

WV A

1 Ramesses VII

EAST VALLEY

2 Ramesses IV

3 Son of Ramesses III
46 Yuya and Tjuyu
4 Ramesses XI
41

8 Merenptah
7 Ramesses II

5 Sons of Ramesses II

KVC
6 Ramesses IX
55 Tiye and Akhenaten cache

62 Tutankhamun
9 Ramesses V/VI
35 Amenophis II
12   KVL,M   58
56 'Gold tomb'
45 Userhet
57 Horemheb
48 Amenemopet
16 Ramesses I
17 Sethos I
44
49–52   53
KVP,Q   KVN
36 Maiherpri
28
27
KVO
10 Amenmesse
18 Ramesses X
21
61
11 Ramesses III
KVG
13 Bay   KVR,T
29
54 Tutankhamun
embalming cache
47 Siptah
KVS
20 Hatshepsut/Tuthmosis I
14 Tawosret/Sethnakhte
60
40   26
38 Tuthmosis I
19 Mentuherkhepshef
30   59
43 Tuthmosis IV
31
15 Sethos II
37
32
KVB
42 Hatshepsut-Meryetre
KVF
34 Tuthmosis III   33

Amenophis I (?) 39

'My birth is the birth of Re in the west!'

Litany of Re

With the steady accumulation of archaeological information and an ever-closer analysis of images and texts, much has been learned about New Kingdom theologies of death. For Pharaoh, the cessation of life was but a step in the timeless and immutable transition from rule on earth to kingship in the beyond. The royal tomb was not only a portal to this underworld, but an underworld in its own right, a machine for life planned, constructed and equipped according to long-established patterns.

Beyond the tombs' common purpose, yet within the set pattern, each monument was unique, the form, decoration and furnishings reflecting the rich philosophical imaginings of the ancient priests. These imaginings were realized with time-transcending beauty as a testament not only to the god-king but to the hundreds of artists, craftsmen and labourers by whose considerable efforts the tomb had been brought into being. And the glimpses we have of the lives and work of this far from faceless crew help us to see the Valley and its divine occupants in a far more human light.

Detail from the astronomical ceiling in the burial chamber of the tomb of Sethos I.

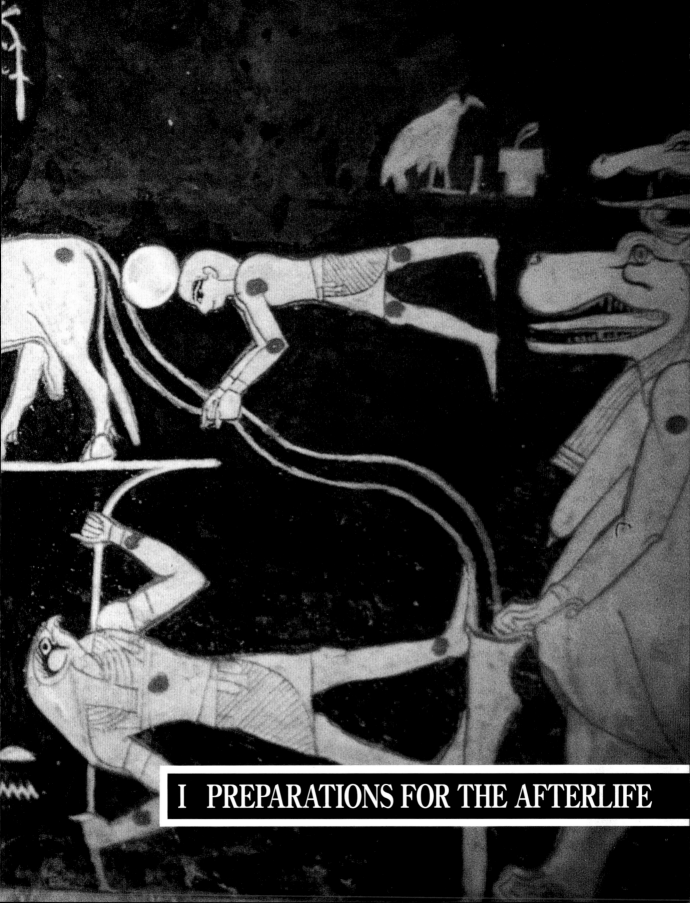

I PREPARATIONS FOR THE AFTERLIFE

Royal Tombs After the Pyramids

> 'The writings of the Hidden Chamber, the place where the souls, the spirits and the gods stand . . . the gate of the Western Horizon.'
>
> From the Amduat

At the dawn of Egypt's New Kingdom, a line of Theban princes initiated an era which would carry Egypt to a level of power unequalled in her history and which would continue, essentially unbroken, for 500 years. Beginning with Amosis (*c.* 1550 BC), the king credited with the establishment of this period at Thebes, more than 30 monarchs of three successive dynasties ruled Egypt. Even when the necessities of ancient *Realpolitik* carried the political centre of gravity northward to the established administrative city of Memphis, and later to royal residence cities in the Delta, Thebes continued to be acknowledged as a spiritual capital and dynastic home of the age; and it was there – in the southern city then called Waset – that virtually all the monarchs of the New Kingdom were buried.

First Intermediate Period tombs

The Theban area had in fact been used as a royal necropolis during the First Intermediate Period, between 2134 and 2040 BC. During this time at least three rulers of the local 11th dynasty (Inyotef I, II and III) built their tombs on the west bank of the Nile in the region of el-Tarif, to the northeast of what would become the Theban necropolis.

Although similar in type to provincial tombs built elsewhere in Egypt in this period, the monumental size and architecture of these tombs set them apart. The sepulchres of these Theban princes consisted of a large court (the largest some 300 m (980 ft) in length) cut into the sloping desert surface and backed by a row of door-like openings which give the structures their name of *saff* tombs, from the Arabic for 'row'. The doorways lead into chambers which evidently served as the funerary chapels of the king and also for members of his family and high officials of the court; shafts led to burial chambers in the rock below. A brick-built 'valley' temple completed the mortuary complex of these *saff* tombs which, despite the apparent lack of a pyramidal superstructure, nevertheless approximated in their form the essential elements of the classic Egyptian pyramid complex.

The Middle Kingdom and after

Mentuhotep I (2061–2010 BC), first ruler of the Middle Kingdom, constructed a highly innovative tomb in the amphitheatre-like basin of Deir el-Bahri in western Thebes. This impressive monument consisted of a terraced and columned mortuary temple overlying twin subterranean corridor burials, perhaps symbolizing the dual royal burial and cenotaph utilized by many Egyptian kings since very early times. Earlier reconstructions of Mentuhotep's tomb show a pyramidal superstructure, but recent analyses indicate that (as with the earlier *saff* tombs) no pyramid was present – a development which may have influenced subsequent royal tombs at Thebes. Only in northern Egypt did the Old Kingdom tradition of building pyramids for royal burials continue into the Middle Kingdom era.

At the close of the Middle Kingdom, control of much of Egypt passed to the Asiatic Hyksos who invaded and settled in the region of the Delta. Some Theban princes, however, maintained a degree of independence and a number of kings of the 17th dynasty ruled at Thebes. The site chosen by these

(Right) A comparison of the interior chambers of Unas's pyramid at Saqqara (on the left) with the tomb of Amenophis II (on the right) shows the basic similarity of the bent axes found in most Old Kingdom pyramids and the early New Kingdom royal tombs.

(Opposite) The mortuary temple of Mentuhotep I at Deir el-Bahri combined the mortuary temple of earlier pyramids with a subterranean burial complex.

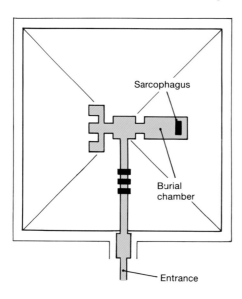

Sarcophagus

Burial chamber

Entrance

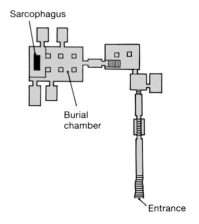

Sarcophagus

Burial chamber

Entrance

southern princes for their burials was at Dra Abu el-Naga, between el-Tarif and Deir el-Bahri; the Abbott Papyrus records an official inspection of these burials conducted in Ramessid times. Though the tombs are now lost from view, the coffins of three rulers, Inyotef V, VI and VII (now in the Louvre and the British Museum), were found in this area, and the site is now under joint excavation by the University of California at Los Angeles and the German Archaeological Institute of Cairo.

The New Kingdom

After the expulsion of the Hyksos, the Theban rulers of the 18th dynasty continued the tradition of burial at Thebes, but began to build tombs of a new style commensurate with their status as kings of all Egypt. While we are unsure as to the exact location and identity of the very earliest of these 18th-dynasty tombs, it is likely that Amosis, the founder of the dynasty, who constructed a tomb or cenotaph at Abydos, also had a tomb made in the Theban necropolis. The burials of Amosis's successor, Amenophis I, and that king's mother, Queen Ahmose-Nofretiri, have not yet been firmly identified, although there are contending claims for tombs both in the Valley of the Kings and at Dra Abu el-Naga (pp. 88–90). The special veneration accorded this pair by the subsequent builders of the royal tombs might suggest that these monarchs were either the first members of the dynasty to be buried in the Valley of the Kings or the first to establish officially the location as a dynastic royal necropolis. Yet currently the honour of being the first pharaoh definitely to cut his tomb in the royal valley belongs to Amenophis's successor, Tuthmosis I. It was not long after this event that the monarchs of this same line moved their political base north to Memphis. Inevitably, however, perhaps due to what had become accepted tradition or the growing importance of the Theban god Amun, for 500 years these kings and their successors of the 19th and 20th dynasties returned in death to 'the Great Place' of Thebes.

(Above) The temples of Mentuhotep I (left) and Hatshepsut (centre right) at Deir el-Bahri, with the Valley of the Kings behind.

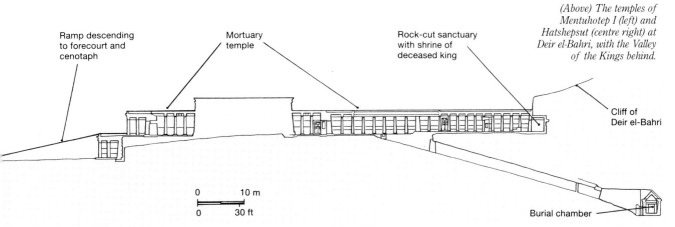

Ramp descending to forecourt and cenotaph

Mortuary temple

Rock-cut sanctuary with shrine of deceased king

Cliff of Deir el-Bahri

Burial chamber

0   10 m
0   30 ft

The Topography of Western Thebes

Western Thebes in New Kingdom times: the Theban massif seen from the Nile. The cliffs of western Thebes resemble the shape of the akhet or 'horizon' hieroglyph and it was here, where the sun set, that the New Kingdom pharaohs built their necropolis.

'Giving praise to the Peak of the West, kissing the ground to her *ka*.... For the Peak of the West is appeased if one calls upon her.'

Hymn to Meretseger, goddess of the peak above the Valley of the Kings

Although geographically Thebes was imperfectly situated for effective rule over the whole country, the natural topography of the area nevertheless made it the perfect location for a royal necropolis. A flat plain on the western side of the Nile – the area associated by the Egyptians with the sinking sun and the afterlife – stretched from the river to a mountain chain with numerous secluded valleys threading their way through tall, soft stone cliffs. The plain was ideal for the location of royal mortuary temples – natural developments of the structures in which the funerary service of the departed king had been celebrated since the pyramid age – while the secluded valleys beyond provided ample sites for the construction of fine rock-cut tombs.

The Egyptians chose the ravine now called the Valley of the Kings as the main royal burial ground for practical and symbolic reasons. Certainly the site was relatively remote and its narrow access points easily guarded, but symbolic aspects were perhaps even more compelling. When viewed from the city of Thebes across the Nile, the whole Theban massif resembles in its shape a giant *akhet* or 'horizon' hieroglyph (⌒) – the symbol used by

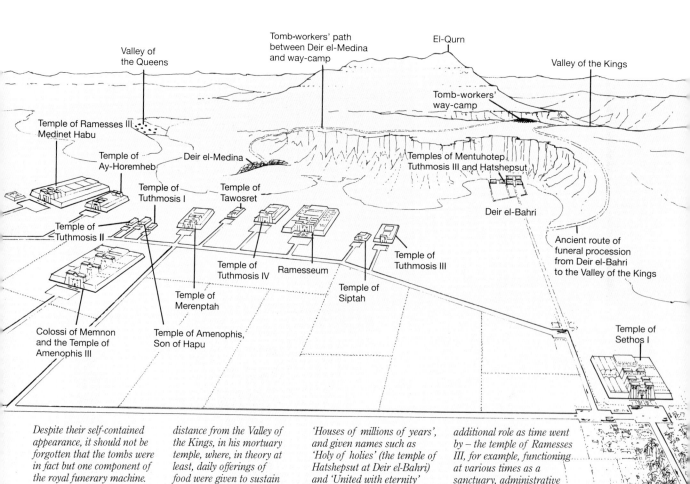

Valley of the Queens

Tomb-workers' path between Deir el-Medina and way-camp

El-Qurn

Valley of the Kings

Temple of Ramesses III Medinet Habu

Tomb-workers' way-camp

Temple of Ay-Horemheb

Deir el-Medina

Temples of Mentuhotep Tuthmosis III and Hatshepsut

Temple of Tuthmosis I

Temple of Tawosret

Deir el-Bahri

Temple of Tuthmosis II

Temple of Tuthmosis IV

Ramesseum

Temple of Tuthmosis III

Ancient route of funeral procession from Deir el-Bahri to the Valley of the Kings

Temple of Merenptah

Temple of Siptah

Colossi of Memnon and the Temple of Amenophis III

Temple of Amenophis, Son of Hapu

Temple of Sethos I

Despite their self-contained appearance, it should not be forgotten that the tombs were in fact but one component of the royal funerary machine. The actual cult of the deceased king was celebrated in the Theban plain, some distance from the Valley of the Kings, in his mortuary temple, where, in theory at least, daily offerings of food were given to sustain his spirit.

The royal mortuary temples were designated 'Houses of millions of years', and given names such as 'Holy of holies' (the temple of Hatshepsut at Deir el-Bahri) and 'United with eternity' (that of Ramesses III at Medinet Habu). Some royal mortuary temples took on an additional role as time went by – the temple of Ramesses III, for example, functioning at various times as a sanctuary, administrative centre and fortress.

the Egyptians to represent the area of the rising and setting sun; and the sun does set in this western region from the perspective of Thebes. Throughout much of the New Kingdom, a royal funerary cortège deliberately followed this western passage of the sun, processing from the king's mortuary temple in the Nile Valley, over the Theban cliffs and down into the Valley of the Kings behind the western horizon, assimilating the king into the solar cycle. Deir el-Bahri, where Mentuhotep constructed his mortuary temple (p. 15), and the Valley of the Kings, which lies directly behind, sit at the centre – the horizon point itself, as it were – of the topographical *akhet*. A number of individual tombs also appear to have been situated at the base of *akhet*-shaped clefts in the rugged valley sides. The topography of the royal necropolis was thus directly linked to its symbolic function.

Another symbolic attraction of the valley may well have been its situation at the foot of a pyramidal peak known to the ancients as *dehenet* and today as el-Qurn. The 450 m (1,500-ft) mountain was sacred to Hathor and later to its own special goddess Meretseger, 'She who loves silence'. Its shape would certainly have reminded the Egyptians of those earlier royal burial places, the pyramids. Little effort was made, however, to enter the mountain from the northern side, as was traditionally the case in the man-made pyramids, and the tombs cut around it were not connected with – or even usually oriented towards – the mortuary temples in the Nile Valley. In this respect the New Kingdom royal tombs decisively broke with the past.

The topography of the royal valley

Topographically, the Valley of the Kings is actually composed of two separate branches: the main, eastern branch in which most of the royal tombs are located, and a larger, western branch in which

(Left and below left) The main branch of the royal valley and el-Qurn, the pyramidal peak at the valley's heart. Known to the ancient Egyptians as Meretseger, 'She who loves silence', the peak was venerated as a major deity of the necropolis to whom hymns were written and shrines dedicated.

(Below) The West Valley. A number of tombs of the late 18th dynasty were cut in this branch of the royal valley.

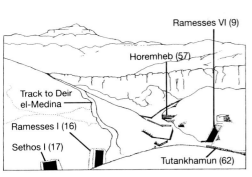

Ramesses VI (9)

Horemheb (57)

Track to Deir el-Medina

Ramesses I (16)

Sethos I (17)

Tutankhamun (62)

only a few tombs are known. The valley opens into the Theban massif about 5 km (3 miles) from the Nile at its nearest point and runs upward from the plain to the west and northwest until it turns and swings south shortly before branching into its two halves. The eastern branch with the majority of the tombs was called *ta set aat,* 'the Great Place', by the Egyptians or, more informally, simply *ta int,* 'the Valley'. Today this is the branch known as the Wadi Biban el-Muluk, 'the Valley of the Doors of the Kings'. The inner central part of this valley is not extensive, yet it is large enough to contain several minor forks such as that known today as 'the Valley of the Tomb of Ramesses VII', which leads a short distance to the north, and 'the Valley of the Tomb of Ramesses XI', which branches off to the south. These and other minor branches and ravines provided the sheltered positions selected for many of the royal tombs.

The second branch of the royal valley, known specifically today as the West Valley, leaves the main branch in a westerly direction (by the new tourist resthouse) and then continues southwest through towering rock-formations, ending in a large natural amphitheatre whose rock walls rise

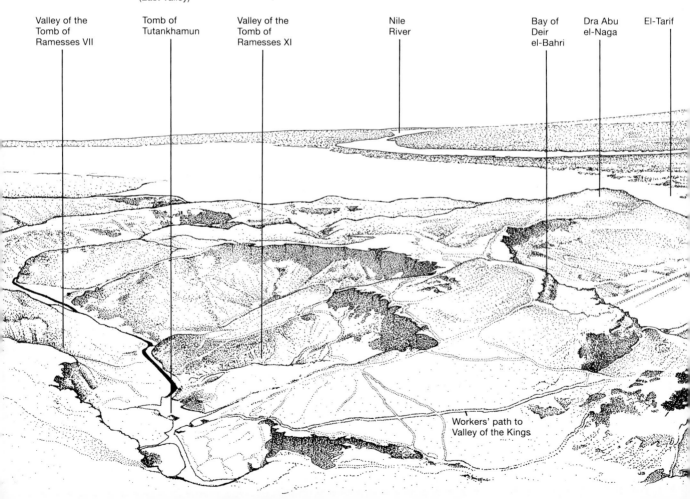

VALLEY OF THE KINGS
(East Valley)

Valley of the Tomb of Ramesses VII

Tomb of Tutankhamun

Valley of the Tomb of Ramesses XI

Nile River

Bay of Deir el-Bahri

Dra Abu el-Naga

El-Tarif

Workers' path to Valley of the Kings

many metres to the desert plateau above. The cliffs of the West Valley are penetrated by hundreds of secluded bays and minor ravines, which would have made it an ideal place for secret royal burials. In fact, were it not for the wadi's more remote position, and (perhaps of greater importance) its association with the monarchs of the heretical Amarna age – Akhenaten's first tomb was at least begun here (p. 116) – more kings might have chosen the western branch of the Valley of the Kings as their burial place during the latter part of the New Kingdom.

In pharaonic times the nearest centres of civilization were many hours' walk away from the Valley of the Kings, if one followed the natural winding route through the wadi. However, the front range of the Theban massif – which separates the royal valley from the plain of the Nile – stands only 130 m (425 ft) above the plain at its lower points; the Great Place could be reached in half an hour going by foot over the steep mountain paths from Deir el-Bahri or from the village of the tomb makers at Deir el-Medina. Mountain-ringed and secluded as it may have been, the Valley of the Kings was far from impenetrable, as history would show.

(Opposite) The eastern valley and its subsidiary branches seen from the height of el-Qurn. The small rectangle in the lower centre of the picture is the enclosure of the tomb of Tutankhamun.

(Left) The Valley of the Tomb of Ramesses VII. Numerous smaller valleys such as this intersect the main, eastern branch of the Valley of the Kings.

(Below) Panorama view from el-Qurn, the high point of the mountains of western Thebes, showing the main branch of the valley on the left with the tomb-workers' way-camp at the centre and their permanent settlement of Deir el-Medina on the right.

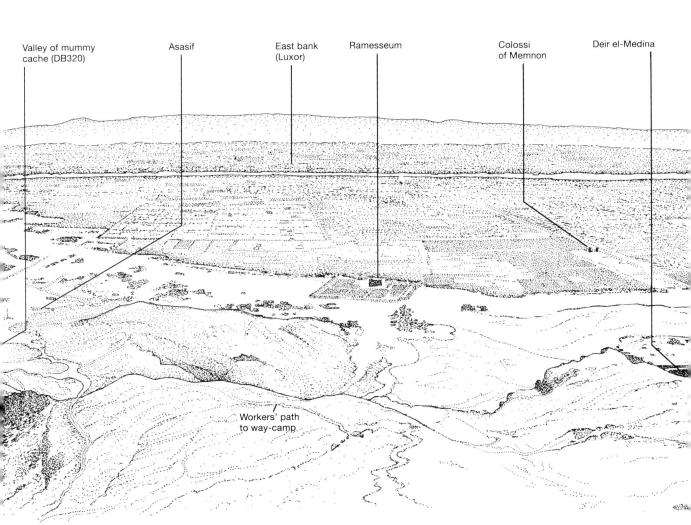

Valley of mummy cache (DB320)

Asasif

East bank (Luxor)

Ramesseum

Colossi of Memnon

Deir el-Medina

Workers' path to way-camp.

The Geology of the Royal Valley

The hills on each side are high steep rocks, and the whole place is cover'd with the rough stones that seem to have rolled from them.'

Richard Pococke

Formation of the royal valley

The Nile Valley was an area of intense land building and movement in distant geological history. Over the millennia, fluctuating ocean levels meant that the Mediterranean Sea repeatedly invaded low-lying land and covered much of what is now Egypt as far south as present-day Aswan. This led to the laying down of three successive sedimentary rock formations known to geologists as the Dakhla chalk, Esna shale and Theban limestone. It is main-

(Below) Geological map of the royal valley showing the surface distribution of the major types of rock in this region. (Bottom) Vertical section (A–B) across the Valley of the Kings showing how the various rock types overlie one another.

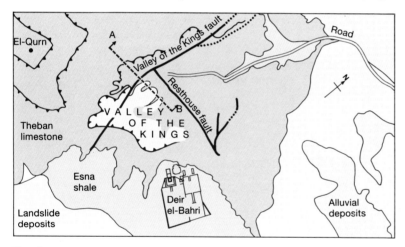

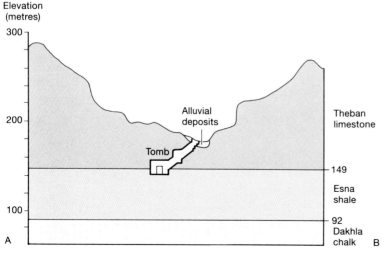

ly the last two levels which are visible in the royal valley, the limestone formation being about 300 m (1,000 ft) thick from its highest point to where it eventually merges into the shale which lies in a band some 60 m (200 ft) thick beneath it. The interface between these different sedimentary formations may be seen at a number of points in the valley and even in some of the tombs, such as that of Sethos I, where the upper part of the burial chamber walls were cut through the Theban limestone and the lower part excavated from the underlying shale.

These different rock formations were extensively affected by geological uplifting in the late Tertiary Period and by erosion caused by the Nile and smaller tributaries during periods of increased rainfall into the early Pleistocene. In pluvial periods such as these, thousands of streams and rivers scoured the Theban limestone, creating millions of tons of boulders, fragmented rock and sand. In this way, the rugged limestone cliffs and rock-strewn scree or talus slopes of the valley were formed, along with the now dry river beds which snake between them.

The very processes which created the valley, however, now threaten to destroy the tombs dug into it. The relatively soft rock formations, ideal though they may be for tomb construction, are particularly susceptible to water infiltration and expansion. Thus, although rainfall in this area is sparse, occasional intense rains on the surrounding high desert lead to massive and disastrous flooding in the valleys below. Unchecked, these rare but destructive floods have scoured and choked many of the royal tombs and damaged the surrounding rock through penetration, expansion and uneven drying.

Where the tombs are found

The intrepid 19th-century explorer Giovanni Belzoni (p. 56) seems to have been the first to describe the basic geology and topography of the Valley of the Kings – including the drainage patterns which led to the specific positioning of some of the tombs. More recent study has shown that three groups of tombs may be distinguished on the basis of these geological and hydrological factors – the three groups closely corresponding to the three dynasties which utilized the valley as their necropolis. Tombs of the early to mid-18th dynasty are usually cut into the rock walls of the valley's cliffs and often in, or close to, rock clefts and dry waterfalls (for example, the tomb of Tuthmosis III). The entrances to these tombs were blocked with dry stone walls covered and sealed with plaster after the burials were installed. The flood waters which later poured over the clefts effectively buried the tomb entrances with water-borne debris.

Tombs constructed towards the end of the 18th dynasty and throughout the 19th dynasty are usually lower in the valley, away from the rock walls

and often cutting through the talus slopes (as, for example, with the tomb of Amenophis III). More susceptible to water damage because of their location, many of these middle period monuments – such as that of Ramesses II – have been severely affected by flooding. Due to their siting low down in the valley floor, some of these tombs make contact with the underlying shale, and are thus prone to expansion damage.

The final group of tombs consists mainly of 20th-dynasty monuments, often situated at ground level, unconcealed, on the ends of rock spurs produced by run-off channels which cut down on each side. This positioning gave some protection from floods, a factor which may have encouraged the use of such locations, although they were also among the few areas not already taken by this time in the later history of the valley. Despite their better siting, many of these tombs have nevertheless been invaded by water, either through their entrances or through cracks in the surrounding rock.

Geological faults

Due to the ancient loss of ground water and resulting earth movement over time, the valley's rock formations are fractured by a number of geological faults. The largest (known appropriately as the Valley of the Kings Fault) runs in an almost north–south line along the western side of the valley and breaks the surface in a number of areas including the hillside above the tomb of Ramesses III. This fault is also the most dramatic of the valley's rock fractures, a displacement of almost 30 m (100 ft) at some points, though its average width is

considerably less. Smaller vertical faults also exist in the Valley of the Kings, and in some cases pose a considerable threat to the tombs which they intersect. In the tomb of Ramesses III, a fault in the left wall of the burial chamber let in large amounts of water which flooded the lower half of the tomb in the early part of the present century. The rock formations of the valley also exhibit hundreds of open fissures which are not technically geological faults because they do not show any signs of slippage on either side. These rock-joints, as geologists refer to them, are especially noticeable in the lower valley and were often used by ancient quarrymen in the selection of tomb sites and in cutting the tombs.

(Above) The locations chosen by tomb builders changed with time. Early tombs were cut into the cliffs (e.g. Tuthmosis III, left). Beginning with Amenophis III (centre), tombs were placed lower in the slopes or in the valley's floor, and in the Ramessid period in rock spurs projecting from the valley's sides (e.g. Ramesses VI, right).

Widened rock-joint above the tomb of Ramesses III. Such 'faults' affect the geological characteristics of the valley.

Pharaoh's Workforce: The Villagers of Deir el-Medina

'[On that day] came the vizier . . . and read to them a letter saying that Nebmaatre Ramesses Amenherkhepshef-meryamun [Ramesses VI] . . . had arisen as the great ruler of the whole land . . . and he said: Let the gang come up.'

From an ostracon

It is one of the ironies of history that we know more about the humble workmen who cut the New Kingdom royal tombs than we do about the god-kings for whom the tombs were made. One of the best-preserved ancient settlements in all Egypt, the workmen's village at Deir el-Medina is situated southeast of the Valley of the Kings on the Nile side of the western mountains in a barren, water-less pocket in the hills. Both from a great pit outside the village, and from the remains of the stone-built houses, storerooms and other structures in the village itself, have come thousands of ostraca (pot-sherds and small limestone flakes used for writing, see p. 31) as well as numerous papyri, inscribed with letters, notes, records and many other kinds of evidence concerning the lives of the men and their families. Due to the pillaging of 19th-century explorers and collectors, objects from Deir el-Medina are now present in virtually every major museum in the world.

Investigating Deir el-Medina

The site first underwent scientific excavation by the Italian archaeologist Ernesto Schiaparelli in 1905–09 and was completely cleared by the French between 1922 and 1951 under the direction of Bernard Bruyère and with the assistance of the brilliant Czech Egyptologist Jaroslav Černý. Many scholars have worked on the material since then. The settlement was founded sometime early in the 18th dynasty, though by which monarch is uncertain. A wall enclosing the village has many bricks clearly stamped with the name of Tuthmosis I – the first pharaoh definitely to be buried in the Valley of the Kings – though it is known that the previous king, Amenophis I, and his mother, Ahmose-Nofretiri, were revered and regarded as patron deities by the workmen of Deir el-Medina. Nevertheless, most of the extant evidence from the site dates to the 19th and 20th dynasties, when the village almost doubled in size; and for these later periods a great deal of information has come to light. In addition to the names of the viziers and other high officials who oversaw from Thebes the excavation of the royal tombs, the names, families and other details of the lives of many of the scribes, foremen and workers who lived at Deir el-Medina are known (p. 24).

A cosmopolitan community

The many documents and inscriptions recovered from the village show that 100 or more individuals (including children) lived in the community for

(Below) View of the workmen's village of Deir el-Medina.

(Below right) Way-camp on the ridge between Deir el-Medina and the Valley of the Kings. Workmen spent their nights here between weekends and holidays.

much of its history and that it was a surprisingly cosmopolitan village – over 30 foreign names have been identified there. Many of the inhabitants were literate, and, in addition to their everyday records, left writings ranging from humorous satirical notes and sketches to pious religious inscriptions. That religion was extremely important to these people is indicated by the many votive stelae offered to the gods as well as the 16 or more small temples and chapels which served the community. A wide range of deities was venerated, from national gods such as Osiris, Hathor and Ptah, to local deities like Meretseger, the goddess of the peak above the Valley of the Kings, and deified kings and queens such as Amenophis I, Queen Ahmose-Nofretiri and Ramesses II. In addition, numerous shrines and stelae honoured the ancestors of the workmen.

The workers' homes were generally small, yet relative status is evident in the size and design of many. A number of the inhabitants augmented their income by producing furniture and funerary items for surrounding communities. During their weekly labour of tomb building the 'Servants of the Place of Truth', as the workers were called, often stayed in a small way-camp (itself having over 50 small shrines) built on the ridge above the royal valley, returning to their homes for 'weekends' and holidays, or to take care of necessary family business. Nominally under the direction of the vizier, the workmen were divided into a 'Right Side' gang and a 'Left Side' gang (according to the side of the tomb on which the particular gang worked), the size of which would vary depending on the point the construction had reached. The term *iswt* or 'gang' signified a military or naval unit, with each gang working under a foreman who controlled the everyday tomb-building activity, and with several scribes in attendance to record the work that took place, workers' absences, payments, supplies received etc. (see 'Cutting the Tombs', p. 28).

Beginning in the 19th dynasty, these same men also plied their trades in the Valley of the Queens, producing the finely-made tombs of the chief royal wives and children. The village was finally abandoned at the end of the New Kingdom when royal burials in the Valley of the Kings came to an end. The villagers removed the valuable wooden doors and supporting columns from their houses when they left, causing the collapse of the two-storey structures.

The women of Deir el-Medina

As most of the men of the community were absent for the greater part of each 10-day week, the village was for much of the time a community of women. Women were not only entrusted with many responsibilities of their own, but there is also at least one instance of a foreman's wife paying out the men's wages in the absence of her husband. That many of

The Tomb-Workers' Strike

Carpenters constructing a wooden shrine-like object. Detail from the private tomb of Nebamun and Ipuky at Thebes.

The massive scale of Ramesses III's construction programme at Thebes seems to have severely depleted the grain reserves used to pay the workmen of the royal necropolis. This situation was exacerbated by the effects of corrupt administrators, so that the workers' grain rations were considerably and intolerably reduced. A letter sent by the scribe Neferhotep around Ramesses' 25th year states, 'One and a half *khar* of grain [about 168lbs] have been taken from us . . . we are dying, we cannot live . . .' and while the situation may not have been as desperate as the letter implies, the delays and shortages of payments seem to have propelled the workmen into the world's first known labour dispute.

In the summer of Ramesses' 29th year, *c.* 1165 BC, the scribe Amennakhte personally delivered a formal complaint about the situation to the Temple of Horemheb, part of the large administrative complex of Medinet Habu. Although a payment was soon forthcoming, the poor conditions continued and later that same year the men of the two gangs stopped work and marched together to one of the royal mortuary temples where they staged what would now be called a sit-in. This action was repeated on the following day within the compound of another temple, until the men's complaints were recorded by the priests and sent across the river to the administrators of Thebes. Only then were the delinquent rations finally distributed to the angry workmen. Perhaps more importantly, however, a precedent had been set, and the events of this strike would be repeated several times before the reign of Ramesses III was over.

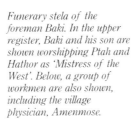

Funerary stela of the foreman Baki. In the upper register, Baki and his son are shown worshipping Ptah and Hathor as 'Mistress of the West'. Below, a group of workmen are also shown, including the village physician, Amenmose.

the wives were literate has been inferred from the messages sent to them at times when it is doubtful that scribes were present in the village. A good number of the documented women bore religious titles, such as chantress, singer or priestess, indicating their involvement in various cults – including some major temple cults outside the village. The legal rights of these women are also evident in cases such as that of Naunakhe, the widow of the scribe Kenherkhepshef, whose willed distribution of goods to her sons during the reign of Ramesses V shows total personal control of her estate.

Stela of the woman Henut offering to an ancestor bust, from Deir el-Medina. Women were important in the village community, and carried out many religious duties, including those of chantress, singer or priestess.

The Men Who Made the Tombs

The vizier Paser's family participating in the presentation of offerings. A detail (after J. G. Wilkinson) from Paser's tomb at Thebes.

(Below) Intermarriage and interaction between selected members of three families during the years 1224 BC (Merenptah) to 1163 BC (Ramesses III). Although many positions became hereditary, opportunities could, and did, occur for individuals to change profession and social status.

The roles, life histories and even characters of many of the men who constructed the royal tombs in the Valley of the Kings are known in some detail – as the following brief sketches of three representative individuals show.

Paser – vizier: The son of a high priest of Amun and the chief of that god's harem, Paser became vizier of Upper Egypt during the reign of the pharaoh Sethos I and continued to serve under Ramesses II. He was buried with his wife Tiy in an impressive tomb at Thebes, where inscriptions show that as most senior adviser to the young Ramesses,

Paser was given the titles 'Beloved of the God' (i.e., the king) and 'God's Father'. As vizier, he organized and directed major projects of state, supervised commerce, production, law and order and officiated at major religious festivals. Like the king himself, Paser even wrote to foreign sovereigns such as the Hittite monarch Hattusil and his wife, Pudukhepa. His many duties included overseeing the construction of the tomb of Sethos I, one of the greatest achievements in the valley (p. 137), and it

was Paser who enlarged and reorganized the royal tomb workforce, taking direct control of the project and dividing the responsibility for the actual work between a chief scribe and foreman of each work gang.

Hay, foreman: A foreman of the Left Side gang (see main text) and village elder, Hay seems to have spent all his long life working in the royal valley. The son of the foreman Inherkau, Hay worked with his father from boyhood and eventually inherited the foremanship when his father died in the last year of Merenptah. About 35 at this time, Hay continued in the position for some 40 years (c. 1214–1174 BC), serving five kings of the 19th and 20th dynasties – Amenmesse, Sethos II, Siptah, Sethnakhte and Ramesses III. Respected by his workmen, Hay seems to have been a kindly and pious individual, and an inscribed stela showing him in worship is known. Living mostly in troubled times, Hay had the additional misfortune of working opposite the difficult and notorious Paneb, who was foreman of the Right Side gang for a number of years. Hay was accused of speaking against the king at this time – perhaps at Paneb's instigation – but steadfastly denied the charges and the case against him was dropped. Hay lived to a ripe age of about 75 and was able to build a tomb for himself on the Nile side of the western mountains. His daughter became the wife of the scribe Amennakhte.

Amennakhte, scribe: Born to the foreman Amenemopet or 'Ipy', Amennakhte did not follow in his father's footsteps but became a scribe appointed to work on the royal tombs during the reign of Ramesses III. The position was to prove a lasting one, as Amennakhte served under four monarchs and became the founder of six generations of scribes. The writings of this important scribe give many details of the disputes and difficulties in which he was involved during his long career, and especially the workmen's strikes at the end of the reign of Ramesses III (see feature). An intelligent and cautious man, Amennakhte recorded the legitimate complaints of the men yet also supported the administration he served as much as possible. Along with the foreman Inherkhau, it was Amennakhte who seems to have done much to defuse the strikes. It was perhaps Amennakhte who drew the famous plan of the tomb of Ramesses IV now in Turin (p. 27), and a portion of this papyrus contains the scribe's will.

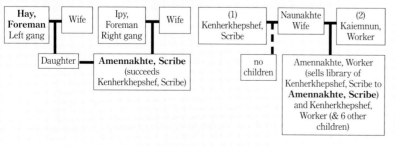

Hay, Foreman Left gang	Wife	Ipy, Foreman Right gang	Wife	(1) Kenherkhepshef, Scribe	Naunakhte Wife	(2) Kaiemnun, Worker
Daughter		Amennakhte, Scribe (succeeds Kenherkhepshef, Scribe)		no children	Amennakhte, Worker (sells library of Kenherkhepshef, Scribe to **Amennakhte, Scribe**) and Kenherkhepshef, Worker (& 6 other children)	

Despite certain underlying commonalities of design, no two monuments in the Valley of the Kings are alike, and unique features of design or decoration were incorporated in the planning of each structure. In this way the royal tomb underwent a complex and ever-changing development throughout the New Kingdom. Broadly speaking, however, the monuments developed through three major stages: the early tombs with curved or bent axes (such as that of Amenophis II); the intermediate tombs with parallel axes where the entrance corridors 'jog' to one side at the first pillared hall, about mid-way into the tomb, but then continue in the same direction (such as that of Horemheb); and the later tombs with straight axes (those tombs from Merenptah onwards). The three stages occur, with some overlapping, during the 18th, 19th and 20th dynasties.

Eighteenth dynasty: development

From relatively early in the 18th dynasty the royal tomb consisted of a series of four passages (beginning with the entrance stair) which alternated in having steps or sloping ramps as their floors. Each section of the entrance into the subterranean tomb was known as one of the passages of 'the Sun's Path', suggesting the nocturnal journey of the sun under the earth, a symbolic concept which was enhanced by the decoration inside the tombs (p. 35). The third passage had broad niches cut on each side which became known as the 'Sanctuaries in which the Gods of the East/West Repose', and the fourth passage opened on a chamber containing a well or pit (called the 'Hall of Waiting' or 'Hall of Hindrance'). Beyond this well was a small pillared hall (the 'Chariot Hall') leading through further passages to a second, larger pillared hall (the 'House of Gold') and its subsidiary storerooms which contained the king's burial assemblage. As time progressed, this basic plan was elaborated with the whole sequence of passages and halls being virtually repeated, but the basic aspects remained constant.

The bends and turns in the axes of the 18th-dynasty tombs may have been a continuation of the crooked corridors of the Middle Kingdom pyramids, which perhaps represented the twisting routes of the netherworld envisaged in Egyptian mythology as seen in the Middle Kingdom Book of Two Ways and in the fourth and fifth hours of the New Kingdom Amduat (or Book of What is in the Underworld: p. 37). As the Egyptologist Erik Hornung has written, 'The architecture of the tomb is thus conditioned by the topography of the Beyond, while the texts and representations fre-

quently take up the theme of the "bent" or "winding" waters in the landscape of the realm of the dead.' It is also possible that some of the earliest tombs of the 18th dynasty curved in order to follow the natural clefts of the subterranean rock or in an attempt to avoid bad stone, and that this curving construction took on symbolic significance by the time it was formalized as the bent axes of the later 18th-dynasty Tuthmosid tombs.

Many architectural features first incorporated for practical reasons continued for symbolic ones even when the original reason for their inclusion no longer existed. The 'well' cut in royal tombs from the time of Tuthmosis III may have originated as a barrier intended to stop flood waters (and tomb robbers); it seems in time to have developed mythological significance as a symbolic burial shaft associated with the mortuary god, Sokar, and the well room was retained after the time of Ramesses III even when the well shaft itself was not excavated. The niches on the east and west sides of the third

Planning a Royal Tomb: Design and Symbolism

Sequential development of the three types of tomb plan. The straightening of the tomb's main axis may have its origins in Akhenaten's tomb at Amarna. It was perhaps solar-related in its significance.

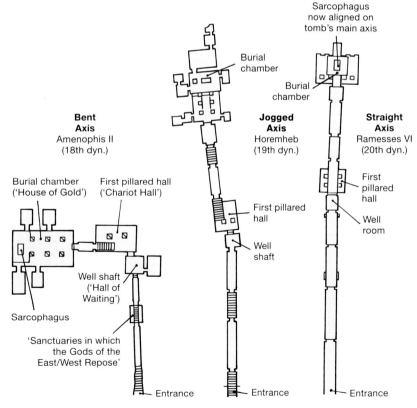

Bent Axis
Amenophis II
(18th dyn.)

Burial chamber
('House of Gold')

First pillared hall
('Chariot Hall')

Well shaft
('Hall of Waiting')

Sarcophagus

'Sanctuaries in which the Gods of the East/West Repose'

Entrance

Jogged Axis
Horemheb
(19th dyn.)

Burial chamber

First pillared hall

Well shaft

Entrance

Straight Axis
Ramesses VI
(20th dyn.)

Sarcophagus now aligned on tomb's main axis

Burial chamber

First pillared hall

Well room

Entrance

passage may also have had a functional origin in early 18th-dynasty tombs, as these tombs usually descend steeply, and the niches, which were originally placed along the length of the first steps inside the tomb, may have been used in the difficult task of lowering the sarcophagus into the burial chamber, a function which became obsolete as the angle of descent in the tombs levelled out.

Many design details of the 18th-dynasty burial chambers are less than certainly understood. The distinct oval shape given to several of the earliest burial chambers has been thought to echo the shape of the royal cartouche (as do some of the sarcophagi in these tombs), or an opened papyrus scroll (which the wall decorations certainly reflect in their colour and inscriptional styles), or, yet again, to be based on either the circuit of the sun or the topography of the netherworld.

(Below) Eighteenth-dynasty tombs, such as that of Horemheb, have steeply descending passages with sets of stairs alternating with sloping, ramp-like floors. Wooden doors were infrequently used.

(Below right) Later tombs of the 19th and 20th dynasties, such as that of Ramesses IV shown here, employed less steep or even horizontal passages. From the time of Ramesses II, stairs and ramps were sometimes combined in the same passages, and later tombs often used only ramps where stairways had been placed before. In these tombs, wooden doors were placed at the entrance and at numerous points within the structure.

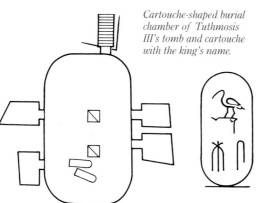

Cartouche-shaped burial chamber of Tuthmosis III's tomb and cartouche with the king's name.

Nineteenth dynasty: change

With the beginning of the 19th dynasty, many aspects of the royal monuments undergo change. Most noticeably, with only one major exception – that of the tomb of Ramesses II – the bent axis of earlier tombs was abandoned from the time of Horemheb on. The impetus for this straightening of the tombs' passages into a single, linear axis may lie in the influence of the Amarna tomb of Akhenaten, though the connection is not as clear as is often believed (p. 118). The descent of the tombs into the earth also became progressively less steep in this period, the form of the sarcophagus hall was modified in a number of ways, and from the time of Ramesses II on wooden doors were increasingly employed to close entrances and passages walled off and sealed in the earlier tombs. While serving to some degree as further protection against illicit entry, these doors could also be opened by the guardians of the necropolis for routine inspections. An interesting new development in this period is that of the side room built off the first pillared hall. This feature appears first in the tomb of Sethos I (p. 137), where it may have been intended as a false burial chamber, but continues (with the exception of the unfinished tomb of Sethos II) till almost the end of the dynasty, and even reappears later in the tomb of Ramesses III.

Regardless of actual orientation, it is known that in the 18th dynasty the builders of the royal monuments often viewed the entrance to the royal tomb as being in the south and the burial chamber in the north; the back of the tomb symbolically represented the northern zenith of the sun's nighttime under-

The Tomb Plan of Ramesses IV

The most detailed ancient plan of a royal tomb known today is this drawing on papyrus of the tomb of Ramesses IV, now in the Egyptian Museum, Turin. The plan is drawn at a scale of 1:28 with double lines enclosing the (white) interior of the tomb on a brown background. The king's sarcophagus is clearly depicted within the four shrines and pall frame which enclosed it; a similar arrangement was found in the tomb of Tutankhamun. Most parts of the tomb are named and their dimensions given in hieratic script. Apart from the peculiarities of Egyptian architectural representation, which produce a bent perspective relative to doors and groundlines, the plan shows errors in proportion, scale and location – such as the ratio of length to width of the rooms, the size of the doorways and the sarcophagus relative to the size of the tomb, and the misplaced location of some of the niches and anterooms (as may be seen by comparing the ancient with the modern plan beneath). Parts of this tomb described on the plan as having been 'drawn in outline' and 'engraved with chisels' are also undecorated. Yet the plan is a reasonable drawing which may have been made before the tomb was cut, or after it had been sealed.

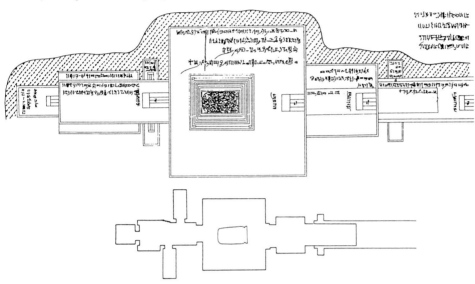

(Above) The ancient plan of the tomb of Ramesses IV was perhaps prepared after the completion of work, at the time the tomb was ritually dedicated for its owner. (Below) A modern plan of the tomb for comparison.

world journey, just as during the day the sun is at its highest in the south at noon. The niches cut into the sides of the passages – the 'Sanctuaries in which the Gods of the East/West Repose' – gave a symbolic fourfold orientation: the north–south axis of the tomb's passages and the east–west axis of the side walls. However, beginning in the 19th dynasty and continuing throughout the 20th dynasty, we find the development of what appears to be an east–west symbolic orientation of the tomb's main axis based upon the east–west path of the sun (p. 35). In the second half of the 19th dynasty, the design of the tomb begins to take on a more regular and symmetrical appearance, which may well be based on the underlying concern with the symbolic axes.

Twentieth dynasty: simplification

The essential tomb plan was greatly simplified in the 20th dynasty, and for economic and other reasons none of the tombs constructed after that of Ramesses III (with the exception of the tomb of Ramesses VI, which was built for two kings) was of comparable size. Yet the proportions used by the tomb architects continued to expand so that the last six tombs to be built in the valley all have corridors more than 3 m (10 ft) wide and 4 m (13 ft) high. This continued enlargement could not be maintained in every aspect, however, and the plans of the latest tombs are considerably curtailed from those of their forerunners. It is curious that the size of certain elements in the tomb – such as the well room – was not increased while that of most others saw a fairly constant increase in proportion.

Most noticeable is the fact that from the beginning of the dynasty the orientation of the royal sarcophagus was realigned along the tomb's major axis, with the head end now being placed towards the end of the tomb – even when there was sufficient space in the burial chamber to maintain the old alignment across the axis. This meant that it was now always aligned towards the west according to the symbolic east–west orientation of the tomb, so that the deceased monarch always looked towards the symbolic east and the rising sun, a factor which may have been related to the increased attention to the solar aspects of Egyptian religion found in the 20th dynasty.

A limestone ostracon in the Cairo Museum, with a working sketch of an unidentified tomb.

Cutting the Tombs

'Fourth month of the *peret*-season, day 21, the day of issuing chisels to the gang.'

From an ostracon

Selecting a site

It is known that a full year elapsed after the coronation of Ramesses IV before the search was begun for a site for his tomb; this kind of delay was perhaps unusual, and a tomb site was probably selected very early in the reign of most kings. In fact, foundation deposits (see below), including cartouches with the name of Tuthmosis IV found at the entrance to the tomb of Amenophis III (WV22: p. 110), indicate that during a king's reign work was occasionally begun on a tomb for his heir.

The specific location for a new royal tomb seems to have been chosen by the vizier accompanied by the chief stonemasons and architects, though the site would undoubtedly have been visited and approved at some point by the king himself. Different criteria were used in choosing tomb sites during different periods. As we have seen (p. 20), during most of the 18th dynasty the favoured positions were usually fairly high in the sides of the cliffs which ring the valley, often within natural rock cracks and beneath storm-fed waterfalls. In the tomb of Amenophis III, constructed in the second half of the 18th dynasty, for the first time the entrance was brought down to the talus slope beneath the cliff, and it continued to be located there throughout most of the following dynasty. Finally, in the 20th dynasty, when many of these low talus-slope sites were exhausted (and their proclivity for flooding by this time fully realized), the major tombs were cut in the ends of solid rock spurs which jutted from the valley's sides.

For the early tombs, ease of concealment was clearly a desirable factor in the choice of a site; later kings abandoned this approach and made larger tombs with impressive and visible entrances. In all periods, however, it is likely that certain symbolic and ritual factors were involved in choosing the specific sites; the external topography of many tombs suggests that they may have been located to lie in natural *akhet* (▱) or 'horizon'-like settings symbolic of the setting and rising sun (p. 16), and indeed there are ancient representations showing private tombs sited in this way.

Foundation Deposit Objects from the Tomb of Amenophis III

(found by Howard Carter and Waseda University)

Copper/bronze model tools:
Chisel blade (8)
Adze blade (3)
Knife blade (2)
Axe-head (2)

Wooden objects:
Symbolic knot (3)
Mshtyw object (2)
Rocker (3)
Hoe (3)
Brick mold (1)
'Wedge' (1)

Plant and animal products:
Rush sieve (2)
Rush tray (1)
Rush basket (1)
Bundle of papyrus fibres (1)
Bundle of leather strips (1)

Faience objects:
Throne name cartouche plaque (53)
Birth name cartouche plaque (45)
Uninscribed cartouche plaque (1)
Beads (several)

Model stone objects:
Limestone jar (2)
Alabaster saucer (1)
Alabaster oval (1)

Model pottery vessels:
Cups (97)
Saucers (19)
Jars (29)

Food offerings:
Head and foreleg of calf (4)
Fruits and other foodstuffs (various)

A selection of foundation deposit objects discovered by Howard Carter outside the entrance to WV22.

The Egyptians must have made numerous maps of the valley in order to avoid running into already existing tombs, though none have survived. Nevertheless, collisions did occur, as when the workmen cutting the corridor of Ramesses III's tomb accidentally broke into the nearby tomb of Amenmesse. The slope of KV9, the tomb of Ramesses VI, also had to be hastily adjusted to avoid a similar collision with the earlier tomb KV12.

The foundation ritual

Once the tomb site had been chosen, ritual ceremonies similar to those conducted for the foundation of a temple were evidently enacted. It was perhaps at this time that foundation deposits were placed in shallow pits dug in front of, and in some cases to the side of, the tomb entrance, arranged symmetrically with one central deposit before or behind. The arrangement may well have been patterned on temple foundation deposits, which were located at the four corners of the hallowed area with a fifth deposit placed along the building's main axis. The pits contained various offerings, along with models of the tools used in the construction of the temple or tomb and various objects of ritual significance.

It is probable that such foundation rituals were carried out at the inception of all royal tombs, though actual deposits are only known for Hatshepsut (KV20), Tuthmosis III (KV34), Tuthmosis I (KV38), Hatshepsut-Meryetre (KV42), Tuthmosis IV (KV43), Amenophis III (WV22), Ramesses IV (KV2), Ramesses X (KV18) and Ramesses XI (KV4). Why some tombs should have been equipped with such deposits and others apparently not remains a mystery, however; perhaps some were destroyed through time or have simply not been found.

Construction of the tomb

After foundation ceremonies had been completed, the work crews first removed the surface sand and debris. They then proceeded to quarry down into the underlying limestone, with the entrance doorway usually being cut as soon as the bedrock was penetrated to a depth sufficient to allow a solid lintel with perhaps some overhang above the doorway. The subsequent quarrying of the tomb's passages and chambers was a matter of considerable skill, for, unlike the construction of a temple or palace which could be mapped out on the ground ahead of time with the help of lines and markers, the interior sections of the tomb had to be driven straight and true without any such aids.

The cutting of the rock was accomplished using copper or bronze chisels struck by wooden mallets; although the soft white limestone fissured easily, it was frequently seeded with nodules of much harder flint which slowed the quarrying process consid-

erably. Occasionally, the embedded flint nodules were of such a size and intractability that the workers despaired of cutting them away and they were left – as in the case of a large boulder which may still be seen projecting from the side of the first pillared hall in the tomb of Merenptah.

The entrance passages of early tombs, such as that of Amenophis II seen here, were roughly hewn yet follow carefully orientated plans.

(Right) A wooden mallet found in WV24 of the type used by the stonecutters in making the royal tombs, and (below) a vivid sketch of a stonemason using a similar mallet on an ostracon from Deir el-Medina.

*(Right) A flint boulder
protruding into the first
pillared hall in the tomb of
Merenptah. Workmen
laboured for days to cut
away the intractable rock
and finally left it projecting
from the wall.*

*(Above) Red pottery oil lamp
from KV20 used with a
twisted linen wick or 'candle'.*

*(Below) A partly plastered
wall in the burial chamber of
the tomb of Horemheb. Note
the plaster filling irregularities
in the lower portion of the
wall; also the mason's or
draughtsman's graffito in the
centre showing the cardinal
orientation of the wall.*

*(Below right) Comparative
plans of abbreviated tombs
showing how construction
was cut short and the plans
adapted to incorporate burials
in the pillared hall (left – tomb
of Ay) or passages (right –
tomb of Sethos II).*

In addition to chisels and mallets, tools and supplies used in the construction of the tombs included spikes and stone pounders, and wicker baskets or leather buckets for the removal of the stone chips. Substantial quantities of oil and twisted linen wicks or 'candles' used to illuminate the action were also required once work had progressed deep into the rock. Salt may have been burnt with the oil or grease to inhibit smoke. As the stonecutters drove the tomb's passages into the heart of the limestone cliffs, other workers smoothed and dressed the floors, walls and ceilings of the corridors and chambers with the aid of hard polishing stones and simple levels and set-squares. Plasterers patched damaged and uneven surfaces and applied a uniform layer of fine gypsum plaster to make the walls ready for decoration.

The various stages of this work may be seen in a number of tombs, including those of Ramesses XI (KV4) and Prince Mentuherkhepshef (KV19), where partially completed corridors were left unfinished. Little detail survives about how the day-to-day work in the tombs was conducted. The records kept by the scribes simply affirm that work was done on a given day and occasionally recount particular problems that were encountered. Certain details may be surmised, however. Judging by the recorded numbers of candles burnt by the workmen, it would seem that they worked in two shifts, a 'morning' and 'afternoon' of about equal duration, with a midday break for rest and a meal. Relatively few men could have worked at the cutting face of the rock while the entrance corridors were under construction, but more and more men would have been needed to carry out the baskets of rock chips as the excavation progressed. More stonecutters must have been employed as the halls and side chambers of the tomb advanced, and even more men would then have been needed to carry out the cut rock, so that the number of workers must have varied greatly depending on the particular point of construction. The ancient records speak of as few as 30 men working on a tomb to as many as 120 at one time.

The scribes assigned to the tomb made regular progress reports. Periodic inspections by the vizier or his appointed aides were also noted. An ostracon in the Egyptian Museum in Cairo records that the vizier visited the valley to make a plan of a tomb, probably in order to check the work done against the architect's original designs. Occasionally, given more time or resources than expected, tombs were expanded and other elements added which were not in the original plans. In the tomb of Ramesses III, the small niche-like rooms off the third corridor must have been added in this manner, for their doors are cut through finished inscriptions on the corridor walls.

More often than not, however, work on the tombs was cut short by the king's death, and the majority of the tombs in the royal valley are unfinished to a greater or lesser degree. The death of the king left only a short time – essentially the 70 days required for the mummification process, and a little beyond – to bring to a close all quarrying and decoration, and to stock the tomb in preparation for the king's afterlife. The accession of the new monarch meant the beginning of a new age and usually, with little delay, the beginning of a new project and the continuation of the cycle.

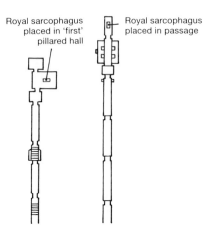

Royal sarcophagus
placed in 'first'
pillared hall

Royal sarcophagus
placed in passage

'The vizier Neferrenpet came . . . and also the king's servant Hori and the king's servant Amenkha . . . to search for a place to cut a tomb for Usermaatre-setepenamun [Ramesses IV] . . .'

From an ostracon

Graffiti and Ostraca

Thousands of graffiti have been found in the mountains of western Thebes, many of them left by individuals connected with the work in the royal valley – from humble workmen to important officials such as viziers and high priests. Thus the graffiti themselves range in length and degree of formality from crudely scrawled names to finely written records of official inspections.

Often, the writers speak of their own actions or circumstances, or simply record their presence in the area. Sometimes useful genealogies are inadvertently set down. In one location, for example, the workman Kenherkhepshef wrote his name and those of his children next to a graffito left by his mother's first husband who had died childless and whose name the younger man continued (p. 24). The elder Kenherkhepshef had recorded his own descent from the earlier scribe Panakhte so that a veritable family tree was inscribed.

Many graffiti are accompanied by sketches of the gods to which they are dedicated, and often include the representation of the artist in pious reverence before the deity. Sometimes the sketches are less serious or respectful, however, as in the case of the famous sketch found just outside the Valley of the Kings in a small cave above the temple of Hatshepsut at Deir el-Bahri. Here, a female pharaoh (undoubtedly Hatshepsut herself) is shown engaged in sexual activity with an unidentified male. In other cases graffiti are of a purely utilitarian nature. In the settlement on top of the ridge between the royal valley and Deir el-Medina, and in spots around the tombs in the valley itself, graffiti record the fact that a certain stone seat or a rock used as a seat is reserved for this or that foreman – for the graffito can also be a mark of possession. Jaroslav Černý spent over 20 years of his life collecting and studying hundreds of graffiti from the Theban mountains, publishing them between 1956 and 1974.

Graffiti have helped locate some of the monuments in and around the royal valley, and at least one tomb – that of Nefrure the daughter of Hatshepsut – was identified by Howard Carter in a desert wadi from the evidence of a graffito close to its entrance. Graffiti left by some of the ancient scribes and workmen also provide clues to the process of tomb construction, and stonecutters' and other workmen's marks, notations and signs are still visible in many of the monuments. In some cases – where the tombs lay open in antiquity – graffiti have been found ranging from the pharaonic period down to Greek, Roman and Christian times. Almost a thousand Greek and Latin texts have been counted in the tomb of Ramesses VI (known as the tomb of Memnon to the Classical writers) alone, and an equal number have been recorded in other Ramessid tombs open to the ancient traveller (p. 50).

Today, many of these graffiti, like the decorated walls upon which they stand, are under threat from

(Left) Many graffiti, such as this from an area to the north of the Valley of the Kings, underline the piety of workmen and others associated with the royal tombs. The kneeling figure worships before a ram-headed form of the god Amon-Re.

Coptic graffito on the wall of KV2, the tomb of Ramesses IV. Many such texts were left by the early Christians who inhabited some of the royal tombs. Strangely, unlike the images of the Egyptian gods in the temples which were often defaced by Christians, representations of the old gods in the royal tombs were rarely 'killed'.

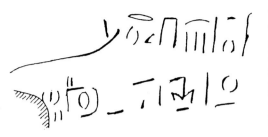

the touristic onslaught. The need for accurate recording still exists, since many graffiti supply vital historical data; they are a major source of information about the reburials of the royal mummies at the end of the New Kingdom (p. 205), and not infrequently the original burials themselves. For example, a graffito only recently found at the entrance to the tomb of Tawosret and Sethnakhte (KV14) records the previously unknown date of interment of Sethos II in that king's nearby tomb.

Ostraca: inscribed flakes and potsherds

The evidence of the graffiti is augmented by many thousands of ostraca – small inscribed limestone flakes and potsherds – found in and around the

Valley of the Kings. The ubiquitous chips were used for letters, lists, reports and receipts, as well as for miscellaneous notes and musings. Ostraca bear everything from sketches of formal royal motifs and tomb plans – details of work in progress, sometimes with dimensions and other labelling to confirm the identification, have been found for the tombs of Sethos II (KV15), Ramesses IV (KV2) and Ramesses IX (KV6) (p. 69) – to the casual and often lighthearted expressions of their artists. Not least in this regard, the ostraca (like certain graffiti) reveal in words and pictures the thoughts and feelings of the individuals who made them far more directly and honestly than the formal autobiographical texts of their age.

Ostraca showing offering scenes and other acts of religious devotion – found in a number of tombs, particularly those of Ramesses VI and IX – have been recognized as votive offerings left by workmen in these especially sacred places. Other figured ostraca are clearly preliminary drawings prepared by the artists in advance of decorating the tomb walls and occasionally, perhaps, when the motifs are alien to the tombs' subject matter, by assistants apprenticed to senior members of the work gangs.

An ostracon with a sketch of a Ramessid king and captives, a motif not found in the decoration of the tombs themselves. As is occasionally the case, the proportions of the king's figure (and the diminutive size of his captives) have been adjusted to fit within the limited size of the stone flake.

Decorating the Walls: Art, Religion and Symbolism

The decoration applied to the walls and ceilings of the royal tombs provided far more than a colourful patina, for the artists were in effect making an eternal underworld for the deceased king. The exigencies of tombs curtailed and hurried burials may have thwarted this goal on many occasions, but what the artists did achieve stands nonetheless among the greatest art of the ancient world.

The process by which these decorations were achieved is quite well understood. In some cases, though not all, draughtsmen laid out the representations using grids made by measuring rods and paint-covered strings snapped against the walls. The images and inscriptions were then applied in red paint outlines which were corrected as necessary in black. The care involved at this stage is seen in that sometimes errors in the texts from which the inscriptions were copied were noted and the term *gem wesh,* 'found defective', was written on the tomb wall. From the time of Horemheb on, carvers cut back the surrounding areas from around the representations before they were painted, or incised the individual hieroglyphs and figures depending on whether raised or sunk relief was chosen. The former, more costly, method was used throughout several of the 19th-dynasty tombs, but usually only in the entrances of later monuments.

In the next stage, painters carefully filled in the reliefs and their backgrounds, applying their pigments by reflected sunlight near the entrances, and by the light of oil lamps deeper within the tombs. No more than six colours were commonly used in the Valley of the Kings – black, red, blue, yellow, green and white – but these were occasionally blended to create gradations and variations of hue and tone. In the early burials it seems that the decoration was applied only when the excavation had been completed and before the actual interment. In later burials, because of their larger size and more extensive decoration, construction and painting of the tomb seem to have progressed side by side. Even here, stonecutters and painters probably took turns working so as to avoid jams in the confined spaces and damage to the freshly painted surfaces from airborne dust. Towards the end of the valley's history, declining resources may sometimes have caused things to be done differently: the decoration of the tomb of Ramesses IX was evidently begun during the king's reign, but only completed later, after his death.

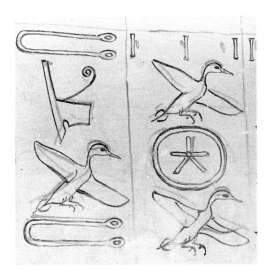

(Below left) Hieroglyphs from the tomb of Horemheb, showing the initial drawing in red paint and the final, corrected version in black.

(Below) Goddess from the tomb of Tuthmosis IV. The striations visible in the goddess's wig indicate brushstrokes, with individual dots of paint along the wig's leading edge representing curls of hair. The preliminary lines of the artist may be seen above the eye and eyebrow and beneath the chin.

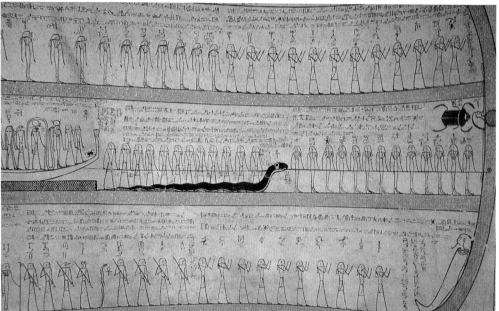

(Above) A comparison of images from the tomb of Amenophis II (left) (c. 1427 BC) and the tomb of Ramesses III (right) (c. 1184 BC) shows the simple paint on plaster of the earlier tomb and the carved and painted relief technique of the later monument. The differing treatment of individual features, for example the mouth, ears, stomach and pupil of the eye, is usually diagnostic of specific periods.

(Left) Burial chamber of Tuthmosis III. In the early painted tombs of the 18th dynasty, the decoration was wrapped scroll-like around the curving surfaces of the burial chambers and filled with cursive figures and script in the style used for writing on papyrus.

Meaning and purpose of the decoration

The wall paintings of the royal tombs are, in a sense, the most singular aspect of these monuments, for not only do they distinguish the tombs from the sepulchres of non- and lesser royalty, but they also provide a more detailed visual map or model of the beyond than is found anywhere else in the Egyptian record. This model of the afterlife at first represented the underworld alone, but later the heavens also, and thus the complete cosmos. The main themes of this decorative programme have been linked to the three successive dynasties which utilized the royal valley: the journey of the sun beneath the earth (18th dynasty); a divided emphasis on the journey of the sun in the heavens and the importance of Osiris and various earth gods in the netherworld (19th dynasty); and a combined stress on the sun's path through both the earth and heavens (20th dynasty).

This gradual change of focus may be seen in the varying choices and locations in the tombs of the funerary books, or in the depictions of scenes from them (see feature). In the early 18th dynasty, only the burial chamber received decoration – this taking the form of an unrolled papyrus of the Book of the Amduat, accurate in shape, colour and inscriptional style – but, from the time of Tuthmosis III, various deities were also shown on the walls of the antechamber and the well. In the 19th dynasty, decoration was carried into all parts of the tomb, and the idea that the axis of the tomb represented the sun's east–west journey into the tomb (and its west–east return) seems to have been paramount.

From the time of Ramesses II on, the solar disc of Re containing the god's morning and evening manifestations was placed above the entrance to the royal tombs. In this exterior position, the disc is invariably painted yellow, the colour of the daytime sun; whereas within the tomb the same image is painted red, indicating its evening and nighttime appearance as it follows the east–west progression of the tomb's axis. Just within the entrance to the

royal tomb, Pharaoh is depicted greeting the sun god Re-Horakhty before the Litany of Re – now placed in the first and sometimes second corridors – which enumerated and pictured the many forms of the solar deity in his daily cycle.

Tomb of Merenptah. From the 19th dynasty on, the upper reaches of the royal tomb were decorated with primarily solar-related texts, such as the Litany of Re with its familiar frontispiece of the king before Re-Horakhty.

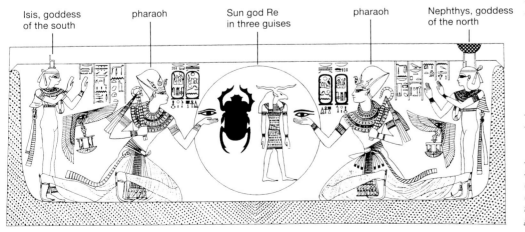

Isis, goddess of the south   pharaoh   Sun god Re in three guises   pharaoh   Nephthys, goddess of the north

A detail from the entrance of Ramesses X's tomb (KV18). The kneeling king presents 'The Eye of Horus' – which symbolizes offerings – to the sun god in ram-headed (evening) and beetle (morning) forms. The royal image is flanked by the goddesses Isis and Nephthys.

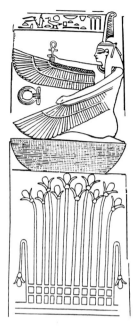

The goddess Maat, the daughter of Re, seated upon a lily plant, the heraldic plant of Upper – southern – Egypt. From the tomb of Tawosret.

The goddesses Isis and Nephthys, symbolically associated with the south and north respectively, were now shown flanking the sun disc above the tomb entrance and at points along the interior passages – as in the tomb of Sethos I. Beginning with the tomb of Ramesses II, two opposing figures of the goddess Maat were painted on the jambs of the tomb entrance, each kneeling upon a basket which was supported on the left-hand (south) wall by a lily plant and on the right (north) by a papyrus clump. This use of the heraldic flora of Upper (southern) and Lower (northern) Egypt at the sides of the tomb – flanking the east–west passage of the sun – seems also to stress the symbolic east–west alignment of the main axis of these royal burials.

Osiris and Re

Another aspect of this symbolic orientation of the tomb, developed in the 19th dynasty, is the logical division of the tomb into a front (entrance) half (symbolically the east) and back half (symbolically west), giving precedence to Re in the front half, and Osiris, 'Foremost of the Westerners', in the back. The conscious division is seen especially clearly in the large so-called 'Osiris shrine', with its opposed images of the underworld god, which was placed on the far wall of the first pillared hall – the dividing point of the tomb – above steps leading into the lower reaches of the monument. There the sun god continues to appear, but his images are often much smaller than those of Osiris. Beginning with the tomb of Horemheb, in fact, it is Osiris and the

Hathor, Mistress of the West

Osiris, supreme god of the underworld

Sethos I, pharaoh

Horus, falcon-headed god associated with kingship

Amduat

Amduat/Astronomical ceiling   Books of Gates

Book of Gates

Tomb of Sethos I

Antechamber

Burial chamber

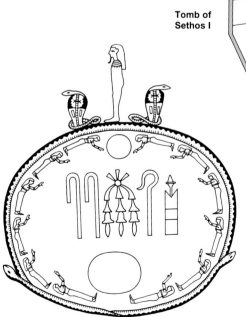

(Left) The name of Ramesses III enclosed within a representation of the sun's endless circuit, linguistically and symbolically fusing the name of the king with the solar deity.

underworld deities which dominate the lower reaches of the 19th-dynasty tombs; and on royal sarcophagi prepared after Ramesses I, the image of the king as Osiris is invariably carved in relief upon the outer surface of the lid.

The 20th dynasty saw further developments in the symbolism of the royal tombs, especially that relating to the association of the deceased king with the sun god and the supremacy of the god in the heavens and netherworld alike. In the burial chamber of Ramesses III, for example, the name of the king was inscribed within a disc formed by the

The Major Afterlife Books

While the Amduat, the oldest of the royal funerary works, continued to be used through most of the valley's history, other works were added and sometimes substituted as time progressed. In the later Ramessid tombs there is a new stress on specific texts concerning the underworld and the heavens.

Books of the Beyond

The theological works which decorated the royal tombs provided detailed maps or models of the beyond. Most of these 'books' were derived ultimately from the earlier Pyramid Texts used by the

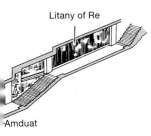

Litany of Re

Amduat

kings of the 5th and 6th dynasties, though each developed unique aspects. The commonly used names of these works are all modern. No tomb attempted to include all these texts, and usually only selections of the works chosen were utilized – in the same way that a modern Christian funeral might include certain hymns but not the entire hymnal.

	Tomb of:	Tuthmosis I	Hatshepsut	Tuthmosis III	Amenophis II	Tuthmosis IV	Amenophis III	Tutankhamun	Ay	Horemheb	Ramesses I	Sethos I	Ramesses II	Merenptah	Amenmesse	Sethos II	Siptah	Tawosret/Sethnakhte	Ramesses III	Ramesses IV	Ramesses V/VI	Ramesses VII	Ramesses IX	Ramesses X	Ramesses XI
Amduat: 'That Which Is in the Underworld' was called by the Egyptians 'The Book of the Secret Chamber'. It is the earliest work detailing the sun god's journey through the 12 divisions of the underworld corresponding to the 12 hours of the night. Complete copies were inscribed in the burial chambers of Tuthmosis III and Amenophis II, and partial versions are found in most tombs.																									
Litany of Re: Originating in the 18th dynasty, the two-part Litany of the Sun acclaims the sun god Re under 75 different forms and also praises the king in his union with the sun god and other deities. First appearing on pillars of the burial chamber of Tuthmosis III, this work was utilized in the entrances of most tombs from the time of Sethos I.																									
Book of Gates: This work appears late in the 18th dynasty and was inscribed in the burial chamber and first pillared halls of most later tombs. The name of the composition refers to the 12 gates which divide the hours of the night. The most complete versions were inscribed in the tomb of Ramesses VI and on the calcite sarcophagus of Sethos I.																									
Book of the Dead: Called by the Egyptians 'The Book of Coming Forth by Day', this is actually a collection of spells, many derived from the earlier Coffin and Pyramid Texts. First used by commoners, extracts from the Book of the Dead appear in the antechambers of a number of Ramessid tombs.																									
Book of Caverns: In this work the underworld is envisaged as a series of caves or pits over which the sun god passes. It lays great stress on afterlife rewards and punishments and on the ultimate destruction of the enemies of the sun god. Usually placed in the upper parts of the later tombs, a complete version appears in the tomb of Ramesses VI.																									
Books of the Heavens: Texts composed during the late New Kingdom which describe the sun's passage through the heavens. Three of the better known are the Book of the Day, Book of the Night and Book of the Divine Cow. These books are found in a number of Ramessid burial chambers and also in several passages in the tomb of Ramesses VI.																									
Book of the Earth: Religious composition originating in the 20th dynasty which describes, in four parts, the sun's nocturnal journey through the underworld. It appears in the burial chambers of several of the later Ramessid tombs, and on anthropoid sarcophagi of the same date.																									

c. 1504 BC ──────────────► c. 1070 BC
── 18th dynasty ► ── 19th dynasty ► ── 20th dynasty ►

entwined bodies of two serpents. By placing his name within this device, Ramesses identified himself directly with the solar deity and joined its cyclical daily journey. The same idea is also expressed in other ways. In the tomb of Ramesses IV the king's royal titles are inscribed along the centre of the ceiling of the hall which leads into the burial chamber. Surrounded by golden stars on a blue ground representing the heavens, the king's names follow the path of the sun and once again identify him with the solar journey – the king and god being fused in the path of the sun.

Because of their location and significance, the lower reaches of the 20th-dynasty tombs were decorated to represent the complete cycle of the sun in both its diurnal and nocturnal phases. The Books of the Heavens were inscribed on the ceiling of the sarcophagus chamber, and texts and illustrations from the Books of the Earth and Underworld were placed on its walls. The Egyptian royal tomb, in the fully developed decorative programme of the late New Kingdom, represents the cosmos which was depicted not only in its images and texts, but also by the specific location of these symbolic elements.

Stocking the Chambers: What the Dead Took with Them

The Osiris Tutankhamun: (below) the king's second coffin found nested within his outermost anthropoid coffin, which itself was enclosed by a rectangular quartzite sarcophagus (right) in the burial chamber.

'Hail to you Osiris! . . . Control the offerings of those who are in their tombs. . . . May you be with them in your mummy-form.'

Book of the Dead

Although almost all the royal tombs were anciently plundered, the list of goods originally placed within them can still be reasonably well reconstructed. Our knowledge is based on evidence from the substantially intact tomb of Tutankhamun, augmented by the remnants of equipment left in the tombs of Tuthmosis III (KV34: p. 97), Amenophis II (KV35: p. 100), Tuthmosis IV (KV43: p. 105) and Horemheb (KV57: p. 130), as well as minor items recovered from other royal tombs. Some royal burial items are also depicted on the walls of the tomb of Sethos II (KV15: p. 152) and elsewhere. Together, this evidence indicates that from the middle of the 18th dynasty, the typical royal burial assemblage consisted of the mummified body of the king contained within several coffins nested one inside the other. These coffins were placed within a stone sarcophagus surrounded in turn by a number of gilded wooden shrines. A large range of other objects intended for the eternal sustenance, protection and use of the deceased king was also deposited in the burial chamber. In some monuments, such as the tomb of Merenptah (KV8: p. 147), there is evidence that the process of stocking the tomb began years before the king's death.

The mummy

The unrifled remains of Tutankhamun (KV62: p. 122) show that the royal mummy itself was prepared with items both to protect and to sustain in the beyond. The carefully crafted face mask preserved the image of the deceased ruler and associated him with named deities whose powers or attributes would be beneficial in the afterlife, while the items of insignia placed upon him guaranteed his rulership in the next world. The various amulets enclosed within the mummy wrappings also provided magical assistance in various ways with some, for example the vulture amulets placed at the neck, apparently being reserved for royal mummies alone. Understandably, few items from this group survived the robbers and dismantling parties (p. 190).

The coffin

The royal mummy was contained within a coffin – usually itself nested within one or two further coffins – made of gilded wood or precious metal. While many early Egyptian coffins were decorated to resemble tombs and houses, by the Middle Kingdom an anthropoid coffin shape had appeared which copied the appearance of the mummy and symbolically provided an alternative 'body' for the deceased's spirit. This is the form used in New Kingdom royal burials. As with the sarcophagus (see below), the figures of the goddesses Isis and Nephthys, the four sons of Horus (see below) and other deities connected with Osiris were routinely added to the decoration of the coffin walls in order to provide a ring of protection around the deceased

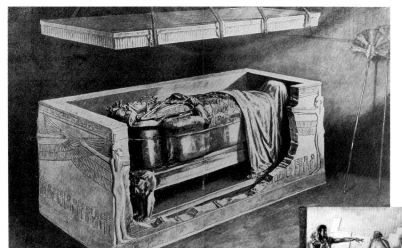

the box. Radical stylistic changes took place during the second half of the 18th dynasty. From Amenophis III on, the favoured material was red granite. The sarcophagi of Tutankhamun, Ay (WV23: p. 128) and Horemheb are all rectangular, shrine-like boxes with a cavetto cornice running around their tops. The protective figures of the goddesses Isis, Nephthys, Neith and Selkis adorn the four corners, though Anubis and the four sons of Horus continue to be represented on the sides. In the 19th dynasty, royal sarcophagi were usually constructed of red granite and were made considerably larger, being as much as 3.7 m (12 ft) in length

Drawings produced at the time of the discovery of Tutankhamun's tomb to illustrate the three principal stages in the burial of the king, the most complete ever discovered: (top) the three nested coffins, draped with a linen shroud, are placed upon a gilded wooden bier within the quartzite sarcophagus; (centre) having erected the first three gilded wooden shrines around the closed sarcophagus, the spangled linen pall is unrolled over its gilded wooden frame; (bottom) finally, the fourth shrine, of gilded wood richly inlaid with blue faience, is erected in sections around the whole.

(Opposite) A selection of the types of funerary objects which accompanied Tutankhamun beyond the grave.

'Osiris'. Many attributes of the god Osiris – such as his curved beard, tripartite 'divine' wig, and hands crossed on the breast – could be added to the form of the royal coffin. Another type of anthropoid mummy case, which developed in the Theban area during the Second Intermediate Period, is the so-called *rishi* (Arabic for 'feather') coffin, named for the patterning which covers much of the lid. This feather patterning represents the mummy as a bird-like *ba* or 'soul' of the deceased himself; it is often augmented by the overlay of the enfolding wings of goddesses such as Isis, Nephthys, Nut and Nekhbet. Although abandoned in private burials early in the 18th dynasty, this coffin type continued to be used for royal burials throughout the New Kingdom – for example in the coffins from the tomb of Tutankhamun, which combine the symbolism of the basic anthropoid form with that of both the Osirid and *rishi* types.

The sarcophagus

Stone sarcophagi were used for royal burials at least from the time of Hatshepsut, and were designed to hold the inner coffin or coffins. In the 18th dynasty, sarcophagi were at first made of quartzite: the earliest known models were copies in stone of the wooden coffins used throughout the Middle Kingdom, but with the upper surface of the lid carved in the form of the royal cartouche. Eventually, corners became rounded and the box itself followed in the shape of the cartouche. During this time the figures of Anubis and the four sons of Horus were carved on the sides, and Isis and Nephthys adorned the head and foot ends of

and 2.7 m (9 ft) high. Weighing many tons, they thus became part of the security of the tomb itself, with inner anthropoid sarcophagi, of calcite, sometimes placed within. Ramessid royal sarcophagi were inscribed with scenes and texts from books of the netherworld; and from the time of Merenptah, the top of the sarcophagus lid was decorated with an image of the king, carved in raised relief between Isis and Nephthys, while the underside of the lid depicted the outstretched form of the goddess Nut. Under Ramesses VII (KV1: p. 166) standards declined, with the presumably coffined royal mummy being simply buried in a pit cut into the burial chamber floor and covered with a huge granite lid.

The funerary shrines

The largest items placed in the royal tomb were the gilded wooden shrines enclosing the sarcophagus. The Turin plan of the tomb of Ramesses IV (p. 27) shows a similar configuration to that actually encountered in the burial of Tutankhamun: four shrines, nested one within the

Gilded wooden figure of the king as Horus on a papyrus skiff, his arm raised to spear the hippopotamus of Seth.

Calcite canopic chest, containing the embalmed internal organs (liver, lungs, stomach, intestines).

The goddess Selkis, one of the guardian deities of the gilded wooden canopic shrine.

Life-sized ka-figure, one of two placed at the walled-up entrance to the burial chamber.

Osiris-shaped tray, filled with Nile silt and planted with grain intended to germinate after the tomb was closed.

Wooden image of Anubis – guardian of the dead – from the top of a gilded shrine equipped with carrying poles.

Model of the mummified king recumbent on a lion bier – a gift to Pharaoh's burial from the necropolis official Maya.

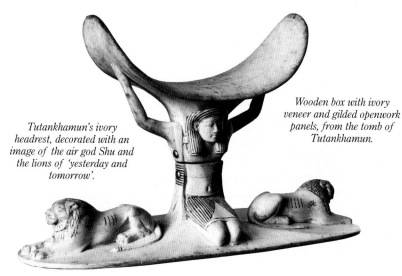

Tutankhamun's ivory headrest, decorated with an image of the air god Shu and the lions of 'yesterday and tomorrow'.

Wooden box with ivory veneer and gilded openwork panels, from the tomb of Tutankhamun.

Large blue faience shabti-figure of Sethos I, one of a number buried in the tomb to work on the king's behalf in the next life.

other, with a pall-frame covered with a sequin-studded shroud inserted between the outermost and second-outermost shrines. The dimensions of a number of burial chambers in the Valley, together with the recovery of several gilded bronze pall-sequins and actual shrine fragments, indicate that such structures were standard fare. The remains of a gilded wooden shrine recovered by Theodore Davis from Tomb 55 (p. 117), prepared by Akhenaten for the Amarna burial of his mother Tiye, indicate further that their use was not restricted solely to the king himself. Whereas Tutankhamun's shrines are decorated with texts and scenes from the underworld books, Tiye's shrine was decorated in pure Amarna style, with images of the royal family under the protective, life-giving rays of the solar disc.

The canopic chest and containers

The mummification process (p. 44) involved the removal of the internal organs, or viscera – liver, lungs, stomach and intestines. These organs were embalmed and wrapped separately and placed in four containers known as canopic jars within a canopic chest. (The term 'canopic' is a misnomer, coined by early antiquarians linking these jars with the pilot of Menelaus, who was worshipped at Canopus in the Delta in the form of a human-headed jar.) Several complete and fragmentary sets of canopic equipment are known from the Valley of the Kings.

The royal canopic chests of the early New Kingdom were at first made of quartzite like the sarcophagi they resembled, calcite later becoming the favoured material from at least the reign of Amenophis II on (KV35: p. 100). That of Ramesses II was inlaid (KV7: p. 140). Decoration (except for the canopic chest of Akhenaten from el-Amarna, which employed figures of the falconiform Re-

Horakhty) consisted of the protective presence of the goddesses Isis, Nephthys, Selkis and Neith, usually set at the corners. Shrine-like in shape, the chests were divided internally into compartments to receive four jars, or else made with four cylindrical borings in the solid stone into which mummiform canopic coffinettes, perhaps of gold (as in the tomb of Tutankhamun), containing the embalmed viscera could be inserted. The jars or hollows were closed with human-headed stoppers.

The canopic chest could be inserted in a pit dug at the foot-end of the sarcophagi, or stored in a separate niche or small room – as, for example, in the tomb of Tutankhamun, where the canopic furniture was installed in the treasury – off the burial chamber. The boy-king's equipment was further enclosed within a large shrine of gilded wood, and fragments of other shrines have been tentatively identified in the tomb of Amenophis III (WV22: p. 110). The use of canopic chests was evidently abandoned in the 20th dynasty, when individual jars of large size again came into vogue. One surviving example is that of Ramesses IV (KV2: p. 162).

Ritual figures and models

The tomb of Tutankhamun has preserved the largest and most spectacular array of ritual figures ever found, stored in upright, resin-coated wooden shrines. Many of the figures are heavily gilded, unlike the less complete and more modest sets which have been recovered from ransacked tombs in the Valley of the Kings (including those of Amenophis II – KV35 – Tuthmosis IV – KV43 – and Horemheb – KV57). The two principal figures in Tutankhamun's burial were the life-size *ka*-statues guarding the sealed entrance to the burial chamber. Among the smaller royal images may be noted statuettes of the king striding, harpooning

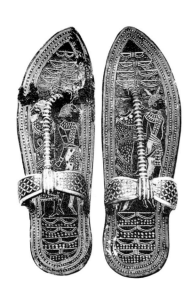

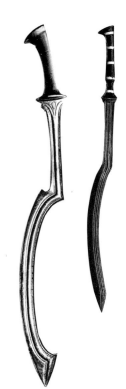

A pair of Tutankhamun's sandals. With every step, the enemies of the Egyptian state would be symbolically crushed underfoot.

Weapons from Tutankhamun's arsenal – a golden dagger and two examples of the Egyptian khepesh *or sickle sword.*

or set upon the back of a leopard. Some 28 statues of the gods included Atum, Duamutef and Sakhmet, as well as more obscure deities such as Mamu and Menkeret.

Tutankhamun was buried with a staggering 413 *shabti* figures – magical fieldworkers for the next life, produced in stone, faience and wood. Most other royal tombs seem to have contained far fewer (Hatshepsut had only one), or none at all (as with Tuthmosis III and Ay), though the tomb of Sethos I (KV17: p. 137) is said to have contained as many as 700–1,000 when first uncovered by Belzoni. With the figures were often interred model hoes and other implements, the tools of the *shabti*'s trade.

Other classes of ritual object frequently encountered in 18th-dynasty royal burials are the 'Osiris-beds' – wooden trays in the shape of this god planted with seeds of grain which would germinate after the tomb had been closed, to symbolize the continuation of life after death. Model boats and chariots were also included in the burial, perhaps as a symbolic means of transporting the dead king through the underworld, and large ritual couches with a similarly symbolic purpose.

Their meaning usually more obscure than obvious, a host of other ritual objects have been found buried in the royal tombs, including faience forelegs, amulets, amuletic vessels and other arcane offerings. Most of the large royal burials also included protective deposits of 'magic bricks' surmounted by divine images, placed in niches in the walls of the burial chamber. The tomb of Tutankhamun possessed four such niches, that of Amenophis III as many as eleven.

Objects of daily life

Although a great deal of the material buried with

Pharaoh was ritualistic in nature, an extraordinary number of objects of daily life was also deposited in the tomb so that the god-king's life in the next world would be not too different from that on earth. In this respect, the royal tomb was much the same as that of the well-to-do commoner. The inventory typically included personal clothing and precious jewels, perfumes and cosmetics, games and game-boxes, musical instruments, writing materials, weaponry, heirlooms and other personal mementoes, elegant tableware in precious metals, stone, pottery and glass, and plentiful food supplies – such as boxes of preserved meats, grain, fruits and copious supplies of wine and beer. Practical furniture, too, has been found, including chairs, stools, beds (both folding and fixed), boxes, chests and baskets, and lamps.

The reuse of royal burial equipment

Although a new royal tomb was normally cut for each monarch, old excavations were occasionally taken over and adapted for a new owner. In the same way, a number of funerary objects can be recognized as having been taken over and reused by later individuals. Two types of reuse should be distinguished: the earlier, in which unused and surplus burial equipment never actually removed from store was pressed into service by a later king to bolster his funerary trousseau – as with Tutankhamun's employment of funerary objects demonstrably discarded by Akhenaten (a number of the ritual figures, as well as other items) and Ankhkheprure Nefernefruaten (including the canopic coffinettes and mummy bands); and a later type of reuse, when previously used burial furniture was taken over by a new, and not necessarily royal, owner at the time the earlier burial was dismantled, because of its inherent magical potency (p. 206).

Pharaoh Joins the Gods

'My seat with Geb is made spacious, my star is set on high with Re, I travel to and fro in the fields of offerings, for I am that Eye of Re which . . . is conceived and born every day.'

Pyramid Texts, Spell 698

The death of every Egyptian monarch of the New Kingdom and the accession of his successor were hailed with a respectful announcement formula: 'The falcon is flown to heaven and [his successor] is arisen in his place.' This dual affirmation, 'The king is dead – long live the king!', was the turning point upon which the new king took effective control of the land and the deceased king underwent the necessary preparations for burial.

The process of mummification

Traditionally, the royal body was first washed and anointed, after which mortuary priests removed the viscera by way of a small incision in the left side of the abdomen. By the 18th dynasty, the removal of the brain was also common – usually through the nostrils, but occasionally in other ways (the cranial tissue of King Amosis was removed through an incision at the back of the neck). The liver, lungs, stomach and intestines were extracted, treated and stored in canopic containers and the body packed with absorbent materials which hastened the process of desiccation. The body was then placed on a slanted bed and covered with powdered natron. After 40 days the body would have lost some 75 per cent of its weight through the dehydrative action of this salt-like compound and it was then rewashed, dried, bandaged and adorned with protective amulets – each stage of the process being carried out with the recitation of appropriate spells and incantations.

Care was taken to preserve the natural appearance of the body as much as possible, as may be seen in the mummy of Queen Ahmose-Nofretiri, the wife of Amosis. Because this queen had lost

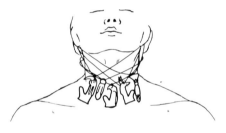

(Above) The possible mummy of Tuthmosis II. Great care was usually taken to preserve the actual appearance of the king in the course of the mummification process – especially as the New Kingdom progressed. Despite its early 18th-dynasty date, the features of the mummy of Tuthmosis II are remarkably well preserved.

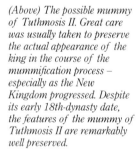

(Right) During the unwrapping of Tutankhamun's mummy, Carter counted some 150 jewels and amulets – a small selection shown here – on the body or folded into the bandages. Each amulet had its own special place on the body (the neck and chest were very important areas) and played a specific protective and strengthening role.

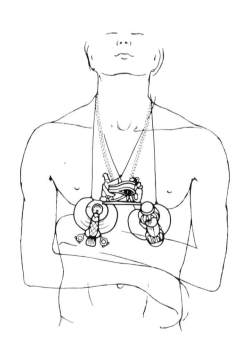

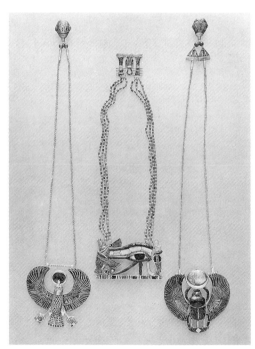

most of her natural hair, her mummy was given additional plaits of human hair which were carefully attached to the head. Care was also taken to retain the fingernails and toenails, which were bound to the body or held in place by tube-like metal stalls. In some cases, even the eyelashes have been preserved. Experimentation and innovation are apparent in the mummification process throughout the New Kingdom. With the mummy of Amenophis III, linen and resin packing was introduced under the skin of the neck, arms and legs so that these parts of the body retained their natural fullness after drying, a practice which only became common somewhat later. The body cavities of some later pharaohs were packed with dried lichens (Siptah, Ramesses IV) or sawdust (Ramesses V) instead of the usual resin-soaked linen; and small figures of the four sons of Horus were found inside the mummy of Ramesses III, which was also the first of several royal mummies to be given artificial eyes.

The ritually prescribed pose of the mummy also saw development and change. At the beginning of the 18th dynasty the arms of the royal mummy were placed along the sides of the body, or sometimes extended with the hands placed over the genital region. This attitude was modified later in the dynasty by placing the arms, crossed and with fisted hands, over the chest – a pose which lasted until the end of the 20th dynasty. With the mummies of Sethos I and his successors, the hands were laid flat upon the shoulders.

The whole process of preparation for burial took 70 days (a ritually significant period – the length of time that most of the stars remain hidden beneath

The feet of Tutankhamun, with toe-stalls and sandals of sheet gold in position.

the horizon). While the main royal residence was located at Thebes the mummification process was naturally completed there, but once the residence moved to the north, the embalming process was undoubtedly carried out in the new location before the body of the king will have been taken on the journey up-river to the royal necropolis – an assumption supported by the fact that the mummy of Ramesses II has been found to harbour traces of marine rather than riverine sand.

Funerary rites and afterlife beliefs

The burial itself involved various ritual ceremonies performed along a processional route from Thebes to the king's mortuary temple – if one had been built – on the west bank of the Nile and from there to the Valley of the Kings. Judging from representations in the tomb of Tutankhamun and other evi-

Tutankhamun's funerary cortège depicted on the east wall of the king's burial chamber. After mummification the body of the king was moved in procession to his mortuary temple on the Nile's west bank and taken from there to the tomb prepared in the Valley of the Kings.

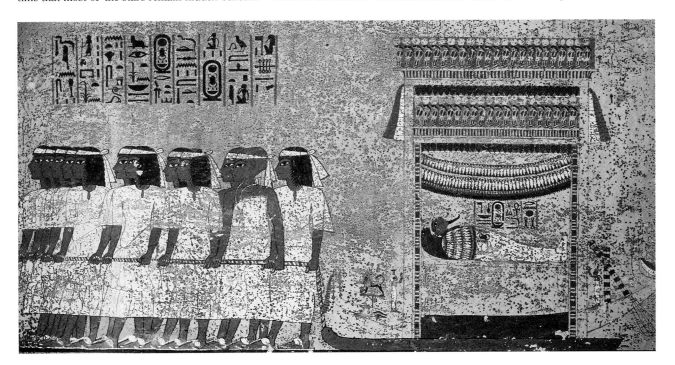

*The 'opening of the mouth'
ritual of reanimation,
performed by Tutankhamun's
successor Ay on the mummy
of Tutankhamun. This scene,
unique to the royal tombs,
illustrates one of the final
ritual activities before the
actual burial of the deceased
king.*

dence, the funerary cortège might be led by the new king, and include the two viziers and various high officials and priests, offering bearers and mourners. The dead king's encoffined body was drawn on a sledge pulled by oxen, followed by a second sledge which held the canopic chest. Masked and costumed priests and priestesses represented the mortuary deity Anubis and the protective goddesses Isis and Nephthys. When the tomb was reached, the final rituals were enacted: the 'opening of the mouth', by which the physical senses of the mummy were 'restored', and the holding of a ritual funerary banquet. The dead king was then placed within the sarcophagus and this and the tomb itself sealed. The finality of this action was mitigated by the belief that the king had now entered the realms of the afterlife.

By the beginning of the New Kingdom, the Egyptians' beliefs concerning the nature of this afterlife had developed considerably from those held by the kings of the pyramid age. Yet new beliefs were continuously assimilated without older

ones being discarded, so that the beliefs of New Kingdom times were a curious mix of ideas based on the association of the dead king with the sun god Re, the stars of the heavens and the netherworld deity Osiris. To some extent these theologies were conflated. By the end of the New Kingdom, Re and Osiris were commonly fused, with Osiris seen as the body of the god and Re as his soul. The deceased king thus became one with both deities and is identified as such in many of the royal tombs.

The pre-eminent gods of the heavens and the underworld were not the only deities with whom the king was believed to unite, however. Various images of gods of the earth, such as Geb and Sokar, also figure in the tombs, and although these deities are often themselves associated with the underworld realm or with Osiris, they are given separate identities frequently enough to show their individual importance. The same is true of those goddesses of the heavens, such as Nut and Hathor, who, although associated with Osiris or Re in cer-

Two representations of the sun god Re in the solar barque from the tomb of Ramesses IX. The sun god was believed nightly to traverse the underworld and to overcome its dangers, returning each day in renewal from death.

tain mythological relationships, maintain their identities as divine mother or eternal mistress of the king. Although somewhat more important in the earlier royal tombs, Hathor continues to appear throughout the 19th and 20th dynasties; and the figure of Nut is prominently featured in some of the very latest tombs.

Thus, the deceased king was not simply assimilated into the line of his predecessors; he joined them in becoming one with Osiris and Re – an aspect, as it were, of these pre-eminent gods. At an even more abstract level, the king was believed to become one with the heavens and earth – with the cosmos itself – while maintaining his own individuality as a distinct god. This was a mystery which is never directly spelled out in any of the afterlife books found in the royal tombs, but is alluded to constantly and was the perceived reality to which every burial in the Valley of the Kings aspired.

The Royal Wives and Pharaoh's Children

The Valley of the Kings was the burial place not only of Pharaoh: a number of tombs were employed for the burial of favoured nobles (p. 174), and for several of the royal wives and their offspring. Hatshepsut, as queen regnant, arranged for burial within KV20, the tomb of her father Tuthmosis I (p. 91). Tuthmosis III prepared a sumptuous tomb (KV42: p. 102) close to his own sepulchre for his chief queen Hatshepsut-Meryetre – though she seems in the end to have been interred within KV35 (p. 100). Amenophis III made provision for two of his queens – Tiye and probably Sitamun – within WV22 (p. 110), though again the likelihood is that neither was ever buried there (p. 118). The form of the supplementary queens' chambers within WV22 is quite distinctive, each having a single central pillar and a small subsidiary room. The configuration is shared by KV21 (p. 115), and we may reasonably identify this tomb, too, as 18th dynasty in date and intended for the use of one or other members of a king's immediate kin.

The presence of royal family members has been noted in several other pharaohs' tombs, including those of Amenophis II (KV35: p. 100), Tuthmosis IV (KV43: p. 105) and Tutankhamun (KV62: p. 122). From the reign of Ramesses I, a new necropolis was established for members of the immediate royal family – the Valley of the Queens. The Valley of the Kings still had its attractions, however, and during the 19th dynasty Merenptah appears to have shared his tomb (KV8: p. 147) with the great royal wife Isisnofret, while Tawosret, as queen regnant, initially began to prepare a joint tomb in the Valley for herself and her deceased husband Sethos II (KV14: p. 157). The king's mother Takhat and possibly the great royal wife Baketwerel were apparently interred within KV10, the tomb of Amenmesse (p. 150), and a similar honour was conferred upon the two Ramessid princes buried in the abandoned KV13 (p. 154).

Other tombs in the Valley of the Kings employed by members of the royal family include KV5, the vast family mausoleum prepared by Ramesses II of the 19th dynasty (p. 144), KV3, prepared for an unknown son of Ramesses III (p. 161), and KV19, taken over by the 20th-dynasty prince Mentuherkhepshef (p. 170) – while the famous 'Gold Tomb' (KV56: p. 153) may be the burial of a child of Sethos II and Tawosret.

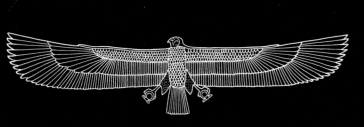

For centuries, the Valley of the Kings has attracted a steady stream of adventurers, tourists and scholars, all drawn by curiosity, the majority infected by romance – and an unhappy few held by obsession. To excavate among the magnificent, decorated tombs of the Theban royal cemetery was the ultimate addiction: it offered the possibility of enormous reward – and the reality of enormous disappointment. In the Valley of the Kings, wrote Lord Carnarvon, 'You either find grand things, or nothing at all.'

Before the 19th century, hints at the potential of this pharaonic Klondyke were few and far between – the tombs themselves, strewn with bones, wrappings and broken images in wood and stone, the odd fleck of gold glinting on the painted sepulchre-walls and shards by the thousand crunching underfoot. These were the sole, meagre pointers to the wealth once lavished on Egypt's kings and their favoured courtiers; but they were an inspiration to dig deeper. In time, further, better preserved tombs would be uncovered: Sethos I, Amenophis II, Maiherpri, Yuya and Tjuyu, the mysterious Tomb 55, the jewel-laden Gold Tomb; and, of course, the unparalleled riches of the boy-pharaoh, Tutankhamun.

Here, in the barren wadis of Egypt's Valley of the Kings, was to unfold one of the most exciting, extraordinary chapters in the history of archaeological endeavour.

II AGENTS OF DISCOVERY

Tourists in Ancient Times

The Roman emperor Hadrian inscribed a record of his visit to Egypt in AD 130 on one of the Colossi of Memnon.

'I, Philastrios the Alexandrian, who have come to Thebes, and who have seen with my eyes the work of these tombs of astounding horror, have spent a delightful day.'

Greek graffito

Greeks and Romans

When, before 1000 BC, the last royal burial had been made in the Valley of the Kings, the need for the permanent workforce which had serviced the necropolis for half a millennium (p. 22) evaporated. There was, as we shall see, sporadic activity of sorts; but the workers dispersed, and the quarrying ceased. For a further 500 years, the Valley of the Kings would remain a backwater of inactivity – until the coming of the Greeks.

Egypt had always had its fair share of foreign visitors, but the first serious touristic interest in the country, and in Thebes and her monuments in particular, followed in the wake of Alexander the Great.

'It appears that those [tombs] open in the time of the Ptolemies were Numbers 1, 2, 3, 4, 6, 7, 8, 9, 10, 11, 12, 14, 15, and 18, fourteen out of the seventeen mentioned by Diodorus...'

John Gardner Wilkinson

Egypt was at its height as a destination for the curious between the end of the third century BC and the second century AD. During this relatively settled and prosperous time thousands of travellers from across the Classical world (including the emperor Hadrian in AD 130) ventured up the Nile to view the monuments of Egypt's fabulous past, guidebooks in hand. High on the list of things to see were the famed 'Colossi of Memnon' – the gigantic seated statues fronting the destroyed mortuary temple of Amenophis III, one of which gave out an eerie sound when struck by the rays of the early-morning sun – and the tombs of 'the Memnonia', the name the Greeks gave to the area of western Thebes as a whole. And, within 'the Memnonia', the most important places to visit were the 'syrinxes' (as the pipe-like corridors of Wadi Biban el-Muluk were referred to by Pausanias and other Classical authors) – tombs into which the intrepid sightseer could clamber with fire-brand and candle to admire the wall decorations and drink in the eeriness of it all.

Graffiti

Here, in the Valley of the Kings, as to a lesser extent

The Copts in the Valley of the Kings

'I beseech thee, Jesus Christ, my Lord, suffer me not to follow after my desire; let not my thoughts have dominion over me; let me not die in my sins, but accept Thy servant for good.'

Coptic graffito within KV2 (Ramesses IV)

Christianity came to Egypt relatively early, and by the 4th century AD had taken a firm hold. By the end of the Classical period, during the 6th century AD when Governor Orion visited the valley to inscribe his graffiti, the abandoned royal necropolis had been settled by a small Coptic community. Traces of this community may be discerned in several tombs. In that of Ramesses IV (KV2), among the 50 or so extant Christian graffiti, two Copts – 'Apa Ammonios, the Martyr', and another – are sketched on the right wall behind the entrance. Other Coptic graffiti may be found in the tomb of Ramesses XI (KV4), and more particularly within the princely tomb KV3 which had been adapted by the Christian inhabitants of the area as a chapel (p. 161). The doleful prayers and mundane scribblings of these early Christians are similarly found in graffiti, ostraca and papyri from other sites within the Valley of the Kings, together with more general evidence of their daily life – domestic debris (including, apparently, at least one gravestone, now in the British Museum – that of a woman named Souaei), and shells from the hallucinatory *Balinites* nut which perhaps offered the Copt some relief from what seems, on the whole, to have been a rather dreary lot.

Coptic platter (with restoration) from KV3.

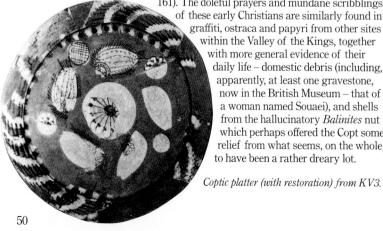

The Colossi of Memnon. In Roman times, the northern statue emitted an eerie tone each dawn – a baleful cry of greeting from the warrior-king to his mother, Eos.

Greek and Latin Graffiti in the Royal Tombs

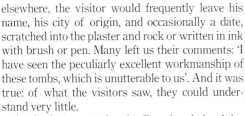

Tomb	No. of graffiti	Location: at entrance	throughout tomb
Ramesses VII (KV1)	132		●
Ramesses IV (KV2)	656		●
Ramesses XI (KV4)	58	●	
Ramesses IX (KV6)	46		●
Ramesses II (KV7)	4	●	
Merenptah (KV8)	121	●	
Ramesses V/VI (KV9)	995		●
Amenmesse (KV10)	7	●	
Ramesses III (KV11)	19	●	
Sethos II (KV15)	59		●

Total no. of Greek and Latin graffiti noted by Baillet: 2,105

Greek graffiti (nos. 514–15) in KV2.

elsewhere, the visitor would frequently leave his name, his city of origin, and occasionally a date, scratched into the plaster and rock or written in ink with brush or pen. Many left us their comments: 'I have seen the peculiarly excellent workmanship of these tombs, which is unutterable to us'. And it was true: of what the visitors saw, they could understand very little.

At the last count, by the French scholar Jules Baillet, over 2,000 Greek and Latin scraffiti and graffiti left by the Classical globe-trotters have been located, together with a lesser number of texts in Phoenician, Cypriot, Lycian and other exotic languages, and a whole multitude, as yet uncounted, of scribbles in demotic (studied by the Egyptologist Georges Bénédite, but never published) and in Coptic left by native Egyptian visitors. Almost half the Classical texts are found in the tomb of

Entrance corridor of KV1 (Ramesses VII) covered with tourist scribbles in Greek (nos. 67–72).

Ramesses VI, whom the Greeks identified (on the basis, perhaps, of a garbled pronunciation of the king's epithet *mery-amun*, 'beloved of Amun') as Memnon himself.

The earliest datable graffito in the Valley of the Kings (in the tomb of Ramesses VII) may be assigned to 278 BC, and the latest, left by Orion, governor of Upper Egypt, to AD 537. In between, there were chronicled visits during the reigns of the Roman emperors Augustus, Claudius, Vespasian, Trajan, Hadrian, Antoninus Pius, Marcus Aurelius and Lucius Verus, Commodus, Septimius Severus and Caracalla, and Diocletian. The Valley of the Kings was silent no more.

The guide books: Diodorus Siculus and Strabo

All 10 tombs in which graffiti have been found are Ramessid, with large, prominent entrances which in antiquity, as now, were easy of access. The tombs without graffiti are for the most part 18th and early 19th dynasty in date, with low-lying entrances which were more easily lost to view. That these latter tombs were known to exist, however, may be inferred from the works of Diodorus Siculus (who visited Egypt between 60 and 56 BC) and Strabo, a friend of Aelius Gallus, prefect of Egypt during the reign of Augustus (travelling 25–24 BC). Their accounts, based upon the records of the Egyptian priesthood, give the total number of Theban royal tombs as '47' (of which it was at the time believed only 17 remained undestroyed) and 'around 40' respectively. Lost, but clearly not forgotten, the rediscovery of the missing tombs would fall to later generations.

Favourite seasons for visiting the royal tombs

(Based upon the Greek and Latin graffiti)

Autumn (September–December):
11 dated visits
Winter (January–April):
24 dated visits
Summer (May–August):
10/11 dated visits

Early Travellers

'Tis whence the greatest part of Mummy, or flesh buried and rosted in the sand is gotten . . .'

Vincent le Blanc of Marseilles

The lifting of the veil

Generally speaking, the Christian occupants of the Valley of the Kings appear to have taken but little interest in the cemetery which was their home, and this apathy was inherited by the Arab invaders of AD 641/2. While sites farther north would continue sporadically to appear in the journals of pilgrims and merchants, southern Egypt was far more difficult of safe access; it would be a thousand years and more before the Wadi Biban el-Muluk was

again seriously to attract the attentions of the curious. By the end of the 16th century the veil had begun to lift.

In the early days, the few enterprising travellers who passed through Luxor seem to have been unaware of its true identity – despite the fact that the location of Homer's 'Hundred-gated Thebes' was clearly marked on Abraham Ortelius's map of 1595. One such traveller was Father Charles François, who visited 'the place of the mummies called Biban el Melouc' in 1668 without realizing its significance.

The first to make the connection was another Frenchman, Father Claude Sicard, head of the Jesuit Mission in Cairo, who travelled widely in Egypt between 1714 and 1726. He, too, visited the Valley of the Kings, in 1708, and this time he was able to appreciate its true nature. Sicard located 10 open tombs (one evidently KV2, prepared for Ramesses IV), 'tunnelled in the rock, and of astonishing depth'. Their preservation was equally astonishing: 'Halls, rooms, all are painted from top to bottom. The variety of colours, which are almost as fresh as the day they were done, gives an admirable effect. . . .'

Richard Pococke: 'Observations on Egypt'

Although Sicard left a complete list of all the sites he visited, his thoughts and conclusions were for

(Below) Richard Pococke's 'map' of the principal Valley of the Kings. The accompanying plans (right) have enabled modern scholars to identify most of the tombs visited by the explorer.

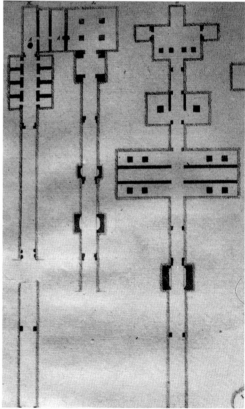

Pococke's Tombs

Pococke designation	KV no.	Owner
A, filled?	KV1	Ramesses VII
B, plan A	KV2	Ramesses IV
C, plan B??	KV7??	Ramesses II
D, filled?	KV8	Merenptah
E, plan C	KV9	Ramesses V/VI
F, filled	KV12	
G, filled	KV13?	Bay
H, plan G	KV14	Tawosret/Sethnakhte
I, plan H	KV15	Sethos II
K, plan K	KV11	Ramesses III
L, plan L	KV10	Amenmesse
M, plan M	KV18	Ramesses X
N, filled	KV6?	Ramesses IX
—, filled	KV4?	Ramesses XI
O, plan N	KV3?	son of Ramesses III

In addition, Pococke may have observed the positions of KV5 (sons of Ramesses II), KV20 (Tuthmosis I/ Hatshepsut), and perhaps KV27 and/or KV28.

(Left) Bruce's romanticized 'copy' of one of the harpists in the tomb of Ramesses III, published in 1790, was very much a product of its time and owed precious little to the original. Compare the later Champollion-Rosellini copy (p. 64).

(Below) The bewigged, 18th-century Scottish explorer James Bruce.

the most part lost with the notes detailing his travels; all that remains to us today are a few letters and maps. As it is, we owe the first significant published account of the Valley of the Kings to an English traveller by the name of Richard Pococke, the first volume of whose narrative, *A Description of the East, and some other countries*, appeared in 1743 as *Observations on Egypt*.

Pococke, who later became Bishop of Ossory and subsequently Bishop of Meath in Ireland, visited Egypt in the late 1730s. He was one of the first to follow the ancients' example and scribble his name for posterity – on 16 September 1739 – before beating a hasty retreat; the graffito was observed by a later traveller, William Hamilton, but its precise location is a mystery today. In the course of his visit to the Valley of the Kings, Pococke noted 'signs of about eighteen [tombs] . . . if I made no mistake . . . [though] now there are only nine that can be enter'd into.'

James Bruce

In the steps of Pococke, in 1768, followed James Bruce, a Scotsman hailing from Kinnaird who visited Luxor and likewise crossed the river to explore the Valley of the Kings. The royal tombs he describes as 'magnificent, stupendous sepulchres', sited in 'a solitary place'. Like his predecessors, Bruce visited the tomb of Ramesses IV; but his principal claim to fame is his description – hardly his discovery, since the tomb already lay open and was probably among those entered by Sicard – of the tomb of Ramesses III (KV11), which would henceforth be known as 'Bruce's Tomb'. For Bruce, the principal feature of this tomb were the scenes, 'in fresco, [of] three harps, which merited the

utmost attention, whether we consider the elegance of these instruments in their form, and the detail of their parts . . . , or confine ourselves to the reflection that to how great a perfection music must have arrived, before an artist could have produced so complete an instrument.'

In view of their fame, it is ironic that the highly embellished renderings of the royal harpists which appear in Bruce's *Travels to Discover the Source of the Nile*, first published in Edinburgh in 1790, should offer such a poor impression of the originals; indeed, a later traveller in the valley, William George Browne (who was to be brutally murdered *en route* to Samarkand in 1813), commented wryly that 'his engraved figures seem to be from memory'. Accurate or not, they would, nevertheless, immortalize Bruce's name.

William George Browne

Browne's own visit to Biban el-Muluk took place in 1792, in which year he left his name in one of the rooms off the burial chamber of KV11 (Ramesses III). His *Travels in Africa, Egypt and Syria* is important because it preserves one of the few extant accounts of Arab interest in the valley – indeed, the first account of any excavation of the site. According to Browne, the site had been explored 'within the last thirty years' by a certain son of one Sheikh Hamam, 'in expectation of finding treasure'. Whether Sheikh Hamam's son was successful or not in his search is unknown. However, Browne suggests that, since three of the tombs to which he himself had had access seemed not to tally with descriptions given by Pococke of the tombs *he* had seen, these were perhaps to be numbered among the fruits of the Arab's labours.

Antiquaries
and Savants

'Curiosity and a passion for learning.'

Jean de Thévenot

The collecting urge

The renewed interest shown in Egypt from the Renaissance on had brought with it a fascination for the collecting of all things ancient, curious and artistic. One of the first organized expeditions to Egypt with the aim of procuring antiquities was that of the German Father J. B. Vansleb. Vansleb's commission, from Louis XIV of France, was 'to seek . . . the greatest possible number of good manuscripts and ancient coins for His Majesty's library. Should he find also among those ancient monuments any statues or bas-reliefs by good masters, he will try and obtain them'. The Vansleb expedition, commissioned in 1672, was less than successful; but it did point the way for the future.

By 1693, the French Consul in Egypt, Benoît de Maillet, was promoting the idea, not just of a collecting trip, but of a thorough survey of the country 'by persons wise, curious, and adroit'. And this call for a more scientific approach to the study of the country's antiquities was taken up by Paul Lucas, Vansleb's successor as proto-Egyptologist to Louis XIV. Lucas was sent out to Egypt with the aim, among other things, of carrying out a detailed exploration of the ruins of Thebes – a commission which might have met with greater success had Sicard's identification already been made and Lucas actually been able to find the site.

Scholars

'You have perhaps heard talk of a secret expedition, the object of which is completely unknown to the public, and of which I have only the slightest inkling. It is a matter of a very great scientific, political and military venture.'

Prosper Jollois, letter to his father

On 1 July 1798, Napoleon Bonaparte landed his forces in Egypt with the ultimate aim of securing a new passage to India and an empire in the east via the Isthmus of Suez. And, in the light of earlier French interest in Egypt, it should come as no surprise to find the 4,000-strong army accompanied by a team of 139 *savants*, whose role was to study every physical aspect of the country, ancient and modern. Among their number, though not formally part of the team, was the artist-philanderer Baron Vivant Denon. Denon's *Voyages dans la Basse et la*

The artist Vivant Denon, who accompanied Napoleon's Egyptian Expedition between 1798 and 1799.

Haute Égypte, published in 1802, would whet the public's appetite for the official survey to come – and in the process render Egypt *à la mode*.

The Expedition, however, was to have a shaky and demoralizing start. Following his victory at the Battle of the Pyramids, Napoleon entered Cairo in triumph; a mere eight days later, Nelson had destroyed the French fleet at the Battle of the Nile in Abukir Bay, and the company's means of return to Europe was cut off. There was nothing to do but press on – which the Expedition did, for three dangerous and uncomfortable years, the *savants* losing a third of their number in the process.

But any despondency they might have felt soon gave way to awe as the French military progressed upstream under General Desaix; even the common soldiers were amazed by what they saw and, as they arrived at Thebes for the first time on 26 January 1799, the troops clapped with delight. Shortly afterwards, they visited the Valley of the Kings, Vivant Denon in tow.

'I had merely time to pass on from one tomb to another: at the end of the galleries were the sarcophagi . . ., composed of a single block of granite . . . but . . . these vast blocks of stone . . . have been [unable] to preserve

The Tombs of the French Expedition

Tomb	*Descr. d'Ég* no. or designation	Owner
KV1	Ier Tombeau	Ramesses VII
KV2	IIe Tombeau	Ramesses IV
KV3	1er Tombeau	son of Ramesses III
KV4	2e Tombeau	Ramesses XI
KV5	Commencement d'excavation ou grotte bouchée	children of Ramesses II
KV6	3e Tombeau	Ramesses IX
KV7	Commencement d'excavation ou grotte fermée	Ramesses II
KV8	IIIe Tombeau	Merenptah
KV9	IVe Tombeau	Ramesses V/VI
KV10	4e Tombeau	Amenmesse
KV11	5e Tombeau	Ramesses III
KV13	Commencement d'excavation ou de grotte fermée	Bay
KV14	Ve Tombeau	Tawosret/Sethnakhte
KV15	VIe Tombeau	Sethos II
KV18	Excavation commencée	Ramesses X
KV20	Commencement de grotte taillée circulairement dans le rocher	Tuthmosis I/Hatshepsut
WV22	Tombeau isolée de l'Ouest	Amenophis III

the relics of the sovereigns from the attempts of avarice; all the tombs are violated . . .'

Vivant Denon

In his *Voyages*, Denon describes the frustration he felt at the mere three hours he was able to spend in the six tombs accessible to him: 'How was it possible to leave such precious curiosities, without taking a drawing of them? How to return without having a sketch at least to shew? I earnestly demanded a quarter of an hour's grace: I was allowed twenty minutes; one person lighted me,

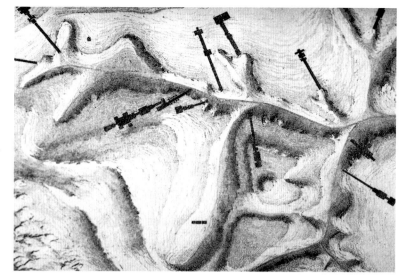

while another held a taper to every object that I pointed out to him, and I completed my task in the time prescribed with spirit and correctness.'

'I found on this occasion, as on all others, that a visit to Thebes was like the attack of a fever, it was a kind of crisis which left behind an impression of indescribable impatience, enthusiasm, irritation, and fatigue.'

Vivant Denon

Jollois and de Villiers

Denon returned to France with Napoleon in 1799, to write up his notes and publish his memoirs, leaving behind the scholars of the French Expedition – now organized as the *Institut d'Égypte* – to explore and document rather more thoroughly the royal wadi which had so captivated him. The fortunate *savants* to whom this task fell were two young and enthusiastic engineers, Prosper Jollois and Édouard de Villiers du Terrage.

The French Expedition's map of the royal wadi was the first accurate survey of the site ever to be carried out, and strikingly different from the primitive rendering of the site presented by Pococke some 60 years previously. In this map, Jollois and de Villiers record the position of 16 tombs. Moreover, they report for the first time the existence of a western annexe to the royal valley: the remote, atmospheric and seldom visited West Valley. And within this annexe they note the existence of one of the most beautiful and important royal sepulchres of all – the tomb of Amenophis III, now numbered WV22 (p. 110).

The results of Jollois and de Villiers' work in the Valley of the Kings were made accessible with the publication of the mammoth *Description de l'Égypte*, which appeared in instalments between 1809 and 1828. The 19-volume report was to be the only tangible result of Napoleon's extraordinary ambitions in the east. But what a result: it would change the face of Egyptian studies for good.

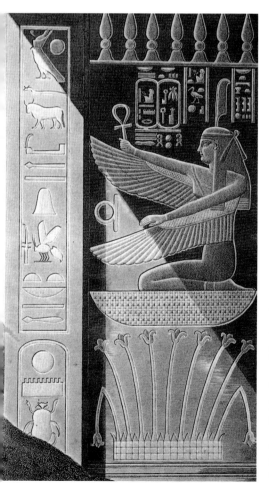

(Above) White-crowned head from a calcite shabti *figure found in the tomb of Amenophis III by Jollois and de Villiers in 1799, as reproduced in the plates of the* Description.

(Left) In the plates of the Description de l'Égypte, *quality of draughtsmanship and high drama sometimes win out over archaeological integrity – as here, in this fanciful, composite representation of the entrance to the tomb of Ramesses III.*

Belzoni
the 'Patagonian Sampson'

'Nile-land was then, as now, a field for plunder; fortunes were made by digging, not gold, but antiques; and the archaeological field became a battle plain for two armies of Dragomans and Fellah-navvies. One was headed by the redoubtable Salt, the other owned the command of Drovetti…'

Richard F. Burton

'…the history of relic-gathering in those days is that of one long *imbroglio*.'

Alexander Henry Rhind

Drovetti and Salt

Napoleon's Expedition, and the chance discovery of the Rosetta Stone, eventual key to the reading of the mysterious hieroglyphic script (p. 65), promised to set the understanding of Egypt and her antiquities on a scientific footing for the first time. But orderly study, for the moment, still lay in the future.

Another legacy of the French Expedition, rather different in flavour, was Bernardino Drovetti. Drovetti was a Piedmont-born colonel who had served in Bonaparte's army and, intermittently over the next 30 years, continued to serve France as her Consul-General in Egypt. Drovetti's passion was for antiquities, and he dedicated his time in Egypt to their collection – by whatever means necessary, including dynamite, and with little appreciation of context.

Drovetti's British opposite number was Henry Salt, who arrived in Egypt in 1816. Although more of a scholar than Drovetti, in order to compete with his rival in the collection of antiquities, Salt had perforce to play by the same rules. And between them, the two Consul-Generals laid personal claim to all that the pharaohs had left behind:

'a line of demarcation is drawn through every temple, and those buildings that have withstood the attacks of *Barbarians*, will not resist the speculation of civilized cupidity, virtuosi, and antiquarians.'

Sir Frederick Henniker

The search for tombs

'…it is plain that the entrances [to the tombs] have been choked up by the loose stones that have fallen down in the course of time from the slopes of the mountain, and …that if by the exertions of the curious and the liberal, they ever come to be explored anew, the sculptures and

paintings in them must be untouched, and the… sarcophagi…unhurt…'

William Hamilton

'…there are many [tombs] which still remain untouched …[and] it is not improbable that the discovery of many objects of considerable importance would be the result of further excavation.'

Thomas Legh

Salt's field man in this Anglo-French *imbroglio* was Giovanni Battista Belzoni – the six-foot-seven hydraulic engineer who (to his subsequent embarrassment) had in his early career earned his living as a circus strongman, the 'Patagonian Sampson'. Belzoni had first arrived in London in 1802, just as the Rosetta Stone was being placed on public view for the first time in the British Museum – though there is no reason to believe that the event would have interested the Italian at this time. He did not travel to Egypt until 1815, drawn there by the possibility of making his fortune with a novel water-lifting device which, he believed, he might sell to the man who was doing his best to modernize the country, Mohammed Ali. Sadly, he could not, and Belzoni was forced to seek gainful employment elsewhere. He had found it with Henry Salt.

Salt, recognizing the worth of Belzoni's engineering background in stealing a march on his French rival, commissioned him to arrange the transportation of a colossal head of Ramesses II from the king's mortuary temple (the Ramesseum) to the river, for eventual shipment back to London. This task, which had confounded Salt's rival, Belzoni carried out in two weeks with barely a hitch.

Salt was delighted, and directed Belzoni, under the supervision of his secretary, Henry William Beechey, to turn his attentions to the Valley of the Kings – specifically to the tomb of Ramesses III, 'Bruce's Tomb', and the removal of the king's sarcophagus box which Bruce had seen in 1769. With careful planning and much pushing and heaving, this piece too was satisfactorily manoeuvred from the desert to the river, to be sold in due course, as part of Salt's second collection, to Louis XVIII of France and later deposited in the Louvre; the lid eventually found its way to the Fitzwilliam Museum in Cambridge in 1823. All in all, Belzoni had proved his worth, and Salt was keen to retain his services.

First discoveries: the West Valley

Belzoni, however, seems to have harboured greater ambitions. These would ultimately alienate his English employer by denying, as Salt saw it, the credit for the discoveries he, Salt, had sponsored.

When Belzoni first took it into his head to spend time exploring Biban el-Muluk, he was able to distinguish 'Nine or ten [tombs]…of a superior class, and five or six of a lower order'. The Italian was well aware of the fact that the Classical authors

(Below) Henry Salt, the British Consul-General in Egypt, and (bottom) his erstwhile employee, Giovanni Battista Belzoni.

Plan and coloured section of the tomb of Sethos I, from the plates accompanying Belzoni's Narrative of the Operations and Discoveries in Egypt and Nubia.

(Below) A detail of the burial chamber of 'Belzoni's Tomb', showing the position of the alabaster sarcophagus when found, over the entrance to the mysterious 'Nun corridor'. The complex wall-decoration, though it bears a passing resemblance to the content and composition of the original, was evidently sketched from memory.

had put the total as high as 47; he would look for the rest, and in due course add a further eight to the list of tombs then known.

Belzoni's first discovery came early on, at the end of 1816: the tomb of the pharaoh Ay (WV23), which he located in the West Valley, further up from the tomb of Amenophis III (WV22) 'discovered' by Jollois and de Villiers in 1799 (p. 128). This find was followed in August–September 1817 by the discovery of another tomb in the West Valley – the unfinished and uninscribed WV25, which had subsequently been employed as a ready-made family vault during the 22nd dynasty (p. 116).

These finds had offered an amusing diversion. 'The result of my researches gave me all the satisfaction I could desire, of finding mummies in cases, in their original position.' But, apart from the tomb of Ay, these were private burials; the prize Belzoni sought was the kings themselves. And for these he decided he must return to the main wadi.

Excavations in the main valley

Unlike his predecessors, and the great majority of his successors in the field, Belzoni possessed the rare ability of reading a landscape; this understanding explains the disconcerting ease with which he was able, again and again, to discern the presence of 'new' tombs. The first would be KV19, the beautifully decorated sepulchre of prince Mentuherkhepshef (p. 170), like WV25 occupied by intrusive mummies, two in number, of the Third Intermediate Period. The second discovery would be the queenly KV21 (p. 115), in which Belzoni again discovered two mummies, 'females, and their hair pretty long, and well preserved, though it was easily separated from the head by pulling it a little'.

But, with the exception of Ay, the pharaohs still eluded him. And so it was a matter of great rejoicing when, on 10/11 October 1817, word was brought of the discovery by his men of a painted tomb – that of Ramesses I (KV16) (p. 134) – still containing its decorated sarcophagus and a range of the wooden funerary statuettes which are now familiar from the beautifully gilded examples discovered by Howard Carter in the tomb of Tutankhamun in 1922. Like Ay's tomb, its plan was abbreviated, since the king evidently died before the full form of the tomb could be achieved. And here again Belzoni discovered two mummies – but once more these were intrusive and non-royal, having been installed in the tomb following the removal of the king's own remains at the end of the 2nd millennium BC.

'Belzoni's Tomb'

A matter of days after his discovery of the tomb of Ramesses I, Belzoni directed his men to dig at a point in the adjoining hillside to the east, an area which seemed, in the past, to have acted as a drain for the floodwaters which occasionally hit the valley. And Fortune again favoured.

He uncovered here the tomb of Sethos I, KV17 (p. 137), which proved to be the finest so far found in

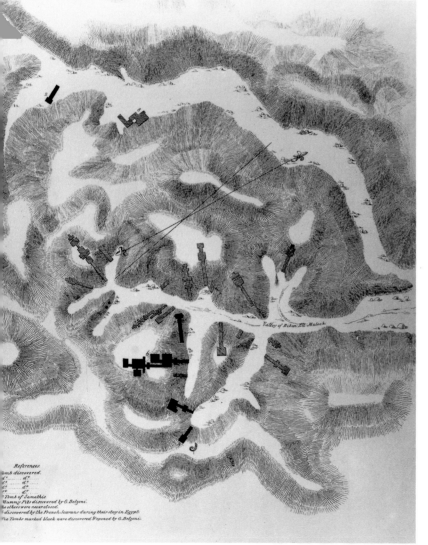

Belzoni's map of the valley, with his new discoveries marked.

Belzoni's Discoveries in the Valley of the Kings

Tomb	Belzoni no.	Tomb owner	Remarks
KV16	3	Ramesses I	
KV17	6	Sethos I	
KV19	5	Mentuherkhepshef	
KV21	4		
WV23	1	Ay	
WV25	2		
KV30	7		Lord Belmore's tomb
KV31	7		Lord Belmore's tomb

The Egyptian Tomb Exhibition

(Below) The striking façade of the Egyptian Hall, Piccadilly, London, the venue for Belzoni's show. The contents of the exhibition were later sold (right).

'The mechanical ingenuity and indefatigable diligence by which Mr. Belzoni has been enabled thus to transport to the arena of European controversy the otherwise immoveable excavations of Egypt reflect no less credit on him as an artist than his sagacity and success in discovering the subject matter of this extraordinary exhibition has distinguished him above all European travellers in modern times.'

The Times

At the time of Belzoni's discovery of the tombs of Ramesses I and Sethos I, the hieroglyphs could not, of course, be read, though a start had been made in that direction by Dr Thomas Young, the celebrated physicist, author of the wave theory of light. Young's attempt at a reading of the characters contained within the many cartouches of 'Belzoni's Tomb' was 'Psammis'. And it was by this translation (subsequently to be changed to 'Ousirei' before the current reading 'Sethos', or 'Seti' was settled upon) that the tomb's owner would be known when Belzoni, in 1821, opened his exhibition on 'The Egyptian Tomb' at the appropriately named Egyptian Hall in London's Piccadilly.

In this exhibition, Belzoni displayed not only a one-sixth scale model of the entire tomb (measuring over 15 m (50 ft) in length), but full-sized reproductions of scenes from two of the most impressive chambers. These scenes, cast in

plaster from wax moulds taken from the original reliefs (removing, in the process, much of the reliefs' ancient pigment), were coloured on the basis of paintings made on site by Belzoni himself and a compatriot, Alessandro Ricci – paintings a few of which, by a happy chance, have survived to the present day in the collections of the Bristol City Museum.

The Egyptian Hall exhibition opened on Tuesday, 1 May, 1821, having been previewed the previous Friday. One thousand nine hundred visitors paid half a crown for the privilege of visiting the show, which was reviewed in *The Times* as a 'singular combination and skilful arrangement of objects so new and in themselves so striking'. Among the odds and ends on display was the rope which the last party to enter Sethos I's tomb in antiquity had used.

Belzoni's curious decision to auction the displays and most of the antiquities in June 1822, after the London exhibition had closed, compromised the success of a follow-up in Paris, which, to make matters worse, was staged in wholly unsuitable premises. With the explorer's death, plans to carry the show to other European capitals were abandoned, but a final exhibition on the theme of The Egyptian Tomb was arranged by his widow, Sarah, in the spring of 1825, at 28 Leicester Square, London, 'for the support of Mr Belzoni's aged mother and numerous relatives at Padua'.

the Valley of the Kings. Its architecture was perfectly proportioned, its walls beautifully decorated (and at that time in bright, pristine condition), and its floors were still littered with remains of the king's original funerary equipment; Belzoni would not recognize the worn out cavern we see today. The centre-piece was the king's sarcophagus, 'of the finest oriental alabaster . . . [which] is transparent, when a light is placed in the inside of it'. Subsequently shipped to England and offered to the British Museum for the sum of £2,000, it was foolishly rejected by that institution – after the greatest possible prevarication – in a decision condemned at the time as 'worthy of low shopkeeping'. The sarcophagus was subsequently acquired by the architect Sir John Soane in May 1824, who installed it in the 'crypt' of his house in Lincoln's Inn Fields where it still resides.

Belzoni was amazed by 'his' good fortune – Salt had already been forgotten – and by the splendour of the tomb: 'I did not expect to find such a one as it . . . proved to be'. Reactions in Egypt varied enor-

The sarcophagus of Sethos I in Sir John Soane's house at Lincoln's Inn Fields – together with a ticket to view issued by the new owner.

THE BELZONI SARCOPHAGUS
AND OTHER ANTIQUITIES;

TO BE VIEWED BY LAMP LIGHT

ON

AT 8 O'CLOCK,

WITH M<small>R</small> SOANE'S COMPLIMENTS TO

mously. The interest of the Turkish Governor of Qena rapidly evaporated when he learned that rumours of a golden cock filled with jewels were, to say the least, somewhat exaggerated; while Drovetti, who had ceded to Belzoni any claims he might have had on the Valley of the Kings, expressed 'speechless astonishment'. Abroad, the tomb would cause a storm of public enthusiasm and bring Belzoni such fame as he could never have dreamed.

Decline and fall

'Salt was genuinely perplexed. . . . As he told Belzoni . . . , he looked upon him with the same high regard that a gentleman would have for the architect whom he had commissioned to build his house. All the merit belonged to the one, but the other supplied the means and the house was his. The analogy was lost on Giovanni . . .'

Stanley Mayes

A somewhat naïve copy, by Belzoni, of a scene in the tomb of Sethos I. The king is shown seated before an offering table piled high with loaves of bread; the hieroglyphs above record his two principal names and his divine filiation – 'son of Amun and born of Mut'.

Shortly after the discovery of the tomb of Sethos I, Belzoni was visited in the valley by Lord and Lady Belmore and their party who, expressing an interest in digging on their own account, had two likely spots pointed out to them by their host: 'they turned out to be two small mummy pits', perhaps to be recognized today as the private tombs now assigned the numbers KV30 and KV31 (pp. 109 and 183), one of which was found to contain a large, anthropoid sarcophagus of painted sandstone, now in the British Museum. Further explorations of the royal wadi followed Belzoni's departure, with Henry Salt, anxious for glory on his own account, labouring long and hard for a further four months in search of yet more tombs. There are no indications that he experienced any success in this enterprise, though it is possible that several of the royal funerary objects now in the British Museum (particularly those from the tomb of Ramesses IX, KV6) are to be associated with this spate of activity. John Gardner Wilkinson, further, was of the opinion that Salt – either independently or through Giovanni ('Yanni') d'Athanasi, his excavator at Thebes between 1817 and 1827 – cleared some 55 m (180 ft) into the tomb of Ramesses II (KV7); if so, nothing is known of the results.

Belzoni, observing this frenetic activity with some amusement, expressed his view on future prospects in the Valley of the Kings: 'It is my firm opinion, that in the Valley of Beban el Malook, there are no more [tombs] than are now known'. It would prove to be as mistaken a view as that later expressed by Theodore Davis in 1912 (p. 80).

Giovanni Battista Belzoni died of dysentry at Gwato, Benin, on 3 December 1823, *en route* to Timbuktu and his next adventure – the discovery of the source of the Niger. He bade his own farewells:

Britains farewell my friends adieu
I must faraway from the happy shore
My hart will remain hever with you
Should I the dear land see no more
I scoff at my foes, and the Intrigoni
If my friends remember their true Belzoni.

His former employer, Salt, outlived him by only four years, dying aged 48 on 29 October 1827. Bitterness and jealousy at Belzoni's hijacking of what Salt considered to be rightfully his, heightened by immense sadness at the unexpected loss of a beloved wife, clouded his memories of the Paduan giant to the end. Writing to his agent in London, Bingham Richards, on what had become a sore subject – the sale of the sarcophagus of Sethos I:

'Nothing vexes me so much as the circumstances that you should have . . . given reason to suppose . . . that I have been in collusion all the time with that prince of ungrateful adventurers [Belzoni]. . . . I have but one wish, never to have my name coupled with his.'

'Sir G. Wilkinson, Mr. Hay, and Mr. Burton, . . . laboriously examined and sketched the figures on the walls by the dim light of wax candles, rather than injure the paintings with the smoke of torches.'

Alexander Henry Rhind

The Dilettantes

John Gardner Wilkinson

'I have not indeed seen any person here who has entered with so much spirit into the study of the hieroglyphicks as Mr W. and . . . he cannot fail making considerable progress; more especially as he works *like a horse at it.*'

Henry Salt

John Gardner Wilkinson, one of the fathers of modern Egyptology, was born in Chelsea on 5 October 1797, and educated at Harrow and Oxford. Originally destined for a career in the army, the young Wilkinson was encouraged by the antiquarian Sir William Gell, a long-time resident of Naples and staunch supporter of the nascent discipline of Egyptology, to travel up the Nile. Wilkinson evidently required little persuasion. He would spend the greater part of his life in Egypt, copying and studying in particular the scenes and inscriptions of the Theban tombs, while carrying out limited excavations in 1824 and 1827–28 – all at personal expense, as was most work carried out between the time of Napoleon and Champollion. The scholar's notes and copies are today preserved in 56 large volumes in the Bodleian Library, Oxford, and, like his published works, are still consulted with profit today.

Wilkinson was in Egypt at an immensely stimulating time, when the quickening decipherment of the hieroglyphs allowed the monuments to be appreciated for more than simply their architectural or artistic form. The door was beginning to open on the study of Egyptian history and thought, and Wilkinson was to be one of the first through it.

The value of the Valley of the Kings in establishing a chronology of the New Kingdom was obvious to Wilkinson from the start, and as a preliminary to his study in 1827 he physically assigned in paint at each tomb entrance a numbering sequence still visible today; except for the West Valley (where Wilkinson numbered the tombs in a separate sequence, W1–W4) the system has been continued to this day. Tombs KV1–21 are marked upon the map of the main valley in Wilkinson's six-map *Topographical Survey of Thebes* of 1830. However,

Two sumptuously padded thrones (above) and two Nile sailing boats (below) – details of scenes in the tomb of Ramesses III, copied by Wilkinson and reproduced (with much loss of quality) in his Manners and Customs of the Ancient Egyptians.

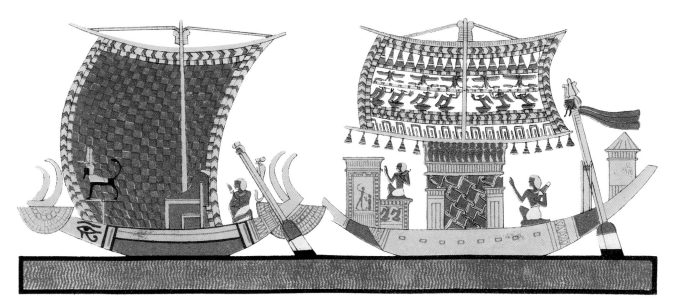

Crudely modelled calcite shabti *of Ramesses VI, painted in black wax, found by John Gardner Wilkinson in the king's tomb.*

if we add the additional tomb-indications from his unpublished sketch map of the valley, a total of 28 tombs may be assumed as known at this time – and this is the figure echoed by at least one contemporary traveller, the Frenchman Marie Théodore Renouard de Bussierre in 1829.

'. . . and I think I have observed several places where other tombs might be found in various parts of this valley.'

John Gardner Wilkinson

James Burton

As his records show, Wilkinson was by inclination more of a copyist than an excavator. James Burton, a contemporary of Wilkinson in Thebes and brother of the architect Decimus Burton, was a much more practical individual. Burton carried out a number of excavations in the Valley of the Kings, both to elucidate and consolidate. He made his survey tomb by tomb, counting a total of 24 or 25, which he identified by letter rather than number: B–I, K–T, V–X, plus several others without reference. His most forward-thinking work was carried out in the vicinity of KV17, 'Belzoni's Tomb', which he made safe from flooding by emptying the well shaft which Belzoni had filled to facilitate human

ingress and egress, and where he (perhaps with Robert Hay) completed the series of dykes which Belzoni had begun at the entrance to divert flood waters.

Burton's curiosity led him to begin a clearance of the extraordinary KV20, work which had to be abandoned, as Wilkinson records, 'owing to the danger of mephitic air'; the clearance would be completed, and only with the greatest difficulty, by Howard Carter on behalf of Theodore Davis 80 years later (p. 91). A similar curiosity led Burton to examine, albeit superficially, KV5. This tomb, currently being excavated by Kent Weeks of the American University in Cairo, is slowly revealing itself as the largest tomb ever found in Egypt. It was evidently prepared as a mausoleum for the family of Ramesses II, the tomb's association with which king Burton was the first to note (p. 144).

James Burton published no details of his work in the valley, though thankfully some 63 volumes of the immensely valuable drawings, plans and notes he made while in Egypt were presented to the British Museum after his death in 1862. The full potential of this archive has yet to be tapped.

Robert Hay

'Mr. Hay's portfolio is the most magnificent which has ever been brought from that country.'

George Hoskins

Another frequent visitor to Thebes during the 1820s and 1830s was the antiquarian Robert Hay, by chance a distant cousin of James Burton. Here in the royal wadi Hay for a time made his base – in the tomb of Ramesses IV (KV2), with that of Ramesses

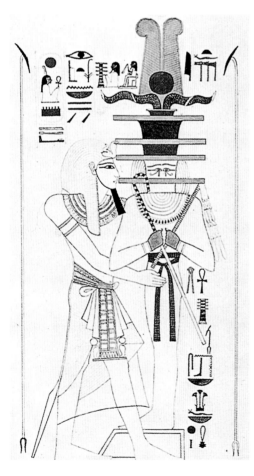

Sethos I embraces the anthropomorphized djed-*pillar of Osiris; a watercolour copy by James Burton of a pillar in the king's tomb.*

(Right) An early photograph of Robert Hay dressed in Turkish costume, c. 1855.

Tomb	Wilkinson sketch	Wilkinson *Top. Survey*	Burton	Hay
KV1	1	1	O	1
KV2	2	2	N	2
KV3	3	3	P	3
KV4	4	4	Q	4
KV5	5	5	M	8
KV6	6	6	L	9
KV7	7	7	K	10
KV8	8	8	I	14
KV9	9	9	H	15
KV10	10	10	G	16
KV11	11	11	F	17
KV12	•	12	—	18
KV13	—	13	E	19
KV14	S	14	D	20
KV15	T	15	C	21
KV16	16	16	X	11
KV17	17	17	W	12
KV18	18	18	V	13
KV19	19	19	S	6
KV20	20	20	R	7
KV21	•	21	T	—
KV26	—	—	•	22
KV27	•	—	—	—
KV28	•	—	—	—
KV29	—	•	•	—
KV30	—	—	•	23
KV31/32	—	—	•	24
KV33	—	—	•?	—

• existence noted but no number assigned.

VI (KV9) and others available for guests and co-workers – who included Edward William Lane in 1826/27 (later to become famous for his *Manners and Customs of the Modern Egyptians*, published in 1836, and for his translation of *The Thousand and One Nights*, 1838–40); the sculptor and draughtsman Joseph Bonomi, from 1824 on (in 1861 to be appointed Curator of Sir John Soane's Museum); Francis Arundale in 1832 (later co-author, with Bonomi, of *Gallery of Antiquities Selected from the British Museum,* 1843–45); and, in 1832–34, Frederic Catherwood (later to become famous for his volumes on the antiquities of Central America). It was an idyllic life, as the antiquary and traveller George Hoskins, a member of Hay's artistic entourage, recalls in his memoirs:

'After drawing almost from sunrise to sunset, I spent the evenings in reading and writing. Sometimes Mr. Hay … smoked his pipe with me; and on Sunday, which, though we had no church to go to, we invariably made a day of rest, I dined with him. On Thursday evenings also the artists and travellers at Thebes used to assemble in his house, or rather tomb I should call it; but never was the habitation of death witness to gayer scenes. Though we wore the costume, we did not always preserve the gravity of Turks; and the saloon, although formerly a sepulchre, threw no gloom over our mirth …'

Hay, like James Burton, published no record of his work in the Valley of the Kings, though the notes and drawings he made during his time in Egypt are preserved in 49 volumes in the British Library. They represent a further resource of great Egyptological worth.

Two of Hay's watercolours, (above) a scene from the tomb of Ramesses IX, with the king shown offering an image of the goddess Maat ('Truth'), and (below) Ramesses III, wearing an elaborate atef-crown, before Re-Horakhty.

The Great Expeditions

'The turn which these [expeditions] have often had a tendency to take has in a great degree depended on the fact that even, or indeed chiefly, when under the auspices of Governments, the economics of a mining speculation rather than the scope of a scientific survey, have been imported by them into the fields of research, – the condition being imposed or implied that for so much expenditure so many tangible returns were expected.'

Alexander Henry Rhind

Champollion and Rosellini

'. . . two of [Champollion's] employees are gone being disinclined to stop longer than they contracted for with a man of his temper. His portfolio is infinitely less rich than Rosellini's which is another source of his displeasure.'

Joseph Bonomi

Champollion visited Egypt in 1828–29, naturally anxious to see the country he had studied at a distance for so long but also keen to put his philological theories to the test in the field. A joint Franco-Tuscan expedition, in part financed by the Grand Duke of Tuscany, was organized by Champollion and Ippolito Rosellini, who since 1824 had been Professor of Oriental Languages at the University of Pisa. The expedition's guide was to be Alessandro Ricci, who had previously assisted Belzoni in preparing copies of the scenes in the

tomb of Sethos I. Among the team of 12 architects and artists accompanying the expedition in the two *dahabiyas* in which they travelled upstream was Champollion's young student, Nestor L'Hôte. L'Hôte's excellent drawings and notes still survive, in the Louvre and in the Bibliothèque Nationale in Paris, to shed much light on the expedition and its work.

Champollion landed at Thebes in March 1829, on his return from a three-month sojourn in Nubia, and in the Valley of the Kings parked himself, like Hoskins before him, in the tomb of Ramesses VI (KV9). This would be his base for the two months the expedition would spend in the necropolis, copying the scenes and their details – not always with enthusiasm. L'Hôte's letters home reveal a very human side to the work: 'God! Hieroglyphs are so boring and depressing! We are all sick of them!' Though L'Hôte's comments will strike a chord with many Egyptologists, the disenchantment behind them would ultimately bring the expedition to a premature end.

The Champollion-Rosellini team appears to have had access to 16 tombs in the main valley: KV1–4, KV6–11, and KV14–19, with clearance work being carried out within KV16 (Ramesses I) and perhaps KV7 (Ramesses II) also. From the tombs, the expedition copied a veritable 'who was who' of the valley's occupants, together with other interesting details which would eventually occupy 44 plates in

Deciphering the Hieroglyphs

The discovery at Fort Rashid in the Delta of the trilingual (hieroglyphic, demotic and Greek) decree of Ptolemy V Epiphanes dating to 196 BC – better known today as the Rosetta Stone – was to provide the long-sought key to understanding hieroglyphic writing and so to the reawakening of ancient Egyptian after its two-millennia-long slumber.

The code would finally be cracked by the brilliant young French scholar Jean-François Champollion, but before that much crucial groundwork was laid by Thomas Young. Young had understood, as early as

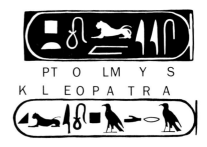

1816, that the demotic section of the Rosetta Stone was a cursive version of the more formal hieroglyphic text which stood above it; and, by 1819, he had been able to recognize the name 'Ptolemy' within one of the hieroglyphic 'cartouches', and to suggest an alphabet. Following on from Young, William Bankes, a member of Salt's Egyptological circle, suggested that a second cartouche which occurred in association with the name 'Ptolemy', on the Philae obelisk Belzoni had carried back for him to Kingston Lacy, was to be read as 'Cleopatra'. The English had made a sound beginning, but could advance no further.

Despite his notorious self-confidence, Champollion's first steps, outlined in 1822 in his *Lettre à M. Dacier . . . relative à l'alphabet des hiéroglyphes phonétiques*, were equally faltering. In this study, he correctly identified 10 alphabetic signs, though erred either in whole or in part in his identification of a further eight, while missing four further alphabetic signs. But by 1824 he was up and running. In his *Précis du système hiéroglyphique*, Champollion was able to demonstrate the key fact that the Egyptian writing employed a combination of ideographic and phonetic signs, with a grammar closely akin to that of Coptic. Egyptology was born.

(Left) Jean-François Champollion was the first to crack the code of the hieroglyphic script, building upon the pioneering work of Thomas Young and William Bankes (above).

Champollion's posthumous *Monuments de l'Egypte et de la Nubie* of 1845 and several more in Rosellini's *I Monumenti dell'Egitto e della Nubia* of 1832. The party's record, however, was not without blemish: for, from within the tomb of Sethos I, in the corridor leading into the chamber referred to by Belzoni as the 'Hall of Beauties', Champollion and Rosellini would physically remove from the walls two complete, practically mirror-image scenes for the collections in the Louvre and for the museum in Florence. The scholarly mining destined to damage so irreparably one of the most beautiful tombs of the Valley of the Kings was off to a flying start

In 1838, six years after Champollion's untimely death at the age of 42, L'Hôte paid a nostalgic return visit to Biban el-Muluk:

'This Valley, where so many precious memories are reborn for me, seems to have taken a forsaken air, a tinge of more austere melancholy, deeper than ever. I have put my bed in the place that was occupied by [Champollion], and my fancy has been happy to make his image live again; if only I could also evoke the genius that has immortalized him!'

In a way, he did. For L'Hôte's visit convinced him that the Valley of the Kings had not yet revealed all of its secrets, and that there were still more tombs to be uncovered, despite Belzoni's conviction that all was done. The supreme irony, as Leslie Greener observed, was that, 'only a few feet beneath the tomb of Ramses VI, the very spot where he wrote ..., lay the unparalleled wealth of Tutankhamon'.

Carl Richard Lepsius

'Thebes, the 25th February, 1845.
We have now been inhabiting our Theban Acropolis, on the hill of Qurna, above a quarter of a year, every one busily employed in his own way from morning to evening, in investigating, describing, and drawing the most valuable monuments, taking paper impressions of the inscriptions, and in making plans of the buildings; we have not yet been able to complete the Libyan side alone, where there are at least twelve temples, five-and-twenty tombs of kings, fifteen belonging to the royal wives or daughters, and a countless number belonging to private persons, still to be examined.'

Carl Richard Lepsius

So far in the history of exploration in the Valley of the Kings, the Germans had been poorly represented. With the arrival upon the scene of the energetic Carl Richard Lepsius, a former student of Baron Bunsen and Alexander von Humboldt, they would soon make up for lost time.

Thanks to the influence of his two teachers, Lepsius's first visit to Egypt was at the head of an official Prussian expedition commissioned by Friedrich Wilhelm IV, which would remain in Egypt for four years, 1842–45. The expedition had the twin aims of surveying the standing monuments and of collecting antiquities – of which Lepsius would send home a staggering 15,000

An early photograph of the great German Egyptologist Carl Richard Lepsius.

Adventurers and Scholars in Egypt, 1815–1845

Year	Salt	Belzoni	Wilkinson	Burton	Hay	Champ/Ros	Lepsius
1815	•						
1816	•	•					
1817	•	•					
1818	•	•					
1819	•	•					
1820	•						
1821	•		•				
1822	•		•	•			
1823	•		•	•			
1824	•		•	•	•		
1825	•		•	•	•		
1826	•		•	•	•		
1827	•		•	•	•		
1828			•	•	•	•	
1829			•		•	•	
1830			•		•		
1831			•		•		
1832			•		•		
1833			•				
1834			•		•		
1835			•				
1836							
1837							
1838							
1839							
1840							
1841							
1842							•
1843							•
1844							•
1845							•

pieces. The results of the expedition's work would be published between 1849 and 1859 in 12 volumes (each so large as to require a special 'cradle' for viewing). This was the famous *Denkmäler aus Aegypten und Aethiopien*.

Lepsius's team, which included among its number Joseph Bonomi, who had previously worked with Robert Hay, was in the Valley of the Kings from October 1844 until February 1845, copying the scenes and carrying out clearance work and excavation within KV7 (Ramesses II), KV8 (Merenptah) and KV20 (Tuthmosis I/Hatshepsut). Sadly, as in the earlier expedition of Champollion and Rosellini, there were excesses: in the tomb of Sethos I, as Rhind records, Lepsius's team overthrew 'a decorated column to secure a portion of it, leaving the remainder a scattered wreck of the floor of the chamber.'

Twenty-five tombs are marked on the expedition's published map (21 in the main wadi and a further four – WV22–25 – in the western annexe), building upon the system of Wilkinson to establish the sequence still in use today.

Alexander Henry Rhind

'... it has been part of [my] plan throughout, that the various details should exhibit some realisation at once of the conditions under which, and those by means of which, Egyptian relics have been procured.'

Alexander Henry Rhind

With the second half of the 19th century, archaeology began to find its conscience. Thanks to the influence of far-sighted individuals such as Auguste Mariette, who laid the foundations for a national Egyptian museum and for a government antiquities service, the days of the free-booter were drawing to a close. No longer would architectural plundering of the sort carried out by Champollion, Rosellini and Lepsius be so readily tolerated.

The importance of context, too, was beginning to be appreciated, one of the earliest advocates being a Scotsman by the name of Alexander Henry Rhind. Born in Wick, Caithness, Rhind first visited Egypt in 1855, as with so many before and after, for the sake of his health. He undertook his first, model excavations at Qurna, bringing to light an interesting collection of mummy labels associated with lesser members of the 18th-dynasty royal family (p. 204). Immediately after, in the winter of that same year, he turned his attentions to the Valley of the Kings.

Sadly for us (for any discoveries would have been carefully documented), his trial excavations in the main valley, with two 20-strong teams of workmen, came to naught: 'One after the other the experimental trenches proved fruitless, and the daily ride over the mountain came to be a round of laborious duty unrelieved by interest.' The closest Rhind came to a discovery, near the door to the sepulchre of Sethos I, were what looked like signs of the beginning of a tomb entrance. But he was to be unlucky – it was merely a natural cleavage in the rock. He sought to console himself with the thought that there probably was, after all, nothing left to find:

'... having dug at I believe every available spot it presented, not bearing evidences of previous search, I feel reasonably confident that no more sepulchres except those already known, exist within its proper limits.'

The intention was to continue the following season 'in and near the Western Valley. There and thereabouts it is undoubtedly most likely that any royal tombs of the series in question, yet to be disclosed, have their place.' But Rhind's already weak constitution gave way and he had to abandon the project. It was to be many years before excavation in the valley would be in such competent and understanding hands.

Auguste Mariette

'The number of open tombs in the principal valley was twenty-one in 1835; since our excavations, it is twenty-five.'

Auguste Mariette

The Valley in Transition 1844–1899

Alexander Henry Rhind was not alone in his concern for the preservation of Egypt's ancient past, but few converted their fine words into action. One who did was an extraordinarily talented Frenchman, by the name of Auguste Mariette. Sent to Egypt by the Louvre to collect Coptic papyri, Mariette diverted his funds towards clearance work in the Memphite desert, where he stumbled upon the Serapeum – the burial place of the sacred Apis bulls. His employers were less than happy, but the discovery aroused enormous interest and encouraged Mariette to remain in Egypt and continue with archaeological fieldwork. By 1858 he had been appointed as the Khedive's Director of Egyptian Monuments, going on to set up the first Egyptian museum at Bulaq in 1863.

Mariette's intentions may have been of the highest, but the results of his massive excavating programme – employing over 7,000 workmen in total, and taking in most of the well-known sites – were disappointing. Since the work was poorly supervised, little could be expected beyond a few interesting sculptures and inscriptions; in the Valley of the Kings it is even uncertain which were the tombs Mariette brought to light.

Auguste Mariette, the first Director of Egyptian Monuments and founder of the national museum at Bulaq.

(Left) The reverse of an inlaid gold pectoral from the mummy of Queen Ahhotpe, found at Thebes in 1860, which alerted the world to the rich potential of the Theban necropolis.

(Right) A wall scene from the tomb of Tawosret and Sethnakhte – a typical example of Lefébure's rough but informative copies of the scenes in the royal tombs.

Mariette, however, was a pioneer, and it is to his energy and enthusiasm that we owe the existence of the Egyptian Antiquities Service. The foundations he laid would be built upon by another Frenchman, Gaston Maspero, during whose two periods in office – 1881–86 and 1899–1914 – excavation in the Valley of the Kings would be pursued with a vengeance.

Eugène Lefébure

'The interest [of the Deir el-Bahri cache] . . . is in the piece of theatre, the dramatic and sudden bringing to light of the assembly of kings which brings close to us that which we had thought so remote . . .'

Eugène Lefébure

Mariette's most famous discovery – or, more strictly, recovery – had been the coffin and collection of jewellery belonging to the 17th-dynasty queen Ahhotpe, whose intact mummy fell into the hands of the Governor of Qena in 1860. Although the mummy itself was abandoned to its fate, the discovery set the scene for the find of royal mummies at Deir el-Bahri a few years later (p. 194). And this, in its turn, inspired Eugène Lefébure's 1883 survey of the Valley of the Kings.

Our hero had been born in Prunoy, Yonne, on 11 November 1838, and enjoyed a humdrum if safe career in the French Postal Service until, following the death of his wife, he took the plunge – he resigned his position and joined the French Archaeological Mission in Cairo. By 1881 he had become its head, in succession to Gaston Maspero, who had resigned to become Director of the Antiquities Service following the death of Mariette.

The new Director of the French Mission was like a dog with a bone. Once he embarked upon his work in the valley, at the end of January 1883, he continued without a break, outlasting the majority of his assistants who seem to have thrown in the towel at a relatively early stage. By April, Lefébure had achieved the miraculous feat of copying in his spidery hieroglyphic hand the tomb of Sethos I in its entirety, and was well advanced with the documentation of KV2, the tomb of Ramesses IV (which for a time served as his base). In addition, he

The energetic, if unpopular, Victor Loret. Émile Brugsch, his assistant, described the previous director as 'but a small devil' compared to Loret, who was 'twenty devils…'.

had crawled and wriggled into every hole he could find in the valley, roughly plotted the plan of every accessible tomb and copied the principal texts and any visible graffiti. More than this: within four years the enterprise had been published fully in two thick volumes, in 1886 and 1889, as *Les Hypogées royaux de Thèbes*. It was, admittedly, a somewhat rough and ready work, the sketched figures lacking any artistic pretension and intended solely to convey a point. But it was precisely what was needed: a basic compendium of information on the royal tombs. Here we encounter for the first time, if unnumbered, the plans of KV26–29, 37, 40 and 59 in the main wadi, and WV24–25 and WV A in the west, and a whole mass of new information besides, which, in many instances, has yet to be superseded.

It is ironic that the Director of the French Mission, despite his achievements, should since have been written off in the standard biographical dictionary of Egyptology as 'not physically fitted for field-work'. He returned to the Egyptology lectureship in Lyon in 1884, never to set foot in the Valley of the Kings again.

Victor Loret

'In the Valley of the Tombs of the Kings M. Loret has made discoveries of the highest importance. [Here,] for several years past . . . the Arabs have offered to reveal the secret of new royal tombs to wealthy tourists, and now the new Director of the Department of Antiquities has had the good fortune to discover two royal sepulchres, the earliest, and in some respects the most interesting of all yet known in the valley.'

Francis Llewellyn Griffith

The years immediately following Lefébure's survey saw a continuation of the French Institute's work of recording, with Jules Baillet and Georges Bénédite making a start on copying the Greek, Roman and demotic graffiti left by visitors to the valley in Classical times (p. 50). In addition, a small amount of clearance work was carried out in 1888 within the tombs of Ramesses VI (p. 164) and Ramesses IX (p. 168) (KV9 and KV6 respectively) by Georges Daressy of the Bulaq Museum. The most notable of the finds made by Daressy was a large group of pictorial ostraca, many of which are probably votive in character. The best known carries a sketch plan of the tomb of the later Ramessid king, one of the very small number of such drawings known from ancient Egypt.

Gaston Maspero had retired as Director of the Egyptian Service des Antiquités two years previous to Daressy's clearances, in 1886. He was succeeded by two other French nationals: Eugène Grébaut, who held the position until 1892; and Jacques de Morgan – who may himself have carried out a clearance of the tomb of Ramesses III (KV11) in 1895 – who was Director from 1892 until 1897. De Morgan, in turn, was succeeded by yet another Frenchman, Victor Loret, whose equally short stint in the top job – he was not a popular figure – would nevertheless be one of the most productive ever in terms of effort and achievement in the Valley of the Kings.

Loret's interest in the site went back a long way. He had arrived in Egypt in 1881, at the height of the hysteria engendered by the discovery of the royal mummies (p. 194); and he was a survivor of Lefébure's manic 1883 survey, work which had inevitably suggested to the young Egyptologist areas which seemed worthy of examination. Now he was in a position to follow up his hunches.

And, for whatever reason, Loret's hunches were good: between 1898 and 1899 he would add 16 tombs to the map of the principal Valley of the Kings, of which only five (KV26–28 and KV30–31) seem to have been known to earlier explorers. Sadly, his record of publication was less impressive – we have a preliminary report for only two of his discoveries: the second cache of royal mummies within the tomb of Amenophis II (KV35) (p. 198) and the discovery of KV34, the tomb of Tuthmosis III (p. 97) – but no substantial body of notes relating to these two years of excavation has yet surfaced.

Our evidence for reconstructing the scheme of Loret's work is meagre: an extensive series of photographs – unpublished – preserved among the excavator's archives in Lyon; and Charles Edwin Wilbour's annotated map of Loret's work in The Brooklyn Museum. This important document, rediscovered by John Romer in the late 1970s, suggests the following basic chronology for Loret's work in the valley:

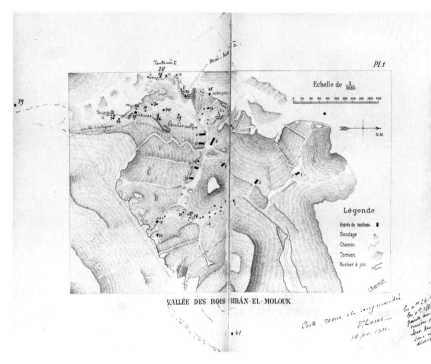

VALLÉE DES ROIS BIBÂN-EL-MOLOUK.

1898	1899
KV26	KV29
KV27	KV36 (Maiherpri)
KV28	KV37
KV30	KV38 (Tuthmosis I, second tomb)
KV31	
KV32	KV39 (?Amenophis I)
KV34 (Tuthmosis III)	KV40
KV35 (Amenophis II)	KV41
KV L–M	

(Above) Map showing the extent of Loret's work in the valley in 1898–1899, with annotations and additions by the excavator.

(Below) Ground plan of KV6 on a limestone flake, from Georges Daressy's clearance of that tomb in 1888.

In addition, entries in the accessions book of the Cairo Museum (the *Journal d'Entrée*) suggest that Loret may have also explored a number of previously numbered tombs – KV2 (the tomb of Ramesses IV), KV17 (that of Sethos I) and WV22 (the burial place of Amenophis III) – perhaps during the 1899 season.

Loret's method in the valley was that of *sondage* – a hit-or-miss technique which entailed locating likely-looking spots and sinking pits there. But his enormously high rate of success makes it difficult to believe that he could have relied solely on chance. Like Belzoni before him, whose understanding of the landscape enabled him to recognize instinctively the types of location favoured by the early Ramessid architects, Loret (or, perhaps more likely, his Egyptian *reis* – supervisor – Ahmed Girigar) quickly grasped the low-lying nature of many of the sites which 18th-dynasty builders tended to select – the period to which all his discoveries may be assigned.

Howard Carter and the Service des Antiquités

The return of Gaston Maspero to the Directorate of the Egyptian Service des Antiquités in 1899 after a gap of 13 years marked a turning point in the archaeological history of the Valley of the Kings. Victor Loret had achieved much, but it was with the energetic work of Maspero's protégé, the young Howard Carter, that the exploration – and the conservation – of the New Kingdom royal necropolis was really to get under way.

Howard Carter's reinstallation of the mummy of Amenophis II, newly illuminated by electricity, is admired by a party of tourists at the turn of the century.

'Amenôthes II and his three companions descend again to the vault, borne by four native workmen. With M. Loret's plan in his hand, Mr. Carter restored the mummies to their cell in the old order ...'

Gaston Maspero

When, in 1899, Carter was appointed as the first Chief Inspector of Antiquities of Upper Egypt he was still a young man, in his mid-20s. He had eight years of practical field experience with the Egypt Exploration Fund behind him, and plenty of ideas and ambition for the future. One of his first jobs for Maspero was the reinstallation of Amenophis II himself and the uninscribed royal mummies which Loret had brought to light in KV35 the previous year (p. 198); the remainder he would carefully pack to ship to the museum at Giza. The tomb would attract immediate attention – and not only from tourists for, within a matter of months, it and its occupants were ransacked by thieves in search of valuables. The culprits were the Abd el-Rassuls, professional tomb robbers with whom Maspero had crossed swords on more than one occasion in the past (p. 194).

Antiquities Service excavations

Carter's first opportunity for tomb clearance in the Valley of the Kings came at the end of 1900, when he was approached by two locals, Chinouda Macarios and Boutros Andraos, who claimed that they knew the whereabouts of a new tomb. By informing the Antiquities Service and paying for the cost of clearance they could, according to the law of the day, be assured of a share of the pro-

Howard Carter (1874–1939)

'... always so pleasant – in spite of his dominant personality.'

Emma B. Andrews

● Born Kensington, London, 9 May 1874, the youngest son of the animal artist Samuel John Carter; without any formal education.

● Through the influence of Lady Amherst, a family acquaintance, sent to Egypt as an artist with the Egypt Exploration Fund, working at Beni Hasan and El-Bersha, joining W. M. F. Petrie at El-Amarna in 1892 and working, again for the EEF, at Deir el-Bahri, 1893–99.

● 1899–1904, first Chief Inspector of Antiquities for Upper Egypt, under Maspero, clearing tomb KV42 (winter 1900) and KV44 (26 January 1901); the first to encourage Davis to dig in Wadi Biban el-Muluk supervising his early clearances of the tomb of Tuthmosis IV (KV43; 18 January 1903)

ceeds. The actual digging, not far distant from the tomb of Tuthmosis III (KV34), was supervised by Ahmed Girigar, chief of the ghaffirs, and within a relatively short time the doorway was reached. The find turned out to be a well-cut, Tuthmosid corridor tomb of royal pretensions, now assigned the number KV42 (p. 102); several objects from here had previously been brought to light by Loret, though the tomb itself seems to have eluded him. Before the discovery here in 1921 of foundation deposits inscribed for Hatshepsut-Meryetre, wife of Tuthmosis III, clearly identifying the tomb as hers, Arthur Weigall and others would identify the sepulchre as the 'missing' burial place of Tuthmosis II, an attribution still sometimes argued.

'. . . my agreement was with the native that either half value or half antiquities shall be the finder's property.'

Howard Carter

The excavation of KV42 was followed, on 26 January 1901, with the discovery and clearance of KV44, a small, New Kingdom shaft tomb which had been reused for a family burial of the 22nd

dynasty (p. 184). The existence of a tomb in the area had evidently been observed, if not by Loret himself, at least by his workers, and the knowledge tucked away for a future rainy day.

During the winter of 1901/2, Carter undertook further excavation work in the Valley of the Kings, digging at the entrance to the tomb of Ramesses X (KV 18) where he turned up portions of a foundation deposit, and elsewhere in the valley (the sites unfortunately not specified) where he brought to light a sandstone door lintel inscribed for 'the scribe Ahmose called Pensekerty, true of voice', a 'sandstone fragment' inscribed with the throne name of Hatshepsut, fragmentary *shabtis* of Sethos I and Ramesses VI, and a number of ostraca and artists' 'trial pieces'.

(Right) Ostracon from Carter's excavations in the valley in 1901/2, with an image in outline of the god Osiris. Ramessid period.

and Hatshepsut (KV20; early February 1903–February 1904) and uncovering two smaller tombs – KV45 (25 February 1902) and KV60 (1903).

● Transfer to the northern Inspectorate in 1904, and resignation from the Service des Antiquités the next year following a dispute with a party of French tourists at Saqqara.

● Following a spell as an independent watercolour artist, 1905–07, employment as archaeologist to the fifth Earl of Carnarvon, excavating at Dra Abu el-Naga, Deir el-Bahri and other Egyptian sites until Davis relinquished his concession for the Valley of the Kings.

● Excavated with Lord Carnarvon in the West Valley, at the tomb of Amenophis III (WV22), spring

(Above) Howard Carter – the young artist newly appointed as Chief Inspector of the Antiquities Service, 1899.

1915, and in the main wadi from 1917 to 1922.

● Discovered the tomb of Tutankhamun (KV62) on 4 November 1922, the work of clearance and conservation extending through to 1932.

● Died in Kensington, London, 2 March 1939.

Watercolour detail of the outer coffin of Tjuyu, painted by Carter for Theodore Davis shortly after the discovery of KV46.

Repair and restoration

Unlike most of his predecessors, Carter believed that one of the prime duties of the Egyptologist was conservation. And so, in part to facilitate tourism, necessary repair work was carried out in a number of tombs during the 1901/2 season – including Amenophis II (KV35), Ramesses I (KV16), Ramesses III (KV11), Ramesses VI (KV9) and Ramesses IX (KV6) – while 'the pathways leading to each tomb have been widened, and a shelter for one hundred donkeys and boys made; the latter being sadly wanted to keep order, and to prevent confusion and litter during the season.' By chance, the total costs in Egyptian pounds for this work are recorded: wages – LE 51.995; materials – LE 37.820; transport – LE 2.640; 'surveillance' – LE15.920.

When the official funding had run out, the energetic Carter looked elsewhere. His best-known source of finance was the successful American lawyer, Theodore M. Davis (p. 73), of whom he – and indeed Maspero – would soon lose control. A more manageable patron was the industrial chemist Robert Mond, to whom Carter turned in 1903/4 to finance essential restoration work in the tomb of Sethos I (KV17) when a pillar collapsed bringing with it part of the ceiling of the burial chamber; another was a lady by the name of Mrs Goff, about whom practically nothing is known. Having evidently taken a shine to the young Chief Inspector, she was persuaded to part with the by no means inconsiderable sum of £10, for 'preserving a special monument'. In fact, the money went towards Carter's clearance of the tomb of Sethos II (KV15); we are expected to believe, perhaps, with Mrs Goff, that the excitement of excavation was a necessary first step before the more tedious work of restoration could be carried out. Carter was, after all, only human.

Lighting the tombs

'It being decided that six of the principal royal tombs at Biban el-Molouk . . . should be lighted by electricity, the necessary project for an electrical installation was drawn by M. Zimmermann, electrician-engineer of the Louxor and Karnak Hotels. . . . The engine was established in the uninscribed tomb no. 18 . . . ; some 900 to 1000 metres of cable and wire were used, and the exterior cables were laid underground, wherever it was possible, so as not to mar the fine prospect of the valley.'

Howard Carter

One of Howard Carter's greatest and best-remembered achievements as Chief Inspector in the valley was the introduction, into the six best tombs, of electric lighting. In the tomb of Amenophis II, with its gruesome occupants, the new-fangled form of illumination was a particular success. Emma B. Andrews, Theodore Davis's travelling companion, records in her diary a visit to the tomb shortly after the power had been switched on:

'We entered Amenhotep's tomb – now lighted with electricity, showing arrangement and decoration delightfully. The rifled mummy has been restored to his sarcophagus, and decently wrapped with the torn mummy cloths – and Carter has arranged the whole thing most artistically. A shrouded electric light is at the head of the sarcophagus, throwing the fine face into splendid relief – and when all the other lights were extinguished, the effect was solemn and impressive. Carter has done wonderful work over there [in the Valley of the Kings] in a dozen different ways. . . . No more stumbling about amongst yawning pits and rough stair cases, with flickering candles dripping wax all over one.'

1903/4 saw Carter embark upon a clearance of the inner chambers of the tomb of Merenptah (KV8), and complete his work for Mrs Goff in the tomb of Sethos II. But time was running out. At the end of 1904 his tour of duty in the south drew to a close, and he was transferred to the north as Chief Inspector for Lower Egypt. He boarded the train to Cairo as a respected and effective servant of the Egyptian government; his return to the valley, in 1915, would be under quite different circumstances.

Lighting the Valley of the Kings, 1903

Tomb	Owner	No. of electric lights
KV6	Ramesses IX	4
KV9	Ramesses VI	12
KV11	Ramesses III	18
KV16	Ramesses I	7
KV17	Sethos I	37
KV35	Amenophis II	21

99 lamps in total, of 10, 16 and 32 candle power

Two faces of a limestone flake from the tomb of Merenptah, showing in both profile and front view the king's inner coffin, with dimensions.

Early days

Theodore M. Davis, the elderly and wealthy financier and lawyer from Newport, Rhode Island, is one of the key figures in the history of archaeological exploration in the Valley of the Kings. Davis had wintered regularly in Egypt since 1889, sailing up and down the Nile on his *dahabiya*, 'Bedawin', with his companion Mrs Emma B. Andrews (from whose diary we learn so much about the day-to-day goings-on). But he came to digging only late – thankfully, some would say – and then quite by chance.

Davis's excavations are among the most important ever carried out in the royal valley. As with Loret, however, Davis's published record did not do justice to his finds; in fact, his reports bristle with ambiguities, errors and omissions. They are supplemented to some extent by a handful of manuscript sources – a few photographs, personal diaries and letters, and a sketch map of work begun by Edward Ayrton in 1905/6, which John Romer found still rolled up in a corner of the derelict dig house in the late 1970s. The human side of the work is very much in evidence, however, and we begin to see for the first time what life on an excavation in the valley was really like.

Davis's interest in excavation seems to have been piqued by Howard Carter, on the look out, as usual, for other people's money to finance his archaeological plans, particularly in the Valley of the Kings. As Carter records in his unpublished autobiographical 'sketches':

'[Davis] often told me that he would like to have some active interest during his sojourns in Upper Egypt. Thus . . . I put the following proposition to him. The Egyptian Government would be willing, when my duties permitted, for me to carry out researches in the Valley of the tombs of the Kings on his behalf, if he would be willing on his part to cover the costs thereof, that the Egyptian Government in return for his generosity would be pleased, whenever it was possible, to give him any duplicate antiquities resulting from these researches. At the same time I told him of my conjecture regarding the possibility of discovering the tomb of Tuthmosis IV . . .'

Carter dangled the bait – and Davis nibbled. In

Theodore Davis: A New Tomb Every Season

January 1902, the young and enterprising Chief Inspector began excavating with the American's money in the area between KV2 and KV7, three days of hard work revealing nothing except rubble from the quarrying and excavation of the Ramesses IV tomb. He then transferred his attention to the area between KV5 and KV3, working 'carefully along the edge of the foothill between the above two points, not leaving a part of the gebel uninvestigated' – to be repaid by the discovery of an ostracon sketched with the profile of a king's head.

By the end of February things had picked up. Digging westwards from KV4, the tomb of Ramesses XI, along the wadi in the direction of KV21, Carter's men stumbled upon a small shaft tomb, now assigned the number KV45. This was opened by Carter on 25 February, and proved to be 'a third full of rubbish', with the remains of two 22nd-dynasty mummies laid out on the top of the heap, each contained in a double coffin but the whole sadly decayed by periodic flooding. Beneath, among the debris, were remains of the original, 18th-dynasty occupants (p. 184). Though not a great find, it was *a* find; the bait was swallowed, and Davis found himself well and truly hooked.

Arthur Weigall the Chief Inspector of Antiquities (second from left), his wife Hortense, Theodore M. Davis (third from left) and Edward R. Ayrton, Davis's excavator (right) standing outside the entrance to the tomb of Ramesses IV.

*(Right) Carter's workmen
remove finds from the newly
discovered tomb of
Tuthmosis IV, 1904.*

On the trail of Tuthmosis IV

Carter's 'conjecture' concerning the tomb of
Tuthmosis IV was strengthened a few days later, on
25 February 1902, by his discovery, in the vicinity
of the long-known KV28, of a fragment of a fine
calcite vessel with an inscription naming the king.
This, evidently, had formed a part of the royal burial equipment, and seemed to hold out the prospect
of more exciting discoveries ahead – more exciting,
certainly, than the pottery, ostraca, broken hoe and
roughly coffined skeleton of a child which made up
the remainder of the season's finds.

But the secret of Tuthmosis IV's tomb would be
kept for a little while longer. Still, as he thought, hot
on the trail, Carter transferred his efforts to the area
in which Loret had discovered the tomb of
Maiherpri (KV36) in March or April 1899. 'This site
was thoroughly dug out', beginning on 26
February, and the effort was rewarded by the discovery, 'In a small hollow in the rock over the tomb
of Mai-her-pri', of a yellow-painted wooden box
inscribed in blue with the name and titles of that
tomb owner. Inside were two leather loincloths,
each intricately cut in a network pattern, among
the finest quality leatherwork ever to have been discovered in Egypt. Close by were scattered ostraca
and broken fragments of Ramessid date, and a
large number of glass and carnelian inlays and broken 'fragments of a wooden box or coffin bearing
the cartouches of Amenophis III', all of this latter
material (now divided between Boston Museum of
Fine Arts and the Cairo Museum) perhaps originating in WV22 (p. 110).

Carter would not pick up the scent of Tuthmosis
IV until the following season, which began in early

January 1903 and would run until the middle of
April. Transferring his men back to the vicinity of
KV21, Carter began steadily to clear the area leading up to the southeast cliff face, his eyes peeled for
the tell-tale, chisel-bruised limestone chips which
would reveal the presence of a tomb in the vicinity.
And, with the luck which characterized so much of
the Davis-financed work in the valley, while clearing in the entrance to the long-known tomb of
Mentuherkhepshef (KV19), Carter and his men
stumbled upon a small and interesting, single-
chambered corridor tomb, no. 60, containing 'two
much denuded mummies of women and some
mummified geese' (p. 186).

On 18 January, the entrance to the tomb of
Tuthmosis IV was at last brought to light, signalled
by the discovery of two rock-cut hollows containing foundation deposits. Further clearance revealed
four sides of a large cutting and, after a further
day's digging, a sunken stairway, as Carter
describes:

'A few eroded steps led us down to the entrance doorway
partially blocked with stones. We crept under its lintel
into a steep descending corridor that penetrated into the
heart of the rock. . . . We slithered down . . . to the brink
of a large gaping well . . . [and eventually] realized in the
gloom that the upper parts of the walls were elaborately
sculptured and painted. The scenes represented the

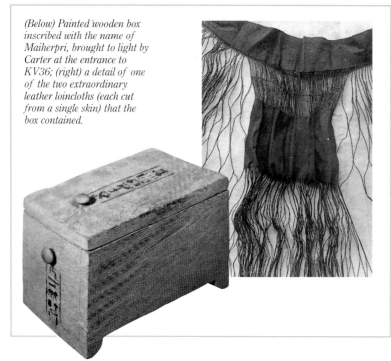

*(Below) Painted wooden box
inscribed with the name of
Maiherpri, brought to light by
Carter at the entrance to
KV36; (right) a detail of one
of the two extraordinary
leather loincloths (each cut
from a single skin) that the
box contained.*

Excavating for Davis

(Below) Theodore Davis's house at the entrance to the West Valley. Designed and built by Edward Ayrton, it was extended (as shown on right in a sketch in one of his letters home) by Harold Jones in 1909.

Life in the field was not all jewels and buried treasure, as the sickly Harold Jones, Theodore Davis's last-but-one field director, bored with finding nothing, records in this down-in-the-dumps letter home to his family on 6 November 1909:

'It's really useless writing for what is there to say? When all else fails one talks about the weather – well, it's still warm, 85° in the shade today and very close even at night – so you can imagine Cyril [Jones, Harold's younger brother and assistant in the work in 1909 and 1910] and I dressed in nothing but trousers, vest and shirts – collarless. We sleep outside at night with two blankets over – the stars above and insects all around. Before sunrise I am awakened by the flies crawling up my nose and so I get up and go indoors with one blanket and finish my sleep on a mattress there. Cyril comes in sleepy around 6.30 to 7 o'clock, turned out . . . because of the sun on his bed! and he generally gets me a glass of milk and then dresses. I, lazy, go to sleep again and get up to breakfast about 8.30 to 9 o'clock. After the porridge etc. the work of the day begins – that is if I have any energy, and so the morning passes with an occasional rest till lunch – then we make a meal of [greens] and cucumbers and whatever meat is going and a milk pudding. (By the way, I have a glass of milk at 10.30.) After lunch it is hot and somehow one feels slack – so I generally have a nap and do a little work before tea and afterwards we go for a short walk till it gets late and then we return and I have a glass of milk – flavoured as Cyril calls it – and then we sit out in the starlight till dinner which comes around 7 – more onion and cucumber and lentil soup, and then we sit out again . . .'

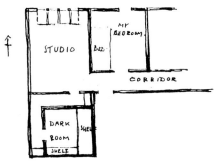

Pharaoh Tuthmosis IV standing before various gods and goddesses of the Netherworld. . . . Here was final proof that I had found the tomb of Tuthmosis IV, which, as you may conceive, gave me a considerable degree of satisfaction . . .'

– not least because future funding for his work would now be assured; for Davis was delighted.

Hatshepsut

'. . . Theo said that when Carter emerged from the tomb he was a horrid object – dripping and wet from the heat, with a black dust over his face and hands – he was very sick too, and had to lie down for sometime. He said the air was filled with a suffocating odour, like ammonia, and that great masses of black stuff like black stalactites were hanging from the ceiling. It is a hard business for him and the workmen . . .'

Emma B. Andrews

By early February 1903, before the dust of Tuthmosis IV's tomb (KV43) had had a chance to settle, Carter had persuaded his sponsor that it might be worthwhile to take a look at the mysterious, uninscribed tomb KV20, which had stood partially open for years but about which practically nothing was known; probably, as we shall see, it was the tomb excavated by Ineni for Tuthmosis I, and subsequently enlarged to accommodate the burial of Hatshepsut (p. 91).

After the easy pickings of Tuthmosis IV, the clearance of KV20 proved an expensive and dangerous slog, dragging on into February 1904. It was the last work Carter undertook for Davis before his appointment as Chief Inspector in the north.

(Left) Watercolour by Howard Carter showing the topsy-turvy state of the burial chamber of KV20 as found: the sarcophagus of Hatshepsut with its displaced lid in the foreground.

The massive outer coffin of Yuya outside the entrance to the richly stocked tomb KV46, uncovered by Davis early in 1905.

hand, assumed a dismissive air in his dealings with Quibell, and his interference in the actual clearance should have alerted Maspero to the dangers of allowing the man to believe the valley to be a playground over which he had complete control. Maspero, however, was weak in this matter, and as a result Davis became more and more unmanageable as his successes mounted. Shortly after the Yuya-Tjuyu find, Quibell transferred to the northern inspectorate, to be replaced by a much more amenable and diplomatic personality, Arthur Weigall, who had already been in on the Davis discovery as Quibell's successor in waiting. Weigall was one of the most gifted archaeologists ever to work in the Valley of the Kings, and he would deal extremely well with the cocksure Davis.

Theodore Davis as independent excavator

'I have now arranged with M. Maspero to the end that "Ayrton" shall be employed for two years to come, by me to conduct explorations in the Valley. I know that you will be glad to escape the bother of looking after my [works?] or at least until I find a tomb, when doubtless the contents will be turned over to your care. It seems to be the best manner of arranging the explorations, and certainly will make life more harmonious!'

Theodore M. Davis, letter to Arthur Weigall

Arthur Weigall soon came to the conclusion that the day-to-day excavations in the Valley of the Kings were taking up far too much of the Chief Inspector's valuable time. He therefore suggested that it would be in everyone's best interest if Davis employed his own man to oversee the digging. Chosen to fill this post was a young Egyptologist by the name of Edward Russell Ayrton (1882–1914), a competent excavator who had worked with the Egypt Exploration Fund at Deir el-Bahri.

Ayrton set to with immense energy and no little flair. We are able to discern system in the work – in strategy, in the use of codes marked on finds to relate them to a master map of the valley, and in the frequent use of a camera for recording purposes. It has been to the detriment of Ayrton's reputation, and indeed to the disadvantage of all today with an interest in Davis's work, that the dictatorial sponsor refused to clutter up his elegant publications with archaeological data of the sort that Ayrton prepared.

Ayrton: a modest beginning

'Ayrton ... was not popular at night; by a consensus, his cot was placed a long distance away from the rest of us. He had dreadful nightmares in which he shrieked in fluent Chinese ...'

Joseph Lindon Smith

Edward Ayrton seems to have begun his work for Davis in the West Valley, clearing the rubbish heaps in the small wadi in which the tomb of

Yuya and Tjuyu

Any sense of relief Carter felt at leaving the valley will very soon have turned sour when his successor as Chief Inspector in Luxor, James Edward Quibell, taking up for Davis where Carter had left off, on 5 February 1905 stumbled upon an unbelievably rich and little-disturbed tomb between KV3 and the tomb of Ramesses XI, KV4. The occupants turned out to be Yuya and Tjuyu, father and mother of Tiye, the principal wife of Amenophis III of the 18th dynasty. The small tomb was stacked to the ceiling with coffins and funerary equipment of the finest quality so far to have come to light in the valley, gold and silver leaf sparkling in every direction.

Carter and Davis had got along well enough; but after 1905 the situation changed. Davis, now the old

Amenophis III had been found by Napoleon's Expedition in 1799. The results were less than encouraging, however, and he soon transferred his efforts to the main Valley of the Kings, where he dug over the ground in the vicinity of KV12, finding nothing and temporarily abandoning the site for the incompletely explored area to the south of the tomb of Tuthmosis IV. Here he had his first success, uncovering the entrance to his first tomb, now designated KV B – though further clearance revealed it to be little more than an unfinished entrance (p. 187).

Further tidying up in front of the tomb of Yuya and Tjuyu (KV46) and KV3 again yielded nothing, and Ayrton turned his attention to the hill containing the entrance to the tomb of Ramesses IV (KV2), trenching in front and to the north and making his first finds: principally ostraca, *shabtis* of Ramesses IV in calcite, faience and wood, and a number of Coptic items including pottery and an unopened letter on papyrus.

Back in the vicinity of KV12, in the western part of the valley, Ayrton began to make further finds of small antiquities, including ostraca, more *shabtis* of Ramesses IV, and one of the most famous of the Davis discoveries: a small faience cup inscribed with the throne name of Tutankhamun – an early clue to the existence of the boy-king's tomb – which came to light at a depth of 3.65 m (12 ft) below the 1905 ground level. And it was perhaps from here also, among chippings quarried from the tomb of Ramesses III (KV11), that Ayrton recovered an unusual ostracon depicting the now extinct Syrian elephant, with its characteristic small ear. Whoever sketched this rare and exotic creature had evidently observed it in life.

Finding Siptah

By November 1905 the loose ends of earlier work had been tied up, and Ayrton embarked upon the more systematic 'policy of exhausting every mountain and foot-hill in the valley', working north from the tomb of Tuthmosis III (KV34). Further interesting finds followed in rapid succession as the diggers ploughed up the wadi, including a faience box knob inscribed with the name of Horemheb found among debris from the tomb of Tawosret (KV14); and, at last, a new tomb – that of Siptah of the 19th dynasty, now assigned the number 47 (p. 155). Like Carter with KV20, Ayrton regretted his decision to clear this tomb (which was filled with rock-hard mud) almost as soon as he had begun. After battling down as far as the burial chamber, he abandoned the work, leaving the job for Harry Burton to complete in 1912.

Animals, nobles and a prince

1905, Ayrton's first season for Davis, was a hectic one. No sooner had he found the tomb of Siptah than he transferred his workers to the small wadi running due west in the direction of the tomb of Amenophis II (KV35). Here more discoveries awaited him: KV49, an unfinished corridor tomb with a long graffito mentioning the necropolis scribe

Edward Russell Ayrton, the architect of much of Davis's good fortune. Under increasing pressure from his master to engineer further and ever-greater discoveries, Ayrton would eventually crack in 1908 and abandon Egyptology for good.

Émile Chassinat's Excavations in the West Valley

'I had noticed, at the end of the gorge, the opening – barely visible – of a doorway to a tomb which had evidently been violated . . . I undertook a complete clearance.'

Émile Chassinat

Despite Theodore Davis's stranglehold over the Valley of the Kings, at the start of 1906 the French Institute in Cairo undertook independent excavations for a period of five weeks in the West Valley under the direction of Émile Chassinat. Precisely why they wished to dig here, and how they managed to bypass Davis, are questions yet to be answered. What we do know is that work was concentrated at the end of the cul de sac at the entrance to which the tomb of Amenophis III is located. Finds included the remains of leather horse harness thrown out from the tomb of Amenophis III; further fragments would be brought to light by later excavators in this small valley. In addition, the small, single-chambered storage tomb WV A was partially cleared (the work since completed by the Japanese under Yoshimura and Kondo: p. 113), the finds consisting primarily of fragments of large pottery jars and sealings. Further work was carried out by the French in the vicinity of WV23, the tomb of Ay, but 'difficulties resulting from the nature of the terrain' brought the work to an early finish with little tangible result.

(Above left) Vessel sealing from WV A, with a reference to Amenophis III's jubilee.

(Above) The West Valley: WV22 and WV A lie at the foot of the cliff face (foreground).

Butehamun written over the entrance (p. 185), and several interesting ostraca; KV50, with its mummified dog and monkey; KV51, containing several mummified baboons, an ibis and a number of ducks; KV52, with a further mummified monkey (p. 185); KV48, the ransacked tomb of the vizier Amenemopet (p. 184); and KV53, from the fill of which were recovered several ostraca and votive stelae (p. 186).

Nor was this all. At the end of February 1906, Ayrton undertook the clearance of KV19, the tomb of Mentuherkhepshef (p. 170), in the entrance to which Carter had discovered the small corridor tomb KV60 in the spring of 1903. The yield included further ostraca, stela fragments, a fire stick and matrix, *shabtis* of faience and resin-coated wood, and fragments of beadwork. As he looked back on the season, Ayrton could feel well satisfied.

The tomb of Queen Tiye

'Gold shone on the ground, gold on the walls, gold in the furthest corner where the coffin leant up against the side. . . . It seemed as if all the gold of ancient Egypt glittered and gleamed in that narrow space [KV55].'

Gaston Maspero

Davis and Ayrton went from strength to strength. The following season, beginning 1 January 1907, Ayrton started to clear an area of some 4 sq. m (40 sq. ft) to the south of KV6, the tomb of Ramesses IX. Here, 'in . . . a recess in the rock' (today designat-ed KV C: p. 168) were uncovered 'several large jars of the XXth dynasty type'; and, at a lower level, the entrance to a tomb. This tomb, KV55, with its dismantled shrine and collapsed coffin, was immediately identified as the tomb of Queen Tiye, whose parents Quibell had uncovered in KV46 two years previously; and this is the attribution to which Davis stuck like glue. As the Rev. A. H. Sayce remarked in a letter to Weigall concerning the find, 'I am afraid you might as well try to stop an avalanche as try to stop Mr. Davis when he is bent upon doing a particular thing'. Thanks to Davis's censoring of Ayrton's contributions to the published report on this important discovery, it represents perhaps the most controversial archaeological discovery ever made in Egypt (p. 117). For Ayrton, and others, disillusionment beckoned.

Tutankhamun, Horemheb and buried treasure

Work on Tomb 55 took up most of that season, and was not completed until the spring of 1908, by which time Davis and Ayrton had had even more success. Digging along the wadi between KV16 (Ramesses I) and the anonymous KV21 resulted in the discovery of foundations for a series of huts employed by the ancient necropolis workers, together with the inevitable ostraca and *shabtis* of Sethos I thrown out from KV17. Here too was brought to light a small pit (KV54: p. 126), which

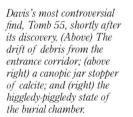

Davis's most controversial find, Tomb 55, shortly after its discovery. (Above) The drift of debris from the entrance corridor; (above right) a canopic jar stopper of calcite; and (right) the higgledy-piggledy state of the burial chamber.

Davis endeavoured to convince himself was all that remained of the burial of the 'lost' king, Tutankhamun. Subsequent events would demonstrate that KV54 contained only embalming materials displaced from the king's actual tomb, KV62, which Davis himself would miss by a hair's breadth, only for it to be uncovered by Lord Carnarvon and Howard Carter at the end of 1922 (p. 122).

Ayrton continued his 1907/8 season by making a partial clearance of KV10, the tomb of Amenmesse (p. 150), the work revealing nothing more than an intrusive calcite *shabti* of Ramesses VI and a calcite 'box' fragment inscribed with the name of Sethos I – both, apparently, washed in from outside during periodic floods.

On 3 January 1908 Davis's man began to excavate the area in which he would make his last important finds, on the western side of the path across from KV11, the tomb of Ramesses III. Ostraca, and yet more ostraca; and then, on 5 January, another tomb: KV56, a small, single-chambered sepulchre from the solidified mud of which Ayrton extracted some of the most splendid 19th-dynasty jewellery ever found (p. 153). And then, six weeks later, on 22 February, the tomb of Horemheb (p. 130) – an immense tomb 'going underground 300 feet about having gorgeously decorated rooms and corridors and a large granite sarcophagus all decorated and heaps of wooden statues of gods . . .'

Ayrton had had a good run for his money, but the strain of working for Davis was beginning to show and, to the relief of everyone concerned, he decided to resign. As the self-righteous Davis wrote cryptically to Weigall on 23 November 1908:

'The disturbing element has passed away, doubtless the sky will be brighter!'

Not for the unlucky Ayrton: quitting Egypt, he landed a post with the Archaeological Survey in Ceylon where, in 1914, he was to drown on a shooting expedition.

Ernest Harold Jones

'As Ayrton is giving up Mr Davis' digging in the Tombs of the Kings next year, Mr Davis has asked me to take it on for £250 for 3 months' work . . .'

Harold Jones

Ayrton's successor as Davis's archaeologist was a young Welsh artist by the name of Ernest Harold Jones – '. . . a dark-haired, small, pleasant young man' – who had had digging experience with John Garstang at Hierakonpolis and with the Metropolitan Museum team at el-Lisht and Heliopolis; he had first encountered the Davis party at the time of the Tomb 55 discovery (p. 119). Jones expressed great excitement in his new post as Davis's field director and artist – but, as he would soon discover, the glory days were over.

By a fortunate chance the day journal kept by Harold Jones has survived among the papers taken over by his successor, Harry Burton, in 1911 and later deposited in the Metropolitan Museum of Art in New York – and so we are able to follow the excavations from day to day, and to see precisely what was turning up and where. Carter and Ayrton had tended to concentrate in their reports on the more imposing discoveries, and it is interesting to see from Jones's journal just how much smaller material was being recovered and, in particular, how many unfinished pits (p. 187) – which previous excavators did not always bother to note:

'Dec[embe]r 4th [1908.] Continuing to E[ast] on N[orth] side of Amenophis II. [KV35] discloses two shallow pit tombs [KV L–M] discovered and emptied by Reis Mohammed in 1898 when Amenophis II was discovered. Broken large bl[ue] gl[azed] bead and fragment of decorated glass found in rubbish.'

Jones began digging for Davis on 18 November 1908, and during the 1908/9 season concentrated his efforts on the area between the tomb of Amenophis II (KV35) and Davis's earlier discovery, the tomb of Horemheb (KV57). The reward for his efforts was a biscuit-tin collection of stray fragments from the Amenophis II tomb – glass sherds, faience scraps, a broken *shabti*, beads, stone fragments, clay seals with the jackal-and-nine-captives motif, ostraca, a 'small piece of gold foil', and three small pits – KV L–N. From in front of the anonymous KV12 Jones turned up two fragmentary calcite *shabtis* of Ramesses VI (presumably removed from that king's tomb via KV12, which those quarrying KV9 had inadvertently broken through into) and a crude limestone figure. More ostraca, coffin fragments, faience inlays, glass fragments and pottery followed until, on 10 January, Jones made what would be his greatest discovery – KV58, the finds including gold foil and other items which had evidently been removed from the tomb of Ay (WV23) in antiquity (p. 186). The digging was fun, but the novelty soon began to wear off:

'The pleasure of excavating is spoilt by Davis' interference – generally ignorant inexperience of the nature of things and of the workmen. He is old and I might almost say stupid at times through his stubborn arrogance. However I find that what gives me less trouble and pleases him most is to give in to him and let the work suffer.'

Harold Jones

Continuing alongside and beneath the valley parking lot – the donkey shed – Jones turned up more funerary detritus, for the most part equally indeterminate, an oddly misplaced funerary cone of Mentuemhet and a further pit, KV O. The monotony would continue throughout the following season, 1909/10, digging between the 'animal tombs' and KV36 (Maiherpri) producing yet more pits –

Ernest Harold Jones – a self-portrait by Davis's new artist and excavator. Jones's initial enthusiasm would soon be put to the test by Davis's dictatorial nature, an almost total absence of finds and chronic ill health.

KV P, Q and R – and broken debris. And so it went on, the work continuing towards KV13 (Bay) and KV47 (Siptah) and up towards the tomb of Tuthmosis III (KV34) revealing, on the way, the archaeologically interesting discovery of a tomb cut and temporarily sealed to await an interment which never in fact came – KV61 (p. 187). Jones then switched his attention to the eastern side of the valley, which too yielded nothing.

Sadly, the end was near, as the tubercular Jones realized:

'. . . latterly the work has been very dusty – being very painful and trying for me – I will be very glad when the excavations are over. I really don't feel up to the work and don't know what I shall do next year. I don't feel up to taking it on again – if I live so long.'

Harold Jones

The next season would be his last:

'Harold Jones is so poorly, so weak, quite incapable of work. But his brother Cyril keeps a certain supervision of the workmen.'

Emma B. Andrews

And so the work continued until, three months later, the tragic Harold was dead, a victim of the consumption which had dogged him throughout his short life.

Harry Burton

'. . . [a man] perfectly suited to archaeological affairs – you know, the isolation, the cramped quarters, the ability to work sometimes with a bunch of people who are about as fascinating as railroad ties.'

'a colleague'

With Jones's death in 1911, Harry Burton would be installed to carry on where his predecessor had unwillingly left off. Born in Stamford, Lincolnshire, Burton was working for the Renaissance art historian Henry Cust in Florence when he met Theodore Davis. Davis engaged him to work in the 'Priest King's Valley' at Thebes in 1910, with a view to promoting him to principal field director once the ailing Jones was dead.

In the Kings' Valley, Burton continued the journal kept by Jones. He records that he began in the spring of 1912 with a clearance of KV3, the long-known tomb prepared for a son of Ramesses III (p. 161), and continued the difficult work of excavating KV47 (Siptah), abandoned by Ayrton (p. 155).

Following a disappointing spell in the West Valley, sinking 'test trenches in search of another tomb', Burton returned to KV47 the following winter, where his time was fully taken up hacking through the rock-hard fill of the innermost parts of the tomb.

Harry Burton evidently relished a challenge – or perhaps he was simply following orders – for the next season, 1913/14, he embarked upon an even more difficult task, the clearance of the tomb of Ramesses II (KV7, p. 140), which was filled with layers of solidified flood debris. He abandoned the work after only a month, and passed the remainder of the season with some desultory poking about in the vicinity of KV8.

All in all, Burton's sigh of relief must have echoed around the valley when Davis finally accepted the conclusion he had first expressed in 1912:

'I fear that the Valley of the Tombs is now exhausted . . .'

Within a matter of months, Davis was dead – and it was perhaps a kindness that he died ignorant of what he had missed. For eight years later, within 2 m (6 ft) of where Davis had stopped work, Howard Carter and Lord Carnarvon would reveal to a stunned world the richest treasure ever found in the valley – the tomb of Tutankhamun.

Theodore Davis: Clearances and Discoveries 1902–1914

Tomb	Owner/description	Excavator	Date
KV3	son of Ramesses III	Burton	7/15 Feb. 1912
KV7	Ramesses II	Burton	11 Dec. 1913–Feb. 1914
KV10	Amenmesse	Ayrton	Dec. 1907
KV11?	Ramesses III	Ayrton?	1905/6?
KV19	Mentuherkhepshef	Ayrton	late Feb. 1906
KV20	Tuthmosis I/Hatshepsut	Carter	early Feb.1903–11 Feb.1904
KV43	Tuthmosis IV	Carter	*c.* 18 Jan. 1903
KV45	Userhet	Carter	25 Feb. 1902
KV46	Yuya and Tjuyu	Quibell	5 Feb. 1905
KV47	Siptah	Ayrton	*c.* Nov. 1905
		Burton	7/23 Feb. 1912–8 Mar. 1913
KV48	Amenemopet	Ayrton	1905/6
KV49	private tomb	Ayrton	1905/6
KV50	'animal tomb'	Ayrton	1905/6
KV51	'animal tomb'	Ayrton	1905/6
KV52	'animal tomb'	Ayrton	1905/6
KV53	private tomb	Ayrton	1905/6
KV54	Tutankhamun		
	embalming materials	Ayrton	1907/8
KV55	Akhenaten	Ayrton	Jan. 1907
KV56	'Gold Tomb'	Ayrton	5 Jan. 1908
KV57	Horemheb	Ayrton	22 Feb. 1908
KV58	'chariot tomb'	Jones	10 Jan. 1909
KV60	In	Carter	1903
KV61	unused tomb	Jones	*c.* 6 Jan. 1910
WV A	annexe to WV22	Burton	1912
KV B	unfinished entrance	Ayrton	1905/6
KV C	cache of jars	Ayrton	Jan. 1907
KV D/E or S	pits	Ayrton	*c.* 1905/6
KV L	pit	Jones	4 Dec. 1908
KV M	pit	Jones	4 Dec. 1908
KV N	pit	Jones	21 Dec. 1908
KV O	pit	Jones	4 Feb. 1909
KV P	pit	Jones	12 Dec. 1909
KV Q	pit	Jones	13 Dec. 1909
KV R	pit	Jones	15/20 Dec. 1909

'Carnarvon . . . was of medium height and slight in build, with nondescript features and sparse hair. The shape of his head was abnormal, flattened on top, sloping abruptly downward, and widened, which gave a curious effect on a slender neck. . . . The unhealthy colour of his complexion was made more conspicuous by the fact that his face was pitted from smallpox. But when he discussed Egyptology, his pale, lustreless eyes lit up with enthusiasm . . .'

Joseph Lindon Smith

Lord Carnarvon and Howard Carter

Several years of intensive digging after 1908 had produced virtually nothing, and to all the world it seemed as if Davis was probably correct in his belief that any further effort in the valley would be wasted. Howard Carter had followed Davis's excavations closely from the start, however, and he was able to discern several points in the valley where further digging might well produce interesting results. The main Valley of the Kings had been explored with great thoroughness, but in extent rather than in depth. Carter realized that the valley floor was in places submerged in chippings to a depth of tens of metres; and until these 'pockets' had been removed, and the wadi explored systematically down to bedrock, no-one was in a position to predict with confidence what secrets the valley might or might not still hold. There was another factor, too: one of the kings for whom a burial in the Valley of the Kings could be demonstrated from stray finds was not represented in the list of tombs then known. This king was Tutankhamun.

Carter's timing, as usual, was good. In October 1912 he had been able to buy on the Luxor antiquities market, on behalf of his then employer, the fifth Earl of Carnarvon, a group of three hardstone bracelet plaques which were rumoured to have been found in the vicinity of the tomb of Amenophis III in the West Valley. They were beautiful pieces, and both Carnarvon and Carter were anxious to explore the tomb from which they came – it had never been fully cleared – to see whether more objects of value might be forthcoming. This Carter was able to do in February 1915 (p. 110), bringing to light several intact foundation deposits at the entrance – indicating that the cutting of the tomb had been begun during the reign of Tuthmosis IV – and many items of Amenophis III's (and Tiye's) burial equipment.

The tomb of Tutankhamun

Carnarvon's interest had been sparked, and he agreed to take up where Davis had left off. In December 1917 Carter began work in the Valley of the Kings proper, the first of a series of short excavations he would fit in during the war and immediate postwar years (Table p. 84). Yet, despite his conviction that there were still things to be found, the results of his labours were as depressing as could be – if worthy enough from an archaeological point of view: ostraca by the dozen, some of signif-

icant interest (in particular, a series of check lists relating to the burial of Ramesses VI, from the 1917–18 season), and a cache of calcite vessels which had once held oils for the embalming of Merenptah (p. 148). But:

'We are working in untouched stuff so one never knows what may come – I hope a hundred times something good . . .'

Howard Carter

(Above) The fifth Earl of Carnarvon, pictured in his study at Highclere Castle shortly after the discovery of the tomb of Tutankhamun.

(Right) Transcript of the opening paragraphs of Lord Carnarvon's permission to excavate in the valley. The terms were essentially the same as those granted to Carnarvon's predecessor in the field, Theodore Davis.

" Ministry of Public Works
" Antiquities Service

" AUTHORIZATION TO EXCAVATE

" I, the undersigned, Director-General of the Antiquities Service, acting " in virtue of the powers delegated to me, hereby authorize the Right " Honourable Earl of Carnarvon, residing at Highclere Castle, to carry " out scientific excavations in the Valley of the Kings, on lands belonging " to the State, free, unbuilt upon, uncultivated, not included within the " Military Zone, nor comprising any cemeteries, quarries, etc., and, in " general, not devoted to any public use, and this on the following " conditions :—

" 1. The work of excavation shall be carried out at the expense, " risk and peril of the Earl of Carnarvon by Mr. Howard Carter ; the latter " should be constantly present during excavation.

" 2. Work shall be executed under the control of the Antiquities " Service, who shall have the right not only to supervise the work, but " also to alter the manner of the execution if they so deem proper for the " success of the undertaking.

Carnarvon was unimpressed: he wanted art, not junk. He was becoming less and less convinced by Carter's ravings that a further tomb remained to be found; and Carter himself was presumably beginning to question his own sanity. But there was still one small triangular area of the valley yet to be cleared, and Carter could not rest until that had been dug. Carnarvon, a betting man, agreed to a final season.

As if to order, on 4 November 1922, a matter of days after work had begun, a step, neatly cut in the limestone bedrock, was brought to light by Carter's workers. Then a second, and a third – until a whole flight was revealed leading down to a mud-plastered doorway stamped over its entire surface with large oval seals bearing the name of – Tutankhamun!

It was the tomb they had been searching for. But the discovery was to be at a price. Within six months of the find, Carnarvon was dead, Carter close to a nervous breakdown, and the face of Egyptology changed for ever.

The legacy of Tutankhamun

The interest and excitement aroused by the discovery of the tomb of Tutankhamun came as a surprise to everyone – not least Carnarvon and Carter. The find was unmatched in the entire history of exploration in the Valley of the Kings, in its immediacy as much as in its splendour. There was gold – everywhere the glint of gold – but there was also romance in the untimely death of a child-pharaoh, the only son of the 'monotheistic' king, Akhenaten. Thanks to the press, the thrill and excitement of Egyptian archaeology were in the public domain – and things would never be quite the same again.

Under Gaston Maspero's all too liberal administration, Theodore Davis had been able to treat the Valley of the Kings as his personal fief, to administer and exploit – as he saw fit. It was a less than perfect situation, and one which Lord Carnarvon

(Left) Tutankhamun's innermost coffin was fashioned from thick sheet gold and weighed over 110 kg.

(Right) The jackal-and-nine-captives motif, one of the seals used to close the doorways in the boy-king's tomb.

(Opposite) The back of the 'Golden Throne', of wood overlaid with precious metals and decorated with rich inlays. The scene, altered in antiquity, shows the king and his wife Ankhesenamun in a floral pavilion receiving the life-giving rays of the Aten.

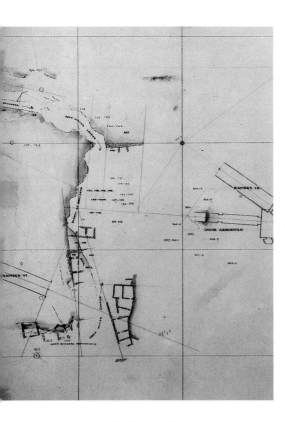

(Right) The entrance corridor leading down into the antechamber of the boy-king's tomb.

(Second right) The three large gilded beds in the antechamber, piled high with boxes, furniture and other funerary equipment.

(Far right) The two lifesize wooden figures guarding the entrance to the burial chamber; the blocking is shown partially dismantled to reveal the large gilded shrines surrounding the sarcophagus.

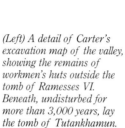

would inherit. In Egypt at this time, a division of finds, while not obligatory, was expected and generally granted as a matter of course. Davis, for all his faults, had not been digging primarily to augment his own personal collection, and so had not pressed this point; he had taken what Maspero had generously allowed him. Lord Carnarvon was a very different kettle of fish: he was a collector first and foremost – and from the tomb of Tutankhamun, 'his' discovery, he wanted his pound of flesh.

The enormous publicity generated by the finding of the tomb (which Carnarvon and Carter appeared to control through their exclusivity deal with *The*

Carnarvon Excavations, 1915–1922

Mod. site ref.	Carter site ref.	Site	Date	Carter find nos.
1	—	WV22 (Amenophis III)	8 Feb.–8 Mar. 1915	1–105
2	A	between KV7 (Ramesses II) and KV9 (Ramesses VI)	1 Dec. 1917–1 Feb. 1918	106–215
3	B	before KV38 (Tuthmosis I)	19–24 Feb. 1919	216–26
4	C	entrance to KV2 (Ramesses IV)	5–10? Jan. 1920	227–42
5	D	between KV7 (Ramesses II) and KV2 (Ramesses IV)	10–15? Jan. 1920	243
6	—	entrance to KV7 (Ramesses II)	15–17? Jan. 1920	244–49
7	E	canyon above KV34 (Tuthmosis III)	17–21? Feb. 1920	—
8	F	entrance to KV8 (Merenptah)	21 Feb.–5? Mar.1920	250–75
9	—	between KV7 (Ramesses II) and KV9 (Ramesses VI)	1–22? Dec. 1920	276–85
10	L	entrance to KV12	1 Dec. 1920	—
11	—	clearance KV4 (Ramesses XI)	c. Dec. 1920	no nos.
12	H	entrance KV9 (Ramesses VI)	23 Dec. 1920–3? Jan. 1921	286–302
13,15	I	valley before KV34 (Tuthmosis III)	3–? Jan.+ 1921	303–19; 326–36, KV F
14	—	between KV6 (Ramesses IX) and KV55	c. Jan.–Mar. 1921	320–25
16	—	south of KV55	before 3/13 Mar.1921	337–50
17	K	vicinity of KV47 (Siptah)	8 Feb.–Mar. 1922	351–432
18	H	entrance KV9 (Ramesses VI)	1 Nov.+ 1922	433 (KV62)–35

Times) fed and nourished rising nationalistic sentiment in Egypt, and it soon became apparent that a division of Tutankhamun's treasures, besides being archaeologically undesirable, was a political impossibility. Despite much gnashing of teeth in the Carnarvon-Carter camp, no formal share-out was ever made.

Today, the principle has gradually been extended to cover all archaeological discoveries made in Egypt, large or small, whether in the Valley of the Kings or elsewhere: everything belongs to the Egyptian state. Today, though happy when new discoveries are made, we dig primarily for information, not things.

(Left) Howard Carter brushes away remains of the linen shroud covering the lid of Tutankhamun's second coffin.

(Right) The treasury, with a large carrying chest surmounted by the Anubis dog and the spectacular gilded shrine surrounding the calcite canopic chest – repository for the king's embalmed inner organs.

'*When we behold the enormous mass of valuable and precious objects found in the small and modest tomb of Tutankhamen, who was a relatively obscure King with a short reign, our imagination will fail us if we try to picture the magnificence and extent of the burial equipment which must have filled the enormous tombs of such Kings as Sety I. and Ramesses II., who had long and prosperous reigns . . .*'

Warren R. Dawson

The discovery, in 1922, of the tomb of Tutankhamun opened the eyes of an awe-struck public to the full extent of pharaonic wealth and power. The boy-king's burial offered a unique insight into what once had been: a valley filled with the kings and queens, royal offspring, officials and pampered pets of three dynasties and five centuries – and the largest accumulation of bullion in the ancient world.

Tutankhamun, if ill-starred in life, in death had been immensely fortunate, escaping the passing of the millennia relatively unscathed. To his fellow travellers, Fate would be less kind: with very few exceptions, their tombs were extensively robbed, comprehensively sacked, efficiently dismantled and pawed over by the curious for more than 3,000 years. So thorough was the destruction that it might reasonably be doubted anything at all should remain to mark their existence.

But it has – and, if in fragments, in abundance. Archaeologists past and present have assembled a vast pool of evidence, and each of the wadi's 80 or more tombs and pits, large and small, decorated or roughly hewn, may be seen to have its own more or less eloquent tale to tell – of kings, priests, nobles, of ritual and magic, and of pharaonic conceit and human greed.

The decorated entrance to the tomb of Merenptah (KV8).

III TOMBS OF THE KINGS

The Search for the Tomb of Amenophis I

The glory of finally expelling the foreign Hyksos rulers of the 15th and 16th dynasties fell to the Theban king, Amosis, son of Kamose and founder of the 18th dynasty and the New Kingdom. By this action, Amosis was to lay the foundations for an Egyptian empire which would ultimately stretch from the Euphrates in the north to the fourth cataract on the Nile in the south.

The precise location of Amosis's burial place is as yet unidentified, but was perhaps at Dra Abu el-Naga. The royal mummy was recovered from the Deir el-Bahri cache in 1881 (p. 194), while a *shabti* of the king, of unrecorded provenance, is preserved in the British Museum.

Amosis was succeeded by Amenophis I, *c.* 1525 BC, who consolidated his father's territorial gains abroad and embarked upon an administrative reorganization of the unified Egyptian state. Together with his mother, Ahmose-Nofretiri, he would be revered as the tutelary god of the Deir el-Medina workforce, whose village community he had perhaps established. The precise location of his burial place is, as we shall see, still a matter of debate; his mummy was discovered in the royal cache at Deir el-Bahri.

Two candidates for Amenophis I's tomb are traditionally suggested: KV39, located on the very edge of Wadi Biban el-Muluk – the choice of Arthur Weigall; and AN B, Howard Carter's preference, situated outside the Valley of the Kings in Dra Abu el-Naga. It has to be said that, while each has features which might justify the claims made

for it, neither tomb fits the bill completely. Other, perhaps less likely, possibilities have been put forward (notably DB320); and it remains to be seen whether the recent candidature of the large, 17th-dynasty-style K93.11, also at Dra Abu el-Naga, should be seriously considered.

The basic evidence we have for the siting of the tomb of Amenophis I is a reference in an official inspection of royal tombs in Year 16 of Ramesses IX, Papyrus Abbott:

'The eternal horizon of king Djeserka[re] life! prosperity! health! son of Re Amenophis [I] life! prosperity! health! which measures 120 cubits down from its *ahay* of *pa a-ka*, so called, north of the temple of Amenophis life! prosperity! health! of the Garden. . . . Examined this day; it was found intact by these inspectors.'

Papyrus Abbott thus locates the tomb 120 cubits down from its *ahay* – a word whose basic meaning would seem to be something which stands up, hence the usual translation 'stela' – and to the north of the 'Temple of Amenophis, life! prosperity! health! of the Garden.' The problem is that neither of these landmarks has yet been identified with any certainty on the ground.

The king's mummy

The mummy of Amenophis I was discovered in the Deir el-Bahri cache (DB320) in 1881, and is one of the few not to have been unwrapped by Maspero. It had been restored in Year 6 of Pharaoh Smendes, 4th month of *peret*-season, day 7, when it had been furnished with a replacement coffin very similar to that given to Tuthmosis II. According to a second coffin docket, the burial was 'renewed' again precisely a decade later – perhaps when it was transferred to a subsequent place of burial (the tomb of Inhapi?) where, by Year 10 of Siamun (according to dockets on the coffins of Ramesses I, Sethos I and Ramesses II) it had come to rest before its final transfer to DB320 during the reign of Shoshenq I.

The coffin supplied for the reburial of Amenophis I's mummy at the end of the New Kingdom, from the royal cache at Deir el-Bahri. It had originally been prepared for a wab ('pure')-priest by the name of Djehutymose.

The cartonnage mask covering the head of Amenophis I's mummy.

Tomb KV 39

'A good morning at the excavation. John found two fragments of sandstone with cartouches on which were clearly readable. He also discovered that the inside of the tomb is different to what he had expected.'

Delyth Rose

Tomb KV39 is one of the most mystifying tombs in (actually on the edge of) the Valley of the Kings, and has only recently been investigated, by John Rose. The most extraordinary feature of the sepulchre is its eccentric plan. KV39 seems to have started out as a fairly standard corridor tomb which was left unfinished beyond the first chamber. Subsequently, it was extended considerably, with a second descending corridor running eastwards, parallel to the first, and a third corridor running out to the south, each of these secondary cuttings terminating in a single chamber. Interestingly enough, the south chamber has a cut in the floor to receive a coffin, this pit then being covered with stone slabs – a feature reminiscent of pre-New Kingdom sepulchres.

Rose's clearance of KV39 has produced over 1,350 bags of finds: potsherds, calcite fragments, pieces of wooden coffins, textiles, fragments of metal, mud jar sealings, cordage, botanical specimens and human skeletal remains – 'of at least nine persons'. Among the inscribed material is a group of unusual sandstone dockets bearing car-

Factfile

Tomb number/location:
KV39, Wadi Biban el-Muluk
Date of discovery:
1899, by Victor Loret
Excavator/report:
John Rose, 1989–, for Pacific Western University: J. Rose, in C. N. Reeves (ed.), *After Tut'ankhamun* (1992) pp. 28–40

(Left) The entrance to KV39 following clearance by John Rose in 1989.

(Right) John Rose (on the right) with two of his Egyptian workers.

touches in blue of Tuthmosis I, Tuthmosis II(?) and Amenophis II. 'A calcite fragment bearing the title of the tomb owner . . . and a gold signet ring bearing the name of a famous pharaoh of the 18th dynasty' were also found, but, tantalizingly, no further details have yet been released.

Arthur Weigall's view was that the mysterious *ahay* of Papyrus Abbott was to be recognized as the group of workmen's huts located on the ridge above the tomb – though he was unable to provide a satisfactory candidate for the 'Temple of Amenophis . . . of the Garden.'

(Below) KV39 comprises an entrance staircase and sloping corridor leading into an unfinished chamber; a further staircase and sloping corridors at 90 degrees to the first and leading to a second chamber with burial pit; and, running parallel to and back from the entrance, a third corridor with two flights of steps leading into another chamber. The complexity of KV39 is as yet unexplained.

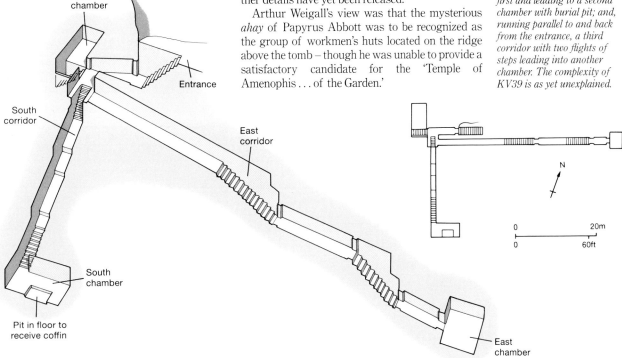

First chamber

Entrance

South corridor

East corridor

South chamber

Pit in floor to receive coffin

East chamber

N

0   20m

0   60ft

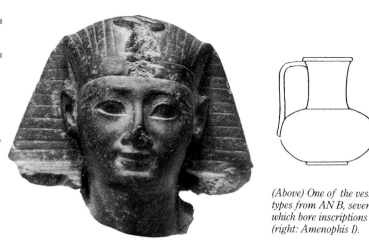

Small greywacke head of a king, of Tuthmosid date, said by Carter to have come from AN B.

(Above) One of the vessel types from AN B, several of which bore inscriptions (right: Amenophis I).

Factfile

Tomb number/location:
AN B, Dra Abu el-Naga
Date of discovery:
before 1907, by locals
Excavator/report:
Howard Carter, 1913/14, for the Earl of Carnarvon: H. Carter, *JEA* 4 (1917) pp. 147–54

Tomb AN B

'I believe I really have found the tomb of Amenhotep I, at all events a great deal of inscribed stone and as to its being a Royal Tomb there is no possible doubt.'

Howard Carter

Until Rose's clearance of KV39, tomb AN B was generally considered the more likely bet for the king's tomb. Discovered by locals, its excavation yielded a number of stone vessel fragments inscribed for: the Hyksos king, Apophis and his daughter, Princess Heret (1 example); Amosis I (3); Ahmose-Nofretiri (8); and Amenophis I (9). There was also evidence of *ex-voto* offerings, in the form of fragmentary royal and private statuettes. For Carter, tomb AN B had held a double burial of Amenophis I and his mother, Ahmose-Nofretiri, the two patrons of the Theban necropolis, who shared a funerary temple (anciently called 'Meniset') on the plain below the tomb, on the edge of the cultivation ('the Garden'?). Carter believed that the burial chamber was a later addition, and is supported in this view by John Romer who asserts that the well – a characteristic feature of kingly burials throughout the New Kingdom – was also cut later.

The basic weakness of Carter's thesis was his reconciliation of the inspectors' measurements recorded in Papyrus Abbott with the *internal* dimensions of AN B: since the tomb of Amenophis I is recorded as having been found intact, the interior was presumably inaccessible. If the attribution to Amenophis I is to be maintained, however, it might be possible to recognize in the Abbott *ahay* the cairn, or pile of rocks, located on Carter's rough map of the area at an appropriate distance to the north of AN B. Such cairns have received little discussion, but it seems undeniable that at least some functioned as markers of some sort.

Carter's finds indicate that AN B was reused during the 22nd dynasty. The burnt finds included 'bronze eye-brows, eye-sockets, pieces of lapis lazuli inlay, and decayed wood, recovered from the bottom of the Protective Well.'

(Right) The well of AN B appears to have been cut as an after-thought at the time the burial chamber was extended. The changes may reflect the expansion of a queen's tomb – that of Ahmose-Nofretiri – to receive the (re)burial of a king – her son, Amenophis I.

(Far right) The entrance to AN B.

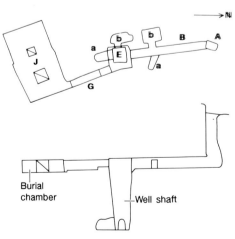

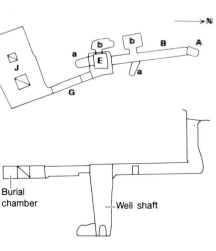

Burial chamber

Well shaft

Amenophis I, who left no male heir, was succeeded *c.* 1504 BC by a member of a collatoral branch of the family, Tuthmosis I, whose claim to the throne was strengthened by marriage to his predecessor's daughter. The new pharaoh would find fame as one of Egypt's greatest warrior kings, expanding the frontiers of the empire to their furthest extent and securing the long-distance trade upon which the extraordinary prosperity of the following years would be based.

The family relationships of the Tuthmosid rulers are a genealogical nightmare. Tuthmosis I died within a decade, and was the first king known definitely to have been buried, in tomb KV20, in the Valley of the Kings. He was succeeded by Tuthmosis II – his son by a secondary wife, Mutnofret. Tuthmosis II married his half-sister, Hatshepsut, daughter of the principal queen, Ahmose, and Tuthmosis I. Hatshepsut produced no male heir and, with the death of Tuthmosis II (whose tomb has not yet been positively identified) in *c.* 1478 BC after a relatively short reign, the crown passed to a son of Tuthmosis II by a secondary wife, the lady Isis. The claims of this son, Tuthmosis III, who was a mere child at the time of his father's death, may have been strengthened by marriage to Nefrure, the daughter of Tuthmosis II by Hatshepsut.

During the minority of Tuthmosis III, the dowager queen, Hatshepsut, held the reins of state, at first as mere regent and thereafter, until her death in her stepson's 22nd year, as joint pharaoh. Perhaps because of this presumption, her memory would be attacked during the latter years of Tuthmosis III's sole reign. Real power during much of this time seems to have been exercised by a mere commoner – Senenmut, tutor of Nefrure and, it has been suggested, an intimate of Hatshepsut. He seems to have fallen from grace, for reasons unknown, three years before Hatshepsut's death.

The sole reign of Tuthmosis III was marked by further campaigns in the north and south and an expansion of the empire, together with extensive construction within Egypt itself, paid for by the fruits of war. It was a policy which would be followed by his son, coregent and successor, Amenophis II (*c.* 1427–1401 BC), who further broadened the Egyptians' horizons and set the scene for the cosmopolitan period to come.

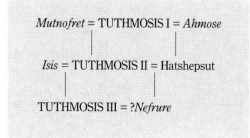

Mutnofret = TUTHMOSIS I = *Ahmose*

Isis = TUTHMOSIS II = Hatshepsut

TUTHMOSIS III = ?*Nefrure*

The Early Tuthmosids

The Tomb of Tuthmosis I and Hatshepsut (KV20)

'I supervised the excavation of the cliff tomb of His Majesty alone, no-one seeing, no-one hearing.'

biographical inscription of the architect Ineni

History and excavation

'It was one of the most irksome pieces of work I ever supervised.'

Howard Carter

Although it was long believed that the tomb quarried by Ineni, the architect of Tuthmosis I, was to be recognized as KV38 (p. 95), this honour, as we shall see, seems now to fall to the anomalous and quite extraordinary tomb KV20, traditionally assigned to Hatshepsut, daughter of Tuthmosis I. KV20 was not Hatshepsut's intended place of burial – at least before her adoption of the royal style: she had previously prepared a cliff tomb in the Wadi Sikket Taqa el-Zeide (WA D), which would later be stumbled upon by Carter in 1916 (see feature).

KV20 had been known for over a century before Carter began to dig in the valley, having been noted both by the French Expedition and by Belzoni. In 1824, James Burton had attempted a clearance, advancing as far as the second staircase but then abandoning the work because of the hardness of the fill, the poor condition of the architecture, and the bad air, 'which extinguished the lights'. Carter's clearance of KV20 was no less difficult, but paid off in that it at last provided a range of inscribed fragments (including a foundation deposit inscribed with the name of Hatshepsut regnant) to suggest the identity of the owner. Carter concluded that KV20 had been excavated by the queen-regnant as a double tomb for herself and her father, whose burial she had transferred from its original tomb, KV38. And this, for 70 years, remained the accepted view.

However, John Romer's able study of the Tuthmosid royal tombs in 1974 demonstrated that the true sequence was rather different. Romer, on the basis of design, has argued that KV38 is several years *later* in date than KV20, and had been prepared during the reign of Tuthmosis III as a secondary place of burial for Tuthmosis I. For Romer,

Incised inscription on a calcite jar fragment – a stray from Carter's work within KV20. The text records the vessel's dedication to the burial of Tuthmosis I by his queen, Ahmose.

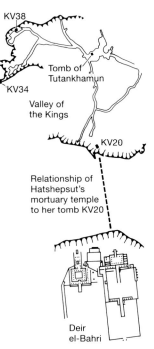

KV38

Tomb of
Tutankhamun

KV34

Valley of
the Kings

KV20

Relationship of
Hatshepsut's
mortuary temple
to her tomb KV20

Deir
el-Bahri

(Above) KV20: its position relative to the temple of Hatshepsut across the cliff at Deir el-Bahri.

(Below) The goddess Isis: a detail from the foot end of the sarcophagus of Hatshepsut altered to receive the body of her father Tuthmosis I.

the tomb prepared by Ineni for Tuthmosis I is KV20 itself – though at the time of the king's burial the excavation seems to have extended no further than the first large chamber; the pillared hall and its satellites were subsequently added by Hatshepsut, Romer argues, to accommodate a double burial of father and daughter, at which time the foundation deposit of Hatshepsut was placed. The proportions of this new suite differ markedly from the rest of KV20, and indeed find an echo in the architecture of Hatshepsut's mortuary temple at Deir el-Bahri. Finally, during the reign of Tuthmosis III, the situation changed yet again, with the body of Tuthmosis I being removed from KV20 for reburial in a new sarcophagus within the recently prepared KV38. The burial of Hatshepsut was abandoned, alone, within KV20; her first kingly sarcophagus, which she had surrendered for the use of Tuthmosis I, was left empty within the burial chamber.

Architecture and decoration

KV20 turns and twists for more than 213 m (699 ft) beyond its entrance, with its burial chamber lying some 97 m (318 ft) beneath the surface. The corridors soon curve from their original axis towards the bay of Deir el-Bahri, swinging first to the south and then back to the west as they descend. Two stairwell chambers, spaced equidistantly along these passages, are more irregular in shape but otherwise resemble those encountered in KV38. The large antechamber is also similar in profile to that of KV38 but, as considered above, was most probably intended originally as the burial chamber. A final stairway descends from a point half way along the right hand wall of this room, and continues through a short passage into the burial hall which was cut with three centrally aligned pillars and three low-roofed storage rooms. The final flight of steps leading from the antechamber is architecturally quite different from the style of the rest of

(Below) The left exterior side of the same recarved monument.

the sepulchre, and this and the burial chamber beyond are presumably additions to the original plan; Romer's observation that the burial chamber uses the same 'metrical system' as that encountered in the temple of Hatshepsut at Deir el-Bahri presumably identifies the author of this change.

Because the shale walls of the deeply cut burial chamber of KV20 were unsuitable for decoration, funerary texts were applied to limestone blocks which were probably intended to line the room. The 15 or so blocks of this kind recovered by Carter are inscribed in black and red and illustrated with 'stick figure' drawings of scenes from the Amduat

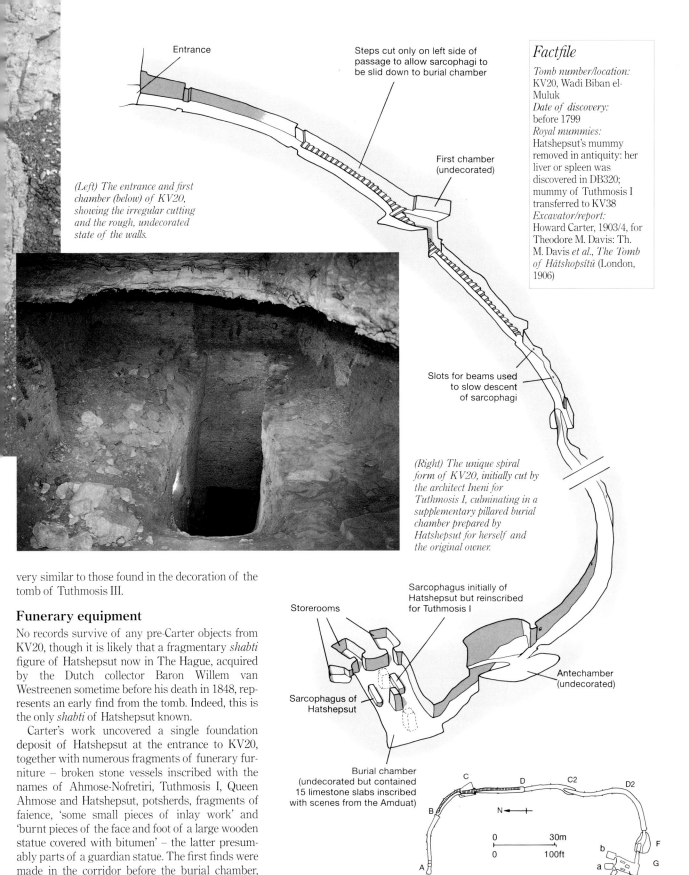

Entrance

Steps cut only on left side of passage to allow sarcophagi to be slid down to burial chamber

First chamber (undecorated)

(Left) The entrance and first chamber (below) of KV20, showing the irregular cutting and the rough, undecorated state of the walls.

Factfile

Tomb number/location:
KV20, Wadi Biban el-Muluk
Date of discovery:
before 1799
Royal mummies:
Hatshepsut's mummy removed in antiquity: her liver or spleen was discovered in DB320; mummy of Tuthmosis I transferred to KV38
Excavator/report:
Howard Carter, 1903/4, for Theodore M. Davis: Th. M. Davis *et al.*, *The Tomb of Hâtshopsîtû* (London, 1906)

Slots for beams used to slow descent of sarcophagi

(Right) The unique spiral form of KV20, initially cut by the architect Ineni for Tuthmosis I, culminating in a supplementary pillared burial chamber prepared by Hatshepsut for herself and the original owner.

Sarcophagus initially of Hatshepsut but reinscribed for Tuthmosis I

Storerooms

Antechamber (undecorated)

Sarcophagus of Hatshepsut

Burial chamber (undecorated but contained 15 limestone slabs inscribed with scenes from the Amduat)

very similar to those found in the decoration of the tomb of Tuthmosis III.

Funerary equipment

No records survive of any pre-Carter objects from KV20, though it is likely that a fragmentary *shabti* figure of Hatshepsut now in The Hague, acquired by the Dutch collector Baron Willem van Westreenen sometime before his death in 1848, represents an early find from the tomb. Indeed, this is the only *shabti* of Hatshepsut known.

Carter's work uncovered a single foundation deposit of Hatshepsut at the entrance to KV20, together with numerous fragments of funerary furniture – broken stone vessels inscribed with the names of Ahmose-Nofretiri, Tuthmosis I, Queen Ahmose and Hatshepsut, potsherds, fragments of faience, 'some small pieces of inlay work' and 'burnt pieces of the face and foot of a large wooden statue covered with bitumen' – the latter presumably parts of a guardian statue. The first finds were made in the corridor before the burial chamber,

C D C2 D2

B

N

A

0   30m
0   100ft

b F
a   G
c J

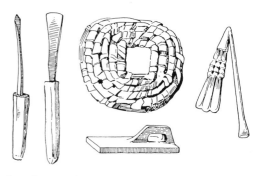

*(Right) Underworld god
seated on a serpent: detail of
a scene from the 7th hour of
the Amduat painted on a
stone lining-slab from KV20.*

*(Far right) Model tools from
the foundation deposit
discovered by Carter at the
tomb entrance.*

with the greatest concentration in the burial chamber itself, which also yielded two yellow quartzite sarcophagi inscribed respectively for Tuthmosis I (originally cut and inscribed for Hatshepsut herself) (now in Boston) and 'King' Hatshepsut (Cairo), a canopic chest similarly inscribed for Hatshepsut, and the lining-slabs of limestone described above.

Human remains

'A king she would be, and a king's fate she shared.'

Howard Carter

The body of Tuthmosis I was evidently removed from KV20 by Tuthmosis III for reburial within a newly-quarried tomb nearby – KV38 (p. 95). Hatshepsut, together with her father's discarded sarcophagus, seems to have remained within KV20 until the turn of the millennium. The present whereabouts of her mummy are not known – unless the body recently exhumed from KV60 by Donald Ryan (p. 187) should prove to be hers. A box recovered from the royal cache (DB320) in 1881 is inscribed with the woman-pharaoh's name, and contains a mummified liver or spleen; evidently salvaged from the debris of KV20 by the reburial commission at the end of the New Kingdom, it eventually found its way to DB320 during or after the reign of Shoshenq I via the *kay*, or cliff tomb, of Queen Inhapi (p. 207). Pieces of Hatshepsut's finely decorated wooden coffin were discovered by John Romer during his clearance (for The Brooklyn Museum) of the deep shaft within the tomb of Ramesses XI (KV4) in 1977–79 (p. 172). This latter tomb had evidently served as a workshop for the dismantling of a number of royal burials during the 'reign' of Pinudjem I.

The Cliff Tomb of Queen Hatshepsut

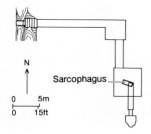

Factfile

Tomb number/location:
WA D, Wadi Sikket Taqa
el-Zeide
Date of discovery:
1916, by Howard Carter
Excavator/reports:
H. Carter, 1916/17, for the
Earl of Carnarvon: H.
Carter, *ASAE* 16 (1916)
pp. 179–82; *id., JEA* 4 (1917)
pp. 114–18

'It was midnight when we arrived on the scene, and the guide pointed out to me the end of a rope which dangled sheer down the face of a cliff. Listening, we could hear the robbers actually at work. . . . [W]hen I reached the bottom there was an awkward moment or two. I gave them the alternative of clearing out by means of my rope, or else of staying where they were without a rope at all, and eventually they saw reason and departed.'

Howard Carter

This well-hidden cliff tomb (plan, *left*), D, 70 m (230 ft) above ground level (*right*), Carter found to be entirely filled with washed in debris which took 20 days, working around the clock, to clear. It consisted of a short staircase leading down into a gently sloping corridor, which after 10 m (33 ft) turns sharply to the right to terminate in a square chamber containing a yellow quartzite sarcophagus and lid, from which chamber a further corridor leads down to a second and smaller unfinished room.

The sarcophagus (now in Cairo) was inscribed for 'the hereditary princess, great in favour and grace, mistress of all the lands, the king's daughter, king's sister, wife of the god, great royal wife and lady of the Two Lands, Hatshepsut.' Apart from this sarcophagus, 'two broken necks of pottery jars such as were used by workmen' and a series of plain limestone slabs (which may have been intended to receive ink-written extracts from the Amduat), similar to other blocks recovered from KV20 and KV38, the tomb was devoid of finds. Following Hatshepsut's assumption of power, tools had been downed and the tomb forgotten.

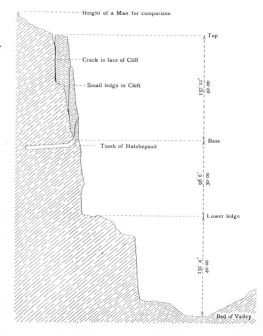

The 'Second' Tomb of Tuthmosis I (KV38)

History and excavation

KV38, as its position in the valley tomb sequence might suggest, was a Loret discovery, made in March 1899 during his sweep of the valley, though John Gardner Wilkinson, as early as 1835, had suggested that a tomb was to be found in the vicinity. The circumstances of the discovery are virtually unrecorded.

Architecture and decoration

Roughly cut steps lead to a small doorway and a single corridor which immediately begins to curve to the left as it descends. The corridor opens into an irregularly cut room, through which the stairwell descends to the burial chamber. This cartouche-shaped room is of substantial size, being about 11 m (36 ft) in length, and has a small, roughly cut storage opening on the left side near the sarcophagus and canopic emplacement. Originally a single square pillar stood at the centre of this room, though this is now broken and no longer visible.

Although the tomb is often said to be undecorated, faded patches of mud plaster with remnants of a decorative *khekher*-frieze are still visible beneath the ceiling of the burial chamber. Fragments of the decoration, inscribed with texts from the Amduat, were removed from the tomb during clearance in 1899, and are now in storage in the Cairo Museum.

Funerary equipment

A listing of the pieces recovered by Loret was published by Georges Daressy in his *Fouilles de la Vallée des Rois*. The principal find was a yellow quartzite sarcophagus inscribed for Tuthmosis I (now in Cairo). At first sight, therefore, the tomb appeared to be his – and, by extension, none other than the famous tomb quarried secretly by the architect Ineni, 'no-one seeing, no-one hearing' (p. 91). The foundation deposits recovered by Carter from outside the entrance in February 1919 were uninscribed, but did not contradict this attribution.

In 1974, however, John Romer drew attention to the extent to which tomb KV38 is based upon and was influenced by the architecture of KV34, the tomb quarried by Tuthmosis I's grandson, Tuthmosis III. This dating finds an echo in certain elements of the surviving burial furniture – notably the sarcophagus and several fragments of glass vessels which, taken together, suggest strongly that KV38 had been prepared for the *reburial* of Tuthmosis I by his grandson, who clearly desired to move the king away from the polluting presence of Hatshepsut and re-equip the burial. The tomb quarried by Ineni must be sought elsewhere – presumably in the guise of KV20 (p. 91).

Factfile

Tomb number/location:
KV38, Wadi Biban el-Muluk
Date of discovery:
March 1899, by Victor Loret
Royal mummy:
transferred from KV20 to KV38; removed from KV38 in antiquity; a body sometimes identified as Tuthmosis I discovered in DB320
Excavator/report:
V. Loret, 1899, for the Service des Antiquités; Georges Daressy, *Fouilles de la Vallée des Rois 1898–1899* (Cairo, 1902) pp. 300–03
Wall documentation: –

(Below left) The entrance to KV38 and its plan and form (below). The roughly cut surfaces and rounded forms are typical of early 18th-dynasty tombs.

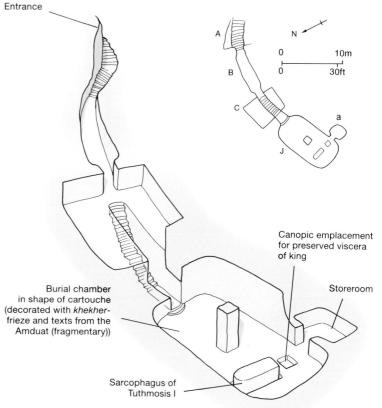

Entrance

Burial chamber in shape of cartouche (decorated with *khekher*-frieze and texts from the Amduat (fragmentary))

Sarcophagus of Tuthmosis I

Canopic emplacement for preserved viscera of king

Storeroom

Graffiti

'1st month of *akhet*-season, day 13. Coming by
Meniunufer [to] open [the tomb of] Aakheperkare . . .'

Heiratic graffito

This graffito is of particular interest, for it records
an opening of the tomb which, to judge from the
personnel involved ('Userhet; Pa[…]; Amenhotpe;
Iuf[?…]amun'), is to be dated to the end of the 20th
dynasty or beginning of the 21st dynasty. This
'opening' was presumably associated with the official policy of dismantling the necropolis set in train
by the High Priest of Amun, Piankh, and gathering
momentum under (and to a great extent explaining
the power and influence of) the High Priests of
Amun, Herihor and Pinudjem I, who were subsequently to adopt royal status (p. 204).

The two wooden coffins of Tuthmosis I, presumably immanent with divine power (p. 206), were
appropriated for Pinudjem I's own use; they were
found, redecorated and newly inscribed for
Pinudjem as 'king', in the Deir el-Bahri cache in
1881. Their dimensions suggest that Tuthmosis I
had originally been provided with an innermost
coffin of precious metal, which had 'disappeared' –
presumably melted down for bullion – at the time
KV38 was finally abandoned.

The fate of the mummy of Tuthmosis I is not
known, the attribution of the body found within the
coffins usurped by Pinudjem I being quite uncertain.

A Tomb for Tuthmosis II?

'No tomb can be positively assigned at present to
Thutmose II.'

Elizabeth Thomas

The tomb of Tuthmosis II has not yet been identified, and, indeed, may still await discovery –
though we do have his mummy, which turned up in
1881 in the Deir el-Bahri cache (p. 196), rewrapped,
docketed (in Year 6 of Smendes, 3rd month of
peret-season, day 7), recoffined like – and perhaps

at one stage associated with – the mummy of
Amenophis I.

Among suggested candidates for the king's tomb
are KV42, Bab el-Muallaq (WN A), and, the best
of a bad lot, DB358, which was brought to light by
Herbert Winlock and the Metropolitan Museum of
Art team in the Deir el-Bahri bay in 1929. On
the basis of design, KV42 is probably post-
Tuthmosis III in date, and the foundation deposits
appear to assign it to Queen Hatshepsut-Meryetre
(p. 102); about Bab el-Muallaq almost nothing
is at present known (p. 197). The claim of tomb
DB358 rests solely upon the presence of a 'well' –
which is, nevertheless, a characteristic feature
of kingly burials. The actual interments found in
the tomb belong to Queen Meryetamun (identified
by Winlock as a wife of Amenophis II), and a
king's daughter Nany – probably a child of the
21st-dynasty pharaoh, Pinudjem I. No funerary
equipment attributable to Tuthmosis II was
discovered.

If DB358 is Tuthmosis II's tomb, however – on
the basis of the kingly well shaft – why should
Tuthmosis II have opted for interment outside the
Valley of the Kings? Although the burial of his
predecessor in KV20 marked a further step in
the gradual movement away from the old, 17th-
dynasty burial ground at Dra Abu el-Naga
(a movement which may perhaps have been
under way as early as the reign of Amenophis I –
p. 88), only with Tuthmosis III did Biban el-
Muluk become firmly established as *the*
royal burial ground of New Kingdom Egypt.
The systemization which we now take for
granted had not yet begun by the reign of
Tuthmosis II.

Factfile

Tomb number/location:
DB358, Deir el-Bahri
Date of discovery:
23 February 1929, by
Herbert E. Winlock
Excavator/report:
H. E. Winlock, 1929, for the
Metropolitan Museum of
Art, New York: H. E.
Winlock, *The Tomb of
Queen Meryet-Amūn at
Thebes* (New York, 1932)

---

*(Right) Plan and sections of
the complex and anomalous
DB358, showing the well
shaft normally associated
with kingly tombs.*

*(Far right) The unwrapped
head of Tuthmosis II: a detail
of the king's mummy, found
in the DB320 royal cache in
1881.*

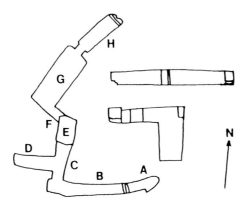

The Tomb of Tuthmosis III (KV34)

History and excavation

'... a fitting climax to two thousand years of development in the design and construction of funerary monuments.'

William C. Hayes

William C. Hayes refers here to the sarcophagus of the king, but his words might be applied equally to the tomb itself – for KV34 is one of the most sophisticated architectural achievements in the Valley of the Kings.

The tomb was discovered in 1898 by Loret's workmen during his absence. On Loret's return, clearance was carried out with care over a number of days, Loret noting on a plan of the tomb the place of each object ('even the smallest') by means of a 24-square grid marked out on the sandy floor of the burial chamber, which, as may now be seen, was numbered from right to left from the entrance doorway to the interior wall.

The two side rooms on the left of the burial chamber were empty, their contents having presumably been swept out onto the floor of the burial chamber as in the tomb of Amenophis II (below). The motive for this action in KV35 had been to accommodate several mummies which had been removed from their original place of burial at the end of the New Kingdom or later. Perhaps KV34 had played a similar role before it was finally abandoned.

Architecture and decoration

'One may gain the impression from Tuthmosis III's tomb that although an exact idea of the shape and function of

(Right) Embracing figure of the goddess Nut: the underside of the lid of Tuthmosis III's sarcophagus.

(Below left) Wall painting from the antechamber of KV34 showing stick-figure representations of the divinities of the Amduat.

(Below) Burial chamber with yellow quartzite sarcophagus of Tuthmosis III. The curving walls of the room are decorated with the hours of the Amduat.

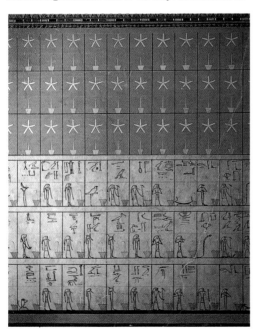

The king suckled by the tree-goddess Isis; from a pillar in the burial chamber of KV34.

(Below right) Four of the series of resin-varnished wooden figures recovered by Victor Loret from the tomb of Tuthmosis III.

some of the rooms and corridors was present at the work's inception, the precise articulation and relationship of these elements was not carefully controlled but left rather to expediency and practicality.'

John Romer

KV34 represents a turning point in tomb architecture in the Valley of the Kings. A skewed entrance gives access to three corridors and a well, which is here seen for the first time in the valley proper. Beyond the well is a hall (antechamber) with twin pillars and a staircase cutting directly down into the burial chamber – again with two pillars and furnished with four storage chambers. Although not truly at right angles, the two arms of the tomb are clearly meant to be so.

The passages are not decorated, but other areas were plastered and painted for the first time. The well shaft received stars on its ceiling (as did the rooms beyond) and a decorative *khekher*-frieze on its walls, and the antechamber also contains a list of 741 divinities of the Amduat, a motif which was not to be repeated (unless planned but not executed in the tomb of Amenophis II). The walls of the burial chamber are decorated – with a brilliant, powerful simplicity – with the three registers of the Amduat wrapped scroll-like around their curving surfaces and filled with the cursive figures and script of the papyrus *Vorlage*. For the first time, seven of the faces of the two columns of the burial chamber are decorated with the Litany of Re, and the eighth face exhibits a unique scene in which the king is shown being nursed by a divine tree goddess labelled 'Isis' (after that goddess, and perhaps also the king's own mother, also named Isis) and followed by his wives and daughters. Romer's study of

the decoration in this chamber suggests that here, as probably in most 18th-dynasty tombs, the decoration was hastily applied after the king's death while preparations for the burial were in progress.

Funerary equipment

Remains of one or more foundation deposits – model tools, plaques, vessels – are included among the finds published by Daressy. Further deposits were later brought to light by Carter in the valley below the tomb entrance.

The principal item of funerary equipment inside the tomb was the cartouche-shaped yellow quartzite sarcophagus of Tuthmosis III, its incised scenes and texts highlighted in red paint. Other finds were relatively few. They included a number of wooden statuettes of the king and funerary deities, pieces of wooden model boats, pottery and bones from a baboon and a bull.

Further fragments associated with the burial of Tuthmosis III were recovered by John Romer from the shaft in the tomb of Ramesses XI (p. 172).

The plundering of the tomb

The condition of the material recovered by Loret makes it clear that the tomb had been heavily plundered, in a very brutal manner. The sarcophagus had been damaged by a rough and ready removal of the lid, gilded wooden images had been thrown with force against the walls, leaving traces of gold foil which still glint in the light of a torch, while all metal fittings and coverings were systematically chopped out or off. Some items may have been removed still whole, to be hacked about elsewhere – notably within KV4 (Ramesses XI). Everything of

Sequence of Work in the Tomb of Tuthmosis III (KV34)

(after Romer)

	Operations	Remarks
1	cutting the tomb	unfinished
2	plastering the walls	
3	painting ceilings and friezes	dados hastily done and unfinished
4	enlargement of doorways C–D, D–E, E–F to allow introduction of larger items of funerary furniture	
5	sealing of side rooms off burial chamber	
6	the funeral	
7	painting of burial chamber texts	chippings still present in tomb
8	repainting of well-frieze (after 4)	
9	tomb closure	

the slightest reusable worth had gone – including large pieces of wood such as the hulls of model boats and the doors and lintels to the four burial chamber side rooms.

Official activity in the tomb, perhaps in connection with one or other phase of its plundering, is attested by a series of graffiti noted by John Romer. Two of these make mention of the late 20th-dynasty scribe, Amenhotpe, but they are otherwise uninstructive.

The royal mummy

The mummy of Tuthmosis III was discovered in DB320 in one of its original wooden coffins, the surface of which had been completely stripped of its gold leaf overlay (p. 207). The badly damaged body had been rewrapped using four model oars to keep it firm. Portions of the original shroud, inscribed in ink with extracts from the Book of the Dead, are in Cairo and Boston. The body had been efficiently stripped of any embellishment, though two strings of gold, carnelian, lapis lazuli and feldspar beads were found by Elliott Smith within the bandages on the front of each shoulder, and a bracelet was revealed more recently, in the course of X-ray examination, on the right arm.

Intrusive burials

'The [presence of intrusive burials] is rather important, since it shows that the hypogées [tombs] in the Valley of the Kings were then visited and appropriated by the inhabitants of the small towns in the plain of Thebes: the plundering continued much later than had been suspected up to this discovery.'

Gaston Maspero

One of the side rooms leading off the burial chamber – that on the left of the crypt – contained two coffined, though disturbed, mummies. According to Elliot Smith, who published the bodies in his *Catalogue général* volume *The Royal Mummies*, these dated from the 'late dynastic or early Ptolemaic period'. The only late activity which may

be discerned within KV34 (albeit indirectly) was during the 26th dynasty or later, when a close copy of the sarcophagus of Tuthmosis III was prepared for the high official Hapimen – the same man, perhaps, who carried off the king's missing canopic chest.

Factfile

Tomb number/location:
KV34, Wadi Biban el-Muluk
Date of discovery:
12 February 1898, by Victor Loret
Royal mummy:
removed in antiquity; discovered in DB320
Excavator/reports:
V. Loret, 1898, for the Service des Antiquités: V. Loret, *BIÉ* (3 série) 9 (1898) pp. 91–7; Georges Daressy, *Fouilles de la Vallée des Rois 1898–1899* (Cairo, 1902) pp. 281–98 (finds)
Wall documentation:
Paul Bucher, *Les Textes des Tombes de Thoutmosis III et d'Aménophis II* (Cairo, 1932)

(Left) The mummy of Tuthmosis III – a photograph taken soon after its removal from the Deir el-Bahri cache. The badly damaged body had been rewrapped in antiquity; the hole in the chest was made in modern times by Arabs searching for jewellery.

(Right) The sophisticated form of KV34, with its cartouche-shaped burial chamber and the first well shaft cut in the royal wadi.

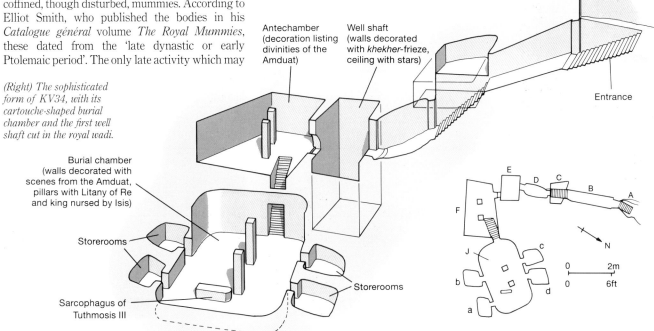

Antechamber (decoration listing divinities of the Amduat)

Well shaft (walls decorated with *khekher*-frieze, ceiling with stars)

Entrance

Burial chamber (walls decorated with scenes from the Amduat, pillars with Litany of Re and king nursed by Isis)

Storerooms

Sarcophagus of Tuthmosis III

Storerooms

The Tomb of Amenophis II (KV35)

The contents of the tomb

As the excavator progressed beyond the well he stumbled upon a large wooden figure of a serpent close to the entrance to the antechamber, noting 'between the [first] column and the right wall' two large funerary barques; between the first and second columns was a third barque. From the entrance to the burial chamber, he was just able to distinguish in the gloom a large wooden Sekhmet figure, and a *shabti* figure (which subsequently proved to have been made for the king's son Webensenu), in grid square 3. Proceeding into the sepulchral hall, in the left angle of the crypt, within grid square 15, he noted a large, virtually life-size cow head. These were the first things which came into view. As he zigzagged across the chambers, exploring the new tomb, a hundred and more other objects passed before his eyes.

The four side chambers off the burial hall Loret found knee-deep in debris. In the first chamber on the left were 'vases of green porcelain [faience], mostly *hes*-vases, others imitating the sign for life [*ankh*] . . .', and a resin-coated wooden 'panther'. The next room down, off the crypt, was filled with the remains of some 30 large storage jars, which had been emptied out, more glazed faience, linen and a mass of embalmed provisions.

'the floor of the chamber itself was hidden by a perfect litter of . . . débris, wooden statuettes of the king and of various gods, *Answerers* [i.e. *shabtis*] . . ., handled crosses . . . and *didu [djed*-pillars] of wood and blue enamel [faience], and [a] thousand [other] articles . . .'

Gaston Maspero

In the first side room on the right, Loret discovered 'three cadavers, side by side at the end, in the left-hand corner, feet pointing towards the door'; the

Discovery and clearance method

'. . . a very important discovery.'

Howard Carter

Victor Loret's discovery of KV35 in 1898 was one of the most significant in the history of excavation in the Valley of the Kings, for the tomb contained not only the burials of Amenophis II, his son Webensenu and probably his mother Hatshepsut-Meryetre, but the cached remains of a further 17 royal burials. The caching of these mummies and the later history of the tomb are considered in detail below, p. 198.

Unlike the first royal cache stumbled upon by Emile Brugsch in 1881, KV35 was cleared with some care, finds being recorded by means of numbered grids superimposed on plans of the antechamber and the sepulchral hall. Sadly, these grids, of 6 and 17 squares, were never published and are now lost, though they can be partially reconstructed from scattered remarks in Loret's preliminary report. Only for grid squares 7–17 within the burial chamber, however, may any firm locations be ventured.

Shabti *of Webensenu, the son*
of Amenophis II.

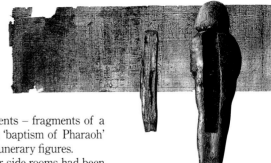

(Left) Pillars in KV35 show the first fully drawn images of the king with various deities.

(Right) Figure from KV35. The interior was hollow and contained a rolled-up papyrus.

vestiges of its original contents – fragments of a calcite representation of the 'baptism of Pharaoh' and a further three wooden funerary figures.

The contents of these four side rooms had been considerably confused since the original, 18th-dynasty stocking of the tomb – though all (with the exception of the walled-up room on the right-hand side of the crypt) preserved vestiges of their original contents in the form of provisions, objects of faience and *shabtis* respectively. The bulk of the contents appears to have been thrown out into the crypt.

Within the crypt, contained within what appears to have been a replacement coffin in the original yellow quartzite sarcophagus, lay Amenophis II himself, bedecked with flowers and undisturbed for almost 3,000 years.

Architecture

Like that of his predecessor, Tuthmosis III, the tomb of Amenophis II is innovative in design, regulating the asymmetry of the previous royal tombs and adding several new elements to the plan. While the sequence of corridors, stairways and chambers is essentially the same as KV34, a room is added at the base of the well shaft; a corridor now separates

Factfile

Tomb number/location:
KV35, Wadi Biban el-Muluk
Date of discovery:
9 March 1898, by Victor Loret
Royal mummy:
found in KV35
Excavator/reports:
V. Loret, 1898, for the Service des Antiquités: V. Loret, *BIÉ* (3 série) 9 (1898) pp. 98–112; Georges Daressy, *Fouilles de la Vallée des Rois 1898–1899* (Cairo, 1902) pp. 62–279 (finds)
Wall documentation:
Paul Bucher, *Les Textes des Tombes de Thoutmosis III et d'Aménophis II* (Cairo, 1932)

right side of the room was taken up with the debris of wooden funerary statuettes and miniature wooden coffins, which had been swept aside to make space for the mummies. Finally, Loret peeped into the last side chamber (to the right off the crypt), which had been walled off; he found nine further corpses, variously coffined. This side chamber too had similarly been swept out, and also contained

(Far left) The burial chamber of Amenophis II, with the entrance to one of the storerooms in the background.

(Left) Image of Isis in sunk relief at the foot of the king's sarcophagus, still preserving much of its original paint.

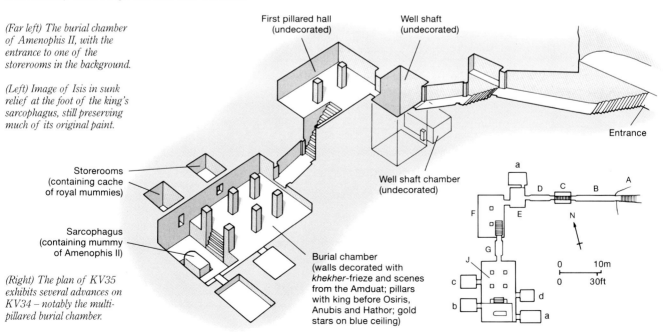

First pillared hall (undecorated)

Well shaft (undecorated)

Entrance

Well shaft chamber (undecorated)

Storerooms (containing cache of royal mummies)

Sarcophagus (containing mummy of Amenophis II)

(Right) The plan of KV35 exhibits several advances on KV34 – notably the multi-pillared burial chamber.

Burial chamber (walls decorated with *khekher*-frieze and scenes from the Amduat; pillars with king before Osiris, Anubis and Hathor; gold stars on blue ceiling)

0   10m
0   30ft

(Above) A selection of objects discovered by Loret in the tomb of Amenophis II: figure of Horus from a composition in calcite representing the 'baptism of pharaoh'; a fragmentary core-formed glass vessel; amulets in wood and faience; a stopper from the king's calcite canopic chest; a painted wooden bull head; and two model throwsticks in faience.

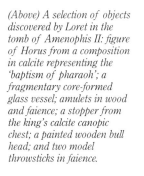

(Below) The head of the mummy of Amenophis II: a photograph taken by Howard Carter following the robbery of the tomb in 1901.

the stair from the first pillared hall and the new, rectangular burial chamber; and the final chamber itself was now divided into two parts, comprising an upper section in which were located six pillars, and a lower part, representing one-third of the chamber's area, usually referred to as the 'crypt' because of the siting here of the royal sarcophagus. Together with the straightening of the arms of the tomb's axes and the regular shape imposed upon its rooms, all these elements continue in the tombs of the king's immediate successors.

Wall decoration

As for decoration, the ceiling of the burial chamber received the now-familiar golden stars upon a ground of dark blue, while the walls exhibit the usual *khekher*-border and a three-register, 'stick-figure' treatment of the Amduat closely similar to that found in the tomb of Tuthmosis III. The decoration of KV35 also exhibits innovations which were to influence subsequent monuments: beneath their *khekher*-borders and framing 'sky' signs, the pillars in KV35 introduce for the first time fully drawn figures of the king performing ritual acts before Osiris, Anubis and Hathor. The motif of the king before a variety of deities continued to be employed on the pillars and well-room walls of most of the later tombs.

The royal funerary equipment

Apart from the sarcophagus, the tomb yielded a large range of funerary objects, both magical and of more mundane use. The former class of finds included royal and divine figures (one containing a papyrus with extracts from the Book of Caverns) and emblems in wood, fragments from the shrines which had contained such images, *shabtis*, a badly broken wooden Osiris bed, and the remains of at least one large wooden funerary couch similar to those later discovered in the tomb of

A Tomb for Tuthmosis III's Queen

KV42, situated in the valley leading up to the tomb of Tuthmosis III, was first entered by Howard Carter on 9 December 1900, having probably been discovered by Victor Loret during excavations in the vicinity some 18 months previously. As Carter later wrote:

'On entering, I at once saw that the tomb had already been plundered in early times … for the funereal furniture, vases and Canopic jars, were [s]mashed and lying about on the ground of the passage and chambers, evidently just as the former robbers had thrown them…'

Architecture and decoration

KV42 is royal in appearance, being larger than any private tomb of definite 18th-dynasty date and having the cartouche-shaped burial chamber found most famously in the tomb of Tuthmosis III (KV34). Although lacking a well (a good indication that the tomb had not been prepared as the primary place of burial of a king) or pillars in the first hall, and with fewer subsidiary rooms leading from the burial chamber than are found in KV34, the design seems to postdate KV34 in all other features, most notably the added corridor between the first hall and the burial chamber.

The burial chamber had been plastered and partially decorated with a *khekher*-ornament dado and yellow-starred blue ceiling; the work had never been finished, and no inscriptions were in evidence.

A tomb for Queen Hatshepsut-Meryetre

At the far end of the burial chamber Carter encountered a rectangular stone sarcophagus, unfinished and seemingly unused. Yet other fragments of funerary equipment showed that the tomb had at one stage contained one or more burials of non-royal status, with the names of the mayor of Thebes, Sennufer, his wife the royal wet-nurse Senetnay, and the 'king's adornment' Baketre

Tutankhamun. The tomb also yielded quantities of fragments of furniture, stone, wood, faience and glass vessels (the latter being particularly numerous and wide ranging), wooden model boats, model vases of faience in the form of *ankh*-signs, faience fruits and flowers, and cosmetic objects. Everything, almost without exception, had been smashed to pieces – either by robbers, or by the 21st-dynasty salvage parties (p. 204).

The mummy of the king

'Absolute silence, a silence that may be felt, is all round; a feeling of awe steals over one as it is realised that here, lying in his lonely coffin, far away from the haunts of man, beast or bird, is the shrouded, silent form of the monarch [Amenophis II] whose word alone was sufficient to make the world tremble.'

May Brodrick

Within its replacement cartonnage coffin the mummy of Amenophis II, when found, was superficially intact, with a simple identifying docket on the outer shroud. Following the robbery of the tomb by the Abd el-Rassuls in 1902 (p. 70), Maspero partially unwrapped the body, and it was later reexamined and commented on by Grafton Elliot Smith in his publication of the royal mummies in 1912.

Beneath the outer shroud, the original linen was visible, heavily gashed, especially around the legs, where it had been chopped away to get at the royal jewellery. Impressions of this jewellery (in particular a beaded broad collar and a beaded belt) were still visible in the hardened resin which covered the body.

For the employment of KV35 as a cache, see below, p. 198.

occurring on the limestone canopic jars and dummy vessels, and an offering table. Carter also noted the remains of wooden 'sledges and coffins', uninscribed items including 'some twenty or thirty, whole and broken, rough earthen jars' in the small side chamber of the burial hall, and 'some gold leaf and an exquisite gold inlaid rosette', found in the entrance corridor.

Carter believed in 1900 that KV42 was the burial of Sennufer and his immediate family. But we know that Sennufer at least had a tomb elsewhere at Thebes (TT96) where he was probably buried. Furthermore, Catharine Roehrig has made the plausible suggestion that the burials of Senetnay and Baketre, rather than being original to KV42, may have been simply cached there following their transfer from original tombs nearby – perhaps KV26 and KV37 – at the end of the New Kingdom.

If the employment of KV42 is thus somewhat uncertain, the *intended* occupant of the tomb was convincingly established in January 1921 when Carter uncovered the foundation deposits placed at the entrance: these carried the name of the great royal wife Hatshepsut-Meryetre, wife of Tuthmosis III and mother of Amenophis II, for whom the husband had evidently excavated the tomb. Whatever Tuthmosis III's intention, however, the lady seems never to have been interred in KV42: to judge from traces in the tomb of the son, it seems that Amenophis II decided that she should rest instead in KV35.

Emptying the burial?

A graffito at the entrance to KV42 reads as follows:

'3rd month of summer, day 23: work was begun on this tomb by the necropolis team, when the scribe Butehamun went to the town to see the general's arrival in the north.'

The reference is clearly to official activity of some sort. Indeed, as Karl Jansen-Winkeln tentatively suggests, KV42 may be the 'tomb of the ancestors' that the High Priest of Amun, Piankh, ordered the necropolis scribe Butehamun to uncover for him – with a view to emptying it, as we shall see (p. 205).

Factfile

Tomb number/location:
KV42, Wadi Biban el-Muluk
Date of discovery:
before 9 December 1900, by Victor Loret(?)
Excavator/report:
Chinouda Macarios and Boutros Andraos, 1900, under the supervision of Howard Carter, for the Service des Antiquités: H. Carter, *ASAE* 2 (1901) pp. 196–200

(Above) A canopic jar from the tomb, inscribed for Senetnay

(Right) The burial chamber of KV42, as first encountered by Howard Carter in 1900.

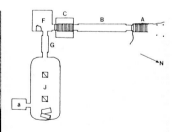

(Above) The ground plan of KV42: a simplified development of the tomb of Tuthmosis III.

Tuthmosis III's warlike nature, which had been shared by his son and successor, Amenophis II, seems not to have been inherited by the subsequent kings, Tuthmosis IV (*c.* 1401–1391 BC) and Amenophis III (*c.* 1391–1353 BC). These two reigns ushered in an extended period of peace and prosperity on a scale Egypt had never before enjoyed. Diplomacy took over from the sword as the principal instrument of Egyptian foreign policy, and peace was made with the kingdom of Mitanni in northern Syria, Egypt's main rival, which now found itself threatened by the Anatolian Hittites. Pharaoh became fat, self-indulgent and ever more convinced of his power and infallibility.

Tuthmosis IV, a son of Amenophis II's second queen, Tiaa, had come to the throne following the premature death of an elder half-brother. Like his two predecessors, he was buried in the main part of the royal valley, within tomb KV43. His son and successor, Amenophis III, was born to the lady Mutemwia and would be married by Year 2 of the reign to Tiye, daughter of the commoners Yuya and Tjuyu, whose burial was discovered by Theodore Davis in tomb KV46 in 1905 (p. 174). Amenophis III's own tomb, founded by his father, was the first to be located in the western Valley of the Kings, better known today as the West Valley.

The Tombs of Tuthmosis IV and Amenophis III

The Tomb of Tuthmosis IV (KV43)

Discovery

'. . . our eyes became more accustomed to the dim light of our candles, and . . . we realized in the gloom that the upper part of the walls of this well were elaborately sculptured and painted. The scenes represented the Pharaoh . . . standing before various gods and goddesses of the Netherworld. . . . Here was final proof that I had found the tomb of Tuthmosis IV . . .'

Howard Carter

The formal opening of KV43 took place on 3 February 1903. However, Carter had first entered the tomb on 18 January to ensure that he had indeed uncovered more than an unfinished pit. The burial had, of course, been plundered in antiquity –

Factfile

Tomb number/location: KV43, Wadi Biban el-Muluk
Date of discovery: 18 January 1903, by Howard Carter
Royal mummy: removed in antiquity; found in KV35
Excavator/report: H. Carter, 1903, for Theodore M. Davis: Th. M. Davis *et al.*, *The Tomb of Thoutmôsis IV* (London, 1904)
Wall documentation: *ibid.*

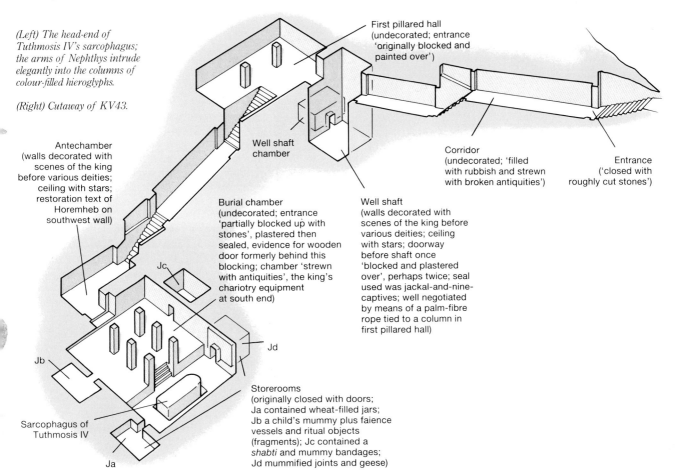

(Left) The head-end of Tuthmosis IV's sarcophagus; the arms of Nephthys intrude elegantly into the columns of colour-filled hieroglyphs.

(Right) Cutaway of KV43.

First pillared hall (undecorated; entrance 'originally blocked and painted over')

Well shaft chamber

Corridor (undecorated; 'filled with rubbish and strewn with broken antiquities')

Entrance ('closed with roughly cut stones')

Antechamber (walls decorated with scenes of the king before various deities; ceiling with stars; restoration text of Horemheb on southwest wall)

Burial chamber (undecorated; entrance 'partially blocked up with stones', plastered then sealed, evidence for wooden door formerly behind this blocking; chamber 'strewn with antiquities', the king's chariotry equipment at south end)

Well shaft (walls decorated with scenes of the king before various deities; ceiling with stars; doorway before shaft once 'blocked and plastered over', perhaps twice; seal used was jackal-and-nine-captives; well negotiated by means of a palm-fibre rope tied to a column in first pillared hall)

Jc

Jd

Jb

Sarcophagus of Tuthmosis IV

Ja

Storerooms (originally closed with doors; Ja contained wheat-filled jars; Jb a child's mummy plus faience vessels and ritual objects (fragments); Jc contained a *shabti* and mummy bandages; Jd mummified joints and geese)

(Left) Interior view of KV43, showing the austere appearance of the carefully finished but undecorated walls and pillars.

(Below) Tuthmosis IV receives the gift of life from a welcoming goddess Hathor. The scene is typical of the decorative scheme of the well shaft and antechamber, with noticeably fuller-bodied figures than are found in earlier tombs.

which was to be expected. The work had been thoroughly done: everything of any conceivable value had been carried off, from the smallest scrap of metal to large, re-usable pieces of wood such as doors and lintels. What was left had been smashed and scattered around the tomb.

Architecture and decoration

Clearly a development of KV35 (Amenophis II), KV43 follows the earlier tomb's location preference (it is the last tomb to be sited under a storm-fed waterfall), size and complexity, while further increasing its precision of plan. The carefully cut entrance stair and first three corridors push in a straight line to a large well with an offset chamber cut at the base of its far wall. The axis then turns 90 degrees into the first pillared hall from which a staircase, sloping corridor and another staircase lead to the anteroom and burial chamber. Different from KV35 is the lowering of the far third of the burial chamber to form the 'crypt', the alignment of the storage rooms and the tomb's more careful cutting. Also, two small rectangles – one on a pillar, the other (in outline) on the entrance wall – represent the first occurrences of the 'magical niches' which are found in all succeeding tombs until the time of Ramesses II.

Despite the careful cutting of the tomb, the burial chamber is undecorated and austere. Only sections of the well shaft and antechamber were decorated, and the representations were evidently hastily prepared. The two decorated areas were afforded similar treatments: the ceilings of both the well shaft and anteroom are painted with yellow stars on a dark blue ground and *khekher*-friezes appear at the top of the decorated walls, which are painted a uniform golden yellow. In the well shaft, six images of the king receive the gift of 'life' (the *ankh*) before various deities, and in the antechamber the king is seen again before images of the same deities. In both locations the representations of the king are virtually identical, and those of the various goddesses are distinguished only by differing patterns in the materials of their dress. The inscriptions are also very similar, and consist only of the names of the deities shown and, alternately, the throne- and birth-names of the king.

Finds from the Tomb of Tuthmosis IV

'Though plunderers had stripped the contents of this tomb of all its valuable gold, they had left much that to us is even more valuable.'

Ambrose Lansing

Besides the royal funerary equipment, Carter recovered fragments of three subsidiary burials, presumably offspring of Tuthmosis IV who had predeceased their father: the king's son, Amenemhet (whose rewrapped and recoffined mummy may be that discovered by the Metropolitan Museum Expedition buried close to the Deir el-Bahri cache a few years later), the king's daughter, Tentamun, and an individual whose name is not preserved. The corpse discovered by Carter propped up against the wall in side room Jb perhaps belongs to one of them. Functional items from the tomb such as wicks and a weight may be associated with the dismantling of the burial at the end of the New Kingdom.

Most of the finds were fragmentary. The following individual objects and classes of object were represented:

Tuthmosis IV
Foundation deposits – model vessels, implements, pebbles and plaques (calcite, wood, bronze, faience)
Sarcophagus box and lid (yellow quartzite)
Canopic chest (calcite)
Statuettes of the king and divinities (wood)
Small shrines (wood)
Shabtis (wood, faience)
Shabti coffins (faience)
Shabti implements (faience)
Magical bricks with figures (wood, clay)
Boxes and chests (wood, faience)
Furniture (wood)
Model boats (wood)
Chariot and associated equipment (wood, leather)
Staves, fans, whips, etc. (wood)
Throwsticks (faience)
Scabbards (leather)
Mace heads (limestone)

Textiles
Gloves (leather)
Armlets (leather)
Amulets (faience)
Vessels (diorite, calcite, limestone, glass, faience, pottery)
Jar sealings (mud)
Labels (wood)
Game board (wood)
Mirror handle (ivory)
Seal(?) (limestone)

King's son Amenemhet
Canopic jars (limestone)

King's daughter Tentamun
Canopic jars (calcite)

Unnamed
Canopic jars (limestone)

Intrusive material?
1-*deben* weight (flint)
oil wicks

Items of burial equipment found by Carter in KV43: model papyrus rolls, vessels, amulets and shabtis *in faience; resin-coated wooden images of the king; a clay Anubis from one of the magical niches; and an embroidered textile fragment.*

(Left) Detail, by Carter, of the plaster relief-decoration found on the interior of Tuthmosis IV's chariot-body: the king as sphinx tramples Egypt's enemies while under the protection of the war-god Montu.

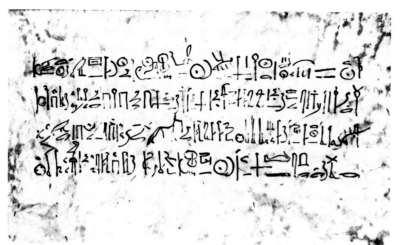

The text refers to a restoration, by the pharaoh Horemheb (1319–1307 BC), of the burial of Tuthmosis IV within KV43, made necessary by illicit entry, perhaps during the troubled years following the Amarna period. Robbery in the valley was evidently a rare occurrence at this time, and the repairs seem to have been carried out with far more care and attention than during later restorations, Carter noting quite elaborate repairs to the tomb's faience in 'blue paste' or 'yellow plaster'. A further response to this 18th-dynasty robbery may have been the plastered blocking erected in front of the original wooden door to the burial chamber, further bolstering the protection it offered. Again, we owe the evidence of this to Carter.

'[Those who carried out the robbery] must have been bold spirits . . . : they were evidently in a great hurry, and we have reason to believe that they were caught in the act. If so, we may be sure they died deaths that were lingering and ingenious.'

A second intrusion may be discerned in the breached reblockings to the doorways at D–E and I–J. This took place at an undetermined date, but it may have been at this time that a number of items removed from the tomb were hidden in KV37 (p. 183). This later phase of theft may also have been the prompt for the official removal of the king's mummy (p. 207). With the king gone, the dismantling of the burial began in earnest. The thoroughness of the workers is shown by the fact that they were concerned to remove even the small bronze eye-surrounds of the royal and divine statuettes, two of which, after treatment, had been casually thrown into the now-empty royal sarcophagus. The job done, they abandoned the tomb to posterity, taking care to close off (albeit with a simple drystone wall) the entrance after they had left.

'. . . it is particularly interesting to observe the ancient rope by which the plunderers ascended, fastened around one of [the] columns [in the pillared hall F], and still hanging down the well.'

Arthur Weigall

Robbers and restorers

Two large and beautifully written hieratic texts on the south wall of the antechamber read as follows:

(1) 'Year 8, 3rd month of *akhet*-season, day 1, under the majesty of the King of Upper and Lower Egypt, Djeserkheprure-setepenre, son of Re Horemheb-merenamun. His majesty life! prosperity! health! commanded that the fan-bearer on the king's right hand, the king's scribe, overseer of the treasury, overseer of works in the Place of Eternity [i.e. the royal necropolis] and leader of the festival of Amun in Karnak, Maya, son of the noble Iawy, born of the lady of the house Weret, be charged to renew the burial of King Menkheprure [Tuthmosis IV], true of voice, in the noble mansion upon the west of Thebes.' (2) 'His assistant, the steward of the southern city, Djehutymose, whose mother is Iniuhe of the city [i.e. Thebes].'

The royal mummy

The mummy of Tuthmosis IV would eventually be cached within a side chamber of the tomb of Amenophis II (KV35), where it was discovered by Victor Loret in 1898 (p. 198). The original coffins had gone, and the king now lay in a rough and unadorned replacement of later date. The fact that the mummy of the child propped up against the wall of side room Jb had not been removed from KV43 with that of the king may suggest that those responsible for clearing the tomb were being deliberately selective in which bodies they restored and reburied. The fate of the second and third subsidiary burials is uncertain, though for Amenemhet see p. 107.

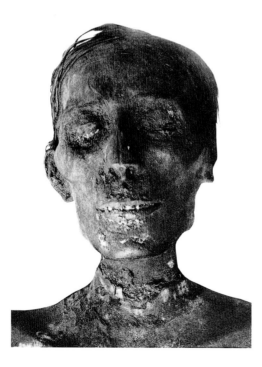

New Kingdom Family Tombs

The Valley of the Kings contains a number of undecorated tombs which may, from their multi-chambered design, have been intended for group burials of immediate members of the royal family. These tombs still await a full and critical study, but current evidence suggests a date for the group in the mid-18th dynasty, a number perhaps showing later adaptation. They may be precursors of that ultimate dynastic tomb, KV5, which would be prepared – perhaps again from an original 18th-dynasty tomb cutting – for the offspring of Ramesses II in the following dynasty (p. 144).

Tomb KV12

Date of discovery: before 1739
Excavator/report: unknown: unpublished

Though its presence was apparently observed by Pococke, the first record of exploration we have of this multi-chambered tomb is by James Burton in the 1820s or 1830s, when it was still encumbered with debris; precisely who swept it out during the past or present century is not recorded. Harold Jones in 1908–09, Howard Carter in 1920–21, and most recently Otto Schaden in 1993–94 have all searched at the entrance, without significant result.

Within the tomb itself, Burton recorded the presence of mummy remains and a graffito on the east wall of the ultimate chamber's side storeroom. The Burton corpse may represent the remains of one of the tomb's occupants; if so, it had probably been interred within the end chamber, which Romer discovered to have been 'anciently sealed with mud plaster'.

This end chamber had been broken into accidentally by workmen quarrying the later KV9, probably under Ramesses VI, at which time any burial within would very likely have been plundered. At the latest, KV12 will have been robbed when KV9 itself was entered by thieves (p. 165) – if, indeed, the robbers of Ramesses VI's burial did not find their way into KV9 via KV12, as a number of *shabtis* of Ramesses VI discovered by Harold Jones at the entrance to KV12 might suggest.

The plan of this strange, undecorated tomb is unique in a number of ways. The entrance, slightly offset, opens immediately into a hall with a single pillar, a stairway and several unfinished offshoots – one of which actually doubles back parallel to the entrance (compare KV39: p. 89). It is possible that this section of the structure was begun in the 18th dynasty, left unfinished, and later incorporated into the present design. While the outermost chambers are roughly hewn in a way reminiscent of earlier tombs, the innermost chambers are much more carefully finished, with a transition between the two areas being clearly visible in the passage beyond the first room. As in royal tombs, the subsequent passage consists of a staircase with side ledges.

Although the lower section of the tomb appears asymmetrical in plan, the outlines of uncut doors around the central main chamber indicate that a balanced arrangement of subsidiary rooms was intended. The irregular form of those subordinate rooms which were cut is due to the presence of veins of impenetrably harder rock.

Tomb KV27

Date of discovery: before 1832
Excavator/report: Donald P. Ryan, for Pacific Lutheran University, 1990: D. P. Ryan, *KMT* 2/1 (spring, 1991) pp. 30–31

KV27 was apparently known to John Gardner Wilkinson and may even be alluded to by Pococke. It was examined, albeit superficially, by Lefébure, who noted the presence of 'mummy remains' of uncertain date. More recently, in 1990, the tomb was entered by Donald Ryan, who notes 'evidence of at least seven different floodings having taken place, which in some areas filled the sepulchre with rock and dirt debris nearly to the ceiling.' A small sampling of pottery from room Bc tentatively suggests a mid-18th-dynasty date, perhaps during the reign of Tuthmosis IV or Amenophis III.

'This architecturally interesting monument resembles the simple plan of tombs 28, 44 and 45, but that three additional rooms seem to have been added to the central rectangular chamber.'

Donald Ryan

KV27 seems architecturally to lie between those shaft tombs which open directly into a single room and those tombs in which multiple rooms open from at least one entrance corridor (as in the Queens' Valley tombs and KV12). The only tomb having a similar design is KV30 (below), which combines the entrance shaft with a single corridor. Preliminary cutting in the east wall of the southernmost chamber may represent the beginnings of another room, or of a niche (though the latter feature is rare in tombs of this type).

Tomb KV30

Date of discovery: 1817, by Giovanni Battista Belzoni
Excavator/report: G. B. Belzoni, for the Earl of Belmore, 1817: unpublished

KV30 is closely similar to KV27 in design. Nothing is known of its archaeology: the only recorded find is a potsherd, which Elizabeth Thomas dated to the 18th dynasty; James Burton noted a quarry mark(?), in 'red characters in chamber of pit', about which nothing more is known. It is uncertain whether the mid-18th-dynasty sarcophagus EA 39 in the British Museum, presented by Lord Belmore, came from here or KV31.

The entrance to the uninscribed tomb KV12, situated in the wadi leading up to the tomb of Amenophis II.

Anthropoid sarcophagus in sandstone discovered by the Earl of Belmore in the Valley of the Kings in 1817. The painted decoration and inscriptions are now badly deteriorated.

The Tomb of Amenophis III (WV22)

Discovery and excavation

'It was in the course of our researches in the Valley of the Kings that crossing the ridges on the west side, we were led, Jollois and I, into a secondary valley where we found a tomb which had not been noticed by any of the travellers who had preceded us.'

Édouard de Villiers du Terrage

Was Queen Tiye Ever Buried Here?

'In the course of [the] work we made the interesting discovery . . . that Queen Tyi had actually been buried here.'

Howard Carter

Such was Carter's view. But is it correct?

There can be little doubt that Amenophis III intended that both his queens, Tiye and Sitamun, should be buried with him in WV22, the two burial suites leading off the main burial chamber having evidently been prepared for them. Both queens appear, however, to have outlived their king; and, since the introduction of one or both at a later date would have involved breaking the sanctity of the burial and destroying the scene which appears to have been painted over the well-shaft entrance, alternative arrangements may have been made for the queens after they died.

Nothing is known of the burial arrangements of Sitamun, who disappears from view soon after the death of Amenophis III. Tiye evidently died during the reign of her son, Amenophis IV-Akhenaten, who provided her with the gilded shrine recovered by Davis from the reburial in KV55 (p. 117) and a red granite sarcophagus. The fragments of this latter monument have been found in the royal tomb at el-Amarna (TA26 – p. 118), and presumably mark the queen's original place of interment.

The *shabtis* of Tiye from WV22 are something of a puzzle. Two of the series are inscribed with her name and the titles 'Great Royal Wife and Royal Mother', the latter indicating that they were prepared under Amenophis IV-Akhenaten. In the light of what has been said above, it is surprising to find Amenophis IV-Akhenaten providing items of burial equipment for his mother's use in WV22. Their presence here would be easier to explain if the reigns of Amenophis III and Amenophis IV-Akhenaten were at one stage concurrent, a view which is again creeping back into fashion. If there were no coregency between Amenophis III and his son, these figures would have to be interpreted not as *shabtis* for the queen's use in the next world, but as votive images offered by the queen to her dead husband's burial.

The tomb prepared for Amenophis III, ninth and most splendid pharaoh of the 18th dynasty, is located in the West Valley. Although it may have been known to the 18th-century traveller W. G. Browne, the tomb was 'officially' discovered in August 1799 by two members of Napoleon's Expedition – Prosper Jollois and Édouard de Villiers du Terrage, engineers who superficially explored the sepulchre, planned it and drew a selection of the objects they found. They were followed during the course of the 19th century by a whole army of enterprising tourists, whose clothing polished to a high gloss the southern wall of the corridor as they squeezed through the only partially cleared debris to the burial chamber below. Most visitors were tempted to carry off a small, innocent souvenir of their visit – a fragment of inscribed wood, or a broken stone *shabti* – Flinders Petrie and Francis Llewellyn Griffith (at the end of 1886) among them; a few, persons unknown, went so far as to carve out from the beautifully painted surface of the walls a series of portraits, now in the Louvre, a brutal defacement of an exquisitely decorated monument (p. 112).

Lord Carnarvon and Howard Carter

Despite a superficial clearance of WV22 said to have been carried out by Theodore Davis (about which details are almost completely lacking), the first serious archaeological interest in the tomb was shown by Howard Carter during the spring of 1915 (8 February–8 March).

Carter's interest had been aroused by his acquisition in October 1912 (from a Luxor antiquities dealer) of three hardstone bracelet plaques inscribed with the names of Amenophis III and his chief consort, Tiye, discarded when the original precious metal mounts had been prized off in antiquity. Hearsay had it that these plaques had been found in the vicinity of the tomb (they were perhaps strays from the Davis excavations), and Carter was

Faience face of a queen, probably Tiye, discovered in the debris of WV22 by Yoshimura and Kondo. It joins a shabti *figure from Carter's work now at Highclere Castle.*

clearly hoping for further finds of comparable interest.

Carter began by clearing the mouth of the water course beneath the entrance of the tomb, almost immediately turning up the broken foot of a *shabti* figure of Queen Tiye, together with fragments of faience and glass thrown out from the tomb in ancient times. Further digging immediately before the entrance uncovered a series of five intact foundation deposits and one robbed emplacement positioned at the time work first began on the tomb – which, to judge from the inscribed cartouche-plaques within the deposits, was during the reign of Tuthmosis IV.

Within the tomb, Carter concentrated his efforts on clearing those parts which Davis and previous explorers had neglected – notably the deep well shaft, which yielded a whole array of objects. Finds included the splendid hub of a chariot wheel and, as if to justify Carnarvon and Carter's initial interest in the tomb, a small fragment of a fourth bracelet plaque, this time in faience. Carter also

Factfile

Tomb number/location:
WV22, West Valley
Date of discovery:
before 1799
Royal mummy:
removed in antiquity; found in KV35
Excavators/reports:
Howard Carter, 1915, for the Earl of Carnarvon: unpublished, but see H. Carter and A. C. Mace, *The Tomb of Tut.ankh.Amen,* I (London, 1923) p. 79; Sakuji Yoshimura and Jiro Kondo, 1989–, for Waseda University: J. Kondo, in C. N. Reeves (ed.), *After Tut'ankhamun* (London, 1992) pp. 41–54; *id.,* in R. Wilkinson (ed.), *Valley of the Sun Kings* (Tucson, 1995) pp. 25–33
Wall documentation:
Alexandre Piankoff and Erik Hornung, *MDAIK* 17 (1961) pp. 111–27

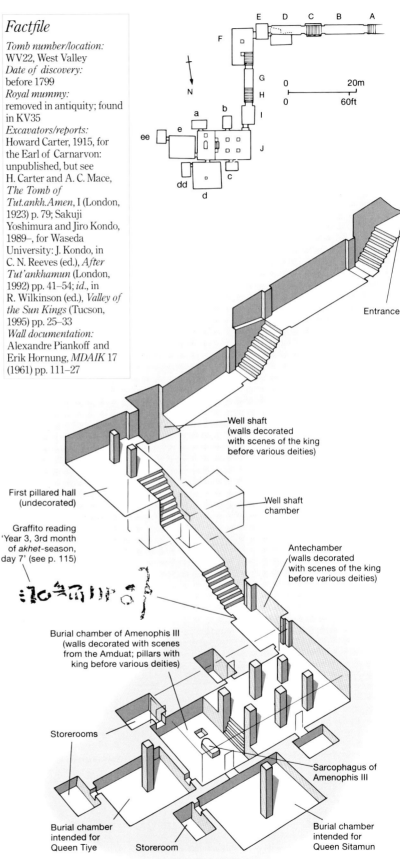

Entrance

Well shaft
(walls decorated with scenes of the king before various deities)

First pillared hall
(undecorated)

Well shaft
chamber

Graffito reading
'Year 3, 3rd month of *akhet*-season, day 7' (see p. 115)

Antechamber
(walls decorated with scenes of the king before various deities)

Burial chamber of Amenophis III
(walls decorated with scenes from the Amduat; pillars with king before various deities)

Storerooms

Sarcophagus of
Amenophis III

Burial chamber
intended for
Queen Tiye

Storeroom

Burial chamber
intended for
Queen Sitamun

(Far left) Calcite head wearing the nemes *headdress, from a* shabti *of Amenophis III; (above) the Japanese excavations at the entrance to WV22; (left) Carter's drawing of the hardstone bracelet plaques which first aroused his interest in the tomb.*

(Right) Amenophis III's tomb is the most developed of the 18th-dynasty bent-axis tombs. Two suites for the king's consorts were later added to the burial chamber.

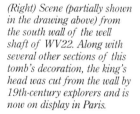

*(Above) Amenophis III
accompanied by the* ka *of his
deified father, Tuthmosis IV –
copy of an early drawing by
Nestor L'Hôte.*

*(Right) Scene (partially shown
in the drawing above) from
the south wall of the well
shaft of WV22. Along with
several other sections of this
tomb's decoration, the king's
head was cut from the wall by
19th-century explorers and is
now on display in Paris.*

reexamined the areas already dug over by Davis's men, bringing to light in the burial chamber the first recorded fragment of the king's calcite canopic chest, other fragments of which would subsequently be recovered from the debris outside.

Waseda University excavations

'Compared with their European colleagues, Japanese archaeologists have been late arrivals in Egyptological fieldwork, but the past 20 years have seen a steady programme of Japanese survey and excavation in Egypt, mainly in the area of Luxor and Cairo.'

Ian Shaw

In 1989 a Japanese team, led by Sakuji Yoshimura and Jiro Kondo of Waseda University, decided to look again at the tomb, as a logical follow-up to Waseda's earlier work in the palace complex of Amenophis III at Malqata to the south. Yoshimura and Kondo initiated a full clearance down to bedrock, both within and outside the tomb. The thoroughness of their approach has paid dividends. A seventh, somewhat smaller (uninscribed) foundation deposit was found before the tomb entrance, and a whole mass – several hundreds of fragments – of broken-up funerary material in undisturbed corners and in the dumps of previous excavators.

Architecture

Located – for the first time for a royal valley tomb – in the talus slope away from the cliff face, WV22 exhibits several changes from the plan of Tuthmosis IV's tomb, though these are mainly changes in the location of specific elements rather than major design modifications. Most noticeable are the position of the room cut at the base of the

well shaft, the connection between the anteroom and the burial chamber, the direction of the latter room and the addition of two large rooms to the crypt, each with a pillar and subsidiary storeroom. The first of these 'suites' (Je) appears to have been designed for the burial of Amenophis III's principal wife, Tiye, and a number of funerary items recovered by Carter and by the Waseda team are evidently to be associated with this (anticipated) burial. The second suite (Jd) seems to have been expanded from an original storeroom (as the chisel marks documenting the adaptation on the ceiling and walls clearly show). The preparation of a second suite finds an interesting parallel at Malqata, where an extra set of rooms was squeezed in between the quarters of Amenophis III and Tiye for the princess Sitamun, presumably in connection with her promotion to royal wife status later in the reign; and the likelihood is that it was for Sitamun that the preparation of the Jd suite was carried out in the royal tomb. A small recess made at one corner of the crypt and a canopic placement are cut in the floor; these elements are roughly prepared, and may be unfinished. A total of 11 niches have been noted at points around the crypt and at the entrances to the adjoining rooms. Wooden doors were also placed at the entrance to the sarcophagus chamber and at the entrances to its two large subsidiary suites.

Decoration

'The condition of the paintings is very poor, but we have started the work of restoration . . .'

Jiro Kondo

Several aspects of the iconography of WV22 are new. For the first time the king is shown with the

figure of the royal *ka* and before the goddesses Hathor and Nut. The Mistress of the West is also now clearly differentiated as a separate aspect of the goddess Hathor. On the walls of the well shaft, Hathor leads one group of deities while Nut leads another group – showing the king's entry into the western realm of the dead as well as into the heavens.

The well shaft also shows the king being received by Hathor along with the *ka* of his deified father, Tuthmosis IV. As Betsy Bryan has recently suggested, this may indicate more than mere filial piety or affection; it may be intended to show that Amenophis considered his father's role in the foundation of the tomb to be an important one which continued on through his own eventual acceptance by the deities of the afterlife. Unfortunately, even at the time of its discovery in 1799 it was in quite poor condition, with considerable portions of the plaster detached from the wall, and, as we have seen, further damage was done to the more intact decorations by souvenir hunters in the following century.

Funerary equipment

Amenophis III died in or after his 38th regnal year, and, as the broken fragments recovered by Carter and the Waseda team clearly indicate, was interred within WV22 surrounded by the same broad range of funerary equipment encountered in the tomb of Tutankhamun (see Table p. 114). The king himself, as we know from fragments preserved, was buried within a series of shrines, a cartouche-shaped sarcophagus – for the first time in red granite rather than quartzite – and a nest of gilded and inlaid anthropoid wooden coffins. Furthermore, there is every reason to believe that, like Tutankhamun a quarter-century later, the royal mummy was furnished with an inner coffin and/or mask of solid gold: an exquisite cobra head of lapis lazuli with inlaid eyes set in gold surrounds was found by Yoshimura and Kondo in the debris of the antechamber, and seems to come from a coffin or mask of just this sort.

Dismantling the burial

The present state of the fragments recovered from WV22 is lamentable. All the wooden objects (by far the bulk of the material recovered) had been chopped into small pieces in antiquity in a deliberate attempt to render them unrecognizable and unusable. All precious metal coverings had been stripped away, and metal fittings and glass and semi-precious stone inlays had been removed and carried off. Some of this salvaged material – hundreds of inlays of coloured glass and semi-precious stone, and a mass of stripped gold foil – appears to have been carried over the cliffs to the main valley, where it was buried, eventually to be brought to light by Carter working for Theodore Davis in 1902, outside the entrance

A Storage Chamber for Amenophis III's Tomb

'In one place [in the West Valley] where I made them dig, following tolerably certain signs, we found ... about ten feet beneath the rubbish, a door and chamber, but these [were] without sculpture. Some remains of earthen vases were, however, brought to light at the same time, which contained the name of a king hitherto unknown.'

Carl Richard Lepsius

WV A, a small staircase tomb, was discovered by Lepsius in 1845, explored superficially by Chassinat in 1905–06, and finally excavated by Yoshimura and Kondo in 1993–94. It retains much of its original blocking, and in the single chamber behind had been stored wine amphorae and blue-painted pottery, dockets associated with the former bearing dates of Year 32 and Year 37 (Amenophis III's third jubilee). The likelihood is that the tomb had been employed as a storage chamber for Amenophis III's own tomb, WV22, situated nearby.

(Left) The entrance to WV A, and (below) the tomb's location relative to WV22.

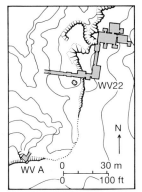

Factfile

Tomb number/location:
WV A, West Valley
Date of discovery:
before 25 February 1845, by Carl Richard Lepsius
Excavators/reports:
C. R. Lepsius, 1845, for the Prussian Expedition: C. R. Lepsius, *Letters from Egypt ...* (London, 1853) p. 262; Émile Chassinat, 1905/6, for the Institut français d'archéologie orientale: É. Chassinat, *EEFAR 1905–06*, pp. 82–83; Sakuji Yoshimura and Jiro Kondo, 1993–94, for Waseda University: J. Kondo, in Richard Wilkinson (ed.), *Valley of the Sun Kings* (Tucson, 1995) pp. 30–32

to KV36, tomb of the fan-bearer Maiherpri (p. 74).

The body of the king himself was removed from WV22 to a side room in the tomb of Amenophis II (KV35), where it was discovered by Victor Loret in 1898; beneath the docketed shroud recording its restoration in Year 12/13 of King Smendes of the 21st dynasty, it was in poor condition. The 'Elder Lady', identified by some as the mummy of Tiye, was recovered from this same tomb, though stripped of its bandages and cached in room Jc.

Graffiti

An interesting graffito was recently observed by the Japanese team between the antechamber and the staircase leading into it, written in black on the east wall 1.72 m (5 ft 7in) above floor level. It reads:

Wooden label found by the Japanese in WV22.

Finds from the Tomb of Amenophis III

Most of the finds were fragmentary. The following individual items and classes of object were represented:

Tuthmosis IV
Foundation deposits

Amenophis III
Large shrines (wood)
Sarcophagus box? (fragment) and lid (red granite)
Rishi coffins (wood, gold?)
Mask? (gold?)
Coffin bier? (wood)
Canopic shrine (wood)
Canopic chest (calcite)
Canopic jars (calcite)
Guardian statues (wood)
Statuettes of divinities, including Sekhmet, Netjerankh (wood)
Small shrines (wood)
Small coffins (wood)
Shabtis (red granite, calcite, serpentine, wood, faience?)
Shabti coffins (faience)
Shabti implements (wood)
Ritual couches (wood)
Boxes and chests (wood)
Furniture? (wood)
Palanquins (wood)
Model boats (wood)
Staves and fans? (wood)
Archery tackle (wood)
Jewellery (faience, gold)
Sandals (papyrus)
Vessels (serpentine, calcite, glass, frit, faience, wood, pottery)
Lamp (calcite)
Labels (wood)

Tiye
Large statues (wood)
Boxes (wood)
Shabtis (calcite, wood?, faience)

Intrusive material
Coffins (wood)
Mummy remains
Shabti (pottery)
Jewellery (faience)
Mallet (wood)
Fire-board (wood)

(Right) Sakuji Yoshimura (right) and Jiro Kondo discuss strategy during the course of their work in the West Valley.

Finds from WV22. (Above) Limestone double-shabti of Amenophis III and Tiye, discovered by the French Expedition and now in the Louvre; (right) wooden door panel from a shrine with an ink sketch of a statue, and (right centre) a painted wooden face from one of the king's shabti figures. (Far right) Lapis lazuli serpent head, with eyes of obsidian set in gold frames, similar to those found on the innermost gold coffin and mask of Tutankhamun. (Below right) Curved fragment, from one of the king's coffins, of gilded wood with rishi *inlay.*

(Left) Wheel-hub from the king's chariot, found by Carter in 1915.

(Far left) The head of the mummy of Amenophis III.

'Year 3, 3rd month of *akhet*-season, day 7.' Although the docket's precise significance is uncertain, the palaeography appears to be contemporary and it is at least possible that the text was written at the time the tomb was closed, following the interment of Amenophis III. The regnal year would in that case be of Akhenaten, tying in with the date at which he first began to prepare his own funerary equipment as king (p. 116) and perhaps indicating the maximum duration of any coregency which may have existed between Akhenaten and his father.

Intrusive burials

Among the finds of the Carter season was a small and evidently intrusive faience ring bezel inscribed with the royal name Usermaatre-setepenre, and several fragments of late burials which had been made in the now empty and abandoned WV22. The throne name on this ring was identified by Carter and others as that of Ramesses II of the 19th dynasty; it seems more likely, however, to belong to a king of the later 22nd dynasty, at which time (or later) the intrusive burials represented among the debris appear to have been introduced.

Ostracon with 'enigmatic' symbols – perhaps an 18th-dynasty attendance register.

The Tomb of Two 18th-Dynasty Queens?

'The entry corridor ends with a steep flight of steps, which usher one into another corridor leading to the burial chamber. The latter is a fairly large room with a single pillar at its center. Deep ledges or shelves carved in the limestone run along two of the walls. The floor is littered with small stones, along with bits of human and animal mummies, pottery shards, wood fragments and other miscellaneous fragmentary artifacts . . .'

Donald Ryan

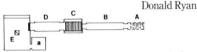

KV21, opened by Belzoni on 9 October 1817, was found to be blocked 'at the end of the first passage' by 'a brick wall, which . . . had been forced through'. This breach led, via a further corridor, into 'a pretty large chamber, with a single pillar in the centre'. In one corner of this chamber 'we found two mummies on the ground quite naked, without cloth or case. They were females, and their hair pretty long, and well preserved. . . .' A room off the burial chamber contained 'fragments of several earthen vessels, and also pieces of vases of alabaster. . . .' An intact pottery jar, 'with a few hieroglyphics on it, and large enough to contain two buckets of water', was found 'On the top of the staircase'.

A re-excavation of KV21 and study of the surviving contents were undertaken by Donald Ryan beginning in 1989. James Burton, writing in the 1820s–30s, had described it as 'a clean new tomb – the water not having got into it'. By 1989 the situation had changed dramatically: the entrance had been buried under many feet of flood debris, the water having penetrated the roughly blocked entrance doorway leaving a tide mark several centimetres above the floor level – carrying in with it half of a calcite *shabti* of Ramesses VI or VII and other debris.

The walls were well cut, with red and black masons' marks still in evidence, and apparently never intended to receive plaster. Several of the items noted by Belzoni were still present, including fragments of 24 large pottery storage jars of typical mid-18th-dynasty form, dating post-Hatshepsut and pre-Tuthmosis IV. These had contained small linen packages of natron, presumably left over from the embalming process, and a number of them were found scattered around the side chamber. Fragments of a blue-painted vessel from the corridor, datable to no earlier than the reign of Amenophis II, may be intrusive. Other finds included pieces of decorated wood and parts of a canopic jar, and five small seals bearing the jackal-and-nine-captives motif.

The most intriguing of Ryan's discoveries, were Belzoni's two female mummies, still present in the tomb, albeit dismembered. Nothing has yet been discovered to suggest their identity, but Ryan was able to observe that they had been 'embalmed in a special pose with their left arm bent at the elbow across the chest . . . with the left hand clenched, the right arm held straight at its side.' This is an attitude adopted by queenly burials such as that of the 'Elder Lady' from the Amenophis II cache, thought by some to be Queen Tiye, wife of Amenophis III (p. 200); in all probability, therefore, the two ladies from KV21 were members of the 18th-dynasty royal line.

The close similarity in the plan of KV21 to that of the two 'queens' suites' prepared for Tiye and (probably) Sitamun in the tomb of Amenophis III (WV22) (p. 111), added to the pose of the mummies, is further evidence that KV21 too was a queenly tomb of comparable date.

(Right) Donald Ryan in the entrance corridor of KV21, and (below) mummified hands and feet in the burial chamber.

Factfile

Tomb number/location:
KV21, Wadi Biban el-Muluk
Date of discovery:
9 October 1817, by Giovanni Battista Belzoni
Excavators/reports:
G. B. Belzoni, 1817, for Henry Salt: G. B. Belzoni, *Narrative of the Operations and Recent Discoveries in Egypt and Nubia* (London, 1820) p. 228; Donald P. Ryan, 1990, for Pacific Lutheran University, Tacoma, Washington: D. P. Ryan, *KMT* 1/1 (spring, 1990) p. 59; *id.*, *KMT* 2/1 (spring, 1991) pp. 29–30

The Enigma of Akhenaten's Tomb

With the premature death of the crown prince Djehutymose, Amenophis III was succeeded by a younger son by Queen Tiye, Amenophis IV (c. 1353–1335 BC). His revolutionary adherence to a single god – the Aten, or solar disc – would irreversibly change the course of Egyptian history. By Year 6 of the reign, the new king had altered his name to Akhenaten, 'He who is beneficial to the Aten', and started work on a cult centre for the new god, Akhetaten, 'Horizon of the Aten', at el-Amarna, where he would in due course be buried. The traditional gods and their human personnel were abandoned, and the empire left to rot.

Before Amarna in the royal valley

Among the many treasures recovered by Carter from the tomb of Tutankhamun were a series of gilded wooden funerary deities wrapped in linen dated to Years 3–7 of Amenophis IV-Akhenaten. These and other related funerary items seem originally to have been prepared for a burial of the heretic king at Thebes, which was evidently projected before Akhenaten abandoned Thebes and moved north to Akhetaten in Years 6–7.

If work on the Theban tomb itself had ever been initiated, two possible candidates at present suggest themselves: WV25, a tomb of royal pretensions and evident late 18th-dynasty date, which had been abandoned before work had progressed beyond the second corridor; or WV23, the tomb subsequently employed by Ay for his burial as king (p. 128) and which is usually assumed to have been taken over from Tutankhamun.

Akhenaten's Theban Tomb (WV25)

Discovery

'The following day. . . . I made a machine not unlike a battering-ram. The walls resisted the blows of the Arabs for some time . . . ; but they contrived to make a breach at last, and in the same way the opening was enlarged. We immediately entered . . .'

Giovanni Battista Belzoni

Tomb WV25 was discovered by Belzoni in 1817, blocked off at the base of the staircase with a well-

(Right) The mouth of WV25 – perhaps Akhenaten's Theban tomb. The entrance proper (below). The scale and proportions of the architecture are characteristic of the late 18th dynasty.

(Left) Seated figure depicted on a New Kingdom limestone ostracon brought to light in the course of Otto Schaden's clearance of WV25.

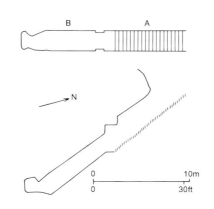

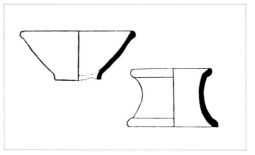

Factfile

Tomb number/location:
WV25, West Valley
Date of discovery:
1817, by Giovanni Battista Belzoni
Excavators/reports:
G. B. Belzoni, 1817: G. B. Belzoni, *Narrative of the Operations and Recent Discoveries in Egypt and Nubia* (London, 1820) pp. 223–4; Otto J. Schaden, 1972–73, for the University of Minnesota: O. J. Schaden, *ASAE* 63 (1979) pp. 161–8

(Above left) Plan and section of WV25, an incipient royal tomb of 18th-dynasty design.

(Left) Two of the New Kingdom pottery types represented in the debris: a dish and jar stand.

built stone wall, beyond which lay two rows of four coffined mummies arranged with their heads to the outside, lying in dried mud. To judge from Belzoni's description, the coffins contained intrusive burials of Third Intermediate Period date; the finds recovered during Otto Schaden's clearance of the tomb in 1972–73, though including a handful of objects which had evidently been washed into the tomb from nearby WV23 (the burial place of Ay), basically confirm this view, while the presence of cartonnage fragments suggests that the assemblage did not predate the 22nd dynasty.

Architecture

'. . . certainly royal in inception and . . . contemporary with the identified tombs of the wadi.'

Elizabeth Thomas

Although begun with care and according to royal dimensions and design, this structure achieved little more than the first two passages of the regular 18th-dynasty royal tomb plan. It is clear that WV25 was far from complete, and the incipient royal tomb appears to have been halted in its construction without any attempt to adapt it for use. The entrance is cut through a deep surface level of hard-packed gravel, and the first seven levels of steps are constructed of blocks set into the earth above the solid rock. Another 18 steps were cut into the rock itself. The doorway at the bottom of this stairway is set into an extension which reaches out from the lowest step in a design not found in the

sepulchres of the monarchs who reigned before Amenophis III or after Ay.

The Mysterious Tomb 55 (KV55)

Discovery and clearance

'An athletic and beflannelled young Englishman [Ayrton], with the aid of an electric burner and surrounded by tin cigarette boxes, was sorting precious stones; . . . half moon-shaped bits of lapis-lazuli in a box of 'Egyptian Beauties', cornelian and turquoise respectively in tins from Demetrius or Nestor Genakalis..'

Walter Tyndale

Theodore Davis's excavator, Edward Russell Ayrton, had been digging in the central portion of the main valley, when, on 3 January 1907, a few metres to the west of the tomb of Ramesses IX (KV6), he uncovered 'a recess in the rock' (now numbered KV C) containing a cache of pottery jars perhaps containing embalming refuse associated with the Ramessid tomb. Three days later the entrance to a tomb was uncovered. The tomb was KV55, today better known in the literature as 'Tomb 55', about which more has been written than almost any other burial in the Valley of the Kings.

The remains of an original cemented door-blocking were encountered, stamped with the 'jackal-and-nine-captives' seal, which had been partially dismantled in ancient times. Subsequently, the entrance had been blocked off with a loosely built

The entrance to KV55 today. Traces of the original blocking are still visible on the jambs of the doorway.

Akhenaten's Burial at Amarna

Factfile

Tomb number/location:
TA26, Royal Wadi, Amarna
Date of discovery:
1887–88?
Royal mummy:
moved in antiquity to KV55?
Excavators/reports:
A. Barsanti, 1891–92, for
the Service des Antiquités,
et al.: G. T. Martin, *The
Royal Tomb at El-'Amarna,*
I–II (London, 1974–89)
Wall documentation:
G. T. Martin, *ibid.*

Akhenaten at Amarna.
(Above) A 'trial-piece' in
limestone from the Amarna
royal tomb, showing the king
and his family offering to the
solar disc. (Left) Fragmentary
faience shabti of Akhenaten
from his Amarna tomb
(below).

Funerary equipment

Most of the finds were
fragmentary. The following
individual items and classes
of object were represented:

Chephren
Vessel fragment (diorite)

Unas?
Vessel fragment (diorite)

Tuthmosis III
Vessel fragment (diorite)

Akhenaten
Sarcophagus (red granite)
Pall sequins (gold, bronze)
Canopic chest (calcite)
Lion bier (limestone)
Embalming blocks (limestone)
Furniture fragment? (wood)
Various boxes and chests (calcite,
faience)
Shabtis (quartzite, sandstone,
granite, limestone, calcite, faience)
Shabti implements (faience)
Model boat (wood)
Sculptor's model (limestone)
Stela (limestone)
Statue fragments (calcite,
limestone)
Uraeus heads (faience)
Inlays (calcite, glass)

Vessels (diorite, limestone,
calcite, faience, pottery)
Jar dockets (pottery)
Jar sealing (mud)
Ostraca (limestone)
Jewellery (gold, carnelian,
turquoise, quartz, steatite,
glass, faience)
Throwstick (faience)
Pounders
(dolerite)
Knife (flint)
Textile

'Meketaten
suite'

Tiye
Sarcophagus

Intrusive
Human remains?
Textiles
Jewellery

Discovery

The royal tomb at Akhenaten's capital city at el-
Amarna was apparently discovered by the locals
around 1887–88, and subsequently explored by
Alessandro Barsanti and others of the Antiquities
Service. The objects and reliefs seemed to indicate
that, although the tomb was never completed, a
number of burials had been made within – including
the king's daughter, Meketaten (in the *alpha, beta,
gamma* suite of rooms), Akhenaten himself (in the
hastily adapted pillared hall beyond the well room),
and the king's mother, Tiye (fragments of whose
sarcophagus, recently and independently identified
by Edwin Brock and Maarten Raven, were found in
the tomb).

Architecture

Different as its plan may be from those of its Theban
precedents, the essential similarity to the established
royal tomb design may be seen in the elevation
drawing of the main axis. The entrance (with the first
New Kingdom royal example of the step-ramp-step
design) is wide (*c.* 3.2 m (10 ft 6 in)) and opens onto a
huge first corridor which basically combines the first
two passages of the normal plan. The two sets of
crudely cut corridors and rooms which branch off
from this corridor are certainly unique, and the
design of the upper suite reflects the elements of a
complete tomb in itself. Cuts in the walls opposite the
doorways to the two subsidiary suites may indicate

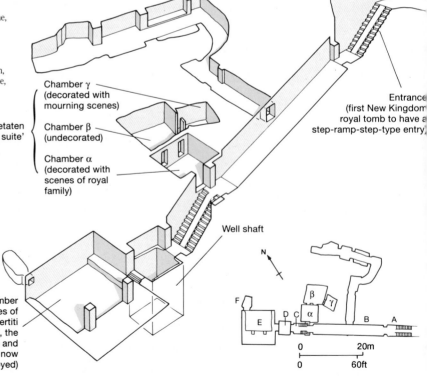

Chamber γ
(decorated with
mourning scenes)

Chamber β
(undecorated)

Chamber α
(decorated with
scenes of royal
family)

Entrance
(first New Kingdom
royal tomb to have a
step-ramp-step-type entry)

Well shaft

Burial chamber
(decorated with scenes of
Akhenaten and Nefertiti
offering to the Aten, the
decoration here and
elsewhere in the tomb is now
almost entirely destroyed)

N

F

β
γ
α

E

D C

B

A

0   20m

0   60ft

that other chambers were also intended on the left-hand side of the tomb. The well room is larger than usual but with a relatively shallow pit (c. 3 m (9 ft 9 1/2 in) deep). This room has a centrally placed exit leading into what was probably intended to be the first pillared hall, but is here adapted (by the removal of two pillars) into a twin-pillared sarcophagus chamber – with a lowered crypt area and sarcophagus plinth. A subsidiary room at the far corner appears to be the beginning of a corridor on an uncompleted bent axis, which if completed would have made this tomb of considerable size. The present straight axis of the tomb is widely believed to have been intended to allow access of the sun's rays to its very back, but the evidence does not support this idea as strongly as might first appear. Akhenaten was buried in the first pillared hall before a bent axis could be cut, and the crypt holding the king's sarcophagus in this pillared hall is offset to one side of the tomb's axis, so that he would not actually have lain in direct alignment with the tomb's entrance or the sun's light.

Decoration

The entrance walls are undecorated, and little now remains of the original decoration in the burial chamber. The painted plaster here was so completely smashed after Akhenaten's reign that only a few cartouches, Aten discs and rays may now be clearly seen around the tops of the walls. Lower sections of the walls retain only traces of Akhenaten and Nefertiti offering to the Aten, which seems to have been the primary decorative motif of this chamber and the well room. As might be expected, given the unsuitability from Akhenaten's 'heretical' point of view of the canonical Egyptian funerary works, relatively few texts seem to have been inscribed in the burial chamber. Among the hieroglyphic traces still evident, however, the name of Nefertiti is surprisingly prominent – indicating the great importance of the queen during this period. Chamber alpha is decorated with scenes of the royal family (including five of the daughters) within a temple court making offerings to the Aten, depicted rising on the east wall and setting on the west. Outside the court, chariots and a military escort also are shown, and in one scene the king, queen and mourners lament the death of a queen or princess while a nurse holds a royal child. Chamber beta is undecorated, but the mourning motif appears again in chamber gamma, where Meketaten is specifically named, and a nurse is also shown with a royal infant – indicating that this particular princess had perhaps died in childbirth.

Although the style of these decorations is clearly similar to that of many of Akhenaten's other monuments, the figures seem to have been somewhat more moderately proportioned and are less caricatured than many from the earlier years of the heresy. Some figures have even been recarved in an effort to modify the earlier style.

wall of limestone resting upon the rubble fill of the stairway beyond. This secondary blocking had itself been breached in antiquity, giving access to a sloping corridor partially filled with limestone chippings which flowed out into the tomb's single chamber.

On top of the corridor fill lay a single door leaf and a large panel from what proved to be a large gilded wooden shrine prepared by Akhenaten for the el-Amarna burial of his mother, Tiye. Further dismantled portions of this shrine were encountered as the excavators gingerly slid their way down the corridor into the burial chamber. The figure and cartouches of the heretic Akhenaten had everywhere been erased from this shrine in ancient times.

'... bits of gold leaf seemed to be flying through the air in every direction. We felt we must be breathing it in. Tyndale whispered to me that he had just sneezed and found seven and six in his handkerchief!'

Charles Trick Currelly

On the southern side of the chamber lay a decayed wooden coffin adorned with crook and flail and carrying an uninscribed bronze uraeus; the cartouches had everywhere been cut out, and the gold face mask brutally torn away below the eyes. Within, slightly displaced, lay a mummy 'crowned' by a gold vulture pectoral and with one arm crossed over the breast. A large niche (the barely begun entrance to a side room) in the south wall contained four calcite canopic jars with portrait-head stoppers, and scattered to the four cardinal points among the debris were four mud 'magical bricks' and a range of other broken funerary items.

A recent sifting of the tomb by Lyla Pinch Brock has turned up further interesting objects. These include a possible fragment of the original hard plaster door sealing, with the remains of a practically illegible impression, blue painted pottery fragments, and a hieratic docket and mud seal

Harold Jones's drawing of Queen Tiye on the dismantled shrine found in KV55. The shrine was commissioned by Akhenaten for the burial of his mother, who is shown in characteristic Amarna style.

The burial chamber of KV55. The coffin is beneath the 'niche' containing its canopic jars; the positions of the sections of Tiye's shrine show that it had originally occupied the centre of the chamber.

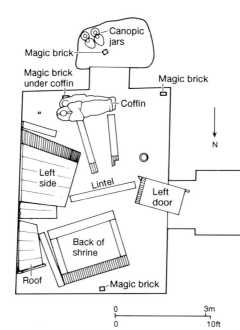
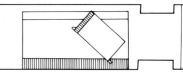

Factfile

Tomb number/location:
KV55, Wadi Biban el-Muluk
Date of discovery:
January 1907, by Edward R. Ayrton
Excavator/report:
E. R. Ayrton, 1907/8, for Theodore M. Davis: Th. M. Davis *et al., The Tomb of Queen Tiyi* (London, 1910)

(Above) Possible plan of KV55, on an ostracon and (above right) plan of the main finds as encountered by Davis.

mentioning 'an estate in Sinai and another estate belonging to Sitamun, a daughter of Amenhotep III.' Most interesting of all is a limestone chip with what may be part of a working plan of the tomb, found by Earl Ertman in the back of the 'canopic niche'.

Whose body?

'Are you sure that the bones you sent me are those which were found in the tomb? Instead of the bones of an old woman, you have sent me those of a young man. Surely there is some mistake.'

Grafton Elliot Smith, letter to Arthur Weigall

Theodore Davis was thrilled at the possibility of having discovered the burial of Queen Tiye, and he at first accepted that the coffined body and calcite canopic jars found in Tomb 55 were hers. Although he was soon forced to change his opinion since the body was evidently male, the find was published in 1910 as *The Tomb of Queen Tiyi*.

Almost a century later, no consensus has yet been reached on the nature of the discovery or the identity of the mummy. What is clear is that the finds fall into two main groups: the first comprising the shrine and a number of minor items of funerary furniture, which may be associated with the burial of Queen Tiye; the second comprising the coffined mummy, canopic jars and magic bricks.

The presence of Tiye's dismantled shrine seems to indicate her original presence in the tomb, though her mummy and most of her funerary equipment were absent, having perhaps been removed when KV55 was stumbled upon by workmen quarrying the overlying tomb of Ramesses IX (KV6) (p. 169). The shrine itself had been abandoned when the workers realized that it could not be extracted without fully clearing the corridor fill. The mummy of Tiye was identified a few years ago, on the basis of the Tiye hair sample found in the tomb of Tutankhamun, with the 'Elder Lady' from the Amenophis II cache (KV35) in 1898 – but the equation has not been universally accepted.

As for the Tomb 55 coffin and canopic jars, these had been prepared originally for a secondary wife of Akhenaten named Kiya, who appears to have fallen from grace sometime after Year 11 of the king's reign. Kiya seems never to have employed the items, and, adapted for their new, kingly owner, they were subsequently employed for the burial found in KV55. Unfortunately, the names of this last owner had been excised from the coffin (the jars

Finds from Tomb 55

Items from KV55: (below) a seal with cryptographic version of the throne name of Amenophis III, and (bottom) a 'magic brick' inscribed with the throne name of Akhenaten.

Object	Names
Shrine and shrine fittings (wood – gilded – bronze)	Amenophis III, Tiye, Akhenaten
Pall rosettes (gold, bronze)	
Bier fragment (gold)	
Coffin and coffin fittings (wood – gilded and inlaid – bronze)	Akhenaten?
Uraeus (bronze) (from statue?)	Aten (late form)
Statue socle (wood)	
Bes figures (faience)	
Earring fasteners (gold)	
Vulture collar (gold)	
Floral collar (gold – inlaid)	
Misc. necklace ornaments, plaques, amulets and beads (gold, lapis lazuli, carnelian, felspar, glass, faience)	(one) Aten (early form)
Foil fragment (gold)	Aten (early form)
Uraeus heads (faience) (from shrine?)	
Canopic jars (calcite)	[Akhenaten, Kiya]
Vessels and lids (haematite, 'amazonite', calcite, glass, faience, pottery)	inc. Amenophis III, Tiye, Sitamun
Head of a goose (silver – from vessel?)	
Boxes and furniture fragments (wood, bronze)	
Hieratic label (wood)	
Tools and fragments (wood, bronze)	
Magic bricks (mud)	Akhenaten
Pesesh-kaf amulets (schist)	(one) Tiye
Model knives, boomerangs, grapes, papyrus rolls, boxes (limestone, faience)	
Misc. 'ritual' items – bricks, pebbles etc.	
Small sealings (clay)	inc. Amenophis III, Tutankhamun
Ostracon with plan (limestone)	

NB Items from the 'Harold Jones collection' in Swansea have no demonstrable connection with KV55

had never been reinscribed), presumably at the time the burial of Tiye was removed from the tomb.

The inscriptions on the magic bricks suggest that the coffin, jars and body ought to be those of Akhenaten himself. Both he and Tiye had originally been buried in the same chamber of the royal tomb at Amarna (p. 118) and, to judge from the seal impressions sifted by Ayrton from the KV55 floor debris, both had been transferred to Thebes (on separate occasions?) by Tutankhamun following the abandonment of the new capital at Akhetaten (Amarna). Indeed, close physical similarities have been observed between the decayed KV55 body and the mummy of Akhenaten's putative son, Tutankhamun, while both corpses shared the same blood group (A_2MN).

'The body was lying in a coffin inscribed with Akhnaton's name; it was bound around with ribbons inscribed with his name; it had the physical characteristics of the portraits of Akhnaton; it had the idiosyncracies of a religious reformer such as he was; it was that of a man of Akhnaton's age as deduced from the monuments; it lay in the tomb of Akhnaton's mother; those who erased the names must have thought it to be Akhnaton's body, unless one supposes an utter chaos of cross-purposes in their actions; and finally, there is nobody else who, with any degree of probability, it could be.'

Arthur Weigall

Weigall's argument is compelling, despite the latest low estimates put forward for the corpse's age at death, ranging between 20 and 25/26, which seem to conflict with the archaeological analysis. The accuracy of these estimates has yet to be proven. Until it is, Akhenaten, on balance, is who our mummy must be.

Architecture

The entrance stair is cut well into the overhanging rock and thus is comparable in design to those of royal tombs in the valley; yet the overall size and form of the tomb are clearly closer to those of a private burial. The single sloping passage and burial chamber resemble the core elements of Tutankhamun's tomb, itself of private origin, although the dimensions of these elements in KV55 are somewhat larger and more impressive and may indicate by their scale an uncompleted royal sepulchre. The fragment of a tomb plan found in KV55 in 1993, on a limestone flake, may show the intended widening of the main entrance, as might masons' marks outside the entrance to the tomb. The small canopic niche in the tomb chamber seems to be the initial opening for an intended side room. And red masons' marks may also indicate where another room was planned in roughly the same position as the annexe in Tutankhamun's tomb.

Unusually, the chamber walls of KV55 were plastered (but left undecorated), possibly indicating the intention to utilize a private tomb for a royal burial as evidently occurred in the tomb of Tutankhamun.

(Left) Pectoral ornament of thick sheet gold, found bent around the head of the coffined mummy.

(Below) The reconstructed Tomb 55 coffin lid. The sheet-gold face mask had been torn off in antiquity (top), and the inlaid cartouches identifying the occupant excised (above).

Tutankhamun and His Successors

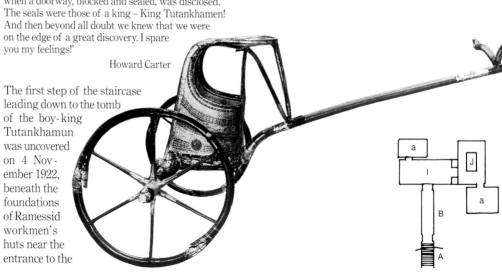

Factfile

Tomb number/location:
KV62, Wadi Biban el-Muluk
Date of discovery:
4 November 1922, by
Howard Carter
Royal mummy:
found *in situ* in 1922;
mummy still in KV62
Excavator/reports:
H. Carter, 1923–32, for the
fifth Earl of Carnarvon: H.
Carter (and A. C. Mace),
*The Tomb of
Tut.ankh.Amen*, I–III
(London, 1923–33); C. N.
Reeves, *The Complete
Tutankhamun* (London,
1990)
Wall documentation:
C. N. Reeves, *ibid.*, pp. 72–4

Towards the end of Akhenaten's reign, the heretic seems to have taken as coregent his wife, Nefertiti, who may well have gone on to rule as pharaoh in her own right (under the name Smenkhkare) following the death of Akhenaten in his 17th regnal year. With the death of Smenkhkare (whose tomb has never been found), the Egyptian throne passed in *c*. 1333 BC to a child no more than nine years of age – Tutankhaten, the only son of Akhenaten, perhaps by the lesser queen, Kiya. In Year 2, Tutankhaten changed his name to Tutankhamun, signalling the abandonment of the Aten's dominance and a return to orthodox religious practice. During much of the reign, power was wielded by two high officials, Ay and Horemheb; one after the other, they would accede to the throne following the boy-king's suspiciously early death in 1323 BC. The reign of Ay (who is recognized by some as the father of Nefertiti) was short – a mere four years – and the royal mummy was interred in the king's small, unfinished tomb in the West Valley (WV23).

The Tomb of Tutankhamun (KV62)

Discovery

'All next day we worked at high pressure, and ere long uncovered what proved to be a sunken staircase cut in the living rock of the valley's bed. The deeper we descended the more evident it became that a find of importance was before us. It was late in the evening when a doorway, blocked and sealed, was disclosed. The seals were those of a king – King Tutankhamen! And then beyond all doubt we knew that we were on the edge of a great discovery. I spare you my feelings!'

Howard Carter

The first step of the staircase leading down to the tomb of the boy-king Tutankhamun was uncovered on 4 November 1922, beneath the foundations of Ramessid workmen's huts near the entrance to the

Annexe
(for Carter equivalent to one of the side rooms off the burial chamber in a full-sized tomb, containing a mix of objects ranging from jars of wine and funerary provisions to jars of oils and unguents and boxes, chairs, bedsteads and stools)

Objects from the tomb of Tutankhamun. (Clockwise from top) Head in gessoed wood of Tutankhamun as the sun-god Re bursting forth from the primeval lotus; gilded wooden figure of a king standing on the back of a large feline; Tutankhamun's gilded canopic shrine and its four protective goddesses; a life-sized mannequin for the pharaoh's clothes, of gessoed and painted wood; and the king's first state chariot, of gilded and inlaid bentwood.

(Centre) The small, private tomb adapted and extended for Tutankhamun's use, with its burial furniture shown in position.

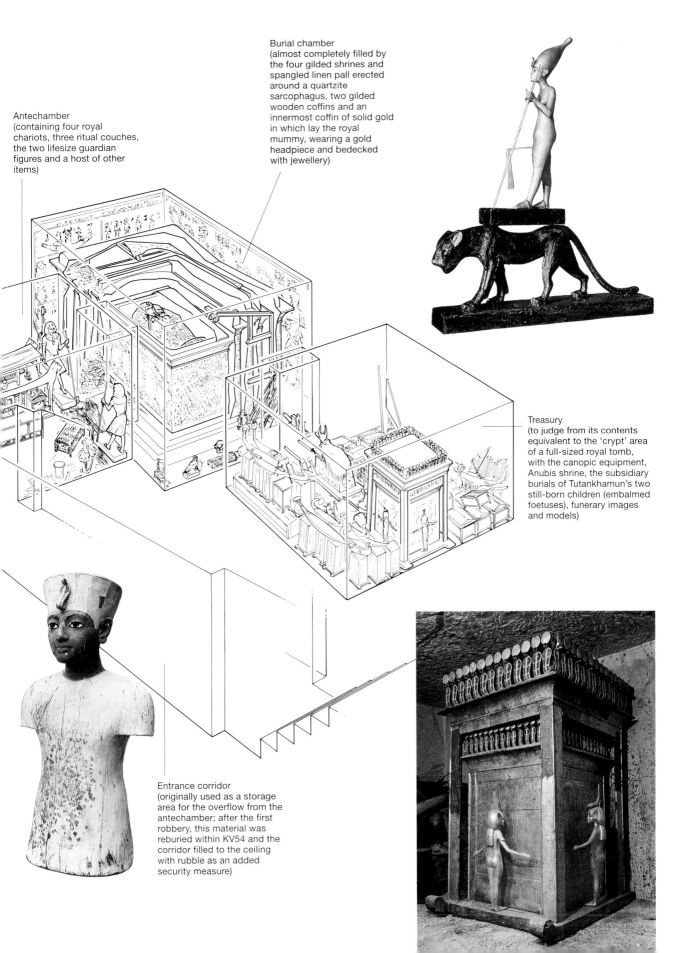

Antechamber
(containing four royal chariots, three ritual couches, the two lifesize guardian figures and a host of other items)

Burial chamber
(almost completely filled by the four gilded shrines and spangled linen pall erected around a quartzite sarcophagus, two gilded wooden coffins and an innermost coffin of solid gold in which lay the royal mummy, wearing a gold headpiece and bedecked with jewellery)

Treasury
(to judge from its contents equivalent to the 'crypt' area of a full-sized royal tomb, with the canopic equipment, Anubis shrine, the subsidiary burials of Tutankhamun's two still-born children (embalmed foetuses), funerary images and models)

Entrance corridor
(originally used as a storage area for the overflow from the antechamber; after the first robbery, this material was reburied within KV54 and the corridor filled to the ceiling with rubble as an added security measure)

tomb of Ramesses VI. By the following day, 5 November, the outer blocking had been revealed and Lord Carnarvon was wired in England. With his arrival, work began on emptying the corridor of its rubble fill; and by 26 November – 'the day of days' – Carter, Carnarvon, Arthur Callender and Lady Evelyn Herbert were able to poke their flickering candle through into the outermost room (the antechamber) and gasp with stupefaction. They were witnesses to an impossible vision: a virtually intact royal tomb, just dripping with gold, from one of the highest points of Egyptian civilization.

'At first I could see nothing, the hot air escaping from the chamber causing the candle flame to flicker, but presently, as my eyes grew accustomed to the light, details of the room within emerged slowly from the mist, strange animals, statues, and gold – everywhere the glint of gold.'

Howard Carter

The clearance of the tomb and the final preparations for transporting the finds to Cairo would take almost a decade of Carter's life. The cost for Carnarvon would be dearer still: bitten by a mosquito (for some, the agent of Pharaoh's revenge), septicaemia set in, Carnarvon sickened, and death soon followed – on 5 April 1923.

(Above right) Tutankhamun receiving life from Hathor in her guise as Mistress of the West. From the south wall of the burial chamber.

(Left) The second of Tutankhamun's life-sized wooden guardian statues, the flesh painted with a treacly black resin and the regalia covered with thick gold leaf. The eyes are inlaid.

Architecture and decoration

While in its essential plan and dimensions KV62 is not unlike private tombs of the period, its complexity is unparalleled among those structures. As Carter pointed out, by rotating the chambers 90 degrees, KV62 could be seen to resemble the typical royal groundplan of the 18th dynasty, and this fact might well indicate the architectural goal of the ancient architects faced with the adaptation of a preexisting private tomb.

After the entrance stairway, the single passage descends to the antechamber with its annexe and, to the right, the sunken burial chamber with the subsidiary room known as the treasury. These last two rooms may have been added at the time of the king's death.

Only the burial chamber received decoration, and this is very similar to that later encountered in the tomb of Ay (p. 128). There is no *khekher*-frieze or dado, and the walls all share the same uniform golden ground. On the west wall are depicted the apes of the first hour of the Amduat (p. 39); on the south wall the king is followed by Anubis as he appears before Hathor, Mistress of the West; while on the north wall the king appears before Nut in a similar manner and, again, with the royal *ka* embracing Osiris. Further along this same wall King Ay performs the opening of the mouth ceremony before the mummy of Tutankhamun, thereby establishing his claim to the throne.

On the east wall, Tutankhamun's mummy is

shown being pulled along on a sledge in the procession to the necropolis (p. 45) – the funerary cortège including the two viziers (distinguished by their dress) and a single, final figure who is perhaps to be identified as the general and future king, Horemheb. Although such representations of the funerary procession are common in private tombs of the New Kingdom, they are otherwise unattested in the royal necropolis.

The south wall of the burial chamber shows Tutankhamun welcomed into the realms of the underworld by Hathor, Anubis and Isis standing behind him (the figure of Isis was destroyed when the plastered partition wall was dismantled to allow the extraction of the shrines).

All the figures in this tomb are rather curiously represented, with those of the north, east and west walls being depicted with the exceptional proportions current during the Amarna period, and those of the south in more traditional style.

The burial of an Egyptian king

With the discovery of Tutankhamun's tomb it was possible to see for the very first time the riches of an Egyptian royal burial – and they were immense. More staggering still is the realization that Tutankhamun was a young and relatively minor king, and that space within his tomb was severely restricted. Imagine the wealth once stored in a tomb the size of that of Ramesses II!

Robberies

'Plunderers had entered . . . , and entered . . . more than once.'

Howard Carter

One of the most interesting aspects of the Tutankhamun burial is the evidence it preserved of at least two robberies, carried out within a short time of the interment and perhaps by individuals drawn from the burial party.

At the time of the first break-in the entrance corridor was empty, save for jars of embalming material and other items which had been stored there for want of space within the tomb proper. Both the outer and inner corridor blockings were broken through at the top left hand corner, giving access to the antechamber which the robbers ransacked primarily for metal but also linen, oils and perfumes. The robbery was soon discovered, order restored, the corridor emptied of funerary goods (and the materials reburied in pit KV54), filled up to the roof with limestone chippings, and the tomb resealed with the seal of the necropolis administration.

A short time later, the tomb was clearly entered again, though this time with far more difficulty than previously since the thieves now had to burrow through the corridor fill. This second band of robbers gained access to the entire tomb, and among their booty was perhaps 60 per cent of the jewellery stored in the treasury. They evidently

(Above) Detail of the king's outermost coffin of gilded wood.

(Left) Feather-block of a richly decorated fan inlaid with the cartouches of Tutankhamun.

The Lost Tomb of Smenkhkare

The name 'Smenkhkare' may well conceal the identities of not one but two rulers of the late 18th dynasty: Ankhkheprure Nefernefruaten, who is very probably identical to Nefertiti, wife of the heretic Akhenaten who seems to have ruled as coregent with her husband; and Ankhkheprure Smenkhkare, who may either be identical with Ankhkheprure Nefernefruaten or represent a separate, male king. The fact that no items of funerary equipment inscribed for Ankhkheprure Smenkhkare have so far been found, while items of clearly feminine funerary material, some inscribed with the name Ankhkheprure Nefernefruaten, were discarded, to be adapted for Tutankhamun's eventual use, might weigh in favour of regarding 'Smenkhkare' as a single individual buried under that name.

Since nothing is known of these burial arrangements – the old association of Smenkhkare with Tomb KV55 (p. 117) being without foundation – could the tomb of Smenkhkare still await discovery? And could it perhaps be intact? The answer to both of these questions is a tentative 'yes'.

The absence of funerary objects bearing the name of this king is highly suggestive, as is the fact that the part of the valley in which one might expect the burial to have been made – the central area, bordered on two sides by KV62 and the KV55 cache – appears never to have been fully cleared.

The king's mummified head, showing the poor state of preservation owing to the over-liberal application of unguents.

entered the tomb at least twice; on the last occasion they must have been apprehended: a knotted scarf filled with booty – eight gold rings – had been confiscated by the authorities and casually tossed back into one of the antechamber boxes. The breached entrances to the burial chamber and at either end of the entrance corridor were closed and resealed with the same jackal-and-nine-captives motif, and the hole dug through the corridor fill reblocked. One of the officials involved with this restoration was the scribe Djehutymose, of whom Carter had earlier found traces, together with his chief Maya, in the tomb of Tuthmosis IV (KV43). Here, in the tomb of Tutankhamun, Djehutymose repacked in a rough-and-ready manner the items the robbers had displaced, and docketed the boxes with their new contents; he left no official record of his visit, but contented himself with a scribbled name in hieratic on the undersurface of a calcite jar stand.

Although the outer shrines had been opened, the robbers had not progressed as far as the king's mummy – the burial proper was intact.

Shabti figure of gilded wood with feminine characteristics, from the tomb of Tutankhamun.

Factfile

Tomb number/location:
KV54, Wadi Biban el-Muluk
Date of discovery:
21 December 1907, by Edward R. Ayrton
Excavators/report:
E. R. Ayrton, December 1907, for Theodore M. Davis; Herbert E. Winlock, *Materials Used at the Embalming of King Tut-'ankh-Amun* (New York, 1941)

Miniature gilded mask from KV54, originally intended for the second of the two foetuses found in KV62.

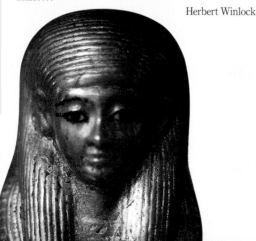

The Embalming Cache

'Originally the jars contained perhaps more than half a dozen flower collars that had been worn by those present at the banquet. Some were torn by Mr. Davis to show how strong they still were. . . . Three have survived almost intact . . .'

Herbert Winlock

Little more than a small abandoned pit, KV54 was pressed into use shortly after the burial of Tutankhamun within KV62, and following the first robbery. The contents consisted of a dozen or so large storage jars containing among other things small clay seal impressions bearing the name of Tutankhamun, fragments of linen bearing hieratic dockets dating to Years 6 and 8 of the reign, some 50 bags of natron (the naturally occurring salt used in embalming), 180 or more linen bandages, 72 offering cups, bones from numerous joints of meat, faded floral collars and a gilded cartonnage mask from the foetus of Tutankhamun's second still-born child. Clearly this was a mix of embalming refuse and materials left over from the funerary meal, which seems originally to have been stored in the corridor of the tomb, and to have been transferred when it was filled with rubble. Most of what Davis spared was rescued by the American Egyptologist Herbert Winlock and is now in the Metropolitan Museum of Art in New York.

(Above) One of two similar staffs, in gold and in silver, surmounted by images of Tutankhamun as a child-pharaoh.

(Left) Tutankhamun's magnificent innermost coffin, fashioned from 2.5–3-cm-thick gold sheet, its surface richly chased and discreetly inlaid.

(Below) The exquisitely carved sarcophagus of red quartzite. Despite a change in the decorative scheme, there is no evidence that the coffer had ever been intended for anyone other than Tutankhamun himself.

Finds from Tutankhamun's Tomb

Object class	Entrance staircase	Corridor	Antechamber	Burial chamber	Treasury	Annexe
Archery equipment		•	•		•	•
Baskets			•			•
Beds			•			•
Bier				•		
Boat models					•	•
Boomerangs and throwsticks			•			•
Botanical specimens		•	•			•
Boxes and chests	•		•		•	•
Canopic equipment					•	
Chairs and stools			•			•
Chariot equipment			•		•	•
Clothing			•	•		•
Coffins (king)				•		
Coffins (other)					•	
Cosmetic objects		•	•			•
Cuirass						•
Divine figures			•	•	•	
Fans			•	•	•	
Foodstuffs			•		•	•
Gaming equipment		•	•			•
Gold mask				•		
Granary model					•	
Hassocks			•			
Jewellery, beads, amulets	•	•	•	•	•	•
Labels		•	•		•	•
Lamps and torches			•	•		•
Mummies				•		
Musical instruments			•			•
Pall and framework				•		
Portable pavilion			•			
Regalia			•		•	•
Ritual couches			•			
Ritual objects			•		•	•
Royal figures		?	•		•	•
Sarcophagus				•		
Sealings	•	•	•		•	•
Shabtis and related objects		•		•	•	•
Shields			•			•
Shrines			•	•	•	•
Sticks and staves			•		•	•
Swords and daggers			•			•
Tools					•	•
Vessels	•	•	•		•	•
Wine jars	•	•	•		•	•
Writing equipment			•		•	•

Factfile

Tomb number/location:
WV23, West Valley
Date of discovery:
winter 1816, by Giovanni
Battista Belzoni
Royal mummy:
not identified
Excavators/reports:
G. B. Belzoni, 1816, for
Henry Salt: G. B. Belzoni,
*Narrative of the Operations
and Recent Discoveries in
Egypt and Nubia* (London,
1820) pp. 123–4; Otto J.
Schaden, 1972, for
University of Minnesota: O.
J. Schaden, *JARCE* 21 (1984)
pp. 39–64
Wall documentation:
Alexandre Piankoff,
MDAIK 16 (1958) pp.
247–51

The entrance to the tomb of Ay photographed prior to its recent, drastic remodelling by the Supreme Council of Antiquities.

The Tomb of Ay (WV23)

'[WV23] contains a broken sarcophagus and some bad fresco painting of peculiarly short and graceless proportions. Of the æra of the king whose name here occurs, I have only been able to ascertain that he was prior to Remeses II., and probably by several ages.'

John Gardner Wilkinson

Discovery

The discovery of the tomb of Ay, in the winter of 1816, Belzoni owed 'merely to fortune, not to any premeditated research, as I went into these mountains [of the West Valley] only to examine the vari-ous places, where the water descends from the desert into the valleys after rain'.

'I cannot boast of having made a great discovery in this tomb, though it contains several curious and singular painted figures on the walls; and from its extent, and part of a sarcophagus remaining in the centre of a large chamber, have reason to suppose, that it was the burial-place of some person of distinction.'

The tomb was cleared fully by Otto Schaden in the summer of 1972, who found firm evidence that it had been employed for a burial – notably traces (though no seal impressions) of a plastered blocking at the entrance to room E, together with remains of 18th-dynasty funerary equipment (below). The tomb has recently been drastically 'restored' – much to the detriment of its archaeology – for opening to tourists.

Architecture

As one might expect, the tomb of Ay exhibits more similarity with the tomb of Akhenaten at el-Amarna than with the earlier tombs of the 18th dynasty. The corridors continue the trend of enlargement, and are even wider than those in the tomb of Amenophis III, if not quite as high. In the first passage, sarcophagus holds – slots cut into the walls to hold a beam used in lowering the heavy stone sarcophagus into the tomb – appear for the first time since their possible use in KV20 (p. 91). No shaft was cut in the well chamber and the exit doorway is positioned, uniquely, on the right-hand side of the wall. What would have been the pillared hall was adapted as the burial chamber, and only a small, 'canopic' chamber was cut beyond this point. As in the Amarna royal tomb, the axis remains straight although, as there, the burial itself was off-set from the axis.

The sarcophagus of Ay had been badly damaged in antiquity (below), but the principal fragments have now been reassembled (right). The lid was recovered by Otto Schaden upturned within the burial chamber in 1972.

Decoration

There are many similarities in the decorative programmes of the burial chambers (the only part of these tombs to be painted) of Ay and his predecessor Tutankhamun, and it is probable that both monuments were decorated by the same artists. In each tomb the *khekher*-frieze is absent, and several of the scenes are virtually identical. Even the famous scene found on the east wall of the burial chamber of WV23 – the only marsh hunting scene on the walls of a New Kingdom royal tomb – is paralleled by the scene of Tutankhamun hunting wild birds on the famous 'little golden shrine', as well as in two statues depicting the king standing with a spear in a small papyrus skiff (p. 41).

The representations of Ay were almost entirely hacked out in antiquity, save one of the royal *ka* figures which was left intact and another which was only slightly damaged, perhaps indicating reverence for other royal ancestors fused in the *ka*. At the end of this same west wall, above the doorway into the canopic chamber, the four sons of Horus (protective deities for the royal internal organs) are depicted for the first time in a royal tomb.

Funerary equipment

Belzoni's work appears to have brought to light little more than the broken sarcophagus. This was removed from the tomb at the end of the last century for restoration and exhibition, and has recently been reinstalled and surmounted by the lid discovered in 1972 during Schaden's clearance. Other items brought to light by Schaden include fragments of wooden deity-figures, several gilded copper pall rosettes and fragmentary human remains of uncertain origin, as well as intrusive pottery of late New Kingdom and Roman date.

The fate of Ay's burial

The extensive damage to the side of the sarcophagus box perhaps indicates robber-activity in the tomb during the Ramessid period, activity which may in turn have brought the tomb to the notice of the authorities and resulted in the post-mortem execration of Ay's memory reflected in the erasures of the burial chamber and sarcophagus. Was Ay's mummy destroyed at this time? Probably not.

The contents of pit-tomb KV58 (p. 186) included a number of crumpled-up sheets of thin gold foil,

in a variety of shapes and embossed with a range of decorative motifs. These, together with three or four calcite knobs and two faience box handles, had been dumped or washed into the tomb's open shaft in antiquity. The name of Tutankhamun occurred three times (twice with that of Akhnesenamun), that of Ay before his elevation to the throne four times, and Ay's name as king a further three times.

The assemblage evidently originates from a single source – the West Valley tomb of Ay – and was deposited in KV58 at the end of the New Kingdom, at the time the tombs in the necropolis were being dismantled. Its presence in KV58 may reflect the reinterment of Ay's body in nearby KV57, which other indications suggest was perhaps being employed as a cache at this time (p. 204).

(Above) This scene with the four sons of Horus above the entry to the canopic chamber is unique in the royal valley.

(Below) WV23, though never completed, shows the characteristic post-Amarna straightening of the axis.

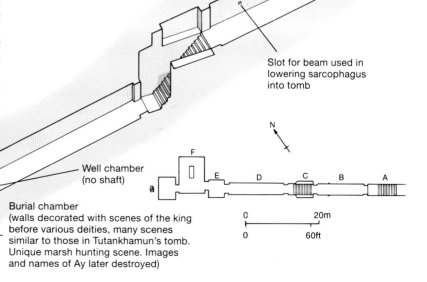

Entrance

Slot for beam used in lowering sarcophagus into tomb

Niches for magic bricks

Sarcophagus of Ay

Well chamber (no shaft)

Burial chamber (walls decorated with scenes of the king before various deities, many scenes similar to those in Tutankhamun's tomb. Unique marsh hunting scene. Images and names of Ay later destroyed)

Canopic chamber (undecorated)

N

F E D C B A
a

0   20m
0   60ft

Horemheb to Sethos I

(Above) A shattered portrait-headed canopic stopper from Horemheb's tomb.

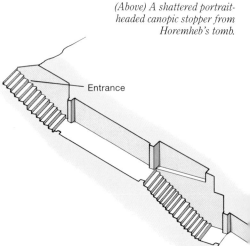

Entrance

Factfile

Tomb number/location:
KV57, Wadi Biban el-Muluk
Date of discovery:
22 February 1908, by Edward R. Ayrton
Royal mummy:
not identified
Excavator/report:
E. R. Ayrton, 1908, for Theodore M. Davis: Th. M. Davis *et al., The Tombs of Harmhabi and Touatânkhamanou* (London, 1912)
Wall documentation:
Erik Hornung, *Das Grab des Haremhab im Tal der Könige* (Bern, 1971)

Horemheb, who followed Ay, had been commander-in-chief of the army during both preceding reigns. His succession in 1319 BC, which may have been less than smooth, marked a final break with the hated Amarna heresy. He was consequently looked upon by the Egyptians as founder of a new dynasty, the 19th.

With the death of Horemheb (who, like all subsequent New Kingdom pharaohs, returned to the main Valley of the Kings to prepare his tomb, KV57), the throne passed in 1307 BC to Ramesses I, another military officer of non-royal birth. Ramesses I's son by Queen Sitre was to rule as Sethos I (1306–1290 BC), and Sethos's tomb (as magnificent as his father's was modest) was brought to light by Belzoni in 1816.

Sethos I's rule ushered in a revival of Egyptian fortunes on the battlefield, re-establishing for a time Egyptian control as far north as Qadesh on the Orontes. The town would find lasting fame as the site of his son and successor Ramesses II's indecisive battle against the Hittites in Year 5 of his reign. Heralded by Ramesses as a great victory, it was in fact little more than a holding action, and a lasting peace with the enemy could not be achieved for a further 16 years.

The Tomb of Horemheb (KV57)

'... here, where vivid and well-preserved wall-paintings looked down on a jumbled collection of smashed fragments of wood and bones, one felt how hardly the Powers deal with the dead. How far away seemed the great fight between Amon and Aton; how futile the task which Horemheb accomplished so gloriously!'

Arthur Weigall

Discovery

The tomb of Horemheb was brought to light in 1908 opposite the tomb of Ramesses III. Slowly the steps leading down to the doorway were uncovered, and the excavators were able to peer through the gloom into a corridor, almost entirely choked with rubble. Two days later this scree, which continued as far as the partially filled 'well', had been cleared and it was possible to proceed. As Weigall records:

'The party which made the entrance consisted of Mr Davis; his assistant, Mr Ayrton; Mr Max Dalison, formerly of the Egypt Exploration Fund; and myself. Wriggling and crawling, we pushed and pulled ourselves down the sloping rubbish, until, with a rattling avalanche of small stones, we arrived at the bottom of the passage, where we scrambled to our feet at the brink of a large rectangular well, or shaft. Holding the lamps aloft, the surrounding walls were seen to be covered with wonderfully preserved paintings executed on slightly raised plaster. Here Horemheb was seen standing before Isis, Osiris, Horus, and other gods; and his cartouches stood out boldly from amidst the elaborate inscriptions.'

Panting heavily from the intense heat and bad air, the perspiration streaming down their faces, the explorers pressed on, climbing down into the well by means of a ladder and climbing up the opposite side. The further wall of the well had originally been blocked, concealing the fact that the corridor continued beyond; this decorated blocking had been breached, however, and the excavators were able to enter the simple chamber beyond, in the floor of which was cut a flight of stairs (again originally concealed) leading into a further corridor, another flight of steps and a final antechamber (originally fitted with a wooden door sealed around the edges), decorated like the well shaft. Beyond lay the burial chamber (also once fitted with a wooden door) with its six crumbling columns and outlined, unfinished decoration, off which lay an elaborate series of storerooms originally intended for the royal funerary equipment.

Architecture

'The whole tomb is of great interest, as showing the transition from the style of the XVIIIth dynasty to that of the XIXth, the plan and style being intermediate between those of the tombs of Amenhetep III and Sety I.'

Edward Ayrton

The architecture of this tomb is quite new, the 'dog-leg' bend of the characteristic 18th-dynasty tomb having been abandoned in favour of a straight – or more precisely, jogged or parallel – axis. The corridors are long, maintaining the trend of enlargement in their height and width, and still descend with the steepness found in the earlier monuments. The first pillared hall is much more square than before, however, as would be the case in all subsequent tombs; and the burial chamber is notable for a number of rather idiosyncratic design features: the slope from the first pair of pillars to the steps of the 'crypt', the second stair in this area, and the addition of a lower room (Jdd) cut beneath storeroom Jd – all features which do not appear again.

Precise cutting was for the first time attempted, though time evidently ran out before the work

(Above) The red granite sarcophagus in the burial chamber of KV57. The design is transitional, incorporating both pre- and post-Amarna features. The gable-ended lid is unique.

(Below) Though the tomb employs a straightened axis, it retains the steep angle of descent of earlier tombs.

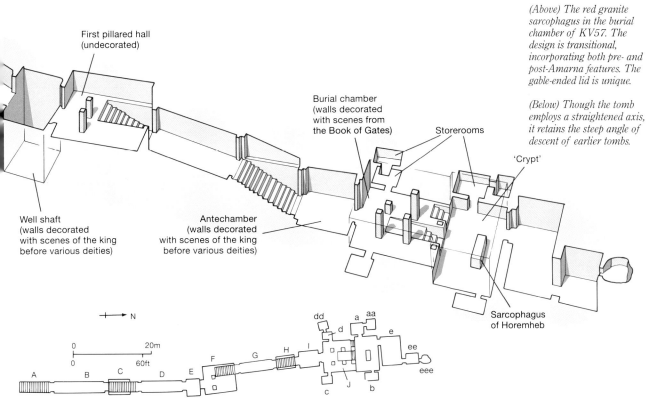

First pillared hall (undecorated)

Burial chamber (walls decorated with scenes from the Book of Gates)

Storerooms

'Crypt'

Well shaft (walls decorated with scenes of the king before various deities)

Antechamber (walls decorated with scenes of the king before various deities)

Sarcophagus of Horemheb

N

0   20m
0   60ft

A   B   C   D   E   F   G   H   I   dd   d   a   aa   e   ee   eee   c   J   b

Scenes from the antechamber of KV57: (right) head of the goddess Isis, showing the exquisite workmanship of the painted reliefs in this tomb; (far right) the god Nefertum, with lotiform headdress symbolizing regeneration and rebirth.

(Below) The king's germinating Osiris bed.

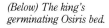

could be completed: unfinished walls are in evidence (with either point-chiselled or flat-chiselled surfaces) and the decoration in the burial chamber (see below) is only partly completed. The tomb thus offers an interesting glimpse of the various stages of work in painted relief – here used for the first time in the Valley of the Kings in preference to mural painting – first the outline grids on the pebble-polished limestone walls, then the freely sketched outlines in red finally corrected in black, then preliminary carving and finally the exquisitely finished, brightly painted reliefs.

Decoration

As in earlier tombs, decoration in the tomb of Horemheb is limited to the well shaft, the antechamber and the burial chamber proper. In the first two areas, similar scenes depict the king appearing before and offering to the gods associated with the hereafter, with the figure of Isis replacing that of Nut found in many of the earlier tombs. These multiple images of the king paired with a protective deity stand in a tradition begun in the tomb of Tuthmosis IV, but here they are produced by more skilful artists who vary the stances, gestures and clothing of the figures, and produce much more dynamic representations. The use of colour is particularly noticeable in this tomb, with multicoloured hieroglyphs and figures accentuated by the blue-grey ground on which they appear. For the first time scenes from the Book of Gates instead of the Amduat were used in the decoration of the

(Left) A ram-headed underworld deity of resin-coated wood, with strangely contorted body.

burial chamber. The figures depicted represent an interesting transition between the late Amarna age and the refined Ramessid style which appears in subsequent tombs.

Funerary equipment

The principal item of funerary furniture still remaining in the burial chamber was the pink granite sarcophagus, containing a skull and several bones, beautifully decorated in delicately painted sunk relief, standing upon a limestone base and 'symbolically supported' by six magical wooden figures (of which five remained *in situ*) set into hollows in the floor on each face. The plain lid, removed in antiquity and thrown to the ground, had shattered across an old break which had previously been repaired by means of butterfly cramps. Additional broken wooden images, resin coated and with yellow detail, royal and divine, were to be seen in the light of the excavators' arc lamps, scattered along with masses of builders' debris and dried floral remains from funerary garlands. Further human remains were recovered from the northeast and lower southwest storerooms.

The royal 'sledge sarcophagus' and coffins were represented by several small fragments of cedar wood and acacia tenons incised with the king's throne name, 'Djeserkheprure-setepenre (heqa maat)', '[Holy are the Manifestations of Re, Chosen of Re (Ruler of Justice)]'. The alabaster canopic chest, with portrait-headed stoppers, smashed and scattered in antiquity, was also recovered and has now been restored. Evidently associated with the canopic chest was a series of four miniature lion-headed embalming tables, again smashed to pieces, which had presumably been employed in the embalming of the king's internal organs, remains of which were also found.

(Left) Further resin-coated wooden images from the tomb (clockwise, from far left): walking feline, originally supporting a statue of the king; hippopotamus head from a large, ritual couch; human- and animal-headed deities, their outstretched hands perhaps originally holding bronze serpents; and an Anubis-dog figure.

Other items of burial equipment included: life-size 'guardian figures'; a hippo-headed couch; a cow-headed couch; a lioness-headed couch; three large Anubis figures, perhaps similar to the one discovered with Tutankhamun surmounting a carrying shrine; a 'germinating Osiris'; 'magical bricks'; model boats; fixed and folding chairs; pall rosettes; faience beads; and wooden and stone containers for embalmed provisions. Of uncertain significance is a single canopic jar with human-headed stopper, of private 18th-dynasty form, inscribed in hieratic 'with the name of a man(?) . . . *Sanoa*, apparently a foreign form'.

Several items from the royal funerary equipment 'leaked' onto the antiquities market at the time of Davis's clearance of the tomb, including a series of wooden funerary statuettes, now in the British Museum, where for many years they were mistakenly labelled as coming from Tuthmosis III's tomb.

For the possible use of KV57 as a cache, see below, p. 204.

(Below) Horemheb makes offerings to Hathor, Mistress of the West, described as 'Chief one of Thebes, lady of heaven, mistress of the gods'.

Factfile

Tomb number/location:
KV16, Wadi Biban el-
Muluk
Date of discovery:
10/11 October 1817, by
Giovanni Battista Belzoni
Royal mummy:
not identified
Excavator/report:
G. B. Belzoni, 1817, for
Henry Salt: G. B. Belzoni,
*Narrative of the Operations
and Recent Discoveries in
Egypt and Nubia* (London,
1820) pp. 229–30
Wall documentation:
Alexandre Piankoff, *BIFAO*
56 (1957) pp. 189–200

*The improvised burial
chamber of Ramesses I, with
sarcophagus and modern
beams supporting the ceiling.
The painted representations
are finished in intense,
saturated hues.*

The Tomb of Ramesses I (KV16)

Discovery and contents

KV16 was discovered by Belzoni's workers in the main valley on or before 11 October 1817, when he visited the site.

'Having proceeded through a passage thirty-two feet long, and eight feet wide, I descended a staircase of twenty-eight feet, and reached a tolerably large and well-painted room . . . seventeen feet long, and twenty-one wide. The ceiling was in good preservation, but not in the best style. We found a sarcophagus of granite, with two mummies in it, and in a corner a statue standing erect, six feet six inches high, and beautifully cut out of sycamore-wood: it is nearly perfect except the nose. We found also a number of little images of wood, well carved, representing symbolical figures. Some had a lion's head, others a fox's, others a monkey's. One had a land-tortoise instead of a head. We found a calf with the head of a hippopotamus. At each side of this chamber is a smaller one, eight feet wide, and seven feet long; and at the end of it another chamber, ten feet long by seven wide. In the chamber on our right hand we found another statue like the first, but not perfect. No doubt they had been placed one on each side of the sarcophagus, holding a lamp or some offering in their hands, one hand being stretched out in the proper posture for this and the other hanging down. The sarcophagus was covered with hieroglyphics merely painted, or outlined: it faces south-east by east.'

Visiting the tomb a few years later, James Burton and Edward William Lane noted the remains of an original plastered blocking at the end of corridor B, though no seal impressions are mentioned.

The sarcophagus displays damage caused in levering off the lid in antiquity to remove the royal mummy at an unrecorded date at the end of the New Kingdom (after which date the tomb was employed for the intrusive burials encountered by Belzoni). Portions of the king's replacement coffin were recovered from the DB320 cache in 1881. Whether or not the royal mummy itself was once present in that tomb is uncertain.

Architecture and decoration

The royal tomb plan was greatly abbreviated in this structure, owing to the elderly Ramesses' short reign: the first corridor is the most abbreviated of any royal tomb in the valley, the two niches at the sides of the second stairway are only half executed, and the improvised burial chamber was cut immediately at the foot of this stairway.

Although only the burial chamber was painted, the artists responsible clearly attempted to imitate and continue the style found in the tomb of Horemheb; presumably, many of them worked on both tombs. Not only is there the same grey-blue background, but intense, saturated hues and a similar choice of colouration are maintained.

Still only a generation removed from the time of the heretical Akhenaten, Ramesses I's artists were careful to avoid the style of that period, portraying their subject-matter with a controlled orthodoxy, though continuing Horemheb's use of the Book of Gates which is not found before the heresy. Various divine scenes, clearly based on those found in KV57 (Horemheb), show the king in the company of a number of deities, with the figures of Pharaoh on the entry walls of the burial chamber being curiously shorter than those of the deities (though in the representations seen on the other walls of this room a clear equality of size is maintained). Pre-eminent is the representation of Ramesses before Osiris and a scarab-headed form of the sun-god which covers most of the west wall of the chamber. Although the symbolic stress on the position of the two deities appears balanced here, the ritual in which the king is engaged is primarily an Osirid one. Above the doorway leading into the Osiris niche in this same wall an unusual depiction shows Pharaoh in a ceremony of jubilation between hawk- and jackal-headed figures representing the spirits of the cities of Nekhen and Pe. These ancestral spirits symbolize the two halves of the land of Egypt and represent one of many examples of the way in which heaven and earth, night and day, and other dichotomous elements are carefully paired in this tomb.

Funerary equipment

The principal item of Ramesses I's funerary equipment to have survived is the red granite sarcophagus, preserved *in situ*. This monument, like the tomb itself, is unfinished, the decoration not carved into the stone but applied in yellow paint – and rather hurriedly at that, to judge from the number of textual errors. The design, which reverts to earlier 18th-dynasty prototypes, is fully preserved on the right-hand side only, though the lost portions happily survive in a copy by Lepsius.

Ramesses I flanked by the falcon-headed 'soul of Pe' and the dog-headed 'soul of Nekhen', representing the traditional regions of Lower and Upper Egypt.

Cutaway view of KV16, clearly showing the manner in which the corridor beyond the second stairway had been hastily adapted as a chamber to receive the king's burial.

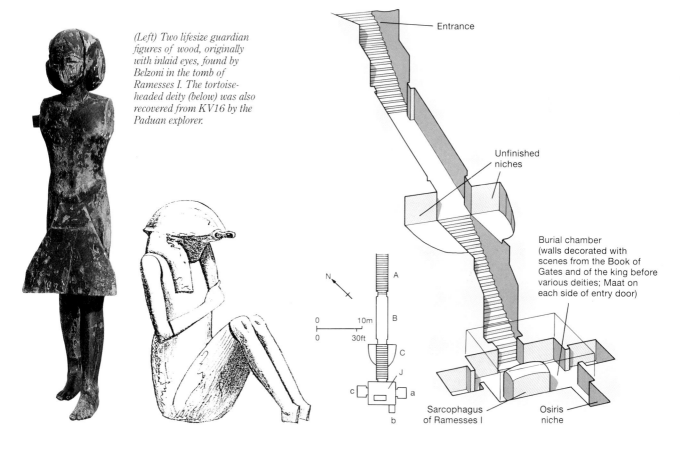

(Left) Two lifesize guardian figures of wood, originally with inlaid eyes, found by Belzoni in the tomb of Ramesses I. The tortoise-headed deity (below) was also recovered from KV16 by the Paduan explorer.

Entrance

Unfinished niches

Burial chamber (walls decorated with scenes from the Book of Gates and of the king before various deities; Maat on each side of entry door)

N

0   10m
0   30ft

Sarcophagus of Ramesses I

Osiris niche

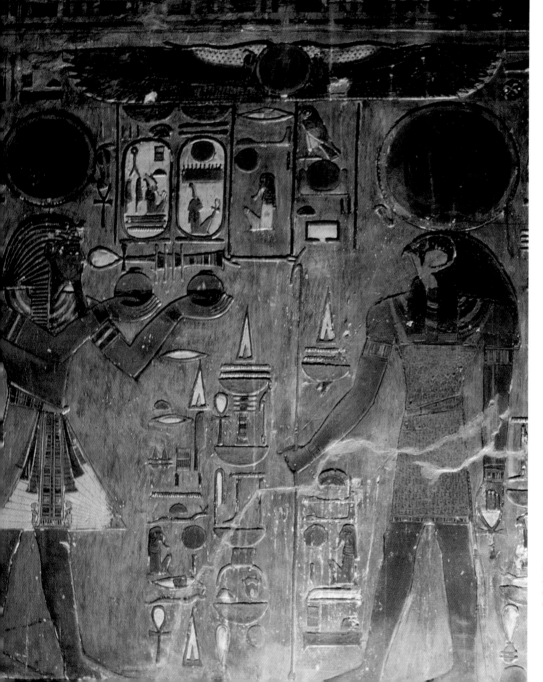

(Above) Kneeling figure of
Isis with wings outstretched,
decorating the tympanum
above the east wall of the
burial chamber in the tomb of
Sethos I.

(Left) Sethos I presents
offerings of wine to Re-
Horakhty in a scene from the
east wall of the burial
chamber.

'Belzoni's Tomb': The Tomb of Sethos I (KV17)

Discovery

'On the 16th [October 1817] I recommenced my excavations in the valley of Beban el Malook, and pointed out the fortunate spot, which has paid me for all the trouble I took in my researches. I may call this a fortunate day, one of the best perhaps of my life . . .'

Giovanni Battista Belzoni

The 'fortunate spot' referred to by Belzoni was the mound of rubble covering the entrance to the tomb of Sethos I (KV17).

The explorer makes no mention of any blocking at the entrance to the tomb, though it is noted that the wall on the far side of the well (which had been negotiated in antiquity by two ropes, found still in position) was closed off and had been penetrated by 'a small aperture'.

Architecture

In complete contrast with the tomb of Ramesses I, structurally the tomb of Sethos I represents the fullest development of royal tomb design in the off-set, or jogged-axis, tombs and is also the longest, deepest and most completely finished of all the tombs in the valley. The basic plan of entrance corridors sloping down to a well shaft and pillared hall is augmented by the addition at this point of a second chamber (perhaps meant to deceive robbers) – an innovation which continues through most of the tombs of the 19th dynasty. The burial chamber is likewise augmented by two pillared subsidiary rooms and a number of ritual niches reminiscent of similar features in the tomb of Amenophis III. For the first time the ceiling of the burial chamber is vaulted. A final innovation is found in the passage which leads down from the floor of the burial crypt, possibly to a real or symbolic burial chamber – note particularly the 'double staircase with ramp' configuration observed by the Theban Mapping Project in 1979 – cut deep in the underlying shale and perhaps intended 'to physically tie the burial place of the king to the primeval waters of Nun, symbolic of creation and rebirth'.

Decoration

'In beauty of execution it far surpasses all the other tombs of Bibân el-Mulûk, and the sculptures on its walls appear to have been executed by the same artists whose works we had the opportunity of admiring at Abydos . . .'

Georg Steindorff

In its decoration, too, the tomb of Sethos I marks an apex of development. It represents the first royal tomb to be decorated throughout all its passages and chambers, and was lavished with extremely fine paintings and reliefs comparable in quality to

The king (on the left with uraeus) before the primeval god Atum: an unfinished scene on a pillar in chamber Fa, sometimes called the 'false burial chamber' of KV17.

those of the king's cenotaph at Abydos. The influence of Horemheb's transitional representations is still felt, though Sethos I's figures exhibit more subtly modelled features, with the larger ears and smaller mouths which form the basis of the new Ramessid style. The decorative programme established here is also followed fully or in part by every succeeding tomb through the rest of the valley's history. For the first time, the Litany of Re appears on the walls of the first two passages, with scenes from the Amduat also in the second passage and at lower points in the tomb. Previously, these works had appeared only in the burial chambers of the royal tombs, and are evidently now given new symbolic emphasis. The well shaft of Sethos I follows the established pattern of scenes showing the king before various gods, but the pillared hall is decorated with scenes from the Book of Gates and with another innovation, the Osiris shrine (p. 36), which marks the transition into the lower reaches of most Ramessid tombs. The lower passages depict scenes from the 'opening of the mouth' ceremony, and the antechamber has various divine scenes similar to those found in Horemheb. In addition to the Book of Gates and Amduat scenes, the burial chamber contains the first occurrence of an astronomical ceiling, with specific constellations of the night sky depicted along with the various decans or calendar units.

Funerary equipment

Belzoni makes mention of several items of burial furniture still present in the tomb at the time of his initial entry, including 'the carcass of a bull . . ., embalmed by asphaltum' in room Je, and (in this same room?) 'an immense quantity of small . . . figures of mummies' – *shabtis* – in wood and faience, while:

'On each side of the two little rooms [Jc and Jd?] were some wooden statues standing erect, four feet high, with a circular hollow inside, as if to contain a roll of papyrus, which I have no doubt they did. We found likewise fragments of other statues of wood and of composition.'

Factfile

Tomb number/location:
KV17, Wadi Biban el-Muluk
Date of discovery:
16 October 1817, by Giovanni Battista Belzoni
Royal mummy:
removed in antiquity; discovered in DB320
Excavator/report:
G. B. Belzoni, 1817, for Henry Salt: G. B. Belzoni, *Narrative of the . . . Discoveries in Egypt and Nubia* (London, 1820) pp. 230–7 and *passim*
Wall documentation:
Erik Hornung, *The Tomb of Pharaoh Seti I* (Zurich and Munich, 1991)

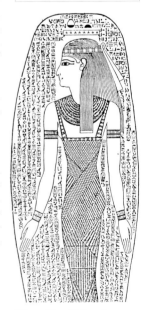

The goddess Nut on the interior of Sethos I's calcite sarcophagus box.

(Above) The ceiling of Sethos I's burial chamber, with astronomical texts shown in the upper half, and constellations flanked by deities in the lower half.

(Below) The mummy of Sethos I following its partial unwrapping by Maspero.

Further broken items from the burial were subsequently recovered by James Burton from the entrance to the tomb, including 'a painting brush with a paint pot or jar'; 'a considerable number of broken jars . . . thrown together in the midst of the shaly earth . . . excavated from the lowest part of the tomb' may have represented the remains of the royal embalming refuse. Other pieces from the tomb have been found widely scattered throughout the Valley of the Kings.

Belzoni's most important find was the magnificent anthropoid sarcophagus of calcite, now in the Soane Museum in London, which is lavishly incised with scenes and texts from the Book of Gates picked out in powdered blue frit. Fragments from its mummiform cover, brought to light at the tomb entrance, show the king wearing the *nemes*-headcloth.

A corner fragment of the king's canopic chest, with cylindrically hollowed interior compartment, is also in the Soane Museum.

The royal mummy

The well-preserved mummy of the king was among the bodies recovered by Émile Brugsch from the Deir el-Bahri royal cache (DB320: p. 194), contained within a version of the original outer wooden coffin which had been restored in or before an unspecified Year 6 by the High Priest of Amun, Herihor. A second restoration seems to have been required after Year 10 and conceivably in Year 15 of Smendes, at the time the mummy of Ramesses II was introduced into KV17. Finally, in Year 7 of Psusennes I, presumably by command of 'King' Pinudjem I, the royal mummy was rewrapped

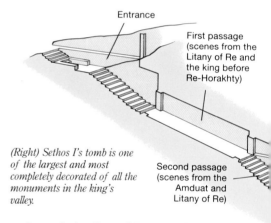

(Right) Sethos I's tomb is one of the largest and most completely decorated of all the monuments in the king's valley.

Entrance

First passage (scenes from the Litany of Re and the king before Re-Horakhty)

Second passage (scenes from the Amduat and Litany of Re)

again employing linen of Year 6 made by the High Priest of Amun, Menkheperre.

A further docket on the king's coffin records the removal of Sethos I from KV17 in Year 10 of Siamun in company with Ramesses I and Ramesses II, and another its reburial three days later in the *kay* of Queen Inhapi (p. 197). By Year 11 of Shoshenq I, Sethos I and the other occupants of the Inhapi cache had been transferred yet again, to DB320 where they eventually came to light in 1881.

As found, the king's mummy was superficially intact, covered in a yellow shroud. Beneath were the remains of the king's original docketed bandages, which had been roughly searched in antiquity for jewellery (overlooking a large *wedjat*-eye on the right forearm and other valuables, only recently revealed by X-rays: p. 204). The head had been detached from the body, and the anterior wall of the abdomen smashed in.

Cenotaphs

Royal cenotaphs (literally 'empty tombs') were dummy sepulchres built at a distance from the real tomb at a place where a king wished to maintain a symbolic presence in the afterlife. In the New Kingdom, the favoured site was Abydos, a site sacred to the god Osiris. The most famous cenotaph is that of Sethos I, associated with the king's Abydos temple.

The cenotaph of Sethos I was a complex underground structure with columns similar to those found in the burial chambers of the Valley of the Kings. Unlike the royal tombs, however, the cenotaph had a false sarcophagus emplacement on an island surrounded by subterranean water which associated the king's 'burial' with both the mythical burial of Osiris and with the forces of original creation. This may explain the strange tunnel which sinks deep beneath the burial chamber of KV17, Sethos I's actual place of burial – for it is possible that this tunnel aimed to reach the deep, underlying groundwater with the same symbolic intent.

(Above) The vaulted burial chamber. The modern barrier in the foreground shields the entrance to the enigmatic passage which descends below the crypt.

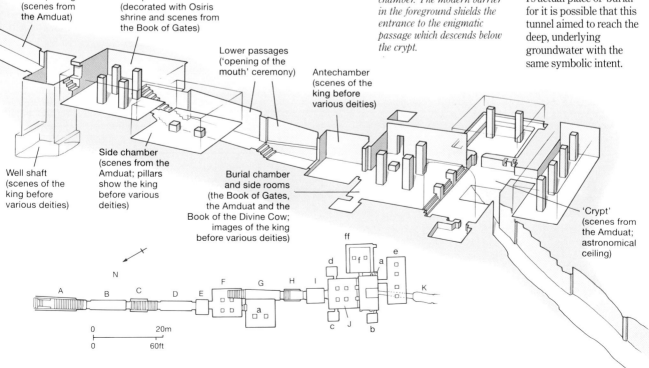

Third passage (scenes from the Amduat)

First pillared hall (decorated with Osiris shrine and scenes from the Book of Gates)

Lower passages ('opening of the mouth' ceremony)

Antechamber (scenes of the king before various deities)

Well shaft (scenes of the king before various deities)

Side chamber (scenes from the Amduat; pillars show the king before various deities)

Burial chamber and side rooms (the Book of Gates, the Amduat and the Book of the Divine Cow; images of the king before various deities)

'Crypt' (scenes from the Amduat; astronomical ceiling)

N

A B C D E F G H I K

ff
d f a e
c J b

0   20m
0   60ft

The Tombs of Ramesses II and His Sons

Factfile

Tomb number/location:
KV7, Wadi Biban el-Muluk
Date of discovery:
open in part since antiquity
Royal mummy:
transferred in antiquity
to KV17; discovered in
DB320
Excavators/reports:
Henry Salt, after 1817:
unpublished; Carl Richard
Lepsius, 1844, for the
Prussian Expedition: C. R.
Lepsius, *Letters from Egypt*
(London, 1853) p. 244;
Harry Burton, 1913/14, for
Theodore M. Davis:
unpublished; Christian
Leblanc, 1995–, for
CNRS/CEDAE: C. Leblanc
EA 8 (1996) p. 14
Wall documentation:
C. Maystre, *BIFAO* 38
(1939) pp. 183–90

Ramesses II fully merits his epithet, 'the Great'. He acceded to the throne in 1290 BC and, during his 67-year reign, built more temples and monuments, took more wives (eight plus concubines) and – according to tradition – sired more children (over 100) than any other pharaoh. His first and favourite royal wife, Nefertari, was buried in the Valley of the Queens in the finest and most beautifully decorated tomb of that necropolis.

Ramesses survived to a great age, over 90, outliving most of his offspring – many of whom, as we know from Kent Weeks's recent discoveries (p. 144), were accorded the privilege of burial in the Valley of the Kings in KV5. It was Ramesses's 13th son, Merenptah, who finally succeeded him as pharaoh in 1224 BC, by which time Merenptah himself was over 60. Merenptah had to contend with incursions from Libya and from the 'Sea Peoples' in the north, and possible rumblings of dissension from the family at home. He was interred in a tomb (KV8) close to that of his father (KV7) and to the mausoleum of his non-ruling brethren (KV5) in the central part of the Valley of the Kings.

Archaeology

The condition of KV7 is poor, immense damage having been wrought by the seven or more distinct 'flooding events' to which the tomb has been subjected over the centuries and by moisture-induced swelling of the underlying shale. The site Ramesses II chose for his tomb was not a good one.

'Sat. 13th [December, 1913]. Clearing 1st passage. It was necessary to pull down a great deal of the ceiling . . . Mond. 15th [December]. First passage finished, commenced 2nd passage. The ceiling very unsafe, pulled down a great deal.'

Harry Burton

Several expeditions have over the years shown an interest in KV7 (which has stood open, at least in part, since antiquity), including Henry Salt, Champollion and Rosellini, Lepsius, Harry Burton (for Theodore Davis), and The Brooklyn Museum. All, in the end, have been deterred by the enormity of the task and the improbability of worthwhile finds, and abandoned the work after a greater or lesser input of time. The fill is rock hard, and major sections of the once beautifully carved and painted walls – among the most magnificent of any tomb in the valley – have flaked from the walls and are sandwiched between the different flood strata. Undeterred by this excavational nightmare, French scholars, under Christian Leblanc, have returned to the fray, and a full clearance of the sepulchre is now in sight.

Architecture

'. . . the sarcophagus chamber is in a very bad state. All the eight columns have fallen and brought down much of the roof with them. My predecessor, who ever he was[,] dug three trenches but apparently found no signs of the sarcophagus.'

Harry Burton

The Tomb of Ramesses II (KV7)

'I have . . . had excavations made in the rock tomb of . . . RAMSES [II] in Bab el Meluk, which was covered over with rubbish, and which Rosellini was mistaken in thinking unfinished; several chambers have already been opened, and if fortune favours us we shall also still find the sarcophagus . . .'

Carl Richard Lepsius

The position of KV7 relative to KV5, the tomb employed for members of Ramesses II's large family. Note also the close proximity of KV8, Merenptah's tomb.

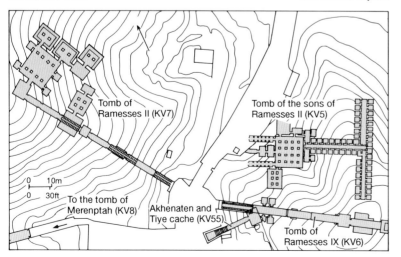

Tomb of Ramesses II (KV7)

Tomb of the sons of Ramesses II (KV5)

0   10m
0   30ft   To the tomb of Merenptah (KV8)

Akhenaten and Tiye cache (KV55)

Tomb of Ramesses IX (KV6)

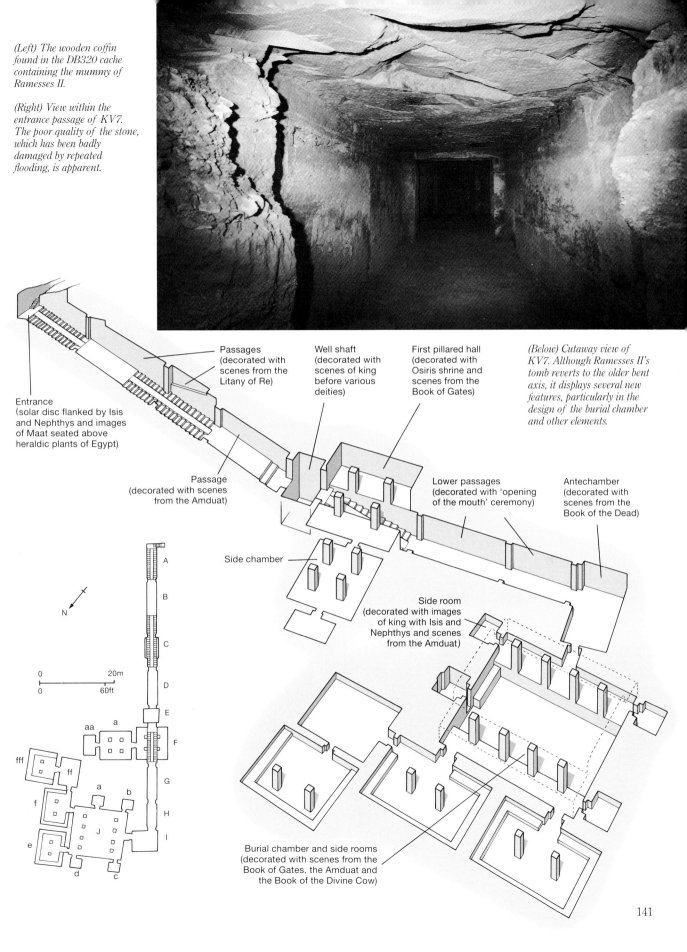

(Left) The wooden coffin found in the DB320 cache containing the mummy of Ramesses II.

(Right) View within the entrance passage of KV7. The poor quality of the stone, which has been badly damaged by repeated flooding, is apparent.

Passages (decorated with scenes from the Litany of Re)

Well shaft (decorated with scenes of king before various deities)

First pillared hall (decorated with Osiris shrine and scenes from the Book of Gates)

(Below) Cutaway view of KV7. Although Ramesses II's tomb reverts to the older bent axis, it displays several new features, particularly in the design of the burial chamber and other elements.

Entrance (solar disc flanked by Isis and Nephthys and images of Maat seated above heraldic plants of Egypt)

Passage (decorated with scenes from the Amduat)

Lower passages (decorated with 'opening of the mouth' ceremony)

Antechamber (decorated with scenes from the Book of the Dead)

Side chamber

Side room (decorated with images of king with Isis and Nephthys and scenes from the Amduat)

N

0   20m
0   60ft

Burial chamber and side rooms (decorated with scenes from the Book of Gates, the Amduat and the Book of the Divine Cow)

141

Shabti *figure of Ramesses II, in bronze. Beaten flat, it had been broken in half for ease of handling, presumably when the tomb was officially dismantled at the end of the New Kingdom.*

Although the tomb reverts to the old bent-axis plan, perhaps to avoid an intrusive bed of shale encountered in its excavation, the structure is not atavistic in design, as can be seen from new elements such as the decreased slope of its passages, the form of its first pillared hall with the added room to the side, the radically new design of the burial chamber, and certain other details such as the form and location of some of the niches, stairs, etc. The reason for turning the burial chamber sideways – and at an angle – is unknown, though the addition of the fourth set of pillars and the large size of this chamber allowed a new emphasis to be placed on the crypt, which was now positioned in the centre of the room instead of at its end. The layout of the subsidiary rooms is interesting, and it may be noticed that, of the four 'corner' rooms, it is the innermost right that is set back in its position on the side wall rather than the left-hand room as in every other tomb since Tuthmosis IV. Although not the longest king's tomb in the valley, KV7 is perhaps the largest in area, the whole tomb covering more than *c.* 820 sq m (8,800 sq ft) and the burial chamber alone some *c.* 181 sq m (1,950 sq ft).

Decoration

'... cleared the centre of Osiris Chamber and found a damaged Osiris figure in high relief in a niche opposite the door.'

Harry Burton

Although much of the decoration of KV7 is badly damaged or missing, it can, for the most part, be reconstructed. While the basic decorative programme follows that of Sethos I, there are a number of important new features. For the first time the entrance doorway is decorated on the lintel with the image of the solar disc flanked by the goddesses Isis and Nephthys (both combining the solar and Osirid beliefs and setting the directional parameters of the symbolic orientation of the tomb). In the same way, the reveals of the doorway are decorated with parallel representations of the goddess Maat kneeling above the heraldic plants of Upper and Lower Egypt (p. 36). All these elements are incorporated into the decoration of succeeding tombs. The entrance corridors have the Litany of Re, followed by the Amduat and other scenes and the Anubis motif; the well room has the usual divine scenes; and the first pillared hall was given the Book of Gates, and the Osiris shrine first found in the tomb of Sethos I. The lower corridors seem to have been decorated in like manner with 'opening of the mouth' scenes. The antechamber decoration shows scenes from the Book of the Dead, a major innovation which future kings would continue in the antechambers of their tombs. The burial chamber and its subsidiary rooms seem to have received a similar treatment to that in Sethos I's tomb, though the decoration of the room set back on the right-hand wall has what appears to be a unique feature in parallel depictions of the king with Isis and Nephthys censing on each side of a wall niche holding a divine statue.

Funerary equipment

Attributable finds are few, but these include a hollow cast bronze *shabti* in Berlin (ex-Minutoli collection) showing the king wearing the *nemes*-headcloth. It has been hammered flat and the legs are broken off; it was obviously treated as scrap, and is perhaps a stray from the late New Kingdom dismantling of the burial which took place following the transfer of Ramesses II's mummy to KV17 (below). As a hieratic graffito in the tomb indicates, Butehamun was involved in this work. Two further *shabtis* of Ramesses II are known, both are made of wood: one is in The Brooklyn Museum; a similar specimen, transformed into a resin-coated Osiris figure on a base at the start of the Third Intermediate Period (p. 206), is now in the British Museum.

Harry Burton's work brought to light only the most meagre scraps, including 'a fragment of a statue, with hieroglyphics on one side, limestone', faience fragments (including pieces of *shabtis*), bits of glass, calcite and limestone lids from vessels, and fragments of calcite from the sarcophagus or canopic chest. Leblanc's ongoing clearance has so far located a definite fragment of the anthropoid sarcophagus, made of calcite and inscribed on both the outer and inner surfaces with extracts from the Book of Gates, as well as fragments of the canopic chest and 'of a blue marble shabti ... of superlative workmanship.'

Reconstruction, by Aidan Dodson, of Ramesses II's canopic chest, of calcite inlaid with blue glass..

Robbery and the testimony of the king's mummy

According to a papyrus preserved in the Egyptian Museum, Turin – the 'Strike Papyrus' – an attempt was made by two individuals to enter the tomb of Ramesses II during the 20th dynasty, in Year 29 of Ramesses III, by stripping stones from above the entrance. Another robber, one Kenena son of Ruta, is recorded in the same document as having made a similar attempt on the tomb of Ramesses II's offspring – KV5 (p. 146).

The mummy of Ramesses II was discovered in the DB320 cache contained within a closely contemporary anthropoid wooden coffin. Cyril Aldred and others have argued on stylistic grounds that this coffin is perhaps likely to have been prepared originally for Ramesses I: it appears to have been marked out for a carved and gilded *rishi*-decoration which may never have been applied – a feature in keeping with the unfinished state of the Ramesses I tomb and of the royal sarcophagus.

The body itself, superficially intact when found,

was unwrapped by Gaston Maspero at Bulaq on 3 June 1886. Beneath the outer bandages was found a hieratic docket recording its rewrapping and reburial in the tomb of Sethos I (KV17) – before its removal to the Inhapi cliff tomb (p. 197) – and a shroud decorated with an image of the goddess Nut. The remains were still articulated, but the genitals were absent.

In September 1975 the king's mummy left Cairo for Paris, where it was to be conserved and studied for eight months before being returned to Egypt. This examination hinted at the opulence of the original burial: linen fragments were discovered within the body, woven in blue and metallic gold. It also provided a possible explanation for the family's devotion to the previously reviled god Seth: Ramesses II, at least, may have been red-haired – as, traditionally, was the god himself. A microscopic examination of sand particles associated with the body suggested that Pharaoh was embalmed in the north of Egypt, at some distance from the Nile since no aquatic-plant pollen was found.

The mummy of Ramesses II: (left) after the removal of its outer, Nut-decorated shroud, restored and docketed by the high priest of Amun, Pinudjem I; (right) fully unwrapped, showing the king's majestic profile.

A Tomb for the Sons of Ramesses II (KV5)

'This is the most exciting find in the Valley of the Kings since the discovery of Tutankhamun's tomb in 1922. Careful archaeological work should now reveal much previously unknown information about Ramesses' enormous family.'

Kenneth Kitchen

Recent excavations by Kent Weeks, 70 m (230 ft) from the tomb of Tutankhamun, have begun to uncover what promises to be the largest ancient Egyptian burial complex ever found. Quite possibly this was the last resting place for most of the 50 or more sons of Ramesses II.

Discovery

'One of the most amazing experiences of my life.'

Kent Weeks

The existence of KV5 has been known for many years, and the tomb was tunnelled into and partially planned by James Burton (who saw little more than the ceiling) sometime before 1835. Howard Carter cleared around and perhaps within the immediate entrance of the tomb, to no avail, for Theodore Davis in 1902; the site was subsequently

hidden by debris from later work in the valley. The tomb was relocated in 1985–86 by Kent Weeks of the American University in Cairo, using sonar and ground-penetrating radar, and re-entered the following season. Only recently, however, has its extraordinary extent become apparent. On 18 May 1995, Weeks made the following announcement:

'Last February, excavating through the flood-borne debris that fills the tomb, my staff and I found a passageway leading past twenty chambers to a statue of the god Osiris. Two transverse corridors, each with another twenty chambers, extend beyond that. At the end of the corridors there are stairs and sloping corridors apparently leading to even more rooms on a lower level. The tomb could be the largest ever found in Egypt...'

An amazing 95 chambers have been located to date, with the clearance still very far from completion. Who was the owner of this vast sepulchre? The wall decoration confirms that KV5 had been intended for the burial not of one individual but of an entire family – the sons (of whom the names of 52 are known) of Ramesses II, whose cartouche was noted at the tomb entrance by James Burton. The interment here of one of these sons, Meryatum, has been proposed on the basis of an ostracon found by Carter while working for Davis, and Weeks's work so far has added the name of the king's eldest son, Amenherkhepshef, of another

Factfile

Tomb number/location:
KV5, Wadi Biban el-Muluk
Date of discovery:
before 1799
Excavator/reports:
Kent R. Weeks, American University in Cairo, 1987–:
K. R. Weeks, in C. N. Reeves (ed.), *After Tut'ankhamun*, (1992) pp. 99–121; *id.,
Minerva* 6 (1995) pp. 20–24

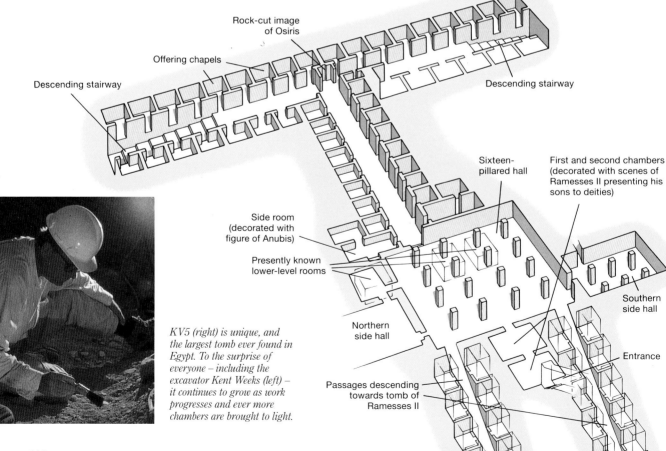

KV5 (right) is unique, and the largest tomb ever found in Egypt. To the surprise of everyone – including the excavator Kent Weeks (left) – it continues to grow as work progresses and ever more chambers are brought to light.

Rock-cut image of Osiris

Offering chapels

Descending stairway

Descending stairway

Side room (decorated with figure of Anubis)

Presently known lower-level rooms

Sixteen-pillared hall

First and second chambers (decorated with scenes of Ramesses II presenting his sons to deities)

Northern side hall

Southern side hall

Entrance

Passages descending towards tomb of Ramesses II

son called Ramesses, and, on a canopic jar fragment from the floor of the second chamber, the name of yet another, Sethy. Other, female members of the family may also have been interred here, but of these there is as yet no trace.

Architecture

'[The tomb is] like an octopus, with a body surrounded by tentacles.'

Kent Weeks

Although KV5 is unique, many aspects of the plan and proportions are similar to tombs of the late 18th dynasty, and it has been suggested that it was during this time that KV5 was originally begun. Typical of several tombs of that period, the relatively narrow entrance opens directly into an actual room rather than a passage and then in this case, another room and a large 16-pillared hall. These subsidiary rooms were evidently added when the tomb was taken over by Ramesses II. A number of the chambers have vaulted ceilings typical of the Ramessid period.

The T-shaped extension to the east, brought to light in the spring 1995 season, has numerous small side chambers. Reaching out from the 16-pillared hall, it is not yet fully cleared, but enough has been revealed to show that the plan of this part of the tomb is unique in the Valley of the Kings. The complications of the plan have increased with the dis-

covery of multi-layered plaster floors (possibly suggesting the presence of rooms beneath) and, at the end of 1995, of two completely new passages sloping down to the west – towards the tomb of Ramesses II – at an angle of 37 degrees. Over 20 further rooms have been revealed.

Decoration

Badly damaged from years of flooding (most recently from a leaking sewage pipe installed in the old valley rest house in the early 1950s), surviving areas of plaster show that, in the first chamber at least, the tomb was decorated with scenes similar to those found in the tombs made by Ramesses III for his sons in the Valley of the Queens (QV42, 43, 44, 55). Decoration so far uncovered within KV5 includes depictions of Ramesses II presenting Amenherkhepshef to Sokar and Hathor, and a rep-

(Above) Rock-cut statue of Osiris, god of the dead, focus of the T-shaped extension of offering chapels at the rear of the tomb.

(Left) A detail of the sporadically preserved wall decoration – vertical columns of text in raised relief, containing the throne name of Ramesses II.

resentation of another son, Ramesses, before Nefertum. The walls and pillars of the 16-pillared hall are also decorated, but as yet uncleared; further finely decorated scenes were cut in the rock and on the plaster of the T-shaped extension, while a rock-cut image of the god Osiris, 1.5 m (5 ft) high, decorates the end wall of its corridors. Further wall decorations may be anticipated as work progresses elsewhere in the tomb.

Funerary equipment

'The objects we have found [within the first two chambers] include thousands of potsherds, a dozen fragments of alabaster canopic jars, pieces of inscribed red granite sarcophagi, the unfinished head of a limestone statue, a piece of a wooden coffin, four inscribed faience ushabtis, numerous clay, faience, and stone beads, amulets, and two hieratic ostraca recording inventories of the grave goods(?) that had been placed with the burials. In one corner, adjacent to a wall whose reliefs had been painted in blue, red, and white, there lay a Canaanite amphora base, filled with blue paint that had spilled onto the floor, probably while the artist was still at work. There were also pieces of human and animal bones, and parts of mummified human remains, well-wrapped fragments of the knee and the thigh of a young adult male.'

Kent Weeks

The 15 m-square (50 ft-square), 16-pillared chamber 3 has not yet been cleared, and work within the vast, T-shaped corridor-system with its 50 and more side (offering?) chambers – with a possible lower level yet to be established – is also unfinished. Clearance of the first 2 m (7 ft) of the corridor leading from the 16-pillared hall has so far yielded 'New Kingdom potsherds, beads, a faience bracelet covered with gold leaf, faience inlays, a few ostraca, and more sarcophagus fragments. In one of the side chambers (the only one . . . examined so far), there were numerous bones of birds and mammals, especially cattle. Again, a few sherds of Roman date lie on the floor, but there is nothing of later date, and there are no artefacts in the debris itself.'

Robbery

'Now Userhat and Patwere have stripped stones from above the tomb of Osiris King Usermaatre-setepenre [Ramesses II], the great god. . . . And Kenena son of Ruta did it in the same manner above the tomb of the royal children of King Osiris Usermaatre-setepenre [Ramesses II], the great god . . .'

'Strike Papyrus'

During the reign of Ramesses III, a number of Theban workmen were charged with entry into tombs in the Valley of the Kings, evidently with a view to plundering them. Among the tombs mentioned in the surviving record of testimony (now preserved in Turin) is KV5, referred to as 'the tomb of the royal children of Osiris King [Ramesses II], the great god', stones from above the entrance to which had been removed by one Kenena son of Ruta. We know nothing definite of this man's ultimate fate, but his interrogation would clearly have been brutal, and most likely followed by impalement on a sharpened wooden stake – the punishment traditionally meted out for this type of violation.

Aerial photograph (with explanatory diagram below) of the central part of the main Valley of the Kings, showing the position of KV5 relative to KV7 (Ramesses II), KV8 (Merenptah), and other tombs.

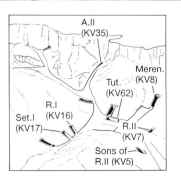

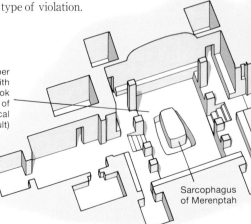

Burial chamber (walls decorated with scenes from the Book of Gates and Book of Caverns; astronomical ceiling painted on vault)

Sarcophagus of Merenptah

The Tomb of Merenptah (KV8)

Archaeology

The tomb of Merenptah has stood open since antiquity and, to judge from the presence of Greek and Latin graffiti, was accessible at least as far as the first pillared hall. The first recorded clearance is that of Howard Carter who, in 1903, emptied the innermost parts. More recently, Edwin C. Brock has carried out further excavation in the floor of the burial chamber and also undertaken a clearance of the well.

Architecture

Royal tomb design was simplified under Merenptah by abandoning the jogged axis used since the time of Horemheb and utilizing instead a single axis which led directly from the entrance of the tomb to its burial chamber. Other innovations are apparent. For the first time, the entrance to the king's monument was made appreciably wider than the internal corridors, so that the effect is of a more imposing façade. This modification was followed by every succeeding king to be buried in the royal necropolis. KV8 is unique, however, in adding a small, niche-like room (apparently dedicated to

Ramesses II) to the chamber cut at the side of the first pillared hall. Merenptah also deleted the antechamber from his tomb plan, instead placing a similarly sized room between the two innermost corridors – a modification employed after this king only by Siptah and, in a somewhat similar manner, by Ramesses III. The door jambs of the tomb were cut out in order to permit the installation of the huge sarcophagus (or the calcite sarcophagus plinth, if this was monolithic), and were replaced by decorated sandstone blocks dovetailed into place. Several of these blocks, displaced in antiquity, were recovered by Brock during his clearance of the well.

Decoration

The tomb's decoration displays a much less radical departure from precedent than its plan. Although

Factfile

Tomb number/location:
KV8, Wadi Biban el-Muluk
Date of discovery:
open since antiquity
Royal mummy:
Removed in antiquity; discovered in KV35
Excavators/reports:
Howard Carter, 1903/4, for the Service des Antiquités: H. Carter, *ASAE* 6 (1906) pp. 116–19; Edwin C. Brock, 1987–88, for the Royal Ontario Museum: E. C. Brock, in C. N. Reeves (ed.), *After Tut'ankhamun* (London, 1992) pp. 122–40

(Below) Among the innovations in KV8 are a straightening of the single axis and alterations in the design of many of the chambers and passages.

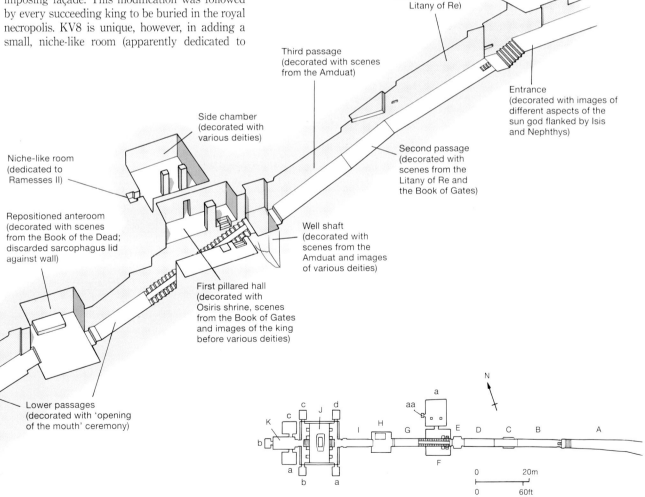

First passage (decorated with image of king before Re-Horakhty and scenes from the Litany of Re)

Third passage (decorated with scenes from the Amduat)

Entrance (decorated with images of different aspects of the sun god flanked by Isis and Nephthys)

Side chamber (decorated with various deities)

Second passage (decorated with scenes from the Litany of Re and the Book of Gates)

Niche-like room (dedicated to Ramesses II)

Repositioned anteroom (decorated with scenes from the Book of the Dead; discarded sarcophagus lid against wall)

Well shaft (decorated with scenes from the Amduat and images of various deities)

First pillared hall (decorated with Osiris shrine, scenes from the Book of Gates and images of the king before various deities)

Lower passages (decorated with 'opening of the mouth' ceremony)

N

0   20m

0   60ft

The passages of Merenptah's tomb exhibit a carefully regulated design and incised, painted decoration on the walls.

(Below right) The Osiris shrine at the rear of the first pillared hall, with dual images of the king before the god.

Howard Carter's drawings of two of a group of 13 calcite vessels found in 1920 across from the entrance to KV8. They carry the cartouches of Merenptah.

much was destroyed by extensive flooding in antiquity, enough painted surface survives through the first pillared hall and elsewhere to show that the tomb was generally decorated along the same lines as those of Sethos I and Ramesses II. As in these predecessors' tombs, the first three passages contained the Litany of Re, followed by scenes from the Amduat, etc., and divided scenes were placed on the walls of the well shaft. The upper pillared hall once again received the Book of Gates and Osiris shrine, with the lower passages having depictions of the 'opening of the mouth' and further divine scenes. The new room built between these lower passages contains a section of the Book of the Dead. Merenptah's burial chamber not only contained sections of the Book of Gates and an astronomical ceiling, but also replaced the traditional material from the Amduat with solar-orientated scenes from the Book of Caverns which were prominently displayed on the right-hand wall. Although the importance of Re and the king's association with that god is clear in this tomb, the importance of Osiris is still evident in a number of areas. In the Osiris shrine of the first pillared hall, for example, Osiris wears a pectoral inscribed with the king's name, thus identifying the monarch directly with the netherworld deity.

Funerary equipment

The burial of Merenptah was equipped with four stone sarcophagi – three outer containers of red Aswan granite and a fourth innermost anthropoid

A Cache of Materials Used in Merenptah's Burial

Until the discovery of the tomb of Tutankhamun in 1922, Carter's most significant find for Lord Carnarvon was a cache of 13 calcite jars discovered on and after 21 February 1920 while digging in the centre of the watercourse on the south side of the tomb of Merenptah (KV8). As Carter records, these had been 'placed side by side in a group, a few stones laid on the top and covered with rubbish – as if carefully buried.'

To judge from the hieratic dockets on these jars, they had been employed in the anointing of Merenptah's body with the 'seven sacred oils' in the funerary tent (the *per-nefer*, 'house of vigour') erected at the time of the funeral. The containers, inscribed with the names of Ramesses II and of Merenptah, were of high quality, but old and damaged when buried.

sarcophagus of creamy-white calcite. The outermost of the three granite sarcophagi comprises a huge (4.1 m (13 ft 5 1/2 in) in length), slightly vaulted, rectangular lid (shifted in antiquity to chamber H), together with fragments (amounting to approximately one-third) of its coffer, the walls of which originally stood some 2 m (6 ft 7 in) in height. Of the second sarcophagus, only the cartouche-shaped lid (discovered by Carter up-turned in the burial chamber) survives, embellished with a reclining mummiform figure of the king, together with approximately one-fifth of the coffer, in fragments. Both outer sarcophagi were decorated with extracts from the Amduat and the Book of Gates.

'Contrary to speculations ... all 4 sarcophagi rested one within the other upon a massive rectangular calcite plinth set into the floor of the burial chamber.'

Edwin C. Brock

The third sarcophagus – a rectangular coffer and lid (again surmounted by a recumbent figure of the king) – had been removed from the tomb during the 21st dynasty for the burial of Psusennes I at Tanis. Inscribed with extracts from the Amduat, the box at least, from the evidence of its cartouches, had been prepared originally for Merenptah as crown prince.

To judge from the lack of room available for manoeuvring within the tomb, these larger containers will of necessity have been installed ready nested one within the other. This introduction may be referred to in Cairo ostracon CG 25504 (dated to Year 7 of the king's reign) from Ayrton's work in the valley in 1905/6.

The innermost, anthropoid sarcophagus of calcite, evidently similar to that discovered by Belzoni in the tomb of Sethos I, is today represented by a large section from the foot end of the coffer in the

British Museum and by other fragments still in the tomb. It repeats, again, extracts from the Book of Gates and the Amduat. This innermost sarcophagus was perhaps intended to contain one or more wooden coffins similar in form to that shown on the well-known ostracon recovered by Carter from the tomb debris, and another, similar, ostracon in the British Museum.

Several fragments of the king's canopic chest are known, one discovered by Carter in 1906 and others found by Edwin C. Brock between 1985 and 1988. These pieces are decorated with the heads of Duamutef and Imseti and protective texts of Neith and Isis.

No *shabtis* are recorded from KV8, and details of other burial equipment are almost wholly lacking.

(Above left) Merenptah, whose name may be translated 'The beloved of Ptah', stands before an image of that deity.

(Above right) Mummified gods preceding the barque of Re – detail of a scene in the first pillared hall, from the 5th hour of the Book of Gates.

(Below) A detail of Merenptah's recumbent image on the granite lid of the king's second granite sarcophagus.

From Amenmesse to Sethnakhte

Factfile

Tomb number/location:
KV10, Wadi Biban el-Muluk
Date of discovery:
open since antiquity
Royal mummy:
not identified
Excavators/report:
Edward Ayrton in 1907 for Theodore Davis: unpublished; Otto J. Schaden – University of Arizona 1992–95, University of Memphis 1996–: O. J. Schaden *NARCE* 163 (1993) pp. 1–9
Wall documentation:
Eugène Lefébure, *Les Hypogées royaux de Thèbes II* (Paris, 1889) pp. 81–5; Earl L. Ertman, *KMT* 4/2 (summer, 1993) pp. 38–46

Merenptah's reign ended after a decade, in 1214 BC, the rightful heir being his son by Queen Isisnofret (II), Sethos II. Whether Sethos II was by-passed, however, and the throne passed directly to a rival claimant, Amenmesse (possibly the son of a daughter of Ramesses II, Takhat), or whether Amenmesse established himself as an independent king in the south, is at present unclear. Amenmesse was certainly regarded by later generations as a usurper, and, following his five-year reign, Sethos II did at last accede.

The *de facto* successor to Sethos II was his second wife, Tawosret, who ruled the country as regent during the minority of the young heir, Siptah, whom some have identified as a son of Amenmesse. The situation is comparable in several respects to that of Hatshepsut and Tuthmosis III during the 18th dynasty (p. 91) – even down to the rumours of sexual misconduct between the queen regent and her highest official of state, Bay.

Siptah died in 1198 BC, after only six years on the throne, and was interred within tomb KV47. The reins of power remained with Tawosret for a short time more, until they passed, perhaps by force, to Sethnakhte, founder of the 20th dynasty. Sethnakhte's own brief period of rule (1196–1194 BC) was followed by that of his son, Ramesses III.

The Tomb of Amenmesse (KV10)

Discovery

The tomb of Amenmesse seems to have lain open since antiquity. Several Classical graffiti are present in the entrance area, together with Arabic inscriptions. The tomb was noted by Pococke on his map of 1743, and examined by Burton and Hay, Champollion, Lepsius and Wilkinson during the early 19th century. Much of the tomb's visible decoration was also recorded in 1883 and later published by Eugène Lefébure. In 1907 Edward Ayrton cleared the entrance passage and apparently used it as a dining or work room.

Beginning in the winter of 1992/93, full-scale study and excavation were initiated by Otto Schaden as a project of the University of Arizona. Although the tomb is now cleared as far as the first pillared hall, with additional trenches and pits beyond this point, it is not yet known if Amenmesse was ever interred in this tomb, or what relationship, if any, Amenmesse bore to the 'king's mother' Takhat and the 'great royal wife' Baketwerel, for whom parts of the tomb were redecorated.

Architecture and decoration

The current excavations have shown that the passages slope considerably less than had been thought; indeed, the fourth passage immediately beyond the well room is virtually horizontal, showing that the more level design first attested in KV7 (Ramesses II) was also used in this monument. No shaft was cut in the well room, but the side room found in all major tombs since Sethos I was partially cut on the west side of the pillared hall. Beyond this point the tomb appears to end in a roughly vaulted passage adapted as a burial chamber.

The original decoration for Amenmesse extended as far as the pillared hall and was almost identical to that found in the tomb of Merenptah (KV8), with the same entrance motifs in raised relief, the first two corridors being decorated with the Litany of Re and the third with scenes from the Amduat. These reliefs were removed and the outer corridors, well room and pillared hall were plastered and painted for the royal women, Takhat and Baketwerel. As recorded by Lefébure, the well scenes consisted of Takhat offering before a number of gods, and the same type of motif was repeated for Baketwerel in the pillared hall along with scenes from the Book of the Dead. A single

Osiris scene on the far wall follows that found in the tomb of Sethos I rather than the dual shrine found in all other tombs since that king. Although a partial, single image of Baketwerel still remains on this wall, most of the rest of the paint-on-plaster decoration has not survived in this tomb.

Funerary equipment

A fragment of limestone discovered in the tomb by Lefébure was originally thought to be part of Amenmesse's sarcophagus, but was probably misidentified. The recent clearance work in the entrance passages revealed items of various periods, including fragmentary *shabti* figures of Sethos I, sarcophagus fragments of Ramesses VI and other intrusive items. Further within the tomb, fragments of alabaster from a canopic jar and a canopic box or sarcophagus were also discovered,

including one with a partial cartouche incorporating the figures of Amun and Re which might possibly be attributable to Amen[ra]messe. Fragments of limestone canopic jars, one of which (found by Carter) was clearly inscribed with the name of Takhat, and part of a red granite sarcophagus lid, also inscribed for Takhat, indicate that this royal woman was probably buried in the tomb.

(Above left) Eugène Lefébure's drawing of Queen Baketwerel led before Osiris – a scene in the pillared hall of KV10.

(Above) A photographic detail of the queen's head from this same scene.

(Far left) Anciently erased image of Re-Horakhty from the first corridor of KV10, with (left) a parallel, undamaged scene from the tomb of Siptah.

(Right) The cutting of KV10 progressed no further than the second passage beyond the pillared hall.

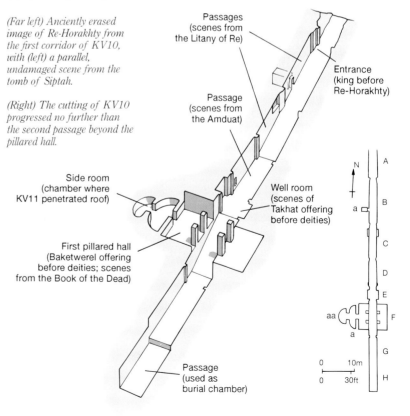

Passages (scenes from the Litany of Re)

Entrance (king before Re-Horakhty)

Passage (scenes from the Amduat)

Side room (chamber where KV11 penetrated roof)

Well room (scenes of Takhat offering before deities)

First pillared hall (Baketwerel offering before deities; scenes from the Book of the Dead)

Passage (used as burial chamber)

151

Factfile

Tomb number/location:
KV15, Wadi Biban el-Muluk
Date of discovery:
open since antiquity
Royal mummy:
removed in antiquity;
discovered in KV35
Excavator/report:
Howard Carter
1902/3–1903/4: H. Carter
ASAE 6 (1906) p. 122ff
Wall documentation:
Eugène Lefébure, *Les Hypogées royaux de Thèbes II* (Paris, 1889) pp. 146–55

Enshrined images in Sethos II's tomb: (right) the king on the back of a feline, similar to actual sculptures found elsewhere; (far right) the king as harpooner on a papyrus skiff – a motif also attested in three-dimensional form.

The Tomb of Sethos II (KV15)

'. . . the [chief] Medjay [necropolis policeman] came, saying: "[The] falcon has flown up to heaven, namely Sethos [II], [and] another has arisen in his place."'

Hieratic ostracon

History and archaeology

Several ostraca exist which relate to the tomb of Sethos II, including one with a preliminary working sketch, with dimensions, of the tomb's single chamber. The complete history of the tomb's construction and employment is still uncertain, however. The body of the king may originally have been interred in the tomb of his wife, Tawosret (p. 157) and only afterwards transferred to KV15, which was hastily and incompletely finished. Later inspection of KV15 by those charged with dismantling the burials and stripping the bodies, evidently led to the removal of the king's mummy – which was eventually found in the KV35 cache (tomb of Amenophis II) in a replacement coffin of later date.

KV15 must have continued to lie open throughout the later Classical period, to judge from the 59 Greek and Latin graffiti to be found on the walls. In more recent times, the entire tomb was accessible to Pococke and to those who followed in his wake. It was completely cleared by Howard Carter in 1903–04.

Architecture

The plan is abbreviated, but a number of innovations are evident. The tomb was located at the base of the *gebel*, and instead of steps cut below a retaining wall, the doorway was cut directly into the cliff face. Unusually, the walls of this entrance were carefully smoothed and covered with a layer of white plaster as elsewhere inside the tomb. The angle of the entrance slope is minimal, and that of the corridors is also very slight, except for the second corridor and the steep descent to the makeshift burial chamber. The niches at the entrance to the well room, which are incipient in Merenptah's tomb, are here fully cut for the first time and continue with only one or two exceptions in all succeeding tombs. The well shaft was never excavated. The burial chamber beyond is no more than an extremely hasty adaptation of a corridor.

Decoration

'It seems they brought in the body before the tomb was finished and then went on working – a large figure of a Deity with outspread wings painted on the ceiling of above the sarcophagus – very rough. Some beautifully drawn figures of the king in red lines.'

James Burton

Due to the summary conclusion of work on this tomb, an interesting change in decorative technique can be observed. Most of the first corridor was decorated in both sunk and raised relief of reasonable quality, but much of the remaining decoration – doubtless applied after the king's death – is far less accomplished and executed in paint alone. The reveals of the entrance jambs feature the goddess Maat kneeling above the heraldic plants, and this motif is utilized in the same areas at further points within the tomb. The first corridor has the Litany of Re, the figures of which continue, as usual, in the second corridor along with extracts from the

(Below) Detail of the kilt of Sethos II at the entrance to the tomb.

The 'Gold Tomb'

KV56 represents one of the most splendid finds of jewellery ever made in the Valley of the Kings. Ayrton's excavation in 1908 unearthed, in the lower of the two strata in the burial fill among other items, a circlet, several finger rings, bracelets, a series of necklace ornaments and amulets, a pair of silver 'gloves' and a silver sandal. Since the deposit included objects inscribed with the names of both Sethos II and Tawosret, Maspero concluded that this was a cache of material salvaged from the burial of Tawosret when her own tomb was usurped by Sethnakhte. Cyril Aldred, however, offered a rather more imaginative interpretation. KV56, he argued, was an essentially intact burial, in which the 'stratum about a half inch thick of broken gold leaf and stucco covering an area of some four square feet'

Factfile

Tomb number/location:
KV56, Wadi Biban el-Muluk
Date of discovery:
5 January 1908, by Edward R. Ayrton
Excavator/report:
E. R. Ayrton, 1908, for Theodore M. Davis: Th. M. Davis *et al.*, *The Tomb of Siphtah; the Monkey Tomb and the Gold Tomb* (London, 1908)

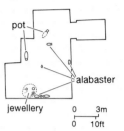

represented all that remained of a completely rotted coffin. The pair of silver 'gloves', containing eight finger rings when found, were presumably coverings for the hands of the mummy.

But whose was this tiny, disintegrated burial? Perhaps, as Aldred suggested, a child of Sethos II and Tawosret, buried during the reign of the former.

In type, the location and design of this tomb clearly assign it to the late 18th dynasty, whatever its subsequent use. The shaft, which is approximately the same depth as that of WV24 (p. 182), but even wider, is the largest in the valley; and the single room, had it been completed, would have been larger than that of any comparable KV pit chamber.

Amduat both here and in the third corridor. The well room was decorated in a manner totally different from any other tomb in the valley. Instead of the usual scenes of the king before deities, the entire room received representations of funerary objects, including symbolic statuettes of gods and kings, some of them identical with actual figures – such as the king standing on the back of a 'panther', or with a harpoon in a small papyrus skiff – found in the tomb of Tutankhamun and elsewhere. Returning to traditional decoration, the walls of the pillared hall were given over to the Book of Gates and an Osiris shrine, but innovation occurs again in the decoration of the pillars, which have only one

figure on each side, two adjacent sides thus forming a 'scene' – a development which was to be used consistently from this time on. The hastily improvised burial chamber also received the Book of Gates and, on the ceiling, an outstretched figure of the goddess Nut.

Funerary equipment

Only fragments of the lid of Sethos II's sarcophagus remain in the tomb; the coffer is untraced, but was perhaps removed for reuse at the end of the New Kingdom. The monument, when complete, would have been the smallest of those New Kingdom sarcophagi still extant and may well have been designed with a view to it nesting within a larger sarcophagus – perhaps, as Aidan Dodson suggests, that ultimately completed and employed by Ramesses III.

Treasure from the 'Gold Tomb': (above left) a pair of silver bracelets inscribed for Sethos II and Tawosret (after a painting by Harold Jones) and gold beads and earrings inscribed for Sethos II (above centre).

(Above) The single chamber, showing the distribution of finds.

(Below) Cutaway drawing of the tomb of Sethos II. As with the tomb of Amenmesse, the quarrying of KV15 was abandoned just beyond the pillared hall.

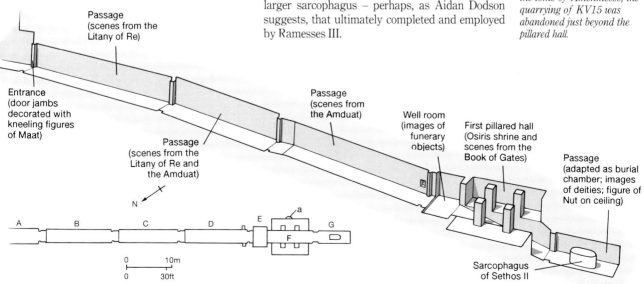

Passage (scenes from the Litany of Re)

Entrance (door jambs decorated with kneeling figures of Maat)

Passage (scenes from the Litany of Re and the Amduat)

Passage (scenes from the Amduat)

Well room (images of funerary objects)

First pillared hall (Osiris shrine and scenes from the Book of Gates)

Passage (adapted as burial chamber; images of deities; figure of Nut on ceiling)

Sarcophagus of Sethos II

A Tomb for Chancellor Bay

Factfile

Tomb number/location:
KV13, Wadi Biban el-
Muluk
Date of discovery:
open since antiquity
Excavator/report:
Hartwig Altenmüller,
1988–94, for the University
of Hamburg: H.
Altenmüller, *SAK* 21
(1994) pp. 1–18

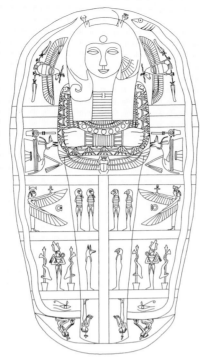

Lid of the recently discovered granite sarcophagus of Amenherkhepshef, found in the burial chamber of KV13. The monument had originally been prepared for Tawosret.

(Below) Plan of tomb KV13.

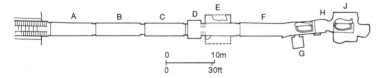

Although KV13, the tomb initiated for the 19th-dynasty *éminence grise* Bay, has stood open since antiquity, it is only recently (1987–94) that a full archaeological clearance has been undertaken by Hartwig Altenmüller for the University of Hamburg – with quite unexpected results.

Bay, originally royal scribe to Sethos II, rose to become chancellor and the 'power behind the throne' during the short six-year reign of the young king Siptah – whose stepmother Tawosret was regent and then supreme ruler on Siptah's death. Bay's status is reflected in the privilege he was granted of a private tomb in the royal valley. But Altenmüller has been able to show that the tomb was left unfinished by Bay and reused during the 20th dynasty by two royal princes – Amenherkhepshef and Mentuherkhepshef. The former seems to have been a son of Ramesses III, while the latter Altenmüller believes could have been a son of Ramesses VI.

Architecture and decoration

Altenmüller discovered that the proportions as far as the pillared hall were almost exactly the same as those of the tomb of Tawosret (KV14). Beyond, the work is extremely rough and unfinished. An elongated corridor ends in an incipient anteroom and an *ad hoc* burial chamber (no larger than the first hall) with two lateral chambers.

The decoration of the outer areas likewise almost exactly mirrors that of the tomb of Tawosret. It consists of scenes of Bay before various deities in the first corridor, scenes and texts from the Book of the Dead in the second and third corridors, and divine scenes in the well room. Although Bay is depicted before the king (Siptah) in the first corridor, it is Bay and not the king who stands before the falcon-headed sun god and other deities, illustrating the adoption of royal prerogatives in the tomb's decoration as well as its design.

In the later use of the tomb for Amenherkhepshef and Mentuherkhepshef the decoration of Bay was usurped, in some cases depictions of the chancellor being replaced by images of a queen who was probably the mother of one or other of the princes.

Funerary equipment

Two sarcophagi were found in the tomb: the first was that of Amenherkhepshef – taken over from its intended owner, Tawosret, by altering the vulture wig and adding a side lock to the queen's image on the lid – positioned in the *ad hoc* burial chamber; and a second, in the corridor before the burial chamber, belonging to Mentuherkhepshef, the lid depicting this prince in the form of a mummy with crossed arms and, again, the side lock of a royal prince.

Funerary material of both individuals was recovered – canopic jar fragments, faience and calcite *shabtis*, inlays and stone and pottery vessels.

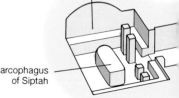

(Left) The burial chamber of KV47 as photographed by Harry Burton in 1912.

(Right) Similar in design to the previous two royal tombs, Siptah's tomb achieved a greater degree of completion, but was not decorated beyond its outer passages.

Burial chamber (undecorated)

Sarcophagus of Siptah

and Burton, it seems that KV47 received the burials of both Siptah and his mother, Queen Tiaa. The burials were eventually disturbed, however, and the king's cartouches erased from the tomb walls – only later to be restored (see below). Unfortunately, the evidence is complex and there is no agreement among Egyptologists as to the exact timing, sequence and motivation of these events.

The bones found by Burton in the sarcophagus of KV47 seem to have belonged to an intrusive burial of the Third Intermediate Period. The mummy identified as that of Siptah by the 21st-dynasty necropolis priests was discovered in the Amenophis II cache (KV35) in 1898. Apart from the somewhat withered and shortened left leg, which was apparently caused by poliomyelitis, the king's body had been much battered in the search for valuable amulets. The mummy's right arm had been reattached with splints at the time of the reburial.

Architecture and decoration

While the outer part of the structure follows the plan of Sethos II's tomb (KV15) quite closely (with the addition of the entrance sarcophagus ramp found in Amenmesse's tomb), the interior of Siptah's monument is unusual in a number of ways. Two corridors, rather than a corridor and stairway, were constructed beyond the pillared hall and, uniquely, a side passage was cut to the left of the corridor after the antechamber. This was abandoned when it ran into the nearby tomb KV32. The shattered burial chamber is also exceptional in having no ancillary storerooms; perhaps this was due to the unsuitable nature of the shale in which this hall was cut. The abandoned passage may have been intended to lead to storage rooms, though it is also possible that a separate sarcophagus hall for the king's mother Tiaa was intended.

(Left) Detail of the lid of Siptah's red granite sarcophagus.

(Above) The withered left foot of the king's mummy, which was recovered from the Amenophis II cache in 1898.

Factfile

Tomb number/location:
KV47, Wadi Biban el-Muluk
Date of discovery:
18 December 1905, Edward R. Ayrton
Royal mummy:
removed in antiquity; discovered in KV35
Excavators/reports:
E. Ayrton 1905: E. Ayrton *PSBA* 28 (1906) p. 96; H. Burton 1912–13: H. Burton, *BMMA* 11 (1916) p. 13–18
Wall documentation:
Theodore M. Davis *et al. The Tomb of Siptah . . .* (London, 1908)

The Tomb of Siptah (KV47)

'Ayrton penetrated as far as the second chamber, but owing to the bad state of the rock he abandoned it as being "most unsafe to work in" . . . Mr. Davis and I inspected the tomb in February, 1912, and as no further collapse had occurred . . . we decided to complete its excavation.'

Harry Burton

History and archaeology

Discovered by Ayrton in November 1905, KV47 was excavated down to the antechamber, but only cleared fully by Burton in 1912. In 1922 Howard Carter cleared the area around KV47, discovering several ostraca and other small objects associated with the tomb. From the finds recovered by Ayrton

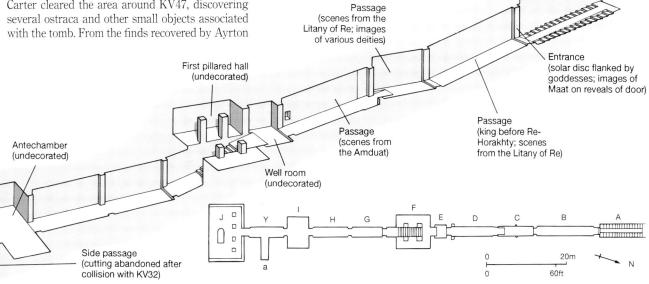

First pillared hall (undecorated)

Passage (scenes from the Litany of Re; images of various deities)

Entrance (solar disc flanked by goddesses; images of Maat on reveals of door)

Passage (king before Re-Horakhty; scenes from the Litany of Re)

Passage (scenes from the Amduat)

Well room (undecorated)

Antechamber (undecorated)

Side passage (cutting abandoned after collision with KV32)

0   20m
0   60ft
N

*A youthful Siptah
before Re-Horakhty –
frontispiece to the
Litany of Re in the first
passage of KV47. To
the left may be partially
seen the motif of the
winged Maat seated
above the heraldic plant
of Upper Egypt.*

*A watercolour detail by
Harold Jones of the reclining
Anubis dog from the second
passage of KV47.*

Only the outer passages of Siptah's tomb were plastered and decorated, and although the motifs are standard ones, the quality of the decoration is high. Beyond the usual entrance motif, perhaps the finest examples of Maat seated on the heraldic plants of the north and south occur on the reveals of the entrance (p. 36). The Litany of Re appears in the first passage and at the beginning of the second, and is followed by a number of scenes stressing underworld deities, including Anubis before the bier of Osiris. Scenes from the Amduat were also placed in the third passage, but these are now largely destroyed.

Funerary equipment

The sarcophagus of Siptah was discovered in the burial chamber of the tomb by Harry Burton in 1912. The sides of the coffer are decorated with alternating triple *khekher*-ornaments and recumbent jackals, above a lower register of underworld demons, a design followed by a number of Siptah's successors. The cartouches are recut, like many cartouches within the tomb, though this fact does not necessarily indicate that the monument was usurped from an earlier king.

Among the mass of as yet unpublished calcite fragments brought to light during the excavations carried out on behalf of Theodore Davis are said to have been discerned the remains of a rectangular sarcophagus, two anthropoid coffins and two canopic chests. These, for the most part, are probably to be divided between Siptah himself and his mother, Queen Tiaa. However, some of the coffin fragments are said to carry the name of Merenptah, and to be associated with the anthropoid coffin fragment of this king now in the British Museum. Their presence within KV47 has not yet been explained.

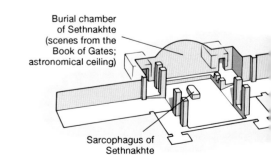

Burial chamber
of Sethnakhte
(scenes from the
Book of Gates;
astronomical ceiling)

Sarcophagus of
Sethnakhte

Factfile

Tomb number/location:
KV14, Wadi Biban el-Muluk
Date of discovery:
accessible since antiquity
Royal mummies:
mummy of Tawosret buried in KV11 and perhaps removed in antiquity; not identified; mummy of Sethnakhte removed in antiquity; found in KV35 (attribution uncertain)
Excavator/report:
Hartwig Altenmüller, 1983–87, for the University of Hamburg: H. Altenmüller, in C. N. Reeves (ed.), *After Tut'ankhamun* (London, 1992) pp. 141–64
Wall documentation:
Eugène Lefébure, *Les Hypogées royaux de Thèbes II* (Paris, 1889) pp. 123–45

The Tomb of Tawosret and Sethnakhte (KV14)

'Found a human skull[,] some bones and some bones of a bull[,] wood sarcophagus etc.'

James Burton

History and excavation

The cutting of KV14 appears to have been begun by Tawosret, the wife of Sethos II, for herself and for her husband, but the tomb was completed by Sethnakhte, who apparently dismantled the earlier burials and prepared the tomb for his own interment. It is likely that Sethnakhte's removal of Tawosret's burial from KV14 was accomplished at the same time as his apparent reburial of Sethos II within KV15.

No certain trace of the queen's mummy has been found (but see p. 199). The remains of the burial of Sethnakhte himself – his cartonnage coffin and perhaps the king's body as well – were recovered from KV35. The remains of a body found in the sarcophagus of the burial chamber in KV14 were probably intrusive and to be dated to the Third Intermediate Period.

The tomb has lain open since antiquity. Some limited, though unrecorded, exploration appears to have taken place early in the present century, as a box knob of Horemheb specifically said to be from KV14 was registered in the Egyptian Museum in Cairo in 1909. Recently, the double tomb has been studied in detail by Hartwig Altenmüller.

Architecture and decoration

In completing the tomb begun for Tawosret and expanded for her as queen regnant, Sethnakhte excavated one of the largest tombs (over 112 m (370

KV14, begun by Tawosret and completed by Sethnakhte on the now standard straight axis, incorporates two burial chambers – a unique feature in the Valley of the Kings.

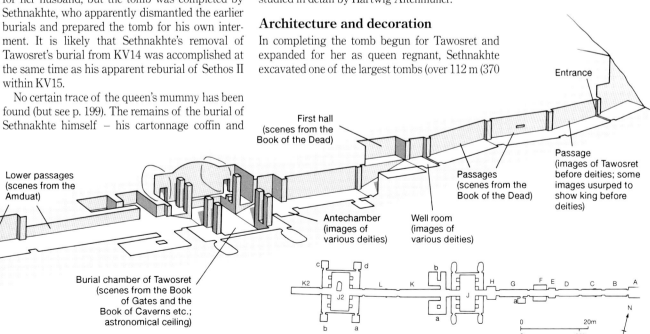

Entrance

First hall
(scenes from the
Book of the Dead)

Passage
(images of Tawosret before deities; some images usurped to show king before deities)

Passages
(scenes from the
Book of the Dead)

Lower passages
(scenes from the
Amduat)

Antechamber
(images of
various deities)

Well room
(images of
various deities)

Burial chamber of Tawosret
(scenes from the Book
of Gates and the
Book of Caverns etc.;
astronomical ceiling)

Detail of the fragmentary sarcophagus lid of Sethnakhte. The monument is closely similar in design to that of Siptah, with the figure of the mummiform king flanked to left and right by images of Isis and Nephthys and two intervening serpent goddesses.

ft)) in the royal valley. Curiously, while the axis of the structure approximates an east–west alignment overall, the various extensions constructed at different times shift slightly in their orientation. The corridors of the first part of the tomb (Tawosret as royal wife) appear carefully to avoid the standard royal canon for this period of five cubits in width (somewhat over 2.6 m (8 ft 6 in)); they are, in fact, one whole cubit less. In the first burial chamber too, the columns are, at 0.6 m (2 ft), rather less than the royal scale of two cubits (0.7 m (2 ft 5 in)) in width – the width of the barely begun secondary chamber

(Ka/Kb) (Tawosret as regnant queen). Similar two-cubit columns occur in the second burial chamber (J2) excavated for King Sethnakhte.

The various stages of development of this unusual tomb are reflected also in its decoration. In the first part of the tomb, several male deities were given grammatically female epithets (as in the inscription above the Osiris shrine), showing attempted assimilation with the person of the queen. The entrance passages were originally decorated with non-kingly material, though the first burial chamber contains royal material such as the closing scene from the Book of Caverns, and it is possible that the abandoned secondary chamber (Ka/Kb) was intended to be decorated in a fully royal manner. The remainder of the tomb (rooms K, L, J2, K2), constructed for Sethnakhte, naturally displays purely royal decoration. As in the tomb of Sethos II (KV15), the king and deity are no longer shown together on the same face of the burial-hall pillars, but rather on separate sides; in Sethnakhte's case, cursory images of the king replace the earlier pillar representations of Tawosret.

Funerary equipment

The sarcophagus of Sethnakhte was smashed in antiquity. The lid is closely similar to that of Siptah, as is the fragmented decoration of the coffer walls. The coffer, at least, appears to have been usurped from a previous owner – perhaps Sethos II.

A battered anthropoid coffin recovered from the KV35 cache was inscribed for Sethnakhte. Despite its modest quality, it perhaps formed part of the original burial equipment.

A 'cache' of materials sometimes associated with the burials of Sethos II and Tawosret was found in the royal valley by Edward Ayrton in 1908 (p. 153).

A pillar from the burial chamber of Sethnakhte: the king wearing the red crown. The combination of single adjacent images to form a complete scene first occurs in the tombs of Sethos II and Tawosret/Sethnakhte.

Sethnakhte's 20th-dynasty successors, nine in total, each bore the name Ramesses, and for all but the fifth (perhaps), eighth and eleventh we have an unequivocal place of burial. The first of the series, Ramesses III (1194–1163 BC), sought to emulate his predecessor, Ramesses II, in both name and deed. He succeeded in warding off attacks from Libya to the west and the 'Sea Peoples' to the north, and retained control of much of southern Palestine. But the sun was beginning to set, and under Ramesses III's successors Egypt fell into decline.

A taste of things to come was the attempted assassination of Ramesses III, the plot hatched in the royal harem; it failed, but it is clear that the status of Pharaoh had diminished. As the endless procession of Ramessid kings ruling from the north came and went, each more colourless than his predecessor and the greatest monument to his life his tomb, a rival dynasty of Amun priests developed at Thebes in the south. By the time of Ramesses XI (1100–1070 BC), the priestly line was sufficiently strong to challenge the status quo and ultimately assume the faded mantle of royalty in its own right.

A Tomb Begun by Sethnakhte and Completed by Ramesses III (KV11)

'Bones of an ox – sarcophagus was in the middle. Yanni [d'Athanasi – *sic*; actually Belzoni] took it.'

James Burton

KV11 was one of the tombs accessible to tourists during Greco-Roman times, at least in its outer portions, and it has stood open ever since. From the 18th century it has popularly been known as 'Bruce's Tomb', after the Scottish traveller James Bruce who reproduced in a poor copy the scene of the blind harpists in room Cd (p. 53).

The tomb was begun by Sethnakhte, who then abandoned it and turned to KV14 where he was buried (p. 157). Sethnakhte's son, Ramesses III, resumed work on KV11 and was interred here.

Architecture

Although the first three corridors were constructed by Sethnakhte, the niche-like side chambers in the first two passages (each, according to J. G. Wilkinson, with a pit, of uncertain purpose) are believed to have been added by Ramesses III. At that time, the third corridor, which had penetrated the roof of KV10 (the tomb of Amenmesse), was turned into a small room from which the rest of the tomb was cut on a shifted axis. Thus the fourth corridor uniquely *rises* to clear the underlying chamber of KV10, and the tomb then continues its planned descent to a well room and to the pillared hall with subsidiary chamber, similar to that in KV10 and not used since that time or again. Another passage then leads to two anterooms and

The Later Ramessids

Factfile

Tomb number/location:
KV11, Wadi Biban el-Muluk
Date of discovery:
open in part since antiquity
Royal mummy:
removed in antiquity; discovered in DB320
Excavator/report:
unknown, 1895, for the Service des Antiquités: J. de Morgan, *BIÉ* (3 série) 6 (1895) p. 140
Wall documentation:
M. Marciniak, *Études et Travaux* 12 (1983) pp. 295–305

Osiris shrine above the stairway giving access to the lower reaches of KV11. Pillars at either side show the king making offerings to Osiris and other underworld deities.

changes to that of Ramesses III. Scenes from the Amduat appear in the fourth corridor, and standard divine scenes decorate the well room. The first pillared hall is decorated with scenes and texts from the Book of Gates, and also depicts Ramesses and various deities on its pillar surfaces. The final corridor contains material from the 'opening of the mouth' ceremony, and the two antechambers show various scenes of deities. Although badly water-damaged, the sarcophagus chamber was evidently decorated with extracts from the Book of Gates and the Book of the Earth. Apparently no astronomical decoration was placed on the ceiling, but the side rooms have various texts and an example of the Book of the Divine Cow (room Jc). At the end of the sarcophagus hall extension, part of the judgment of Osiris was depicted, again from the Book of Gates.

Funerary equipment

It has been suggested (by Aidan Dodson) that Ramesses III's sarcophagus had originally been intended as an outer container for, though never employed by, Sethos II. The wooden trough of Ramesses III's second-innermost coffin – decorated, like the cartonnage of Sethnakhte, with images of

Detail of one of the pillar scenes on p. 159: Ramesses III makes an offering of incense.

the burial chamber, which apparently begins the trend of accommodating the sarcophagus along the tomb's main axis. As in the tomb of Merenptah (KV8), the four subsidiary chambers are symmetrically placed at each corner, and the extension beyond this hall is also cut to a fairly regular plan.

Decoration

'I was riveted, as it were, to the spot by the first sight of these paintings, and I could proceed no further. In one pannel were several musical instruments strowed upon the ground. In three following pannels were painted ... three harps, which merited the utmost attention ...'

James Bruce

Jars (including 'stirrup jars' and other vessels of Aegean design) among everyday objects depicted in one of the side rooms of the second corridor of KV11.

If, technically, the sunk reliefs of this tomb leave something to be desired, their colouring is well preserved and their variety exceptional. The twin Hathor-headed columns which flank the doorway at the entrance to KV11 are unique, though the standard solar disc with goddesses is placed between them. The first three passages were decorated for Sethnakhte (showing that this work must have progressed alongside the actual cutting of the tomb), with the first two corridors carrying the Litany of Re. On the walls of the side chambers added by Ramesses III, unique secular scenes were painted, including the royal armoury, representations of boats, the famous blind harpists of James Bruce (p. 53) and, in the scenes of the king's treasury, many luxury items, some of which were clearly imports from the Aegean. The third corridor shows Sethnakhte before various deities, and from this point on the decorative programme

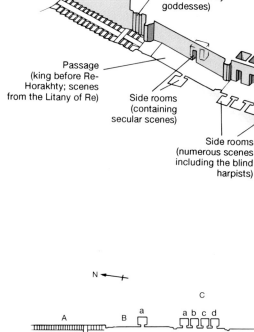

Entrance
(Hathor-headed
columns flanking
doorway; solar
disc adored by
goddesses)

Passage
(king before Re-
Horakhty; scenes
from the Litany of Re)

Side rooms
(containing
secular scenes)

Side rooms
(numerous scenes
including the blind
harpists)

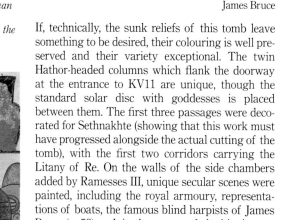

A Tomb for a Son of Ramesses III

Factfile

Tomb number/location:
KV3, Wadi Biban el-Muluk
Date of discovery:
open since antiquity
Excavator/report:
Harry Burton, 1912, for
Theodore M. Davis:
unpublished

KV3, probably among those noted by Pococke, was entered by James Burton in the 1820s or 1830s. Burton noted traces of the cartouches of Ramesses III in the entrance passageway. The tomb was first excavated in 1912 by Harry Burton, though both Quibell and Ayrton had earlier made sundry clearances in the vicinity.

The plan is unusual, and reflects the semi-royal nature of the tomb. Several elements of the standard royal design are lacking, and the tomb is cut straight back into the rock with virtually no descent beyond the entrance. A single corridor leads to a four-pillared hall, both corridor and hall having subsidiary rooms

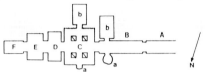

on each side (those on the left unfinished). Three more rooms – one a vaulted burial chamber – lie directly beyond the pillared hall.

Only traces of decoration survive, in the entrance and first corridor, though it is likely that this originally extended throughout the entire tomb since Lepsius, in the 1840s, noted traces of paint on the ceiling of the vault in addition to rows of cartouches of Ramesses III and representations of the king on the walls of the first corridor. As in all royal tombs of the period, the compositions will presumably have been based upon the Litany of Re.

A hieratic ostracon now in Berlin records that in Year 28 of Ramesses III a workgang went to the royal valley 'to found the [tomb] of a prince of His Majesty'. The tomb is probably KV3, though the name of the princely owner is unknown – nor do we know whether he was ever buried here. Tomb KV3 was later employed as a Christian chapel.

---

goddesses and the four sons of Horus – was discovered in the KV35 royal cache in 1898 containing the mummy of Amenophis III. The lid is lost; it had been violently removed in antiquity, the mortise cuts in the trough rim being broken in the process.

Other attributable finds are few, but evidently include five *shabtis* solid cast in bronze, now in the British Museum, in Turin, in the Louvre (2 specimens), and the Oriental Museum, Durham.

Graffiti, the rewrapping of the mummy and other human remains

Champollion recorded three undated graffiti in the tomb, none of them wholly legible. One seems to refer to an inspection, while the second and third, located in the burial chamber, list among other names that of Butehamun (p. 205), the necropolis scribe who directed the 'osirification' of Ramesses III in Year 13 of Smendes I. The work is recorded in a linen notation on the new mummy wrappings of the king (p. 203).

The mummy itself was found in the DB320 cache, contained in a once-gilded cartonnage case within the massive mummy case of Queen Ahmose-Nofretiri. It was stripped by Maspero in 1886. The features were so unappealing that they found fame as the model for Boris Karloff's *The Mummy*.

Human remains noted in one of the side chambers of the tomb (J2) by both the French Expedition and James Burton were evidently intrusive and of Third Intermediate Period date.

The partially unwrapped mummy of Ramesses III from the Deir el-Bahri cache.

(Left) Initiated by Sethnakhte, work on KV11 was abandoned after it collided with KV10. The tomb was later completed by Ramesses III on a realigned axis.

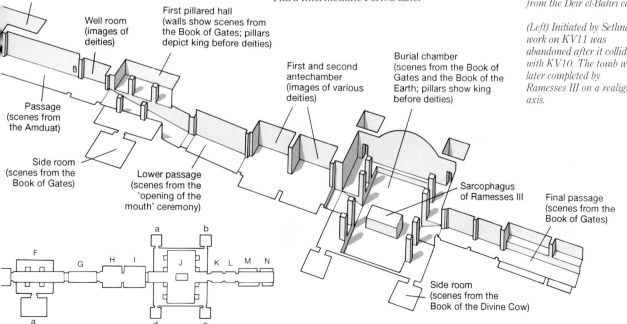

Passage
(where tomb
collided with KV10)

Well room
(images of
deities)

First pillared hall
(walls show scenes from
the Book of Gates; pillars
depict king before deities)

First and second
antechamber
(images of various
deities)

Burial chamber
(scenes from the Book of
Gates and the Book of the
Earth; pillars show king
before deities)

Passage
(scenes from
the Amduat)

Side room
(scenes from the
Book of Gates)

Lower passage
(scenes from the
'opening of the
mouth' ceremony)

Sarcophagus
of Ramesses III

Final passage
(scenes from the
Book of Gates)

Side room
(scenes from the
Book of the Divine Cow)

Factfile

Tomb number/location:
KV2, Wadi Biban el-Muluk
Date of discovery:
open since antiquity
Royal mummy:
removed in antiquity;
discovered in KV35
Excavators/reports:
Edward R. Ayrton, 1905/6,
for Theodore M. Davis: Th.
M. Davis *et al., The Tomb
of Sipthah; the Monkey
Tomb and the Gold Tomb*
(London, 1908); C. N.
Reeves, *MDAIK* 40 (1984)
pp. 228–30 (finds); Howard
Carter, 1920, for the Earl of
Carnarvon: unpublished
Epigraphic documentation:
Erik Hornung, *Zwei
ramessidische
Königsgräber: Ramses IV.
und Ramses VII.* (Mainz,
1990)

The Tomb of Ramesses IV (KV2)

History and archaeology

'[Year 2, second month of inundation], day 17 . . . the city governor Neferrenpet came to the City [i.e. Thebes] and also the king's butler Hori and the king's butler Amenkha, son of Tekhy . . . and they went up to the Valley of the Kings to search for a place for piercing a tomb for Usermaatre-setepenamun [Ramesses IV] . . .'

Hieratic ostracon

KV2 seems to have attracted more attention in antiquity (to judge from the large number of graffiti) and during the 18th century of our era (when it was planned by Pococke, as was the massive, 2.5-m (8-ft) high sarcophagus described by Bruce) than it has more recently. No clearance of the interior of KV2 is recorded, and the only finds known from inside the tomb are the 'bodies' seen by J. G. Wilkinson in the 'recesses' behind the burial chamber. Most probably these were intrusive interments of Third Intermediate Period date.

Far more is known about the vicinity of the tomb entrance, which was cleared by Edward Ayrton in 1905/6 and later by Howard Carter in 1920. Both excavators recovered a large quantity of funerary material, thrown out of the tomb in antiquity – figured ostraca, *shabtis* (in wood, calcite and faience), fragments of faience, glass, and wood, and a group of potsherds 'encrusted with plaster, and . . . with colours', several with the name of Ramesses II, which had clearly been employed as *ad hoc* palettes.

Ayrton's work 'up towards the mouth of the tomb . . . on the north' also uncovered the 'debris of rough Coptic and Roman huts', perhaps for animals, a fragmentary though exceptionally pleasing Coptic trencher (p. 50), fragments of ostraca and an unopened letter on papyrus. For Herbert Winlock, KV2 was one of the most important Coptic dwellings in the valley.

Architecture

'The first of the great entrances . . .'

Elizabeth Thomas

Nine foundation deposits (of which number Ayrton found the remains of one and Carter a further five, intact) were dug before the impressive rock-covered

(Right) The corridors of KV2 (with the royal sarcophagus visible in the distance) exhibit the shallow incline of the later Ramessid tombs.

(Opposite) Although abbreviated somewhat, the finished plan of KV2 includes a number of ancillary niches and other features.

entrance, and this and the first corridor were both given the combined stair-and-ramp configuration found occasionally from the time of Ramesses II on. The second-corridor niches, which had been dropped or modified in a number of earlier sepulchres, also reappear here and continue in succeeding tombs.

The intended design had been abbreviated, presumably owing to constraints of time. The modification entailed the construction of a sloping ramp and burial chamber in what would have been the well and first pillared hall areas.

Two sketch plans of the tomb of Ramesses IV are known, the most famous and complete on a papyrus now in Turin (p. 27), and a detail of the outer doorway preserved on a limestone ostracon discovered by Ayrton in the debris at the tomb entrance. Both show the tomb in its finished state, the papyrus reflecting the abbreviated form of the final plan and both papyrus and ostracon showing the doors closed and bolted. While the ostracon sketch probably represents no more than a casual doodle by one of the workmen, the papyrus plan seems to have had a more serious function, and may have been employed in the consecration ritual performed at the completion of the work. Such 'models' are more commonly recognized in the context of temple foundations, where they usually take a three-dimensional form.

Decoration

'Upon the walls of [room Gb] there are representations of a bed, a chair, two chests, and the usual four canopic vases. These objects were, perhaps, actually placed in this room at the time of the funeral, though this was somewhat against the custom of earlier times.'

Arthur Weigall

The decoration of KV2 is virtually intact, and reveals the original use of several elements. The first two passages contain the usual Litany of Re, but in the third, part of the Book of Caverns appears for the first time. The anteroom has sections of the Book of the Dead, and the burial chamber displays a mixture of old and new works. The walls have selections from the Amduat and Book of

Gates, but beginning with this tomb the Books of the Heavens replace the older astronomical depictions on the vaulted ceiling. Decan lists appear at the sides, framing the twin figures of the sky goddess Nut which are stretched out as a canopy above the royal burial. The rooms beyond the sarcophagus hall are decorated with scenes from the Book of Caverns and representations of objects stored in these final chambers of the tomb.

Dismantling and abandonment

The sarcophagus was broken through at one end in antiquity and the lid displaced. The removal of the king's mummy – which eventually turned up in KV35 (p. 198) – is perhaps documented by a graffito of the scribe Penamun, the same man who, in Year 16 of Smendes, 4 *peret*, day 11, undertook to restore the mummy of Amenophis I for the second time.

(Above) Pharaoh before the sun god: a scene in KV2.

Large wooden shabti *of Ramesses IV (paint restored).*

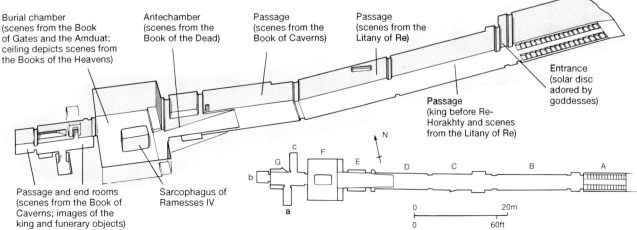

Burial chamber (scenes from the Book of Gates and the Amduat; ceiling depicts scenes from the Books of the Heavens)

Antechamber (scenes from the Book of the Dead)

Passage (scenes from the Book of Caverns)

Passage (scenes from the Litany of Re)

Entrance (solar disc adored by goddesses)

Passage (king before Re-Horakhty and scenes from the Litany of Re)

Passage and end rooms (scenes from the Book of Caverns; images of the king and funerary objects)

Sarcophagus of Ramesses IV

0   20m

0   60ft

Tomb number/location:
KV9, Wadi Biban el-Muluk
Date of discovery:
open since antiquity
Royal mummies:
mummies of Ramesses V
and VI removed in
antiquity; both discovered
in KV35
Excavators/report:
James Burton, 1820s–30s:
unpublished; Georges
Daressy, 1888, for the
Service des Antiquités: G.
Daressy, *ASAE* 18 (1919)
pp. 270–74
Wall documentation:
Alexandre Piankoff and N.
Rambova, *The Tomb of
Ramesses VI* (New York,
1954)

*(Above right) Mask from
the lid of the inner
anthropoid sarcophagus of
Ramesses VI.*

*(Below) KV9, begun by
Ramesses V and continued by
Ramesses VI, is the most
completely executed tomb of
the late Ramessid period.*

The Tomb of Ramesses V and Ramesses VI (KV9)

'I . . . found a number of fragments of small figures
similar to those in Belzoni's tomb but of [calcite] instead
of wood[;] they had hieroglyphics upon them in black
and green – parts of vases of the same material coated
with pitch . . .'

James Burton

KV9 was known to the Romans as the tomb of
Memnon (p. 51), and to the *savants* of the
Napoleonic Expedition as *La Tombe de la
Métempsychose*. The earlier parts of the tomb
before E are inscribed for Ramesses V, with no
trace of usurpation. A wooden box fragment from
the tomb and a possible wooden coffin peg from
Davis's work in the valley are the only funerary
objects of Ramesses V known. Everything else
found in KV9 was prepared for Ramesses VI.
Ramesses V seems not only to have begun the tomb
but to have been interred here in a double burial
with Ramesses VI. The date of Ramesses V's interment (the place unfortunately not specified), in Year
2 of his successor, is recorded on an ostracon.

Architecture and decoration

The parts cut during the reigns of both kings may
be viewed as a single whole. The corridors are larger in width and height than those of Ramesses IV,
but are without the stair-and-ramp configuration
found in KV2. The passage H is unique in having a
horizontal roof combined with a sloping floor,
because here the stonemasons, cutting from top to
bottom, had to drop the level to avoid KV12. The
burial chamber itself is not completely finished,
evident also in the lack of any subsidiary rooms
(though these are omitted in all succeeding royal
tombs) except for the abbreviated extension
beyond the sarcophagus hall.

Although well preserved, the coloured sunk
reliefs are stylistically inferior to those of the preceding 19th dynasty. The decoration differs from
the programme employed since the tomb of Sethos
I, revealing the last major developmental modification to occur in the royal valley. A heavy emphasis
is placed on astronomical texts and representations. The god Re is given greater prominence, in
the outer corridors the Book of Gates (on the left)
and the Book of Caverns (on the right) replace the
Litany of Re, and astronomical ceilings are found
in each passage. The third corridor and well room
are decorated in the same manner, with the addition
of excerpts from the Books of the Heavens, as is
the first pillared hall which retains, however, the
motif of the Osiris shrine. Yet even here the
increased influence of Re is seen, in that Osiris is
identified with the sun god through the addition of
a solar disc and pectoral. In the lower passages and
antechamber, the ceilings show the Books of the
Heavens and various cryptographic texts. The passage walls show sections from the Amduat; and the
antechamber walls scenes of deities and the Book
of the Dead. On the walls of the burial chamber the
Book of the Earth occurs for the first time, and here
the astronomical ceiling combines images from the
Books of the Heavens with the outstretched diurnal
and nocturnal figures of the goddess Nut.

Funerary equipment

Clearance of the single 'sarcophagus pit' in the burial chamber floor by Edwin Brock in 1985 revealed
that the edges had been cut back, perhaps to

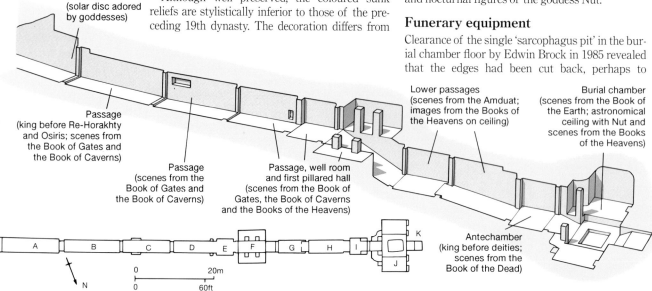

Entrance
(solar disc adored
by goddesses)

Passage
(king before Re-Horakhty
and Osiris; scenes from
the Book of Gates and
the Book of Caverns)

Passage
(scenes from the
Book of Gates and
the Book of Caverns)

Passage, well room
and first pillared hall
(scenes from the Book of
Gates, the Book of Caverns
and the Books of the Heavens)

Lower passages
(scenes from the Amduat;
images from the Books of
the Heavens on ceiling)

Burial chamber
(scenes from the Book of
the Earth; astronomical
ceiling with Nut and
scenes from the Books
of the Heavens)

Antechamber
(king before deities;
scenes from the
Book of the Dead)

A | B | C | D | E | F | G | H | I | K | J

0   20m
0   60ft

N

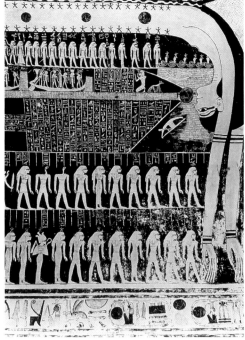

*The goddess Nut, with texts
from the Book of the Day,
one of the so-called Books of
the Heavens – a detail of the
burial chamber ceiling in
KV9. The imagery operates
at differing levels, showing the
sun as a disc being swallowed
and reborn from the body of
the goddess, and also as a god
in the solar barque sailing
upon the celestial waters.*

accommodate the base of a granite outer sarcophagus box – no trace of which was found. The unfinished inner, anthropoid sarcophagus of green conglomerate had been smashed to pieces in antiquity, the best known of the fragments being the large face mask of Ramesses VI now in the British Museum; the lid and sides of the box were lightly incised and painted with figures and texts first found in the sarcophagus of Siptah – the Book of the Earth. The king may also have had an anthropoid innermost sarcophagus of calcite, but the fragments uncovered by Brock are uninscribed and may be intrusive.

No sarcophagi are known for Ramesses V; any prepared had possibly been usurped by his successor. Other finds brought to light by Brock included pottery, fragments of wood and calcite *shabtis* – and a coin of the Roman emperor Maximian.

Robberies and mummies

A unique account of a theft from the tomb of Ramesses VI is preserved in the tomb robbery document (undated) known as Papyrus Mayer B (p. 192). On the assumption that this robbery prompted the visit recorded in the graffito noted by Champollion on the ceiling of the burial chamber, Cyril Aldred suggested that the thefts took place before Year 9 of Ramesses IX.

The mummies of both Ramesses V and Ramesses VI were discovered in the KV35 cache in 1898. The mummy of Ramesses V lay in the base of a white-painted wooden coffin and that of Ramesses VI in a replacement coffin originally belonging to a high priest of Menkheperre named

Re. A fragment of wooden coffin, decorated in a similar manner to the trough of Ramesses III (p. 160), was found with the mummy of Ramesses VI, however, and may well have formed part of the original burial equipment. The mummy itself had evidently been attended to at the same time as that of Sethos II, since the right forearm and hand of this king had inadvertently been wrapped in with Ramesses VI's own badly damaged body.

*The burial chamber of KV9,
with the first occurrence of
the late Ramessid Book of the
Earth beneath images of Nut
and the Books of the Heavens
depicted on the ceiling.*

Edwin Brock directing work at the entrance to KV1.

Factfile

Tomb number/location:
KV1, Wadi Biban el-Muluk
Date of discovery:
accessible since antiquity
Royal mummy:
not identified
Excavator/report:
Edwin C. Brock, 1983–84, 1994, for the Royal Ontario Museum: E. C. Brock, in R. Wilkinson (ed.), *Valley of the Sun Kings* (Tucson, 1995) pp. 47–67
Epigraphic documentation:
Erik Hornung, *Zwei ramessidische Königsgräber: Ramses IV. und Ramses VII.* (Mainz, 1990)

Cutaway view of the tomb of Ramesses VII.

The Tomb of Ramesses VII (KV1)

Archaeology

'Until the recent work to prepare the tomb for access by tourists, the *wadi* in which it is located remained relatively untouched by past archaeological exploration and the site retained much the same appearance that it probably had since antiquity.'

Edwin Brock

The tomb of Ramesses VII is among those accessible since antiquity. Apart from an undocumented clearance in the late 1950s (perhaps at the time Alexandre Piankoff photographed the decoration), it attracted no more than passing attention from archaeologists until Edwin Brock cleared the pit in the burial chamber floor in 1983–84, and a decade later excavated at the tomb entrance, in advance of a repositioning of the tourist path.

Architecture and decoration

Outside the tomb, at the entrance, Brock's 'rescue' clearance brought to light 'two low rubble platforms to either side of the approach . . . composed of construction debris . . . [and] somewhat reminiscent of pylons . . .'; they had been cut through by floods soon after construction. No traces of foundation deposits were found.

The tomb proper consists of only the entrance, a first corridor and the burial chamber with a small extension room and niche. It has been argued that the finish of the masonry and the fine quality of the relief work indicate a planned and executed small-scale tomb, perhaps created with the realization that the king would have little time to complete the structure. On the other hand, the corridor width (3.1 m, or 10 ft 2 in) and height (4.1 m, or 13 ft 5 1/2 in) continue the tradition of expansion in the royal tombs and, together with the unfinished sarcophagus box-turned-lid (see below) and absence of any ancillary features, might indicate that a fully developed tomb was intended.

The decoration generally follows the precedent set in the tomb of Ramesses VI (KV9), yet still maintains several more traditional features including an almost atavistic emphasis on Osiris, whose iconographic presence is perhaps more strongly emphasized here than in any other Ramessid tomb. The entrance corridor has the king before the solar Horakhty-Atum-Khepri on the left and the netherworld Ptah-Sokar-Osiris on the right, followed by sections of the Book of Gates and the Book of Caverns and twin depictions of the king's purification as Osiris. The burial chamber has the goddess Weret-hekau and the composite Sekhmet-Bubastis-Weret-hekau at the entrance, forming another of the complementary symbolic pairs which dominate the decoration of the tomb. The inner walls feature extracts from the Book of the Earth, with the selection of texts being closely parallel to those of Ramesses VI, yet the ceiling combines the double image of the outstretched Nut with depictions of constellations as seen in the royal tombs from Sethos I to Ramesses III. The small room beyond the burial chamber shows scenes of the king before Osiris, shown in judgment on the end wall above the niche. The small *djed*-pillars painted on its sides take Osirid imagery to the very back of the tomb.

Passage
(king before various deities; scenes from the Book of Gates and the Book of Caverns)

The inverted sarcophagus box used to cover the rock-cut pit containing the royal mummy.

End room
(king before Osiris)

Entrance
(solar disc flanked by king and goddesses)

Sarcophagus of Ramesses VII

Burial chamber
(scenes from the Book of the Earth; astronomical ceiling with double Nut image)

A B C D a

N

0 10m
0 30ft

Funerary equipment

The sarcophagus consists of a rock-cut hollow covered by a massive, roughly cartouche-shaped block of stone (actually an inverted sarcophagus box) decorated with lightly incised and green-painted figures of Isis, Nephthys, Selkis and the four sons of Horus on the foot and the interior surfaces. This 'lid' remains in place, access to the royal mummy having been gained via a hole quarried in the foot end. Two circular pits cut into each of the long sides at floor level may have been intended for canopic jars, as Brock suggests.

Extant remains of the king's funerary equipment include a few *shabtis* (including examples in wood, calcite and faience from the burial chamber pit), together with 20th-dynasty pottery amphora fragments. 'Other material [from the burial chamber pit], of uncertain date, included fragments of wood and cloth strips of various types, the former, at least, appearing to belong to wooden coffins which may have been broken up here by tomb robbers.' Brock also found here materials abandoned by the tomb workers – artists' sketches on limestone flakes – and potsherds left from a period when the tomb was reused by the Copts.

In debris from a previous excavation deposited at the tomb entrance, Brock also recovered similar materials to those from the burial chamber pit, as well as basket fragments, a floral garland and fragments of an amphora with a five-line hieratic text on one side and a caricature of a serving scene on the other.

The king's mummy

'The tomb was perhaps unknown to the priests who transferred the royal mummies to their hiding-places, and it may have been found and robbed at a later date.'

Arthur Weigall

Arthur Weigall's opinion is improbable, but it remains a fact that the mummy of Ramesses VII has not yet been identified. Four faience cups of the king found near the DB320 cache may indicate the eventual destination of the corpse, but if so it has yet to be identified among the bodies there.

The Tomb of Ramesses VIII

The burial place of Ramesses VIII, who ruled for only one year, is unknown: neither the royal mummy nor any funerary equipment have ever come to light. It appears that as a mere prince – Ramesses Sethherkhepshef – he began the cutting and decoration of KV19 (p. 170), as Edwin Brock has recently observed; but any thought of interment here will have been abandoned when he ascended the throne.

(Above) The barque of the sun god drawn by attendant deities in the tomb of Ramesses VII. The cabin of the barque is encircled by the coils of the mehen *serpent which helps protect the solar deity in his journey through the netherworld.*

Head from a faience shabti *of Ramesses VII, recovered by Edwin Brock from the burial chamber pit.*

Factfile

Tomb number/location:
KV6, Wadi Biban el-Muluk
Date of discovery:
open since antiquity
Royal mummy:
removed in antiquity;
discovered in DB320
Excavators/report:
Henry Salt, *c.* 1817:
unpublished; Georges
Daressy, 1888, for the
Service des Antiquités: G.
Daressy, *ASAE* 18 (1919)
pp. 270–74
Wall documentation:
F. Guilmant, *Le tombeau de
Ramsès IX* (Cairo, 1907)

(Right) The first passage of the tomb of Ramesses IX, showing the entrances of the side niches and the image of the kneeling king in adoration before the solar disc on the lintel of the doorway into the second passage.

The Tomb of Ramesses IX (KV6)

Archaeology

The tomb of Ramesses IX has stood open since antiquity and attracted the informal comments, scribbled on the walls, of some 46 Classical tourists. It was evidently one of the tombs explored by Henry Salt (p. 60), and a number of objects from KV6 are now among the Salt collection in the British Museum: wooden *shabtis*, figured ostraca, wooden statuettes and a life-sized wooden '*ka*' figure similar to one of the pair from the tomb of Tutankhamun. In 1888 Georges Daressy cleared the sepulchre, his work yielding as many as a hundred ostraca and the runners of a large wooden shrine, identified by Daressy as a sledge used for the introduction of the missing sarcophagus.

Factfile

Tomb number/location:
KV C, Wadi Biban el-Muluk
Date of discovery:
January 1907, by Edward
R. Ayrton
Excavator/report:
E. R. Ayrton, 1907: Th. M.
Davis, *The Tomb of Queen
Tïyi* (London, 1910)

The Embalming Cache

It has been thought that the contents of this pit – 'several large jars of the XXth dynasty type lying together' – might be connected with KV55 (p. 117). However, as Lyla Pinch-Brock suggests, it seems more likely that the jars (not yet published) were embalming containers associated with the burial of Ramesses IX in KV6, just to the north.

Architecture and decoration

'The features of the king are peculiar, and from the form of the nose, so very unlike that of the usual Egyptian face, it becomes very probable that their sculptures actually offer portraits . . .'

John Gardner Wilkinson

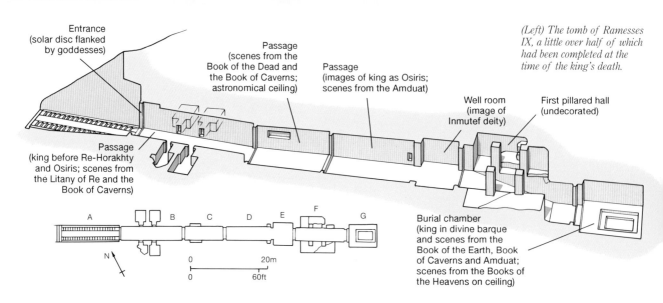

(Left) The tomb of Ramesses IX, a little over half of which had been completed at the time of the king's death.

Entrance
(solar disc flanked
by goddesses)

Passage
(scenes from the
Book of the Dead and
the Book of Caverns;
astronomical ceiling)

Passage
(images of king as Osiris;
scenes from the Amduat)

Well room
(image of
Inmutef deity)

First pillared hall
(undecorated)

Passage
(king before Re-Horakhty
and Osiris; scenes from
the Litany of Re and the
Book of Caverns)

Burial chamber
(king in divine barque
and scenes from the
Book of the Earth, Book
of Caverns and Amduat;
scenes from the Books of
the Heavens on ceiling)

A   B   C   D   E   F   G

N

0   20m
0   60ft

(Left and below) Two wooden figures from Henry Salt's work in the tomb of Ramesses IX: a lifesize ka-statue of the king; and an obscure underworld deity with a lidded compartment at the back to conceal a papyrus roll.

A little over half of Ramesses IX's tomb appears to have been completed by the time of the king's death. After the stair-and-ramp entrance, three well-fashioned corridors were cut, with the first having a series of four niche-like side rooms (the one overlying KV55 left unfinished) similar to those found in the first and second corridors of the tomb of Ramesses III. The well room and pillared hall were also completed, the corridor beyond being enlarged to receive the king's burial.

A sketch on limestone, found here by Daressy in 1888, is usually identified as a plan of KV6 (p. 69).

Only the first corridor of this tomb appears to have been decorated during the life of Ramesses IX, with the remainder of the tomb's decoration completed – with far less care and skill – after the king's death. Plastering was completed in the first corridors and thereafter only in the various door-ways, the far wall of the well room, and the walls

View from the well room into the pillared hall of KV6. The leopard-skin-clad figures with the side locks are of the deity Inmutef or 'bull of his mother' often associated with the royal burials.

(Below) Highly symbolic scenes from the third corridor of the tomb of Ramesses IX include representations from an otherwise unknown book of the netherworld along with enigmatic cryptographic inscriptions.

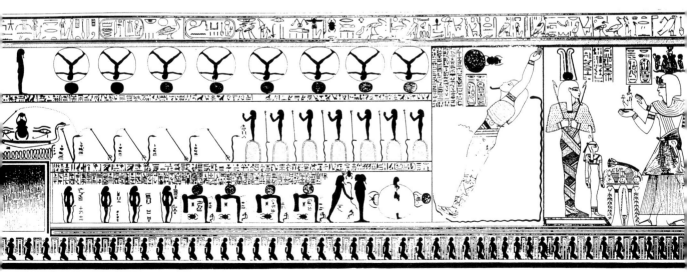

An example of the minutely detailed hieroglyphs found in the wall decoration of Ramesses IX's tomb. The text refers to the 'Great Cat', a form of the sun god.

and ceiling of the burial chamber. The decorative programme essentially follows that established by Ramesses VI, yet with interesting exceptions. The usual solar disc with goddesses motif is modified by the addition of the representation of the king on both sides and another goddess painted above the disc itself. For the first time since Ramesses IV, the Litany of Re appears in the entrance corridors, but alongside the Book of Caverns (introduced by Ramesses VI in this same location). In the second corridor, astronomical scenes – constellations and a list of decans – are shown, and here and in the third corridor scenes from the Book of the Dead and the Amduat were also painted. Scenes of the king and the gods also appear and are used, not always traditionally, in this area. Though several of these scenes of the king with, or as, various deities are unique, the burial chamber follows yet another variation on the decorative plan used by the previous Ramessid kings – the Book of the Earth, the Book of Caverns and the Amduat on the walls, and on the ceiling the Books of the Heavens.

Pharaoh's burial

Little funerary equipment has survived. As in the tomb of Ramesses VII, the floor of the burial chamber was cut with a rectangular, rimmed emplacement for the body, though no trace has been found of the huge lid which would have been required to cover it.

The Tomb of Prince Mentuherkhepshef

The main passage of Mentuherkhepshef's tomb, showing the prince offering before deities such as Ptah, Osiris and Khonsu. The scenes have suffered considerable damage since Belzoni's time.

The unfinished KV19 was discovered by Belzoni in 1817 containing a number of intrusive burials, probably of 22nd-dynasty date. The 20th-dynasty occupant of the tomb had been Ramesses Mentuherkhepshef, a son of Ramesses IX, as the wall scenes indicate, who appears to have been interred here during the reign of Ramesses X. Before him, however, as Edwin Brock has noted, the tomb had

been intended as a royal gift for a prince named Ramesses Sethherkhepshef – who eventually ascended the throne as Ramesses VIII. This king's actual tomb has never been found.

Fragments of the coffin of Mentuherkhepshef are perhaps to be recognized in the faience wig inlays(?) recovered by Ayrton together with fragments of beadwork during his work there in 1905/6; no traces of the prince's physical remains, however, were found.

Architecture

'On entering the tomb one notices on either side the drawings of the swing doors, which, as may be seen from the pivot-holes at the top, actually stood here.'

Arthur Weigall

Both the location (similar to that of the tombs of Ramesses IV–VII) and plan of KV19 suggest that it was initiated for a king; the widths of the entrance (3.6 m (11 ft 9 1/2 in)) and corridors (3 m (9 ft 10 in)) are exceeded only in the tombs of Ramesses IV–VII. However, traces at the bottom of the tomb jambs record that the intended owner had been a mere prince, albeit one who later ascended the throne (as Ramesses VIII).

Quarrying had barely advanced beyond the first corridor when work was abandoned. The shallow pit with covering slabs, and the niches on either side of the incipient second corridor, like the paintings, were evidently adaptations made for Mentuherkhepshef.

Ramesses IX in a posture of praise or adoration before the solar disc; a painted scene from the walls of the king's tomb.

The mummy of Ramesses IX was discovered in the Deir el-Bahri cache (DB320) in 1881, garlanded with flowers and contained in a coffin originally prepared for the lady Neskhons, wife of Pinudjem II. According to a docket on the bandages, the mummy (which is perhaps disarticulated) had been rewrapped at Medinet Habu, the administrative headquarters of the district, in Year 7 of Siamun, with linen dedicated by this same Neskhons.

An ivory veneered wooden casket of Ramesses IX from DB320 had presumably travelled with the mummy from KV6.

Decoration

'The painted figures on the walls are so perfect, that they are the best adapted of any I ever saw to give a correct and clear idea of the Egyptian taste.'

Giovanni Battista Belzoni

The decoration of KV19 is very similar to that found in the tombs of royal sons in the Valley of the Queens, except for the fact that, as an adult son, Mentuherkhepshef is shown alone rather than escorted by his father. At each side of the entrance, on the jambs, were painted twin serpents; beyond them, at the beginning of the first corridor, the leaves of the open doors were depicted, inscribed in hieratic with protective spells from the Book of the Dead.

Within this symbolic threshold, on each side of the first corridor, were painted seven scenes showing Mentuherkhepshef worshipping and offering to the various gods – Osiris, Khonsu, Thoth, Ptah. The figures contrast brightly with the clean white ground of the walls and the golden-yellow bands. The work is among the best in the royal valley.

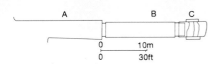

Factfile

Tomb number/location:
KV19, Wadi Biban el-Muluk
Date of discovery:
1817, by G. B. Belzoni
Royal mummy:
not found
Excavators/reports:
G. B. Belzoni, 1817, for Henry Salt: G. B. Belzoni, *Narrative of the Operations . . . in Egypt . . .* (London, 1820) p. 227; Edward R. Ayrton, 1905/6, for Theodore M. Davis: Th. M. Davis *et al., The Tomb of Siphtah; the Monkey Tomb and the Gold Tomb* (London, 1908); C. N. Reeves, *MDAIK* 40 (1984) pp. 233–4 (finds)

The elegant Mentuherkhepshef. The prince's facial features, side lock and robe are carefully detailed and drawn in the finest Ramessid style.

The head of the sun god Re-Horakhty – one of the few images still to be seen in the outer corridors of KV18.

Factfile

Tomb number/location:
KV18, Wadi Biban el-Muluk
Date of discovery:
open in part since antiquity
Royal mummy:
not identified
Excavator/report:
uncleared: unpublished

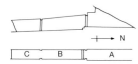

Profile and plan of KV18, the tomb of Ramesses X.

Factfile

Tomb number/location:
KV4, Wadi Biban el-Muluk
Date of discovery:
open since antiquity
Royal mummy:
Ramesses XI probably buried outside Thebes
Excavator/report:
John Romer, 1978–80, for The Brooklyn Museum: M. Ciccarello and J. Romer, *A Preliminary Report of the Recent Work in the Tombs of Ramesses X and XI . . .* (Brooklyn, 1979)
Wall documentation:
The Brooklyn Museum Theban Expedition, *A Report of the First Two Seasons, Introduction* (Brooklyn, 1979) (details only)

The Tomb of Ramesses X (KV18)

Archaeology

KV18, the tomb of Ramesses X, has still not been cleared beyond the first corridor, and no authentic funerary material of the owner has ever come to light. Elements from a foundation deposit – 'blue glaze models of tools (viz.: adze, hoe and yoke)' – were discovered at the entrance by Howard Carter in 1901/2, but these were uninscribed. Ramesses X's mummy has not been found in either of the two principal caches, DB320 and KV35.

Architecture and decoration

So little is known of this still-uncleared tomb that only the entrance area may be considered. The entrance itself continues the Ramessid trend of constant enlargement, being some 10 cm (4 in) wider than the previous king's tomb, but is simple in form, having little slope and no steps. Unusually, two steps do appear at the entrance to the first corridor, which leads into the second corridor where the tomb is currently blocked. The nine-year reign of this king would certainly indicate the likelihood of a fairly extensive tomb, but further details must await full excavation.

Very little of this tomb's decoration remains in the outer, accessible areas. The beautiful example of the Ramessid entrance motif with images of the king kneeling on either side of the sun disc along with attendant goddesses was clear when drawn by Champollion's artists in 1826 (p. 35), but the paint and most of the plaster of this and other motifs have now been lost to subsequent floods. A portion of the left-hand side of the design is still visible, as are traces of other motifs – such as the head of Re-Horakhty on the left wall of the first passage.

The Tomb of Ramesses XI (KV4)

Archaeology

'Ramesses [XI]'s tomb had one feature which intrigued us: in the splendid vaulted burial chamber . . ., more than 250 ft. into the cliff face there was, instead of the usual granite sarcophagus . . ., a vast shaft, some 14 ft. by 10 ft., which dropped straight down into pitch darkness. . . .

To clear it out was going to be an awkward job. But once we had done it, what might we not find? A hidden door to another corridor, and other chambers?'

John Romer

The tomb of Ramesses XI, having stood open since antiquity and been used as a dwelling and a stable by the Copts, attracted little archaeological attention until 1979 when it was excavated by John Romer for The Brooklyn Museum.

Romer did not find his 'hidden door' because Ramesses XI had abandoned the tomb unfinished, opting for burial elsewhere, perhaps in the north. Subsequently the tomb was taken over by Pinudjem I (to judge from a section of the wall decoration where he had added his cartouche: p. 208) with a view to his own interment there – an idea which also seems to have been dropped.

What Romer did find were three of an original four foundation deposits placed at the corners to the mouth of the shaft, and a good many objects which had been tipped into the shaft at the end of the New Kingdom and later – the topmost layers including the remains of a burnt 22nd-dynasty burial with fragments of its cartonnage covering and a wooden coffin, and sundry Coptic pieces. Within the undisturbed layers at the bottom of the shaft, Romer was surprised to find 'broken pieces of burial equipment of several New Kingdom pharaohs': 'two fragments of an extremely large blue faience vessel that bore the Horus name shared by Tuthmosis I and Ramesses II'; fragments of gilded gesso, some perhaps hacked from the coffin of Tuthmosis III; the chopped up remains of royal funerary statuettes originating in KV34, two with yellow hieroglyphs incorporating the throne

Left entrance wall of KV4.
The jambs show the seated
goddess Maat and the wall the
king before Re-Horakhty, the
standard Ramessid preface to
the Litany of Re.

name of Tuthmosis III; fragments of a female
pharaonic coffin, presumably belonging to
Hatshepsut; and three calcite 'lost contour' *shabtis*
of Ramesses IV.

Evidently, during Pinudjem I's reign, the tomb
had been used as an *ad hoc* workshop for
processing material from the burials in KV20
(Hatshepsut), KV34 (Tuthmosis III) and conceivably KV38 (Tuthmosis I). This last phase of activity in KV4 reflects the dramatic change which took
place in official policy towards the royal dead following the last royal burial in the Valley of the
Kings (p. 204).

Architecture and decoration

Although somewhat abbreviated, KV4 is essentially complete, with all the major elements of the
royal tomb plan being present. The tomb displays
several unique features, among them the increased
slope of the second corridor and – even more pro-
nounced – of the descent from the first pillared hall.
Rather than being square in form, this room is elongated like the pillared halls of the 18th-dynasty

tombs, though any functional reason for this adaptation of plan is difficult to ascertain. The inner corridors are noticeably abbreviated, to the point that,
as in Ramesses IX (KV6), there is only a short passage leading from the first pillared hall to the sarcophagus hall, which is unusual in its four
rectangular – rather than square – pillars and in the
deep (over 10 m (30 ft)) central burial shaft, perhaps
intended as an additional security measure.

The entrance corridors retain substantial traces
of yellow painted plaster with a number of scenes
laid out in preliminary red lines. These scenes show
the king before various deities, including the four-
headed ram god Harmachis. Beyond them, the
tomb walls appear to have been left plain, indicating that decoration for Ramesses XI – and
Pinudjem I – was begun only late in the excavation
or even when the work of cutting had stopped.

(Above) Calcite shabti *figure
of Ramesses IV, found during
John Romer's clearance of
KV4.*

*(Below) The tomb of
Ramesses XI, the last royal
tomb to be cut in the Valley of
the Kings, was close to
completion when it was
eventually abandoned unused.*

*(Below, far left) View down
the passage of KV4 towards
the burial chamber.*

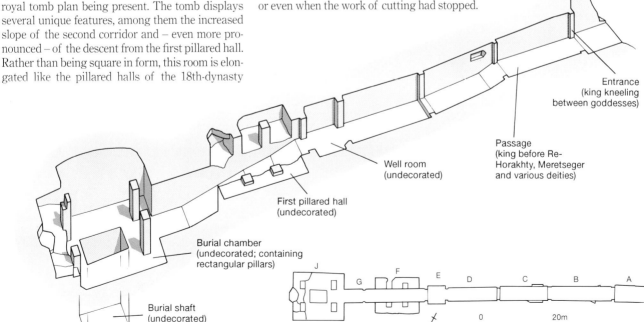

Entrance
(king kneeling
between goddesses)

Passage
(king before Re-
Horakhty, Meretseger
and various deities)

Well room
(undecorated)

First pillared hall
(undecorated)

Burial chamber
(undecorated; containing
rectangular pillars)

Burial shaft
(undecorated)

0   20m
0   60ft

Tombs of
the Nobles

Factfile

Tomb number/location:
KV46, Wadi Biban el-
Muluk
Date of discovery:
5 February 1905, by James
E. Quibell
Excavator/reports:
J. E. Quibell and Arthur
Weigall, 1905, for Theodore
M. Davis: Th. M. Davis *et
al., The Tomb of Iouiya
and Touiyou* (London,
1907); J. E. Quibell, *The
Tomb of Yuaa and Thuiu*
(Cairo, 1908)

*Carter's painting of a casket
on legs from the tomb of
Yuya and Tjuyu, of inlaid
wood decorated with blue
faience tiles carrying the
names of Amenophis III and
Tiye.*

In addition to the tombs of the pharaohs and their immediate families, the Valley of the Kings has yielded several undecorated and uninscribed tombs prepared for highly placed courtiers and influential nobles – and occasionally, it seems, as eternal homes for the king's more pampered pets. Among those few (human) individuals accorded the privilege of burial in the royal wadis (both east and west) may be singled out the royal fan-bearer Maiherpri, who was interred in KV36, and Yuya and Tjuyu, the parents of Queen Tiye, who were buried within KV46. Both of these tombs by chance escaped serious robbery; the bulk of the valley's non-royal burials were completely ransacked in antiquity, however, and the identities of their owners are now a mystery.

Almost all of these lesser tombs appear to have been cut during the 18th dynasty. They may be divided into two basic types: staircase tombs, which are generally larger and more closely approximate to the design of the much larger royal sepulchres; and shaft tombs, which, as their name suggests, are entered by means of a vertical pit or shaft and are for the most part single-chambered.

Both staircase and shaft tombs, as indeed the royal tombs themselves, were commonly reused for family burials during the Third Intermediate Period.

As the importance of these lesser tombs to the history of the valley is increasingly recognized, an ever greater interest is being shown in their relocation and careful re-excavation; particularly important work has recently been carried out by Donald P. Ryan. But much remains to be done, and for many of these burials information from which to draw any conclusions whatsoever is for the moment scant indeed.

The Tomb of Yuya and Tjuyu (KV46)

'Squeezing their way between the wall and the rock ceiling, M. Maspero and Mr. Davis were soon in the midst of such a medley of tomb furniture that, in the glare of their lighted candles, the first effect was one of bewilderment. Gradually, however, one object after another detached itself from the shimmering mass, shining through the cool air, dust-free and golden . . .'

Henry Copley Greene

Discovery and excavation

'. . . so remarkable was the preservation that the silver was still bright, but within three days, and before anything could be moved, it had become black.'

James Quibell

Before the discovery of Tutankhamun, the tomb of Yuya and Tjuyu was one of the most celebrated discoveries in Egyptian archaeology. And, naturally, the discovery was made by Theodore Davis.

*A pottery jar (second item)
and dummy vessels of
gessoed wood, painted to
imitate glass (first and third
examples) and stone. From
KV46, painted by Carter.*

The tomb itself is situated midway between the princely tomb KV3 and KV4, the tomb initiated but never actually employed by the pharaoh Ramesses XI, and chippings from the quarrying of these later tombs wholly overlay the site to provide a useful *terminus ante quem* for ancient activity within the tomb.

The outer doorway 'was closed within eighteen inches of the top with flat stones, about twelve inches by four, laid in Nile mud plaster . . .'. This wall, 'plastered over with mud and stamped in many places' with the jackal-and-nine-captives seal, displayed an opening in the top right-hand corner, at chin height – so clearly it was not to be an intact tomb. Beyond lay a corridor, empty save for a few stray items, leading down to a second blocking, stamped with the seal of the necropolis administra-tion but likewise broken through at the top. On the floor, at the base of the wall, were two pottery bowls containing dried mud – evidence, perhaps, of small-scale plastering work undertaken following the first period of theft (see below) – and the sticks used to apply it. As the excavators peered over the wall an eerie sight met their eyes:

'Imagine entering a town house which had been closed for the summer: imagine the stuffy room, the stiff, silent appearance of the furniture, the feeling that some ghostly occupants of the vacant chairs have just been disturbed, the desire to throw open the windows to let life into the room once more. That was perhaps the first sensation as we stood, really dumbfounded, and stared around at the relics of the life of over three thousand years ago . . .'

Arthur Weigall

(Above) The second coffin of Yuya, with its rich covering of gold and silver foil and abundant glass inlays.

(Left) Gilded cartonnage mask of the lady Tjuyu, mother of Queen Tiye.

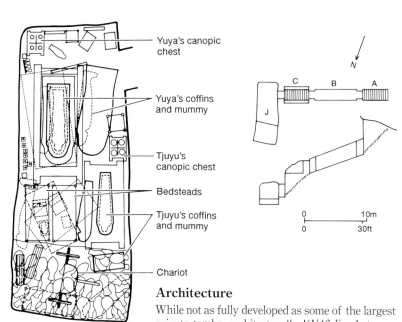

- Yuya's canopic chest
- Yuya's coffins and mummy
- Tjuyu's canopic chest
- Bedsteads
- Tjuyu's coffins and mummy
- Chariot

Plan and section of KV46, and a detail of the single chamber showing the burial equipment in position.

Architecture

While not as fully developed as some of the largest private tombs, architecturally KV46 lies between KV55 and KV21, having one more corridor than the former and one fewer than the latter. The entrance stair leads into a well-cut corridor some 1.76 m (5 ft 9 in) wide and 2.05 m (6 ft 9 in) high – proportions which are respectable for a tomb of this nature (compare 1.68 m (5 ft 6 in) by 2 m (6 ft 7 in) in the tomb of Tutankhamun). A second corridor with stairs and niches is somewhat unusual in that the roof is roughly rounded rather than squared. This and the similar roughness of the irregularly shaped burial chamber have been blamed on the quality of the stone, but might also be explained as the result of the tomb's quarrying being brought to a hasty conclusion. Like KV62, the floor of the burial chamber is dropped approximately 1 m (3 ft 3 in) from the level of the entrance doorway, though only at the left end. In the first two passages a number of black dots spaced about 40 cm (16 in) apart divide the walls into squares; these seem to be masons' marks, since the walls were not smoothed nor was plaster ever applied to them.

(Right) Yuya's wooden coffin-canopy.

(Below) The rifled mummy of Tjuyu.

Funerary equipment *(see also p. 178)*

'The woman [Empress Eugénie, widow of Napoleon III of France] replied, "Do tell me something of the discovery of the tomb."

Quibell said, "With pleasure, but I regret I cannot offer you a chair."

Quickly came her answer: "Why, there is a chair which will do for me nicely." And before our horrified eyes she stepped down onto the floor of the chamber and seated herself in a chair which had not been sat in for over three thousand years! . . .

The visitor turned . . . and said, "I see now where the Empire style came from. Behold these carved heads."'

Joseph Lindon Smith

'One of the vases we uncorked contained thick oil, another almost liquid honey, which still preserved its scent. If it had been left without its cover on one of the steps of the staircase, near the entrance of the corridor, a marauding wasp, having strayed into the Valley of the Kings, would have hovered gluttonously round the jar.'

Gaston Maspero

The mummies

'Again Maspero's voice was heard, this time saying that Mrs. Smith should come down and join him in the tomb. . . . He assisted her over the wall and said: "Doubtless you are the first woman that's been in this tomb chamber alive – there's a dead one over there . . ."'

Joseph Lindon Smith

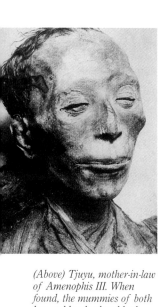

(Above) Tjuyu, mother-in-law of Amenophis III. When found, the mummies of both her and her husband had been partially unwrapped.

The two mummies were in an extraordinary state of preservation; that of Yuya, in particular, is a fine example of the ancient embalmers' craft.

To judge from the differing embalming techniques that the two corpses display, Yuya and Tjuyu died at separate times, and were interred in KV46 on two separate occasions. This view is strengthened by differences in the two sets of funerary equipment – in particular, the canopic jars. As the evidence stands, it is difficult to establish who died first. Maspero believed that it was Yuya basing his view upon the disposition of the man's large wooden coffin-canopy. The style of Yuya's cartonnage mask suggests the opposite.

Robberies

The excavators believed that the burial had been plundered on one occasion only. In fact, KV46 appears to have been entered at least twice and probably on three occasions (see table). Furthermore, the burial was plundered far more efficiently than was originally thought. *All* the more portable valuables had gone – metalwork (including all jewellery not wrapped in with the mummies) and most of the linens not associated directly with the corpses. Perfumes and cosmetics had also been removed – usually evidence of a robbery soon after

KV46: the Robberies

Date	Prompted by	Evidence
time of Amenophis III	knowledge of burial?	absence of oils and perfumes; reclosure; two bowls of mud plaster
time of Ramesses III	quarrying of KV3	small sealings of Ramesses III (intrusive??)
time of Ramesses XI	quarrying of KV4	small sealings of Ramesses III displaced; burial tidied and door reblocked

Wooden shabti *figure of Yuya and its sentry-like box, from a watercolour by Howard Carter.*

the original interment, since such commodities did not keep fresh for long. All that remained were three containers of rancid castor oil, natron and 'a dark red substance' – which the thieves had evidently discarded as worthless.

The tomb was still in a state of disarray when entered by Davis in 1905. The mummies had been disturbed within their coffins, while promising-looking boxes had had their lids ripped off. Several items found in the corridor – a heart scarab, chariot yoke and gilded wooden staff – were either in the process of being carried off by the thieves when they were apprehended, or else had been discarded by them when it was discovered that their value was slight. Following this intrusion, there seems to have been some attempt at restoring a superficial order to the burial: Tjuyu's mummy had been covered with a sheet, some boxes refilled with a jumble of items, and the hole made by the robbers to gain access to the burial chamber roughly blocked again with stones.

(Below) The mummy of Yuya, enclosed, like that of his wife, in a gilded cartonnage framework.

(Above) The profile of Yuya, commander of the king's chariotry. His was one of the best preserved mummies ever found.

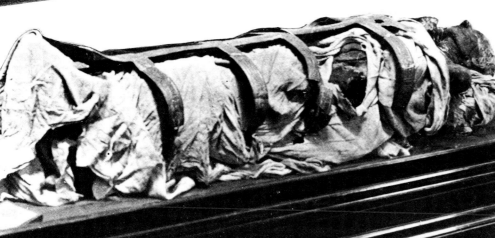

Finds from the Tomb of Yuya and Tjuyu

Sistrum handle of Tjuyu, of gilded wood. The metal shakers had been taken by the robbers.

Elegant calcite vessel filled with a 'dark red substance'.

J. E. Quibell, Antiquities Inspector, Describes the Contents

'Yuaa was laid in four coffins, one inside the other. The outer one can hardly be called a coffin; it is a square box on runners, but has no bottom; it forms a cover or tent over the rest . . . [and] is of wood covered with pitch, and ornamented with bands of inscription in relief on gilt plaster. The second coffin is of the shape of a mummy, covered like the last with glistening pitch and with gilt bands of text. In the third coffin the gilt bands are the same, but the background is of silver leaf. The fourth is gilt all over and has hieroglyphs of glass inlaid in the gold. This coffin was silvered inside and contained the mummy . . . [which] had been thoroughly searched; evidently Yuaa was known to have been buried with jewellery. His gilt cartonnage mask and the bands which encircled the body remained, but were broken.

The mummy itself is in wonderful preservation, better perhaps than any other from Biban el Moluk; the features are not distorted; the powerful and dignified face of the old man strikes one as something human, as a face that one would recognize in a portrait.

The canopic vases of Thuaa are interesting; they each contain, packed in sawdust, some one of the organs of the body wrapped up in cloths so as to form the model of a mummy, over the head of which is placed a small mask of gilt plaster. The vases of Yuaa are much simpler.

One of the most striking objects is a chariot; it bears no scenes in relief to compare with those on the chariot of Thothmes IV., but it is practically complete, and the decorations of spirals and rosettes in gilt plaster make it a very handsome object.

There are two of the Osiris beds, like that in Mahirpra; there is a jewel box decorated with mosaic of ivory, ebony, and faience, with inscription in gold, several other boxes less elaborate in ornament, and besides, a lot of boxes of wood covered with pitch and containing different dried meats, geese, ducks and various joints of veal(?). Lastly there are three beds and three chairs. The beds are like Nubian *angarîbs*, but with head-boards; one of these has panels adorned with bas reliefs in silvered plaster; in another the scenes are gilt; they consist chiefly of figures of Bes.

The chairs are perhaps the most striking objects in the whole collection, and cannot be described in a few words. Two of the three had probably been used before being employed as funereal furniture; they certainly show signs of wear. One, a small one, is gilt all over, and bears on the back a scene of a water excursion; in another the arms are of open-work, representing an ibex; the third and largest is made of veneered wood with designs and texts in gilt; above the front legs and serving as hand-rests are two female heads in the round.'

Item	Yuya	Tjuyu	Un-inscr.	Other
Canopy/box coffin	1	1		
Anthropoid coffins	3	2		
Headpiece	1	1		
Mummy bands/framework	1	1		
Mummy	1	1		
Scarabs		2	1	
Amulets	[2]	[4]		
Truncated cones			2	
Canopic chest	1	1		
Canopic jars	4	4		
Osiris bed			2	
Shabtis	14	4	1	
Shabti boxes	5		10	
Shabti tools			50	
Magical statuette	1			
Papyrus	1			
Model coffin	1			
Scribe's(?) palette			1?	
Osiris cenotaph			1	
Ba-bird	1			
Chariot		1		
Whipstock	1			
Beds		3		
Chairs		2	1	
Boxes	2			3
Wig		1		
Wig basket		1		
Mirror		1		
Sistrum handle		1		
Kohl tube			1	
Mat		1		
Sandals (individual)		24		
Staves	1	1		
Small sealings			3	2
Dummy vessels		28		
Dummy vessels on stand	2			
Stone vessels		2	1	
Pottery vessel			1	
Jars with embalming refuse		52		
Meat boxes		18		
Plant remains		1		

(Left) Yuya's well-preserved chariot.

(Right) Chair of Princess Sitamun, used by Empress Eugénie and (centre) a detail of one of the arm panels.

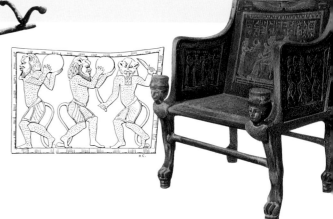

The Tomb of Maiherpri (KV36)

History and excavation

The burial of Maiherpri, a child of the royal nursery and royal fan-bearer, was brought to light by Victor Loret during his second season of work in the Valley of the Kings in 1899, cut into the floor of the wadi midway between KV35 (Amenophis II) and KV13 (Bay). Although KV36 (as the tomb is now numbered) was the first substantially intact burial to have been discovered in the valley in modern times, it never, for some reason, attracted the attention it deserves – perhaps because, like so much work, it was never scientifically published. Indeed, the only account we possess of the burial *in situ* is a semi-popular description prepared by the Egyptologist Georg Schweinfurth. His article, general though it is, does permit a tentative reconstruction of the layout of the burial as Loret first encountered it (plan p. 180).

Who was Maiherpri?

'. . . on the copy of the Book of the Dead found in the tomb . . ., Maherpra is depicted with his face black instead of the normal red, and a detailed examination of his mummy, which showed that he died at about 24 years of age, also showed that he was negroid, but not actually a negro.'

Reginald Engelbach

Factfile

Tomb number/location:
KV36, Wadi Biban el-
Muluk
Date of discovery:
March 1899, by Victor
Loret
Excavator/reports:
V. Loret, 1899, for the
Service des Antiquités:
Georges Daressy,
*Fouilles de la Vallée des
Rois 1898–1899* (Cairo,
1902) pp. 1–62 (finds);
cf. Georg Schweinfurth,
Sphinx 3 (1900)
pp. 103–07

The face of Maiherpri's well-preserved mummy. The body had been rifled in antiquity, though its gilded cartonnage mask was still in position when found.

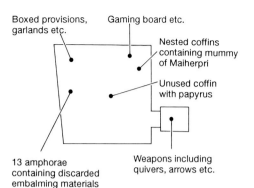

Boxed provisions, garlands etc.

Gaming board etc.

Nested coffins containing mummy of Maiherpri

Unused coffin with papyrus

13 amphorae containing discarded embalming materials

Weapons including quivers, arrows etc.

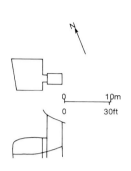

(Above) Plan and section of KV36, with a reconstruction of the layout of items as found.

(Far right) The tomb entrance.

(Right) The tomb owner – a detail from Maiherpri's funerary papyrus.

KV36: the Finds

Box coffin
Anthropoid coffins (3)
Headpiece
Mummy
Jewellery (earrings, bracelets, beads and collar elements, amulets, embalming plaque)
Canopic chest
Canopic jars (4)
Osiris bed
Papyrus
Game box and gaming pieces
Quivers (2)
Arrows (75)
Bracers (2)
Dog collars (2)
Small sealings (4)
Glass/frit vessels (2)
Faience bowl
Stone vessels (2)
Pottery vessels (39)
Rushwork lid
Meat joints (11)
Bread
Plant remains

(Right) Maiherpri's innermost coffin – made too large to fit within his second coffin and discarded, unused, in the centre of the burial chamber.

The mummy of Maiherpri was examined on 22 March 1901, and the results of that autopsy prompted Maspero to put forward the suggestion that the owner was a royal son by a black queen. Since Maiherpri is consistently referred to as 'child of the *kap*', or royal nursery, however, the greater likelihood is that he was no more than a close companion of one of the kings of the early 18th dynasty during his childhood. A linen winding-sheet from the tomb carries the cartouche of Hatshepsut, but most commentators today would date the burial rather later, perhaps in the reign of Tuthmosis IV, on the basis of the tomb's contents.

(Left) Maiherpri's canopic chest, of resin-coated wood with gilded detail.

The problem of the 'extra' coffin

The mummy of Maiherpri lay within two anthropoid coffins and an outer wooden shrine of rectangular form. A third anthropoid coffin, smaller in size, lay unused in the centre of the chamber. Although Maspero's explanation has a charm of its very own ('tired of resting within the one, [Maiherpri] could move over to the other'), the likelihood is that this 'spare' coffin had originally been intended as the innermost of the set. Having been employed to carry Maiherpri's mummy in the funeral procession, on arrival in the burial chamber it was found to be too large to drop smoothly, as intended, into the nested second and third coffins already positioned within the tomb. Interestingly enough, a similar situation faced the workmen charged with placing the second coffin of Tutankhamun (which had perhaps not originally been intended for this king's use) within the first, outermost coffin. But whereas in the tomb of Tutankhamun the problem could be swiftly resolved by a few judiciously aimed adze blows, in the case of Maiherpri's ill-measured innermost coffin nothing could be done. After much fruitless pushing and jamming, Maiherpri's mummy would seem to have been hastily ejected from its overlarge third coffin and placed within the smaller of the two nested coffins around which the large wooden funerary canopy was then erected. The unused third coffin was abandoned where it lay.

The mummy of Maiherpri, and the robbery of the tomb

When Loret entered the tomb, the mummy of Maiherpri still lay within its outer two coffins, though the tenons joining lids to bases had already been broken in antiquity and the mummy rifled – the bandages, over the arms in particular, having been crudely hacked away with an adze. Most of the funerary jewellery had been carried off by the robbers.

Further evidence of robbery could be seen in the general absence not only of jewellery but of all portable metalware, and also of non-funerary linen and clothing. The containers of *ben*-oil had had their sealed linen coverings ripped away, but had then been discarded; the oil was evidently too old to be of interest. Following the plundering of KV36, the tomb appears to have been subjected to a hasty, semi-official tidying up, similar to that seen in the tomb of Yuya and Tjuyu, and reclosed.

All the indications are that the culprits, both here and in KV46, were members of the necropolis workforce who had stumbled upon the tomb in the course of their work (attested by a series of 19th–20th-dynasty ostraca recovered by Carter in 1902) in the immediate vicinity of the shaft entrance, and that the 'restorers' of the damage were their superiors, anxious to avoid scandal, investigation and recrimination.

(Above) Maiherpri's canopic jars, and a selection of painted pottery vessels from the tomb.

(Left) Quiver, arrows, bracer and two collars for the owner's dogs, found in KV36.

(Above) A blue faience cup, decorated with tilapia-fish and lotus flowers.

(Left) Calcite amphora on ring base.

(Above) A handled jar of calcite, the linen covering torn off in antiquity by robbers to determine its contents.

Tomb no.	Owner	Staircase	Shaft
KV26	?		●
KV28	?		●
KV29	?		●
KV30	?		●
KV31	?		●
KV32	?	●	
KV33	?	●	
KV36	Maiherpri		●
KV37	?	●	
KV40	?		●
KV41	?		●
KV44	?		●
KV45	Userhet		●
KV46	Yuya and Tjuyu	●	
KV48	Amenemopet		●
KV49	?	●	
KV50	animals		●
KV51	animals		●
KV52	animals		●
KV53	?		●
KV58	?		●
KV60	Sitre In	●	
KV61	?		●
WV A	storeroom	●	

Tomb WV24

Date of discovery: before 1832
Excavator/report: Otto J. Schaden, 1991–92, for the University of Arizona: O. J. Schaden, *KMT* 2/3 (fall, 1991) pp. 53–61

'It seemed that nearly every basket of *turab* [debris] removed contained tattered mummy wrappings, some bones and some late Roman wares …'

Otto Schaden

WV24 has stood open and neglected for 150 years; during that time it has been noted by Robert Hay and John Gardner Wilkinson and probably entered by Émile Chassinat, Davis's excavators, Howard Carter and several other Egyptologists. Its clearance was undertaken by Otto Schaden in 1991–92.

The tomb consists of a deep and well-cut rectangular shaft which opens at one side of its base into an irregularly cut and evidently unfinished room. Although roughly rectangular, the chamber is rounded at its eastern end, perhaps reflecting its unfinished state (an undamaged mason's mallet was found in the tomb, together with several copper fragments broken from the masons' chisels). A rough, low shelf cut along one side of the chamber is the only feature distinguishing the tomb from the very similar KV44, KV50, KV61 and others, in the main valley.

Excavation of the shaft brought to light the remains of probably intrusive burials of 22nd-dynasty date, including fragments of a wooden child's coffin, fragments of cartonnage, masses of mummy linen, and the remains of at least five human bodies (one that of a child). Later material included fragments of late Roman ribbed amphorae and

cooking pots, presumably of Coptic origin. A coil of ancient rope was also recovered, the leg of a small box or chair, and several fragments of 18th-dynasty glass – including inlay strips and a broken bead which may have strayed from the nearby tomb of Ay (WV23). An interesting fragment of ivory with gold attachments may be another stray from WV23.

The evidence is that WV24 dates from the late 18th dynasty, and most probably had been prepared for a retainer of the owner of WV25. It may, however, represent an ancillary storage chamber for this latter tomb (a similar relationship to that of WV A to WV22 – the tomb of Amenophis III). Roughly the same amount of rock seems to have been removed from both WV24 and WV25, possibly as a result of the two tombs being begun and abandoned at more or less the same time.

Tomb KV26

Date of discovery: before 1835, by James Burton(?)
Excavator/report: James Burton, before 1835(?): unpublished

Virtually nothing is known of this tomb, which may have been first explored by James Burton in the 1820s–1830s. Its position was later noted by Loret, in 1898, but no clearance of the interior has ever been recorded.

For the possibility that the tomb's occupants were transferred eventually to KV42, see above, p. 103.

Tomb KV28

Date of discovery: before 1832
Excavator/report: Donald P. Ryan, 1990, for Pacific Lutheran University: D. P. Ryan, *KMT* 2/1 (spring, 1991) p. 30

'The tomb had been previously "excavated" by an unknown party, so we were, in essence, picking through the leftovers.'

Donald Ryan

KV28, with its shaft leading down to a single, small, rectangular room, was first noted by Wilkinson in the 1830s, and described by Lefébure in 1889 as almost completely clear except for a few mummy bones and wrappings. These remains were still present when the tomb was re-examined by Donald Ryan in 1990, and prove to come from at least two individuals. Other finds included 'fragments of a limestone canopic jar, many pieces of wooden objects and a stray funerary cone from the Theban necropolis.'

Potsherds from the clearance seem to suggest that the burials dated from around the reign of Tuthmosis IV, whose tomb is close by, and that KV28 perhaps belonged to a high official of that king.

Lower section of the shaft of WV24. The well-like entrance to this tomb is among the largest of the royal valley's pit tombs.

Tomb KV29

Date of discovery: before 1832
Excavator/report: unknown: unpublished

Both James Burton and Wilkinson note the position of KV29, but otherwise nothing is known of its plan or contents.

Tomb KV31

Date of discovery: October 1817, by Giovanni Battista Belzoni
Excavator/report: G. B. Belzoni, 1817, on behalf of the Earl of Belmore: unpublished

'Their [the Belmores'] admiration of all that they saw was music in Giovanni's ears. He warmed especially towards Lord Belmore and even pointed out to him a couple of likely spots in the valley where he might care to dig. The noble traveller found only two small mummy-pits [KV31 and KV32]...'

Stanley Mayes

KV31 is now almost completely sanded up. No details are available about either its form or any surviving contents – though presumably it or KV30 (p. 109) was the findspot of the 18th-dynasty private anthropoid sarcophagus of quartz-sandstone later presented by Lord Belmore to the British Museum.

Tomb KV32

Date of discovery: 1898, by Victor Loret
Excavator/report: V. Loret, 1898, for the Service des Antiquités (?): unpublished

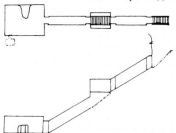

'It was perhaps used as a burial-place of one of [Tuthmosis III's] family, or perhaps for a vizir such as Rekhmara, whose tomb-chapel is to be seen at Shêkh abd' el Gûrneh, but whose burial-pit is not known.'

Arthur Weigall

Very little is known about this tomb, which is apparently unfinished. It was described by Georg Steindorff in the 1902 Baedeker guide as 'probably a royal tomb of the 18th dyn., [which] has not yet been fully explored'. Indeed, no formal clearance appears ever to have been carried out, and no finds are known. According to Harry Burton, the tomb was inadvertently cut into by those quarrying the tomb of Siptah (KV47) – and any burial within KV32 will doubtless have been investigated at that time.

Tomb KV33

Date of discovery: 1898, by Victor Loret
Excavator/report: V. Loret, 1898, for the Service des Antiquités(?): unpublished

KV33 is again hardly known. Baedeker in 1902 described it as 'a small tomb with two empty rooms, reached by a flight of steps'. It has apparently never been fully cleared.

Tomb KV37

Date of discovery: 1899, by Victor Loret
Excavator/report: V. Loret, 1899, for the Service des Antiquités: Georges Daressy, *Fouilles de la Vallée des Rois 1898–1899* (Cairo, 1902) pp. 299–301, *passim* (finds)

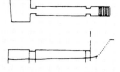

The bone fragments and pieces of large, whitened storage jars noted here by Elizabeth Thomas in the 1960s suggest that the 18th-dynasty tomb KV37 had originally been employed for a burial. The fragments recovered by Loret – a wooden mummiform statuette and fragmentary socle of Tuthmosis IV, the board for a fire drill, some 33 ostraca and a vessel fragment of Sethos I – seem to be intrusive, but may indicate that the tomb had at one stage served as a 'workshop' similar to KV4 (Ramesses XI) (p. 172).

For the possibility that the tomb's occupant(s) were transferred to KV42, see above (p. 103).

Tomb KV40

Date of discovery: 1899, by Victor Loret
Excavator/report: V. Loret, 1899, for the Service des Antiquités: unpublished

No details are available as to either the plan or surviving contents of this tomb.

Tomb KV41

Date of discovery: 1899, by Victor Loret
Excavator/report: V. Loret, 1899, for the Service des Antiquités: unpublished

KV41 was the last of the tombs located by Victor Loret in 1899, and three years later, in 1902, according to Georg Steindorff, it had still not been scientifically examined.

Position of the as yet uncleared KV29.

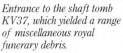

Entrance to the shaft tomb KV37, which yielded a range of miscellaneous royal funerary debris.

Intrusive 22nd-dynasty cartonnage of the lady Tentkerer, recovered by Howard Carter from KV44 in 1901.

Upper part of a wooden coffin lid found by Donald Ryan in 1991 among the debris of KV45.

Tomb KV44

Date of discovery:	26 January 1901, by Howard Carter
Excavators/reports:	H. Carter, 1901, for Theodore M. Davis: H. Carter, *ASAE* 2 (1901) pp. 144–5; Donald P. Ryan, for Pacific Lutheran University, 1991: *KMT* 3/1 (spring, 1992) pp. 45–6

'This Tomb-pit being already known to the reis of Western Thebes, I decided to open it, the work taking only two days to do. The rubbish being removed to a depth of 5 metres 50 cent., the door of the chamber was reached, and I entered on the 26th of January 1901, finding therein three wooden coffins, placed beside one another at one side of the chamber, covered with wreaths of flowers ...'

Howard Carter

Among the 'rubbish' of this tomb, the entrance to which had been roughly closed off with a dry-stone wall, Carter noted 'remains of earlier mummies without either coffins or funereal furniture'. Ryan's reclearance of KV44 in 1990–91 brought to light what was left of this original interment, which contained seven individuals, three of them children and one as young as two years of age. The end piece from a child's coffin was also found, together with a blue cylindrical bead and an uninscribed fragment from a canopic jar. The pottery fragments were too small to be diagnostic, but there seems little doubt that the tomb is to be dated to the mid-18th dynasty, like nearby KV45.

KV45: The Tomb of Userhet

Date of discovery:	25 February 1902, by Howard Carter
Excavators/reports:	H. Carter, 1902, for Theodore M. Davis: H. Carter, *ASAE* 4 (1903) pp. 45–6; Donald P. Ryan, 1991–92, for Pacific Lutheran University: D. P. Ryan, *KMT* 3/1 (spring, 1992) pp. 46–7

'Feb. 25th [1902]: Mr Davis having returned from Aswan, [this] tomb pit was opened in his presence. It proved to have only a perpendicular shaft of about 3 metres deep, with a small chamber on the east side at the bottom containing a burial of the XXIInd dynasty completely destroyed by rain water.'

Howard Carter

The single chamber of KV45 was found by Carter 'a third full of rubbish', on top of which rested the remains of two 22nd-dynasty mummies, each in a double coffin, two wooden *shabti* boxes (with small, crudely made mud *shabtis* of two distinct types, of which Ryan subsequently recovered a total of 44) and the 'scattered remains of wreaths'. The entire tomb was so badly decayed by water that Carter found

'it ... impossible to remove anything excepting the face of the man's mummy case' (later 'modelled' by Miss Jeanette R. Buttles in company with Davis outside the tomb) and 'a small black limestone heart scarab' inscribed for the doorkeeper of the house Merenkhons. 'On the woman', Carter records, 'nothing was found'.

From among the debris underlying the intrusive burials, Carter recovered fragments of canopic jars inscribed for an 18th-dynasty overseer of the fields of Amun called Userhet, evidently an original occupant of the tomb.

Donald Ryan's recent reclearance uncovered 'human skeletal-material and the remains of the water-logged burials, including hundreds of fragments of the highly decayed coffins.... We also found eighty-eight clay ushabti fragments representing at least forty-four figures' – crudely made by pressing mud into a mould. The human remains represented four individuals – presumably the two intrusive burials of the Third Intermediate Period and the original New Kingdom occupants of the tomb. The pottery recovered during Ryan's recent reclearance would date to the reigns of Tuthmosis IV–early Amenophis III.

KV48: The Tomb of Amenemopet

Date of discovery:	January 1906, by Edward R. Ayrton
Excavator/reports:	E. R. Ayrton, 1906, for Theodore M. Davis: Th. M. Davis *et al.*, *The Tomb of Siptah; the Monkey Tomb and the Gold Tomb* (London, 1908); C. N. Reeves, *MDAIK* 40 (1984) p. 232 (finds)

'The shaft was about 20 feet deep by 6 feet broad, with a comparatively large chamber, 16–17 feet by 10–11 feet by 6 feet high, to the south-west. The tomb had been anciently plundered, but a rough wall had been reconstructed to close the chamber door. The floor was covered with some six inches of rubbish, and on this lay the débris from the burial.'

Theodore Davis and Edward Ayrton

The occupant of this tomb was 'a man, tall and well-built' whose mummy 'had been unwrapped and thrown on one side'. On top of the 'rubbish' in the tomb were fragments of the coffin – coated with a black resin and decorated in yellow – together with parts of a 'rough wooden chair' and pieces of whitened pottery storage jars. From the fill were recovered four 'magic bricks', a clay sealing from a papyrus ('bearing the inscription "Amen hears good praises"'), and 'some wooden ushabtis with the titles of Amonmapt, Vizier and Governor of the Town, painted in yellow on a surface of pitch'. These identified the owner and occupant of the burial – Amenemopet called Pairy, brother to Sennufer (p. 103) and mayor of Thebes and vizier under Amenophis II.

The tomb chamber itself was undecorated, 'without even a layer of stucco to fill the irregularities of the rock'. For many years its position had been lost; its site was relocated, however, by means of geophysical prospecting equipment, by Kent Weeks during 1985–86. It has apparently not yet been re-entered.

Tomb KV49

Date of discovery: January, 1906, by Edward R. Ayrton

Excavator/report: E. R. Ayrton, for Theodore M. Davis, 1906: Th. M. Davis *et al.*, *The Tomb of Siphtah; the Monkey Tomb and the Gold Tomb* (London, 1908) pp. 16–17

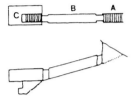

'The only objects in the room were a few scraps of mummy-cloth and fragments of the large whitened jars which occur in burials of the XVIIIth Dynasty. Plunderers had dug a small pit in the second stairway to search for a further door . . .'

Theodore Davis and Edward Ayrton

KV49 appears to be a typical corridor tomb of mid-18th-dynasty date. The doorway still preserves the remains of 'a dry stone wall covered with gritty white plaster'; this wall, the sherds from the large whitened jars mentioned in the quote above and some fragments of cloth noted by Davis and Ayrton are perhaps connected with the two hieratic graffiti, noted above the entrance by Ayrton, written when the tomb was employed as a storeroom for temple linen at the end of the New Kingdom. It is presumably to this period also that an ostracon found by Ayrton and several rough gaming boards with incised grids are to be assigned.

The likely role of this tomb in the restoration of the royal mummies is discussed below (p. 206).

Hieratic inscription on a broken wooden label from KV49, reading 'Corpse oil'.

The Animal Tombs

Tomb numbers/location: KV50, KV51, KV52, Wadi Biban el-Muluk

Date of discovery: January 1906, by Edward R. Ayrton

Excavator/report: E. R. Ayrton, 1906, for Theodore M. Davis: Th. M. Davis *et al.*, *The Tomb of Siphtah; the Monkey Tomb and the Gold Tomb* (London, 1908) p. 17–18

KV50

KV51   KV52

'The children never forgot their trip over to the Valley of the Kings and a visit to Davis's Animal Tomb[s]. They were carried down the shaft of . . . [KV50], into a chamber that was very low and extremely warm.

They both laughed in their delight at the sight of a yellow dog of ordinary life size, standing on its feet, his short tail curled over his back, and with his eyes wide open. The animal looked alive.'

Joseph Lindon Smith

The Valley of the Kings was the final resting place not only for the family and favoured officials of the king, but seemingly of his pets also. A group of three tombs discovered in January 1906 by Edward Ayrton for Theodore Davis appear to represent the 'pet cemetery' of a single animal-loving pharaoh – perhaps Amenophis II, close to whose own place of

burial, KV35, the animal tombs are located. All the animals seem originally to have been mummified and wrapped (sometimes with jewellery) in the same way as a human corpse, and in most cases supplied with a coffin. Furthermore, from within KV51 Ayrton recovered a stucco canopic-package mask, and from KV52 an empty canopic chest. All the tombs had been entered in antiquity and despoiled; the entrance doorway to the burial chamber of KV51 had been reblocked 'with bits of stone, and part of the disused lid of a mummy coffin', presumably following an official inspection.

	dog	monkey	baboon	duck	ibis
KV50	1	1			
KV51		3	1	3	1
KV52		1			

'The most bizarre spectacle [within KV51] was a perfect specimen of a large ape, completely without wrappings, and wearing a necklace of small blue disc beads.'

Joseph Lindon Smith

(Above) A mummified monkey, one of three found by Ayrton in KV51 during the 1905/6 season.

(Left) Monkey and yellow mummified dog in situ in KV50 – from a painting by Harold Jones.

Tomb KV53

Date of discovery: 1905/6, by Edward R. Ayrton
Excavator/reports: E. R. Ayrton, 1905/6, for Theodore M. Davis: Th. M. Davis *et al., The Tomb of Siphtah; the Monkey Tomb and the Gold Tomb* (London, 1908) pp. 18–19; C. N. Reeves, *MDAIK* 40 (1984) pp. 232–3 (finds)

KV53, now inaccessible and never formally planned, is apparently a small, single-chambered shaft tomb. Its clearance by Edward Ayrton resulted in the discovery of a series of limestone ostraca and a limestone stela dedicated to the serpent goddess Meretseger ('She who loves silence') by the chief Deir el-Medina scribe, Hori. Other associated ostraca had been built into one of the 20th-dynasty workmen's huts later erected over the mouth of the tomb – when the tomb was presumably entered.

Tomb KV58

Date of discovery: January 1909, by E. Harold Jones
Excavator/reports: E. H. Jones, for Theodore M. Davis, January 1909: Th. M. Davis *et al., The Tombs of Harmhabi and Touatânkhamanou* (London, 1912) pp. 2–3, 125–34; C. N. Reeves, *GM* 53 (1982) pp. 33–45

'... next day we began going down the pit finding very interesting fragments of furniture all thrown about in the debris and of an interesting period – the end of the XVIII Dynasty the objects bearing cartouches of the Pharaoh Aye and of another called Tut-ankh-Amon, the latter of whom has not yet been discovered or his tomb...'

Harold Jones

KV58 was the one big discovery which Harold Jones, in early January 1909, would make for Davis in the valley. It is therefore rather sad that, in his publication, Davis should give credit for the find to Edward Ayrton in 1907.

The tomb, consisting of a shaft with a single chamber leading off from the bottom, was clearly a satellite tomb of Horemheb's sepulchre, KV57. The bulk of the finds recovered by Jones, however, with the possible exception of a beautiful calcite *shabti* figure, had no connection with the original owner. Fragments of chariot harness, they seem rather to have originated in the tomb of Ay in the West Valley, and to have been dumped into the half-filled shaft at a later date (cf. below, p. 204). The finds from KV58 are considered in more detail above (p. 129).

Gold foil fragments from KV58: (above) Nubian and Asiatic captives back to back; (below) the god's father Ay before the throne name of Tutankhamun.

Tomb KV60

Date of discovery: spring 1903, by Howard Carter
Excavators/reports: H. Carter, 1903, and Edward R. Ayrton, 1906, for Theodore M. Davis: H. Carter, *ASAE* 4 (1903) pp. 176–7; Donald P. Ryan, for Pacific Lutheran University, 1989: D. P. Ryan, *KMT* 1/1 (spring, 1990) pp. 34–9, 53–4, 58

'A small uninscribed tomb, immediately in the entrance of no. 19 (tomb of Ment-hi-khopesh-ef). It consists of a very rough flight of steps leading down to a passage of 5 metres long, ending in a low and rough square chamber, about 4 x 5 metres, which contained the remains of a much destroyed and rifled burial. Nothing was in this tomb but two much denuded mummies of women and some mummified geese.'

Howard Carter

Howard Carter, following his brief examination, seems to have reclosed the tomb, only for it to be stumbled upon yet again by Edward Ayrton, conducting a clearance of KV19 (Mentuherkhepshef), in 1906 when one of the mummies – that of Hatshepsut's wetnurse, Sitre In – was removed to the Cairo Museum. Donald Ryan's recent reclearance of KV60 revealed the tomb in much the same state Carter and Ayrton must have left it, with mummified food-provisions scattered about and, near the centre of the burial chamber, the second mummy, its right arm crossed over the breast in a queen-like pose. The woman had had long hair (found lying on the floor beneath the now-bald head), and had, in life, been quite fat, with well-worn teeth (indicating an older individual). Because of her obesity, the body had been eviscerated through the pelvic floor, rather than through the abdomen. Elizabeth Thomas had believed that this body might well be the mummy of Hatshepsut herself – a possibility the position of the arms does nothing to deny.

Several fragments of funerary equipment were recovered by Ryan, including coffin surfaces which had been hacked off with an adze in antiquity to remove gold-foil overlay. Interestingly, none of the pottery fragments recovered from the tomb can be dated earlier than the 20th dynasty. We may perhaps assume that KV60 had been stumbled upon at the time KV19 was quarried, when it was employed as a storeroom. If so, one or both mummies had perhaps been introduced only subsequently, at the end of the New Kingdom when the burials in the valley were being rationalized (p. 194).

Following Ryan's clearance, we now know that the plan of this tomb is more irregular and somewhat more complex than previously thought. Steep and roughly cut steps lead down to a single corridor with crudely fashioned niches, each with a roughly drawn *wedjat*-eye, one looking in towards the burial chamber and the other looking outwards to the tomb

(Left) The entrance to KV60 following the tomb's recent reclearance.

(Above) The anonymous KV60 mummy, discovered by Carter, abandoned by Ayrton and re-examined by Ryan in 1989. The left arm is flexed at the elbow and crossed over the chest – the pose of a queen.

entrance. The burial chamber itself is asymmetrical and perhaps unfinished. Virtually all surfaces within the tomb are roughly and irregularly cut, and this alone would seem to preclude the structure having been intended originally for an immediate member of the royal family.

Tomb KV61

Date of discovery: January 1910, by E. Harold Jones

Excavator/report: E. H. Jones, 1910, for Theodore M. Davis: unpublished

When it was first uncovered by Harold Jones in January 1910, this small and irregularly-shaped pit tomb 'showed every possibility of [being] a find, the filling of the pit appearing undisturbed and the floor . . . completely built up with stones to the top. However, after two days['] work we cleared to the top of [the] door of the chamber, and on peering inside saw that there was but a small, ill-hewn chamber half filled with debris. . . . [The] work was carefully proceeded with till every corner of the tomb was bare and bare were the results – for never even a potsherd was found'.

The likelihood is that Jones had uncovered a literally virgin private tomb, blocked off by the quarrymen after completion to prevent the chamber filling up with sand before it could be employed. But the anticipated burial never came.

'Tomb-commencements' and Pits

The surface of the Valley of the Kings is pockmarked with several 'tomb-commencements' and pits, of which only a handful have been recorded and designated.

No.	Date discovered	Remarks
KV54	21 Dec. 1907	Embalming materials and other items from the corridor of KV62 (Tutankhamun). See p. 126
KV59	—	Due north of KV37
KV B	—	Close to the cliffs south of KV43 (Tuthmosis IV)
KV C	4/5 Jan. 1907	Group of large jars perhaps associated with KV6. See p. 168
KV D	1907/8	No details
KV E	1907/8	No details
KV F	Jan. 1921	Perhaps a false start for the tomb of Tuthmosis III
KV G	—	Start of a 'potential corridor tomb' to the east of KV18 (Ramesses X) noted by Elizabeth Thomas
KV H	—	East of KV39, noted by Elizabeth Thomas
WV I	—	Close to WV23 (Ay), noted by Nestor L'Hôte
WV J	—	Close to WV23 (Ay), noted by Nestor L'Hôte
WV K	—	Close to WV23 (Ay), noted by Elizabeth Thomas
KV L	1898	Discovered by Loret, cleared by Jones, for Davis, in 1908
KV M	1898	Discovered by Loret, cleared by Jones, for Davis, in 1908
KV N	21 Dec. 1908	Close to KV48 (Amenemopet)
KV O	4 Feb. 1909	'unfinished pit with stone wall built around', possibly a 'workmen's house' (Harold Jones)
KV P	Dec. 1909	Filled with burnt debris – wood, potsherds, flint flakes, straw and bone. Restorers' debris: cf. below, p. 207
KV Q	Dec. 1909	Filled with burnt debris – wood, potsherds, flint flakes, straw and bone. Restorers' debris: cf. below, p. 207
KV R	Dec. 1909	Filled with burnt debris – wood, potsherds, flint flakes, straw and bone. Restorers' debris: cf. below p. 207
KV S	1908	Near KV47 (Siptah). Fill analogous to KV P, Q, R. Same pit as KV D/E?
KV T	1898/99?	South of KV36 (Maiherpri). A Loret discovery? Noted by Jones

The discovery, in 1881, of an extraordinary group of royal mummies in an old tomb in the Deir el-Bahri bay opened a new and wholly unexpected chapter in the history of the Theban necropolis. Egyptologists were forced to recognize that, at the end of the New Kingdom, a dramatic change had taken place in official attitudes towards the royal dead.

The catalyst for this change had been theft: a series of audacious tomb and temple robberies which indicated that security at Thebes could no longer be guaranteed, even for the long-dead ancestors in the Valley of the Kings. The confidence of Pharaoh had been shattered. Ramesses XI downed tools on his partially quarried sepulchre and opted for burial elsewhere, presumably in the north; and with the withdrawal of royal patronage, the morale and prospects of the now-redundant west bank workforce plummeted. The district became more difficult to police than ever, and the determination of the authorities to safeguard the royal tombs began to slacken.

Ruin beckoned – and not only among the Theban locals. For with foreign tribute and campaign booty things of the past, and basic raw materials (including gold and copper) increasingly hard to come by, the Egyptian state itself was spiralling into an economic abyss.

The situation was dire – but how to remedy it?

The answer was simple, pragmatic and inevitable: one problem would be used to cancel out the other. As the robbery of a tomb came to the notice of the authorities, the god's mummy was piously restored and transferred, as necessary, to another, more easily guarded hiding place; while at the same time the violated tomb was stripped of any remaining assets. At a stroke the physical remains of the kings were preserved, the temptation for further robbery removed – and the state left with a profit to show for its efforts.

Sethos I in his coffin: a photograph taken shortly after the mummy's discovery in the Deir el-Bahri cache.

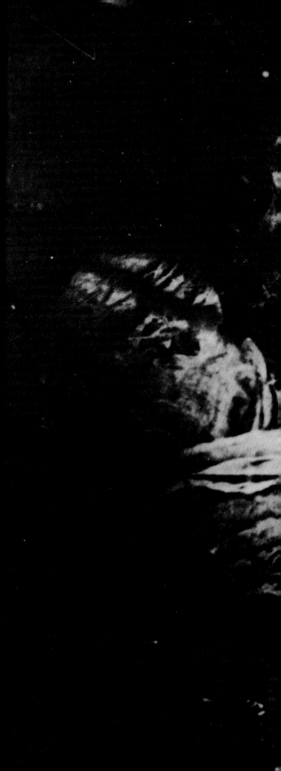

IV DECLINE OF A ROYAL NECROPOLIS

Robbers!

'Sometimes when I have been sitting at work alone . . . [in a tomb in the Valley of the Kings], I have been oppressed by the silence and the mystery . . .; and if, after this lapse of three thousand years, one is still conscious of the awful sanctity . . ., one wonders what must have been the sensations of the ancient thieves who penetrated by the light of a flickering oil lamp into the very presence of the dead.'

Arthur Weigall

The tomb robbery papyri

'Examination. The incense-roaster Nesamun called Tjaybay of the temple of Amun was brought. There was given to him the oath by the ruler, saying, "If I speak falsehood may I be mutilated and sent to Ethiopia."

They said to him, "Tell us the story of your going with your confederates to attack the Great Tombs, when you brought out this silver from there and appropriated it."

He said, "We went to a tomb and we brought some vessels of silver from it, and we divided them up between the five of us."

He was examined with the stick. He said, "I saw nothing else; what I have said is what I saw."

He was again examined with the stick. He said, "Stop, I will tell . . ."'

Papyrus BM 10052

Tomb robbery, if not quite Egypt's oldest profession, clearly ranks a close second. It was practised, to our certain knowledge, since predynastic times and grew in extent with the development of funerary beliefs and the ever-more-lavish provisions made for the next life.

Ordinarily, tomb robbery is known only by its results in the archaeological record, but at Thebes the situation is rather different. The primary source for the study of plundering in the Theban necropolis is a unique group of juridical documents known collectively as the 'tomb robbery papyri'. The bulk of these documents, which seem to have been hidden with other treason records in the temple of Medinet Habu, is concerned with two spates of theft carried out within the tombs and temples of Thebes during two unsettled periods, in the reign of Ramesses IX and under Ramesses XI.

The light these texts shed on the subject is extraordinary – the individuals involved, the types of commodities the thieves were after, and details of official interrogation and retribution. However, only a single text from the principal tomb robbery archive touches directly upon the plundering of the Valley of the Kings – the lamentably broken Papyrus Mayer B (p. 192), a court document which recounts in detail the robbery of bronze and copper utensils and textiles from the tomb of Ramesses VI (KV9); this text is undated but, to judge from a graffito in the tomb, probably pre-dates Year 9 of Ramesses IX. This papyrus may be supplemented by two secondary documents: Papyrus Salt 124, a deposition by a tomb workman which alludes to a casual theft of objects, by the foreman Paneb, from

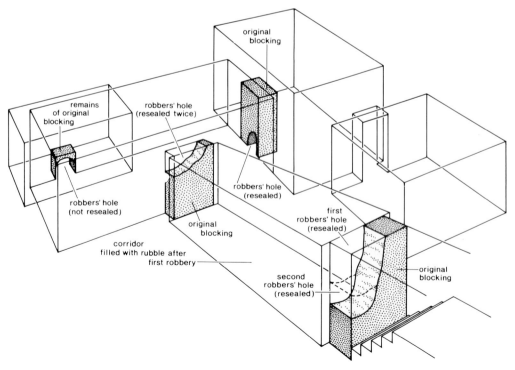

Thanks to the deposit's excellent, undisturbed condition, and its painstaking clearance by Howard Carter, the tomb of Tutankhamun sheds immense light on the activities of the ancient tomb robber – his method of working, what he was after and what he was not. And, because it was robbed more than once, the tomb preserves evidence also of the administration's response.

original blocking

remains of original blocking

robbers' hole (resealed twice)

robbers' hole (resealed)

robbers' hole (not reselead)

original blocking

corridor filled with rubble after first robbery

first robbers' hole (resealed)

second robbers' hole (resealed)

original blocking

the tomb of Sethos II (KV15) some time after the king's burial; and the Turin 'Strike Papyrus', which in passing makes reference to an attempted entry into the tomb of Ramesses II (KV7) and the mausoleum of his children (KV5) in Year 29 of Ramesses III (p. 146).

Archaeological evidence

The evidence of the papyri may be supplemented and to some extent controlled by the archaeological record. As we have already observed, several tombs in the valley show clear evidence of 'robber activity' before and during the Ramessid period. The archaeological evidence may be combined with the inscriptional to produce the following results:

Tomb	Owner	Date of disturbance	Evidence
KV46	Yuya/Tjuyu	Amenophis III	archaeol.
KV62	*Tutankhamun*	*Ay/Horemheb*	*archaeol.*
KV43	*Tuthmosis IV*	*Year 8 Horemheb*	*inscr.*
WV22	*Amenophis III*	*Ay/Horemheb?*	*archaeol.*
KV15	Sethos II	during burial	papyrol.
KV36	Maiherpri	Ramessid	archaeol.
KV46	Yuya/Tjuyu	Ramesses III	archaeol.
KV7	Ramesses II	Year 29 Ramesses III	papyrol.
KV12	*children of R.II?*	*Ramesses V/VI*	*archaeol.*
KV35	*Amenophis II*	*Year 8 Ramesses VI*	*inscr.*
KV9	Ramesses VI	Year 9 Ramesses IX	inscr./pap.?
KV55	*Tiye/Akhenaten*	*Ramesses IX*	*archaeol.*
WV23	*Ay*	*Ramesses IX*	*inscr.*
KV60	*In*	*Ramesses IX/X*	*archaeol.*
KV46	*Yuya/Tjuyu*	*Ramesses IX*	*archaeol.*

Two clear temporal groupings may be discerned (in *italic*):

—the first, coinciding with the dynastic troubles at the end of the 18th dynasty, after which the burials of Tutankhamun, Tuthmosis IV and perhaps Amenophis III required official attention;

—and a second, extended phase of robber-activity during the 20th dynasty, already attested by the papyri, when administrative efficiency was periodically undermined by corruption, inflation, famine and Libyan incursion.

The overall impression gained from the archaeology is that most robberies in the valley were opportunistic in character, and that petty plundering, often carried out by members of the burial party (as, perhaps, in the tomb of Tutankhamun, and as with Paneb in KV15, the tomb of Sethos II), was commonplace. The burial of Yuya and Tjuyu, for example, far from being intact as is sometimes claimed, appears to have been pillaged, and quite extensively, probably three times – following interment, and when it was stumbled upon by those preparing sites for tomb KV3 and later for KV4 (Ramesses XI). The initial plundering of KV10 (Amenmesse), of KV47 (Siptah) and of KV12 will

perhaps likewise have occurred by chance, as a result of the inadvertent 'collisions' which took place during the quarrying of KV14, KV32 and KV9.

What were they after?

The practicalities of tomb robbery are well illustrated by the papyri, which document the entire process from uncovering the entrance to stripping the mummies. Here is the extraordinary confession of the stonemason Amenpanufer, son of Inhernakhte, presented, after suitable 'persuasion', before the court of Ramesses IX in Year 16 of the reign, 3rd month of *akhet*-season, day 23, preserved in Papyrus Leopold-Amherst:

'We went to rob the tombs in accordance with our regular habit, and we found the pyramid-tomb of king Sekhemreshedtawy, son of Re, Sobekemsaf [II], this being not at all like the pyramids and tombs of the nobles which we habitually went to rob. We took our copper tools and forced a way into the pyramid of this king through its innermost part. We found its underground chambers, and we took lighted candles in our hands and went down. Then we broke through the rubble . . ., and found this god lying at the back of his burial-place. And we found the burial-place of Queen Nubkhaas his queen situated beside him. . . .

We opened their sarcophagi and their coffins in which they were, and found the noble mummy of this king equipped with a sword . . . We collected the gold we found on the noble mummy of this god, together with his amulets and jewels which were on his neck. . . . We collected all that we found upon [the queen's mummy] likewise, and set fire to their coffins. We took their furniture which we found with them . . .'

Tutankhamun's jewel caskets neatly arranged in the entrance to the treasury. The seals had been broken in antiquity, and the contents ransacked. The restoration party had repacked what was left and replaced the lids to achieve a semblance of order.

Date	Documents	Description
Uncertain, probably pre-Year 9, Ramesses IX	P. Mayer B	Court record; robbery from tomb of Ramesses VI
Years 16–18, Ramesses IX	P. Abbott P. BM 10053 P. BM 10054 P. BM 10068 P. Leopold-Amherst Parts of the Turin Necropolis Journal	Court records, lists of thieves, booty seized, report on an inspection of tombs; thefts from tombs and temples inc. 17th-dyn. burial of Sobekemsaf II; Valley of the Queens inspected and reported intact
Years 19–20, Ramesses XI	P. BM 10052 P. Mayer A P. BM 10383 P. BM 10403 Abbott - Dockets P. Rochester 51.346.1	Court records, lists of suspects; thefts from tombs of queens and nobles, temples and palaces

Papyrus Mayer B

'The foreigner Nesamun took us up and showed [us] the tomb of King Nebmaatre-meryamun [Ramesses VI], life! prosperity! health! the great god. . . . And I spent four days breaking into it, we being [present] all five. We opened the tomb and we entered it. We found a basket(??) lying on sixty . . . chests(?). We opened it. We found [. . .] of bronze; a cauldron(?) of bronze; three wash bowls of bronze; a wash bowl, a ewer (for) pouring water over the hands, of bronze; two *keb*-vessels of bronze; two *pewenet*-vessels of bronze; a *keb*-vessel, an *inker* [. . .]-vessel [. . .] of bronze; three *irer*-vessels of bronze; eight beds of ornamented copper; eight *bas*-vessels of copper. We weighed the copper of the objects and of the vases, and found it to be) [500 *deben*? (approx. 45.5 kg)], 100 *deben* (9.1 kg) of copper falling to the share [of each man?]. We opened two chests full of clothes; we found, of good quality Upper Egyptian cloth, *daiw*-garments . . ., *ideg*-cloths, 35 garments, [seven garments of] good quality Upper Egyptian cloth falling to the share of each man. We found a basket(?) of clothes lying there; we opened it and found 25 *rewed*-shawls of coloured(?) cloth in it, five *rewed*-shawls of coloured(?) cloth falling [to the share of each man] . . .'

Papyrus Mayer B – a detail.

For robbery in the Valley of the Kings itself, apart from the fragmentary Papyrus Mayer B, nothing quite so eloquent has been preserved. But, in their depleted inventories, the partially plundered tombs KV62 (Tutankhamun), KV36 (Maiherpri) and KV46 (Yuya and Tjuyu) reflect the commodities which interested the thieves. As both archaeology and papyri show, the booty – euphemistically referred to in the texts as 'bread' – was essentially of two sorts: goods of an untraceable nature, which the robbers could dispose of with ease and at little risk; and items, such as gold and silver, made from materials which could be recycled.

Among the first class of anonymous goods were textiles, which are present in abundance in, for example, the intact private tomb of the architect Kha at Deir el-Medina; they are frequently referred to in the lists of stolen items and are almost entirely absent in the pilfered burials of Maiherpri and Yuya and Tjuyu. Fresh perfumes and cosmetics were also sought after, and almost always stolen when a tomb was entered within a short time of the interment – as in the burial of Tutankhamun; when a greater time had elapsed between burial and plundering, as was the case with Maiherpri, such items were generally rejected by the thieves, presumably owing to their limited shelf life.

Top of the robbers' shopping list was naturally metal, precious and not so, which is rarely met with even in burials which have been subjected to the most cursory plundering; gold and silver were the first things to disappear from the tomb of Tutankhamun. Glass, at least during the 18th dynasty, was also of interest to the robbers, though by the end of the New Kingdom (if we are to judge from the quantities of glass still remaining in KV35, the tomb of Amenophis II) its desirability had decreased somewhat. Other raw materials commonly mentioned in the papyri are precious woods and ivory; these again are rarely encountered in the archaeological record – an absence which cannot always be put down to simple disintegration.

Burial restoration

How were thefts from tombs discovered? It is clear that central (and confidential) records were maintained of the positions of tombs (perhaps located by means of cairn markers: p. 190); and during the cooler seasons (as we know from dated documents) necropolis inspections periodically took place – particularly during the late New Kingdom when the threat of tomb robbery seems to have increased, but doubtless as a matter of course in earlier times also.

The nature of the restoration work carried out after a robbery had been discovered is hinted at in the tomb of Tuthmosis IV (KV43). In this burial, which required official attention in Year 8 of the reign of Horemheb, the restoration appears to have been remarkably thorough: broken faience vessels were repaired, other damage and disorder presumably made good, breached door blockings restored and resealed, and the wooden door to the burial chamber perhaps replaced (or supplemented) by a masonry build – a feature discernible also within WV22, the tomb of Amenophis III. With KV62 (Tutankhamun), less care appears to have been taken: the disturbed funerary equipment was merely restored to some semblance of order, and the dismantled portions of the door blockings rebuilt and resealed; while the entrance corridor (which at the time of the burial had been pressed into service as a storage overflow) had been cleared, its contents reburied in a shallow pit, KV54 (p. 126), and the passage filled with rubble to deter future plunderers. This technique of filling up the corridor with chippings seems to have been the norm in Theban corridor tombs, as suggested by the robber's description of the tomb of Sobekemsaf II (p. 191) and by the situation following the burial of Tiye within KV55 (p. 117).

Whose responsibility?

In the case of Tutankhamun, and with Tuthmosis IV also, the official responsibility for reburial and restoration appears to have devolved upon the necropolis administration – as, it appears, did the initial interment in the Valley of the Kings of non-royal individuals such as Yuya and Tjuyu. This is indicated not only by the administrative personnel involved in the restoration of Tuthmosis IV's tomb (one of whom, the scribe Djehutymose, would later be involved in setting right Tutankhamun's burial after the second robbery), but also by the seals found associated with the door blockings of private tombs which are consistently of the jackal-and-nine-captives variety. The numerous priestly officials who applied their seals to the door blockings at Tutankhamun's funeral were evidently not involved in the subsequent resealings of this tomb, or in the closure of non-royal interments.

When a tomb was discovered accidentally by the necropolis workforce, any breach made in the blockings of the tomb to establish its content was either left or else (if the investigation was of an official or semi-official character) hurriedly reclosed with a dry stone wall; and this is how the royal tombs were usually blocked off after the mummies had been removed for reburial elsewhere. In the case of KV46 (Yuya and Tjuyu), two of the officials involved in investigating a disturbance of the tomb during the reign of Ramesses III appear to have resealed a number of the disturbed funerary items with their personal signets. Such resealing was quite unusual, and is not evidenced in any other tomb in the valley; it was certainly not practised by those officials involved in reordering Tutankhamun's burial after its two periods of theft, or in the restoration of the burial of Tuthmosis IV.

Deir el-Medina: poachers turn gamekeepers

Horemheb's repair of the damage which had been caused by thieves in the tombs of Tutankhamun and Tuthmosis IV at the end of the 18th dynasty had been carried out in the course of his reorganization of the west bank administration, which was itself but a part of the wider administrative reforms the new king had imposed on the country as a whole.

With this shake-up, the nature of the necropolis workforce based at Deir el-Medina was completely changed: the pre-Horemheb settlement at the site, populated by a transient, even casual workforce, was a quite different entity from the highly organized and rigidly controlled community which would evolve during the later Ramessid period (p. 22). It may well be that this re-ordering of the workforce was a reaction to the thefts of the recent past – in which those involved in quarrying and stocking the tombs had almost certainly taken part; if so, it had the desired effect and eliminated serious tomb robbery – if not lesser pilfering – during the greater part of the 19th and 20th dynasties. The fact that the later Ramessid rulers ceased to conceal the tomb entrance from view, and in fact chose to signal it by constructing a pair of large 'pylons' from the excavated chippings, is a clear reflection of their continuing confidence. And, despite the incursions referred to in the robbery papyri, it is a design which seems to have survived unchallenged until the very end of Ramessid rule.

Calcite handled jar from the burial of Yuya and Tjuyu in KV46. The linen covering at the mouth was torn away by thieves; discovering that the vessel held only worthless castor oil, they discarded it.

Who was Behind the Robberies?

At least one likely Ramessid 'Mr Big' may be recognized in the extant tomb-robbery documentation – no less a person than Paweraa, the mayor of western Thebes. An investigation initiated in Year 16 of Ramesses IX by the mayor of the east bank, Paser, had managed to extract from one of the tomb robbers his admission of having violated, four years previously, the tomb of King Sobekemsaf II (p. 191). However, a subsequent inspection of the necropolis, headed by the vizier, Khaemwaset (stage managed by Paweraa), reported that Sobekemsaf's was the only royal burial to have been disturbed of the ten royal tombs examined. The case was dismissed.

Paser was suspicious, and engineered a second hearing. Once again Paser's allegations were thrown out by the vizier – only to be upheld 12 months later. The outcome is not preserved, but both the vizier, Khaemwaset, and, ominously, Paser disappear from view, as do the robbers themselves – a number of them members of the tomb workforce.

The double dealing Paweraa survived, and remained in office for several years more. We should not be too surprised to learn that pillaging of the tombs continued.

The Royal Mummies

Factfile

Tomb number/location:
DB320, Deir el-Bahri
Date of discovery:
before 1881, by Abd el-
Rassul Ahmed
Excavator/report:
Émile Brugsch, 1881: E.
Brugsch and G. Maspero,
*La trouvaille de Deir-el-
Bahari* (Cairo, 1881)

The Deir el-Bahri cache (DB320)

Discovery

'For the past ten years or more it had been suspected that the Theban Arabs (whose main occupation is tomb-pillage and mummy-snatching) had found a royal sepulchre. Objects of great rarity and antiquity were being brought to Europe every season by travellers. . . . At length suspicion became certainty . . .'

Amelia B. Edwards

In the late summer of 1881 news began to reach Europe of a great discovery made in the Theban cliffs at Deir el-Bahri on the west bank of the Nile: an ancient tomb, plundered intermittently over the previous decade by local robbers, had at last been located by the Egyptian authorities. In this tomb were assembled the mummified remains and funerary equipment of more than 50 kings, queens, lesser royals and nobles, among them such legendary figures as Tuthmosis III, Sethos I and Ramesses II. Here, for the very first time, Egyptologists could look upon the face of Pharaoh himself.

The precise circumstances of the original discovery are shrouded in uncertainty and contradiction. According to one version of the story (as reliable as any), the mummies first came to light when a straying goat stumbled and disappeared down a partially concealed tomb shaft. The owner of the goat was

Gaston Maspero, Ahmed Kamal and the Abd el-Rassuls at the mouth of the Deir el-Bahri cache, 1881. The original photograph was taken by Émile Brugsch.

an Egyptian, by name Abd el-Rassul Ahmed, a *dragoman* and tomb-robber whose curses must have echoed around the cliffs as he clambered down after the unfortunate creature. The goat was soon forgotten as Abd el-Rassul began to explore. Here before him were dozens of coffins, *shabtis*, *shabti*-boxes, canopic jars and other funerary paraphernalia. But this was no ordinary mummy-pit: as Abd el-Rassul registered the royal cobra decorating the brow of several of the coffins, his eyes must have widened.

The Abd el-Rassul family lived comfortably off the proceeds of their tomb for some time until, in the mid-1870s, the growing number of important funerary papyri reaching the west as well as other objects in circulation on the local antiquities market gave the game away. An official investigation was begun to establish the source of these *antika*, and the authorities' suspicions in due course fell upon Abd el-Rassul Ahmed and his younger brother, Hussein Ahmed. Despite brutal interrogation by the feared *mudir* of Qena, Daud Pasha, the two held their tongues, and after some months Ahmed was released from custody; of Hussein, perhaps ominously, we hear no more. Mohammed Ahmed Abd el-Rassul, an elder brother and head of the clan, was intelligent enough to realize that the chances of successfully exploiting the tomb further were slim. Against his brothers' wishes, he decided to cut the family's losses and claim the *baksheesh* on offer for information on the find. Travelling down to Qena, he told all.

The year was 1881, at the height of the Egyptian summer. Gaston Maspero, head of the Antiquities Service, had returned to Paris, leaving his assistant, Émile Brugsch, temporarily in charge. Upon learning of Mohammed Abd el-Rassul's confession, Brugsch set off to investigate the long-sought tomb, arriving at Deir el-Bahri on 6 July. Although Abd el-Rassul had described the burial, Brugsch was stunned by what he found. In an interview given some years later, he recalled the scene that met his eyes after he had lowered himself down the tomb shaft:

'Soon we came upon cases of porcelain funerary offerings, metal and alabaster vessels, draperies and trinkets, until, reaching the turn in the passage, a cluster of mummy cases came into view in such number as to stagger me.

Collecting my senses, I made the best examination of them I could by the light of my torch, and at once saw that they contained the mummies of royal personages of both sexes; and yet that was not all. Plunging on ahead of my guide, I came to the [end] chamber . . ., and there standing against the walls or here lying on the floor, I found even a greater number of mummy-cases of stupendous size and weight.

Their gold coverings and their polished surfaces so plainly reflected my own excited visage that it seemed as though I was looking into the faces of my own ancestors.'

Émile Brugsch

Brugsch could not afford to day-dream for long. Fearing attack by the locals (who had been stirred up by rumours of a great treasure), he determined to clear the tomb with all possible haste: his large team of workmen laboured around the clock, and within a matter of days the mummies, packed in sail-cloth and matting, were on their way by steamer down to the museum at Bulaq. The finer details of the archaeological record might have been lost along the way, but the greater prize was secured.

Brugsch's recovery from the tomb of some 40 royal (and not so royal) mummies and their coffins – together with 'five thousand nine hundred and odd smaller objects' – aroused a storm of interest and prompted a host of questions. Why had a single tomb yielded such an astonishing number of kings, queens and other notables? And why were the coffins of the greatest in the land so wretched and their bandages so tattered? Where were Pharaoh's fabled riches? The answer soon became clear: the Abd el-Rassuls had stumbled, for the first time, upon an ancient hiding place for the Egyptian royal dead.

The archaeology of the royal cache

As a century of research has shown, the history of the Deir el-Bahri tomb is a complex one, but Maspero saw early on that the mummies fall into two distinct groups: a first, poorly coffined and of Second Intermediate Period and New Kingdom date; and a second, better equipped and dating from the Third Intermediate Period.

Until recently, it was widely believed that DB320 was the tomb of Queen Ahmose-Inhapi, mentioned in a series of hieratic dockets on the coffins of Ramesses I, Sethos I and Ramesses II as their destination following removal from their previous hiding place. This was because a hieratic docket at the bottom of the shaft of DB320, recording the burial within this tomb of the high priest Pinudjem II, carried precisely the same date as the introduction dockets on the Sethos I and Ramesses II coffins. However, the layout of the coffined mummies within DB320, as now established, clearly indicates that the mummy of Inhapi lay not in the interior of

(Left) The hidden entrance to the DB320 cache today. (Inset) The discoverer of the cache, Abd el-Rassul Ahmed, photographed in old age.

(Below left) The mummies and coffins 1–8 had been introduced into DB320 en masse from a tomb in which Inhapi appears to have occupied a central position – evidently the Inhapi kay, or cliff-tomb, mentioned in the coffin dockets inscribed upon the coffins of Ramesses I, Sethos I and Ramesses II. The transfer from Inhapi's tomb to DB320 perhaps took place shortly after the interment of Djedptahiufankh or Nestanebtishru.

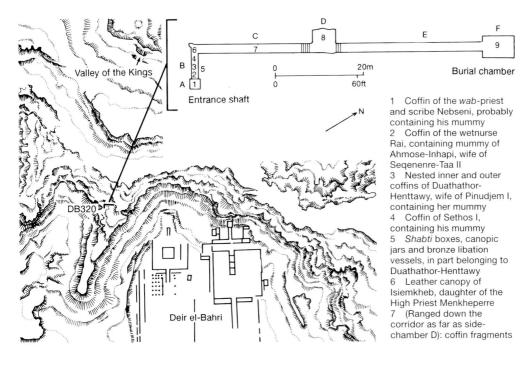

1 Coffin of the *wab*-priest and scribe Nebseni, probably containing his mummy
2 Coffin of the wetnurse Rai, containing mummy of Ahmose-Inhapi, wife of Seqenenre-Taa II
3 Nested inner and outer coffins of Duathathor-Henttawy, wife of Pinudjem I, containing her mummy
4 Coffin of Sethos I, containing his mummy
5 *Shabti* boxes, canopic jars and bronze libation vessels, in part belonging to Duathathor-Henttawy
6 Leather canopy of Isiemkheb, daughter of the High Priest Menkheperre
7 (Ranged down the corridor as far as side-chamber D): coffin fragments of Ramesses I; coffin of Pinudjem I containing the mummy of 'Tuthmosis I'; coffined mummies of Amenophis I and Tuthmosis II
8 Coffined mummies of Amosis I, of his son Siamun, and of Seqenenre-Taa II; coffin of Ahhotpe I, with mummy of Pinudjem I; coffin of Ahmose-Nofretiri, with (a) her mummy(?) and (b) cartonnaged mummy of Ramesses III; and perhaps the coffined mummies of Tuthmosis III and Ramesses II
9 Family vault of Pinudjem II and his principal wife Neskhons, Djedptahiufankh and his (presumed) wife Nestanebtishru, being the last members of the family to be interred here around 935 BC.

195

Name	Mummy	Coffin	Other	Notes
Ahhotpe I		D		contained mummy of Pinudjem I
Ahmose-Hentempet	•	•		
Ahmose-Henttimehu	•	•		
Ahmose-Inhapi	B			mummy in coffin of Rai
Ahmose-Meryetamun	•			mummy in coffin of Seniu
Ahmose-Nofretiri	?D	D	•	coffin also contained cartonnaged mummy of Ramesses III
Ahmose-Sipair	•	•		coffin same as anonymous child's coffin?
Ahmose-Sitkamose	•			mummy in coffin of Pediamun
Amenophis I	C	C		orig. owner of coffin: Djehutymose
Amosis	D	D		
Bakt	?•	•		
Djedptah-iufankh	F	F	F	
Duathathor-Henttawy	B	B	B	inner and outer coffins; outer lid missing
Hatshepsut			•	wooden box with mummified liver or spleen
Isiemkheb	F?	F?	B/C	
Maatkare-Mutemhet	F?	F?	F?	
Masaharta	F?	F?	F?	
Merymose			•	
Nebseni	?B	B		mummy that of unknown man C
Neskhons	F	F	F	one coffin contained mummy of Ramesses IX
Nestanebt-ishru	F	F	F	
Nodjmet	•	•	•	
Paheripedjet		•		contained mummy of Rai
Pediamun		•		contained mummy of Ahmose-Sitkamose
Pinudjem I	D	C	•	coffins usurped from Tuthmosis I
Pinudjem II	F	F	F	
Rai	•	B		mummy in coffin of Paheripedjet
Ramesses I		C?		contained mummy of unknown woman B (Tetisheri?)?
Ramesses II	D?	D?		
Ramesses III	D	D		
Ramesses IX	F??		•	mummy in one of coffins of Neskhons
Seniu		•		contained mummy of Ahmose-Meryetamun
Seqenenre-Taa II	D	D		
Sethos I	B	B		
Siamun	D	D		
Siese			•	canopic jar
Sitamun	•	•		
Sutymose			•	miniature canopic coffin
Tayuheret	F?	F?	F?	
Tetisheri			•	mummy bandages; unknown woman B?
'Tuthmosis I'	C?			mummy in coffin of Pinudjem I
Tuthmosis II	C	C		
Tuthmosis III	D?	D?		
Wepmose			•	canopic jar
Wepwawet-mose			•	canopic jar
anonymous (m)	•	•		unknown man E
anonymous (f)	•			unknown woman B; Tetisheri? Originally within coffin of Ramesses I?
anonymous (f?)	•	•		
anonymous (m?)	•	•		
anonymous (m?)	•	•		
anonymous (m?)	•	•		
anonymous (?)	•	•		box coffin
anonymous		•		child's coffin – of Ahmose-Sipair?

Lettering designates position within the tomb
? preceding – attribution uncertain; ?/?? following – position uncertain;
• – precise position unknown

Ahmed Kamal, Brugsch's assistant in the clearance of the cache, poses beside the enormous outer coffin of Queen Ahmose-Nofretiri.

DB320 but close to the entrance, *behind* the bodies of Ramesses I, Sethos I and Ramesses II – which seems to show that the tomb of Inhapi had been a previous resting place. Evidently the DB320 and Ramesses I-Sethos I-Ramesses II dockets, which first suggested the identification of the Inhapi *kay* with DB320, refer to two separate burials in different places on the same day.

In fact, DB320 turns out to have been the family vault of the high priest Pinudjem II, into which the royal mummies had been introduced only after

Year 11 of Shoshenq I of the 22nd dynasty. The Pinudjem II group of coffined mummies, essentially intact and unplundered when found, occupied the end chamber, while the intrusive coffins were crammed into the corridors and side chamber of the tomb.

(Above left) Smaller finds from DB320, including the Hatshepsut box – centre back.

(Above) Funerary papyrus of Pinudjem II, principal occupant of DB320.

WN A: The Cliff Tomb of Inhapi?

Factfile

Tomb number/location:
WN A, Deir el-Bahri
Date of discovery:
unknown
Excavator/report:
Claude Robichon, 1931–32, for the Institut français d'archéologie orientale: B. Bruyère, *Rapport préliminaire sur les fouilles de Deir el Médineh (1931–1932)* (Cairo, 1934), p. 94

Rough sketch plan by Claude Robichon of the still-uncleared WN A.

'The highest tomb high up in the mountain, large and spacious; called el-Maaleg because it is so high up, being hung as it were in the air.'

Joseph Bonomi

Several of the royal mummies in DB320 had previously been hidden in the tomb of Queen Ahmose-Inhapi, wife of the 17th-dynasty king Seqenenre-Taa II. As the Ramesses I-Sethos I-Ramesses II dockets show, the royal mummies had been introduced into the Inhapi tomb a century before the transfer to DB320, during the reign of Pinudjem I.

The Egyptian word used in the dockets to describe the Inhapi burial place is *kay*, 'high place' – and it seems clear from this that a type of cliff

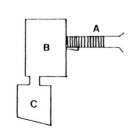

tomb is to be understood, similar to that prepared for Hatshepsut as queen (p. 94), but of no ordinary elevation. A mere 750 m (2,460 ft) to the southwest of DB320, lies the cliff tomb *par excellence* – WN A, explored in 1931/32 and found to be filled up with Roman mummies. The local Arabic name for this sepulchre is [Bab] el-Muallaq, 'The hanging [tomb]'. As a Greek graffito referring to one of the later burials within attests, the name is evidently an ancient one, going back to Roman times at least:

'In this spot the *stolarch* Heraclas, son of Renbuchis, has been placed, in the *khremasterios taphos*, by the sons of Phthonthes and those who loved him ...'

The words used to describe the burial place of Heraclas, *khremasterios taphos*, similarly translate as 'hanging tomb'; and, like the designation 'Bab el-Muallaq', they offer a seductively close approximation of the meaning behind the Egyptian word *kay*.

Could it be that WN A – a sepulchre notable since antiquity for its spectacular position, of appropriate date and within striking distance of DB320 – represents the eyrie of Inhapi from which the royal mummies were removed for reburial in the Pinudjem II family vault at the start of the 22nd dynasty? It is an intriguing possibility, which a reexamination of the tomb will hopefully settle in due course.

The Cache in the Tomb of Amenophis II (KV35)

(For Factfile see above, p. 101)

'The mummies of the hero kings and builders of the empire in the XVIIIth, XIXth, and XXth Dynasties were found at Dêr el Bahri; in the tomb of Amenhetep II. lay the bodies of sovereigns of the same dynasties who enjoyed to the full the fruits of their predecessors' conquests, and of those who reigned feebly. Altogether we now have in the flesh the series of the Theban monarchs of the New Kingdom almost complete.'

Francis Llewellyn Griffith

The second royal cache would be brought to light by the French Egyptologist Victor Loret in 1898, within the tomb of Amenophis II (KV35) (p. 100) – and, like Brugsch before him within DB320, he found it difficult to believe what his eyes were seeing.

In the first of the side rooms located to the right of the burial chamber (Jc), Loret encountered three stripped corpses without coffins: the first, a mummy with long, flowing hair, 'a thick veil [covering] her forehead and left eye' (distinguished by Elliot Smith in his subsequent publication of the royal dead as 'the Elder Lady'); the second, the mummy of a young boy, the head 'shaved except in an area on the right temple from which grew a mag-

nificent tress of black hair'; and the third, the body of a youthful woman, whose face, owing to a dislocated jaw, 'displayed something horrible and something droll at one and the same time'. All three corpses had had their skulls pierced with a large hole, and the breast of each was opened. The identity of none was apparent, and Loret initially assumed that they were simply members of the immediate family of Amenophis II.

The second side chamber, Jb – partially blocked with stones which had originally been employed in Year 13, probably of Smendes (*c.* 1057 BC), to close off the entrance to the burial chamber – held a further nine bodies, this time with the wrappings essentially intact, contained in a variety of ramshackle coffins. At first, Loret assumed that these too were relatives of the king; then he looked more closely:

'The coffins and the mummies were a uniform grey colour. I leaned over the nearest coffin and blew on it so as to read the name. The grey tint was a layer of dust which flew away and allowed me to read the nomen and prenomen of Ramesses IV. Was I in a cache of royal coffins? I blew away the dust of the second coffin, and a cartouche revealed itself, illegible for an instant, painted in matte black on a shiny black ground. I went over to the other coffins – everywhere cartouches!'

The truth began to dawn: 'We had stumbled upon a royal cache, similar to that of Deir el Bahari . . .'

Hole in the skull of the mummy of Ramesses V from KV35. Several royal mummies display similar damage, caused in antiquity by chopping through the bandages with an adze to speed up their unwrapping and to gain access to their jewellery.

Eerie photograph, taken by candlelight, of the three unnamed mummies as found in side room Jc in the tomb of Amenophis II. The mummy of the 'Elder Lady', identified by some as Tiye, is on the left.

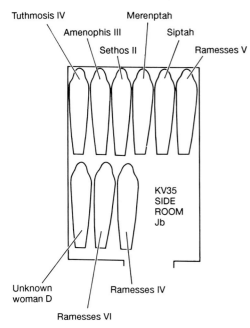

Tuthmosis IV
Amenophis III
Merenptah
Sethos II
Siptah
Ramesses V

KV35
SIDE
ROOM
Jb

Unknown
woman D
Ramesses IV
Ramesses VI

Who's Who in KV35

Name	Mummy	Coffin	Other	Notes
Amenophis II	J	J	passim	
Amenophis III	Jb			
Hatshepsut-Meryetre	?Ea		J	cane
Merenptah	Jb			
Ramesses III		Jb		
Ramesses IV	Jb	Jb		orig. owner of coffin: Aha-aa
Ramesses V	Jb	Jb		
Ramesses VI	Jb	Jb		orig. owner of coffin: Re
Sethos II	Jb	Jb		
Sethnakhte	?F	Jb,●		
Siptah	Jb	Jb		
Tiye?	Jc			
Tuthmosis IV	Jb	Jb		
Webensenu	?Ea		F, J,●	*shabtis*, canopic jars
anonymous (m)	Jc			
anonymous (f)	Jc			

Lettering designates position within the tomb
? preceding – attribution uncertain;   ● – precise position unknown

The roll-call was as awesome as that within DB320: Tuthmosis IV, Amenophis III (in a coffin inscribed for Ramesses III, covered with a lid inscribed for Sethos II), Merenptah (in the lower part of a coffin inscribed for Sethnakhte), Sethos II, Siptah, Ramesses IV, Ramesses V and Ramesses VI, and an anonymous female (the 'unknown woman D' – Tawosret? – lying on the upturned lid of a coffin inscribed for Sethnakhte).

A further mummy, found resting upon a wooden boat in the antechamber of the tomb and probably to be associated with this latter group of bodies, probably represents the Pharaoh Sethnakhte himself.

Interpreting the cache

A recent study of the Amenophis II tomb suggests that the occupants of room Jb had been gathered up from various tombs and earlier caches and walled into the chamber on a single occasion, the timing of this coinciding with the rewrapping of the mummy of Amenophis II himself (which had been labelled in a similar fashion to the Jb dead). The date of these activities cannot be established with any precision; but clearly they did not pre-date the restoration of the burial (*wehem keres*) of Amenophis III which, as a docket on the mummy wrappings records, had taken place within WV22 in Year 12 or 13 of Smendes.

'On the back of the head [of the mummy of Siptah] there is a hole . . . in the right parietal bone . . . deliberately made by means of blows from some sharp instrument [and similar to] openings that I found in the mummies of Seti II, Ramses IV, Ramses VI (and possibly that of

Ramses V also) . . . I was inclined to look upon them as wounds . . . made by plunderers, who . . . chopped through the bandages and so damaged the cranium.'

Grafton Elliot Smith

As for the occupants of the Jc cache, the difference in condition is striking and might indicate that these corpses had been introduced into KV35 only *after* the Jb mummies had been 'treated' – though perhaps by the same officials, since the mummies' original wrappings had been cut away with an adze in the same crude fashion, from head to toe. The three seem originally to have been placed in room Jd (where a stray toe was fished out of the debris) across the burial chamber. They appear to have been displaced during a subsequent rifling of the tomb (when the Jb mummies were also disturbed), and finally stashed at an undetermined date in the chamber they occupied when Loret and his diggers entered the tomb in 1898.

(Above left) The side room Jb cache in the tomb of Amenophis II, the order of the mummies reconstructed from Loret's published description of the find.

The body on the boat, found in the antechamber of the tomb, is probably that of the 20th-dynasty pharaoh, Sethnakhte.

The Face of Pharaoh

(Above) The 'Elder Lady', perhaps Tiye, from KV35.

(Centre) Sethos I, from DB320

(Right, top) Amosis; and the mummy from the coffin of Tuthmosis I/Pinudjem, from DB320.

(Right, below) Siptah, with withered foot, from KV35; and Ramesses III, from DB320.

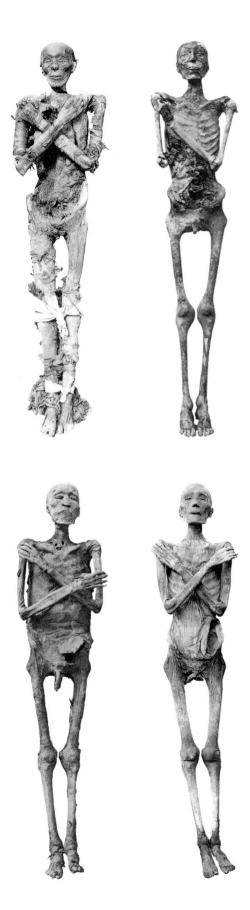

(Above) Merenptah, from
KV35.

(Centre) Ramesses II, the
Great, from DB320.

(Left, top) Tuthmosis II, from
DB320; Sethos II, from
KV35.

(Left, below) Ramesses IV;
and Ramesses V – both from
KV35.

Deciphering the Dockets

The discovery of the royal mummies in 1881 provided the first real insight into what had occurred in the Valley of the Kings at the end of the New Kingdom. Egyptologists soon appreciated the value in understanding the historical process of the hieratic dockets written in ink upon the coffins and on the various layers of bandages wrapping the mummies from DB320 (and later KV35, though the dockets there were on the whole far more concise).

Maspero studied the Deir el-Bahri texts intensively, and in 1889 – within a remarkably short time of the discovery – was able to present an extensive commentary on them in *Les momies royales de Déir el-Baharî*. Like most Egyptologists since, Maspero's view was that the mummies had been callously ripped to shreds by thieves in their search for gold and jewels; the battered mortal remains had later been gathered up by Theban priests, who had lovingly rewrapped the royal dead for secret reburial in a series of old and safely forgotten burial places. But that initial motivation was to become dramatically less pious as time went on.

The royal mummies: are they who they claim to be?

Before considering the evidence of the dockets, a word should be said about their reliability as historical sources. Seeds of doubt were first sown when, in the summer of 1881, the DB320 mummies arrived in Bulaq Museum and it was found that several of the bodies had become separated in antiquity from their intended coffins and replaced in cases to which they had no legitimate claim. In 1898, Loret discovered that the occupants of the KV35 cache had been similarly mixed up. It was clear, therefore, that none of the mummies could be identified with complete confidence from the formal inscriptions of the coffin in which they were contained – a conclusion few would argue with. Rather it was the labelling directly on the mummy bandages that gave the reliable identification.

Unfortunately, the waters were muddied considerably a short time later by Maspero, who argued that one of the DB320 mummies was not the lady she purported to be. Though clearly labelled across the bandages covering the breast as 'The king's daughter and king's sister, Meryetamun, may she live!', Maspero declared that this was, in fact, a mummy of the Middle Kingdom, rewrapped as a replacement for the original, 18th-dynasty mummy, which, he suggested, had been destroyed in antiquity. The anatomist Elliot Smith demonstrated in 1912 that this was an aberration on Maspero's part. But too late; a precedent had been set for dismissing the ancient attribution out of hand where the anatomical data from the corpse seemed to contradict the evidence of the dockets.

Herbert Winlock, one of the clearest thinkers Egyptology has known, pointed out the dangers of such cavalier junking of basic evidence as long ago as 1932:

'... the docket written by the ancient officials must be accepted unless there is very strong evidence against it ...'

To little avail, it seems – for, despite the fact that not a single docketed corpse can be demonstrated to be wrongly identified, it is still widely believed

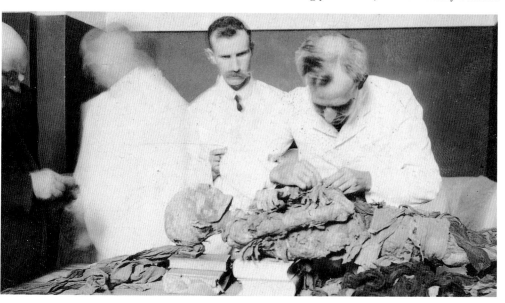

Grafton Elliot Smith unwrapping the mummy of Merenptah in 1907; behind him stands his assistant, Dr Pain, with, at the extreme left of the picture, Maspero himself.

The Coffin and Mummy Dockets from DB320 and KV35

Two basic types of docket are encountered. The first (Type 1) is a simple identifying text prominently displayed on the coffin lid or on the shroud covering the chest of the mummy, containing a record of the deceased's name, often with details of status; for example: 'Nebmaatre-Amenophis, life! prosperity! health!' (docket on coffin employed for Amenophis III).

The second kind of docket (Type 2), more directly instructive than the first, usually contains a date, a record of work undertaken, and the names and titles of the personnel involved: 'Year 12 [or 13] [of Smendes], 4th(?) month of *peret*-season, day 6(?). On this day renewing the burial(?) of king Nebmaatre, life! prosperity! health! by the high priest of Amon-Re, king of the gods, Pinudjem [I], son of the high priest of Amon-Re, king of the gods, Piankh . . . [by?] . . . Wennufer(?).' (docket on mummy of Amenophis III).

A number of the linens employed to wrap the mummies had previously been temple donations, and carry hieratic notations (linen notations) to that effect:

'Linen which the high priest of Amon-Re, Menkheperre, made for his father Amun [in] Year 6.' (linen notation from the mummy of Sethos I).

Name	Tomb	Location	Docket type
Ahmose-Henttimehu	DB320	mummy	Type 1
Ahmose-Inhapi	DB320	mummy	Type 1
Ahmose-Meryetamun	DB320	mummy	Type 1
Ahmose-Sipai	DB320	coffin	Type 1
Ahmose-Sitkamose	DB320	mummy	Type 1
		mummy	Type 2
Amenophis I	DB320	coffin	Type 2 (2 dockets)
Amenophis II	KV35	mummy	Type 1
Amenophis III	KV35	coffin	Type 1
		mummy	Type 2
Amosis	DB320	mummy	Type 1
		mummy	Type 2
Djedptah-iufankh	DB320	mummy	linen notations (3)
Merenptah	KV35	mummy	Type 1
Neskhons	DB320	mummy	linen notation
Nestaneb-tishru	DB320	mummy	linen notation
Nodjmet	DB320	mummy	linen notation
Pinudjem II	DB320	mummy	linen notations (4)
Rai	DB320	mummy	Type 1
Ramesses I	DB320	coffin	Type 1
		coffin	Type 2
Ramesses II	DB320	coffin	Type 2 (3 dockets)
		mummy	Type 2
Ramesses III	DB320	mummy	Type 2
		mummy	linen notations (2)
Ramesses IV	KV35	mummy	Type 1
Ramesses V	KV35	mummy	Type 1
Ramesses IX	DB320	mummy	Type 2
		mummy	linen notation
Sethos I	DB320	coffin	Type 2 (3 dockets)
		mummy	Type 2
		mummy	linen notations (2)
Sethos II	KV35	mummy	Type 1
Siamun	DB320	mummy	Type 1
		mummy	Type 2
Siptah	KV35	mummy	Type 1
Sitamun	DB320	coffin	Type 1
Tuthmosis II	DB320	mummy	Type 2
Tuthmosis IV	KV35	mummy	Type 1

(Below) The mummy of Ramesses III as found, rewrapped and inscribed with a Type 2 docket mentioning Pinudjem I and Butehamun; (below right) Sethos I's refurbished coffin lid, with its large identifying cartouches and three Type 2 dockets written during the high-priesthoods of Herihor and Pinudjem II.

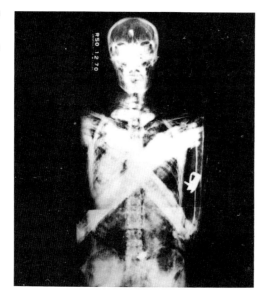

The recent radiographic survey of the royal mummies by James Harris's team has produced a mass of valuable data. This X-ray of the mummy of Sethos I reveals a large wedjat*-eye amulet – missed by robbers and restorers – still in position on the upper left arm.*

One of a group of 21st-dynasty labels brought to light in a plundered tomb at Sheikh Abd el-Qurna in 1857 which carried the names of 10 18th-dynasty princesses – evidently the remains of a cache of lesser royal mummies. Having exhausted the Valley of the Kings, the high priests turned their attentions to more modest fare as the economy of Egypt ground to a halt.

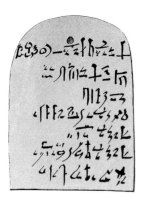

that the restoration parties made frequent errors of identification. The juggling act of bodies and identities which has ensued, based variously on mummification method, craniofacial variation and estimations of age at death, is more like a lottery than science.

Names in ancient Egypt were not bandied about lightly. That we possess several unidentified corpses from both caches clearly indicates that the restorers preferred to leave uninscribed any corpse whose identity was even slightly in doubt; for the rest, unless clear evidence to the contrary is brought to light, we should accept the reliability of those identifications the restoration parties did feel confident enough to make.

Missing mummies: the third cache?

It is clear that DB320 and KV35 were not the only tombs employed as hiding places for the kings' mummies, since several names are absent from the roster of extant royal dead, such as Horemheb, Ay and Tuthmosis I. What happened to these missing mummies?

A group of faint graffiti noted years ago by the English Egyptologist Alan Gardiner at the entrance to the tomb of Horemheb (KV57: p. 130) may offer a clue. The first of these texts refers to the carrying out of an unspecified 'command' of the high priest of Amun, Herihor, in the *per djet* (burial chamber?) of KV57, by the scribe of the army, Butehamun, in an unspecified Year 4; the second and third graffiti record the names of a certain Kysen, and of Butehamun (again) and the royal scribe Djehutymose; while the fourth records a further phase of activity within the tomb in an unspecified Year 6. The precise nature of this later activity is again unclear, owing to Gardiner's uncertainty as to the transcription of the verb in the original hieratic. Two possibilities exist: that this last text

records the removal (*fai*) of the king from the tomb for reburial elsewhere; or that the inscription records an official 'investigation' (*sheni*) and all that implied.

The second option seems the more likely, for, when it was first entered by Theodore Davis and his team in 1908, several dismembered skeletons were in evidence scattered around the tomb, together with abundant remains of Third Intermediate Period funerary garlands. Since the excavators encountered no evidence – coffins, cartonnage fragments, *shabti* figures – of intrusive 22nd-dynasty private burials, there is a strong likelihood that the garlands and skeletal material represent the remains of at least four 'restored' royal mummies. Horemheb is certainly high on the list of 'missing' pharaohs. Ay is another; and, if he had been cached within KV57, this would go a long way towards explaining the presence of fragments of his burial equipment (gilded chariot harness) in the nearby tomb KV58 (p. 186).

The caches in context

Egypt during the reign of Ramesses XI was not only poverty stricken; it was a country on the boil, with relations between north and south becoming increasingly fraught. Years 17–19 witnessed violent confrontation between the viceroy of Kush, Pinhasi and the high priest of Amun, Amenhotep. The general Piankh was dispatched by Ramesses XI to sort matters out. And it seems to have been the ensuing confusion of virtual civil war which would enable the robberies referred to in the papyri of Years 19–20 to take place.

The history of this confusing period is still being written, but it appears that Piankh's repulse of the Ramessid appointee Pinhasi strengthened his hand to the extent that he was able to impose upon Pharaoh a virtual division of the country, in which he and his successor high priests took control of the south while control of the north (and nominal sovereignty over the entire country) was left to Ramesses XI and, after his death, to Pharaoh Smendes. With this division of power was introduced an alternative dating system – the so-called 'renaissance' era (*wehem mesut*, literally 'repeating of births').

Pinhasi, though driven out of Thebes, continued to be a thorn in the Theban flesh. The confusion is vividly mirrored in the 'Late Ramessid Letters' – correspondence principally between Piankh, directing the war against Pinhasi in the south, and the scribes of the necropolis, Djehutymose and his son Butehamun. And it is this correspondence which holds the key to what eventually happened to the tombs in Wadi Biban el-Muluk.

The new policy: search and dismantle

'[To] the fan-bearer on the king's right hand, royal scribe, general, high priest of Amon-Re, viceroy of Kush . . .

Piankh; [from] the two chief workmen, the scribe of the necropolis Butehamun and the guardian Kar, and [the workmen of the tomb]. . . .

We have noted everything about which our master has written to us, [namely]: "Go and perform for me a task on which you have never before embarked and search for it until I come to you" – so says our lord; "What has happened with [the place] you already know about, where you were before? Leave it [alone], do not touch it" – so says our lord. This scribe [Tjaroy, also known as Djehutymose] who was [formerly] here at our head, he is the one who [can] give [advice?] . . . but he is with you [in Nubia]. As soon as he tells us what he knows, we shall require 10–20 days . . .

Now see, you have written: "Uncover a tomb among the tombs of the ancestors and preserve its seal until I return" – so said our lord. We are carrying out orders. We shall leave it [undisturbed] for you and let you find it ready . . .'

'. . . a task on which you have never before embarked'. This letter, written in Year 10 of the 'renaissance' era, fixes precisely the date at which the policy of the high priests of Amun changed from restoration and salvage to ruthless exploitation; the inviolability of Pharaoh was no more.

Robbery in the necropolis had always existed, on a greater or lesser scale – but it would no longer be common thieves who carried out the plundering. Piankh had taken the irrevocable step of emptying the tombs to finance his campaign against Pinhasi in the south and to prop up his régime at home. Once the mining had begun, other uses for these hidden riches would inevitably be devised in the future. The taboo had been broken.

Beyond the Valley of the Kings, the high priest's men roamed the Theban hills, 'seeing the mountains' – looking for the presence of old tombs (private as well as royal) in every conceivable location, marking where they had gone and what they had found, often with a large *wedjat*-eye or *nefer*-signs (perhaps signifying something 'intact' or 'good' in the vicinity – or, when coupled with the hieroglyph *ka* (high), a cliff tomb, as found by Carter in Wadi el-Gharbi). A vast number of such graffiti – around 4,000 – have been noted and copied, testifying to the extraordinary range and thoroughness of the search for tombs which might be 'released' for recycling. More than 130 of these texts are by the hand of one of the main participants in the dismantling process – the necropolis scribe Butehamun.

Digging for gold in the Valley of the Kings evidently continued throughout the high priesthoods of Herihor and Pinudjem I, when it began to be represented as 'restoration'. It shows a noticeable increase just before and after the adoption of 'kingly' status by the latter; indeed, the wealth Pinudjem I was able to accrue may well account for the strength of his position at this time. Herihor had perhaps started the ball rolling by establishing the cache in the tomb of Horemheb (KV57). Amongst the work carried out during Pinudjem I's 'reign' was the establishment of a cache within KV17, and the transfer of the first batch of mummies to the tomb of Amenophis II (KV35). The 'osirification' and reburial of Ramesses III and of the Amosis I group of corpses cached within the *kay* (cliff-tomb) of Queen Inhapi evidently followed, as did the analogous move of Amenophis I, Ahmose-Nofretiri and

An insight into the activities of one of the salvage teams is offered by the burial of Queen Meryetamun, found just as the 'restorers' had left it within tomb DB358 at Deir el-Bahri. The coffins (one pictured above) had been stripped, the mummy slit open, rifled, rewrapped and docketed, and the tomb swept clean. The excavator estimated that the party could have completed its work in the space of a single day.

The Necropolis Scribes Djehutymose and Butehamun

Butehamun's commemoration of Amenophis I, Ahhotpe, Ahmose-Nofretiri, Sitamun, Meryetamun and Sipair – in whose restorations and reburials he probably had a hand. Outer coffin now in the Turin Museum.

The key role played by two 'scribes of the tomb', Djehutymose and his son, Butehamun, in the restoration of the royal mummies and the dismantling of the Theban necropolis was openly acknowledged during their lifetimes. It was also commemorated in the titles and decoration of Butehamun's coffins.

Butehamun is variously styled: 'Opener of the gates in the necropolis', 'Opener of the gates of the underworld (Rosetjau)', 'Overseer of works in the house of eternity', etc. These extraordinary titles emphasize the unique access to, and administrative control over, the tombs and their occupants and contents enjoyed by Butehamun (and presumably by Djehutymose before him) at the end of the 20th dynasty and start of the 21st dynasty.

These scribes' names are found everywhere in the necropolis, and we know specifically from an inscription on the bandages wrapping the mummy of Ramesses III that Butehamun was involved with the restoration of this king (p. 203). Decoration on the lid of Butehamun's outer Turin coffin shows him burning incense before several other members of the ancient royal family – Amenophis I, Ahhotpe, Ahmose-Nofretiri, Sitamun, Meryetamun and Sipair – suggesting that he was involved in the restorations of these earlier burials too.

Where Did the Restorations Take Place?

The temple of Medinet Habu, administrative headquarters of Thebes at the end of the New Kingdom, where the mummy of Ramesses IX was 'restored'.

It is clear that the royal mummies were rewrapped and restored in a number of different places. To judge from a docket found on the wrappings of Ramesses IX, his body was rewrapped at the administrative headquarters of the Theban necropolis, Medinet Habu; he may not have been alone, since several royal funerary objects have been recovered from that site. The mummy of the early 18th dynasty Queen Meryetamun on the other hand, discovered in tomb DB358, appears to have been rewrapped *in situ* (p. 205).

Two graffiti discovered above the entrance to KV49 mention quantities of temple linen brought to the tomb by the scribe Butehamun and other workmen.

These texts appear to indicate that the tomb had been employed as a storeroom for linens used in the restoration of one or other of the royal mummies – an interpretation which is supported by a fragmentary mummy label found here bearing the hieratic inscription 'corpse oil'. The corpse in question was most probably that of Ramesses III, whose tomb stands close by and upon whose mummy a number of 'shawls' similar to those mentioned in the KV49 graffiti (and inscribed as coming from Medinet Habu) were found. Interestingly enough, a hieratic docket on the king's mummy records Butehamun's subsequent involvement in the 'restoration' of this king.

The Reuse of Royal Burial Equipment

Reused burial equipment: (above) gold vessel of Amosis, found at Tanis, perhaps from his as yet unlocated Theban tomb; (right) shabti of Ramesses II refashioned as a private Osiris figure.

One interesting aspect of the dismantling of the Valley of the Kings is the removal and reuse of royal burial equipment. The best known example is the re-employment by 'King' Pinudjem I of two coffins provided by Tuthmosis III for the new tomb of Tuthmosis I (p. 95). These coffins had been entirely reworked by Pinudjem I, and in their finished state the original ownership was wholly undetectable.

Another notable instance is a wooden *shabti* figure of Ramesses II, now in the British Museum, which had been hacked about and varnished during the late 21st or early 22nd dynasty to produce a blackened Osiris figure. Here again, in its final, adapted state, no indication of original ownership was visible. Further examples could be cited – including, we may suspect, a great deal of the jewellery recovered by Pierre Montet from the Third Intermediate Period royal tombs at Tanis.

The explanation for at least some of these appropriations is suggested by a series of funerary papyri from the cache of Amun priests at Bab el-Gasus containing spells whose efficacy was guaranteed by the rubric: 'The book that was found at the neck of the mummy of King Ramesses II in the necropolis.'

A similar benefit presumably attached itself to those Third Intermediate Period papyri influenced by or copied from the walls of the royal tombs (in particular the tomb of Amenophis II). Clearly, royal funerary equipment, by virtue of its associations, was immanent with a magical potency which was widely acknowledged and employed as a result of the dismantling process.

(Right) The lid of Tuthmosis III's original second innermost coffin, its inlaid eyes removed and the surface adzed over by the 'restorers' to remove every scrap of its gilded surface before reburial.

Tuthmosis II, and that of the remains of Hatshepsut, Tuthmosis III and presumably Tuthmosis I.

By the time Pinudjem I died, around 1030 BC, a degree of stability had evidently been achieved in the necropolis: the mummies had been relieved of their valuables (frequently, as we have seen, in a very rough and ready manner) and now lay safe, for the most part rewrapped and docketed, within a handful of easily guarded caches – KV17, WN A(?), KV35 and (perhaps) KV57. Their original tombs were now empty – stripped of their gold, their silver, their linens and perfumes, of handy lengths of wood and slabs of stone – and much of the debris burned.

The status quo seems to have been maintained for a further 60 years until, in Year 10 of Siamun (c. 968 BC), further rationalization was necessary – and after the years of official plunder and pillage one would like to imagine that the motivation was at last wholly pious – with the mummies from KV17 being transferred to the Inhapi *kay*. Forty or more years later, again for reasons unknown, the Inhapi cache was itself abandoned for the Pinudjem II family vault – tomb DB320. Here, the discarded mummies in their cheap coffins would lie shamed if undisturbed, until their rediscovery before 1881 by a less discerning band of robbers – the Abd el-Rassuls.

The Royal Mummies: Who Got Where

The dockets, when studied in conjunction with the graffiti found in and around the royal tombs and with other available archaeological evidence, reveal the routes the mummies followed to reach their final destinations.

Name	Original Place of Burial	CACHES				Inhapi *kay*	
		KV57	KV17	KV35	AN B	(WN A?)	DB320
Tetisheri	?					⇒●	⇒●
Seq.-Taa II	?					⇒●	⇒●
Ahhotpe I	?					⇒●	⇒●
Ahmose-Inhapi	WN A?					●?	⇒●
Amosis I	?					⇒●	⇒●
Ahmose-Nofret.	AN B?				●?	⇒●	⇒●
Ahm.-Hentempet	?					⇒●	⇒●
Ahm.-Henttimehu	?					⇒●	⇒●
Rai	?					⇒●	⇒●
Ahm.-Sitkamose	?					⇒●	⇒●
Siamun	?					⇒●	⇒●
Sitamun	?					⇒●	⇒●
Meryetamun I	?					⇒●	⇒●
Seniu	?					⇒●?	⇒●?
Amenophis I	AN B?/KV39?				●?	⇒●	⇒●
Ahm.-Sipair	?					⇒●	⇒●
Tuthmosis I	*KV20+38*					⇒●?	⇒●?
Tuthmosis II	DB358?				⇒●	⇒●	⇒●
Tuthmosis III	*KV34*					⇒●	⇒●
Hatshepsut	*KV20*					⇒●	⇒●
Amenophis II	*KV35*			●			
Tuthmosis IV	*KV43*			⇒●			
Amenophis III	*WV22*			⇒●			
Tiye?	?			⇒●?			
Ay	*WV23*	⇒●?					
Horemheb	*KV57*	●?					
Ramesses I	*KV16*		⇒●			⇒●	⇒●
Sethos I	*KV17*		●			⇒●	⇒●
Ramesses II	*KV7*		⇒●			⇒●	⇒●
Merenptah	*KV8*			⇒●			
Sethos II	*KV15*			⇒●			
Siptah	*KV47*			⇒●			
Woman D	?			⇒●			
Sethnakhte	*KV14*			⇒●			
Ramesses III	*KV11*					⇒●	⇒●
Ramesses IV	*KV2*			⇒●			
Ramesses V	*KV9*			⇒●			
Ramesses VI	*KV9*			⇒●			
Ramesses IX	*KV6*					⇒●	⇒●
Merymose	TT383?					⇒●?	⇒●?
Bakt	?					⇒●?	⇒●?
Nebseni	?					⇒●?	⇒●?
Siese	?					⇒●?	⇒●?
Sutymose	?					⇒●?	⇒●?
Wepmose	?					⇒●?	⇒●?
Wepwawetmose	?					⇒●?	⇒●?
Paheripedjet	?					⇒●?	⇒●?
Nodjmet	WN A?					⇒●	⇒●
Pinudjem I	WN A?					⇒●	⇒●
Duat.-Henttawy	WN A?					⇒●	⇒●
Maat.-Mutemhet	DB320?						●?
Masaharta	DB320?						●?
Tayuheret	DB320?						●?
Pinudjem II	DB320						●
Neskhons	DB320						●
Isiemkheb	DB320						●
Djedptahiufankh	DB320						●
Nestanebtishru	DB320						●

Occupants of tombs in the Valley of the Kings in *italics*
● original place of burial ⇒● subsequent transfer

Epilogue

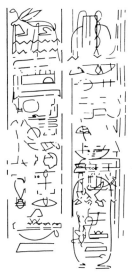

A faint and complex palimpsest text of Pinudjem I in KV4. The decoration of long-open tombs is being scrutinized ever more closely, with surprising results.

'A new interest in their history and archaeology is developing amongst [the] Egyptians; and not long will they permit foreign Egyptologists to work as they have worked before, with greater regard for their own museums and their own public than for the interests of Egypt itself.'

Arthur Weigall

Looking for information not things

For a while, following the discovery and clearance of the tomb of Tutankhamun, archaeology in the Valley of the Kings petered out. This was not only a result of the political tensions which followed on from Howard Carter's discovery. It was generally agreed that, after Tutankhamun, there was nothing new to be found.

Ali Abd el-Rassul's clearance of the mysterious sloping corridor leading down from the burial chamber of the tomb of Sethos I (KV17: p. 137) in the late 1950s was hopefully the last true hunt for treasure the Valley of the Kings will see. Today priorities have changed. There may or may not be new tombs to find. Fresh discoveries are an exciting prospect, but for the moment they are safe where they are. The 80 or more tombs and pits already known, many standing open and vulnerable, are

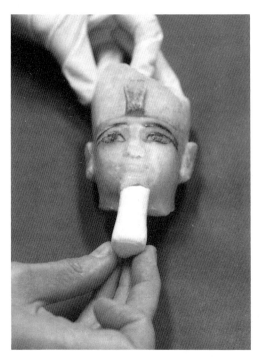

The French Expedition's shabti *head (see p. 55) is reunited with a cast of its long-lost beard, recently brought to light in WV22 by Waseda University archaeologists.*

the new focus of attention; while the aim is not primarily the recovery of further objects, but of information by which the finds already to hand may be better understood.

The new direction archaeology has taken in the Valley of the Kings is largely attributable to one woman – the late Elizabeth Thomas, whose study, *The Royal Necropoleis of Thebes*, appeared in 1966. It is true to say that Thomas's work has inspired and assisted to a greater or lesser degree all work carried out in the valley since its publication.

Although archaeology after Tutankhamun was slow to get off the ground, research proceeded apace in other areas. From 1930 to 1966 the Russian scholar Alexandre Piankoff spent much of his time in Egypt studying the texts and representations in the kings' tombs. Alone and with other scholars, beginning in 1939, Piankoff published a series of ground-breaking studies which inspired a fresh interest in the decoration of the royal sepulchres. *The Tomb of Ramesses VI*, which appeared in 1954, was in fact the first publication to present a complete photographic documentation of the scenes and translations of the tomb's inscriptions.

Archaeology and scholarship today

Scholarly interest in the Valley of the Kings has increased enormously over the past 30 years. Piankoff was followed by Erik Hornung, the Swiss Egyptologist who is today the senior scholar of Valley of the Kings studies. Hornung's many contributions to our understanding of the royal valley include his publications of the religious texts used in the tombs, as well as detailed studies of the art and inscriptions of specific tombs – contributions which are still ongoing. A Polish team directed by T. Andrzejewski and M. Marciniak laboured intermittently between 1959 and 1981, studying the scenes in the tomb of Ramesses III (KV11: p. 159). In 1972 Otto Schaden undertook archaeological clearance of the West Valley tomb of Ay (WV23: p. 128) and of the nearby, unfinished WV25 (p. 116). From 1974 until his death 20 years later, the German scholar Friedrich Abitz published a number of important books and articles which contributed significantly to our understanding of symbolic aspects of the royal tombs.

Between 1977 and 1979 the members of a Brooklyn Museum expedition led by John Romer rebuilt Theodore Davis's house at the entrance to the West Valley for use as a base for their own work in the royal wadi. This had begun in 1975 with geological and hydrological studies of the tombs and the wadis in which they are located; it was followed by epigraphic and photographic surveys of the tomb of Ramesses X (KV18: p. 172) and an important clearance of the tomb of Ramesses XI (KV4: p. 172), the last tomb to be cut in the royal wadi. At the same time, a long-recognized need was addressed when Kent Weeks, then of the University of

California at Berkeley, established the Theban Mapping Project with the aim of providing a detailed survey not only of the Valley of the Kings but ultimately of the entire west bank utilizing modern mapping techniques. In the course of his work, Weeks, ably assisted by Catharine Roehrig of the Metropolitan Museum of Art in New York, and a host of specialists, was able to locate three previously 'lost' tombs – most notably KV5 (p. 144), the huge burial complex prepared by Ramesses II for his sons, the excavation of which is ongoing.

A comprehensive radiographic study of those royal mummies originally buried in the Valley of the Kings and later cached in DB320 and the tomb of Amenophis II was initiated in 1966 by James E. Harris, working in conjunction with Kent Weeks and latterly Edward F. Wente. The results have been impressive, controversial and thought-provoking. In 1982, Edwin C. Brock, former Director of the Canadian Institute in Egypt, initiated his fundamental study of the royal sarcophagi of the 19th and 20th dynasties. In the course of his researches, he has carried out selected clearance work in the tombs of Merenptah (KV8: p. 147), Ramesses VI (KV9: p. 164) and Ramesses VII (KV1: p. 166) and added significantly to our store of knowledge on these sepulchres. In 1983, Hartwig Altenmüller of the University of Hamburg inaugurated a detailed archaeological and epigraphic study of the tomb of Tawosret and Sethnakhte (KV14: p. 157), followed in 1987 with a similar treatment of the tomb of Bay (KV13: p. 154) – the latter project, in particular, producing quite unexpected results which indicate that the Valley of the Kings still has many secrets in store.

In 1989, a team of Japanese Egyptologists and archaeologists from Waseda University in Tokyo, led by Professor Sakuji Yoshimura and Jiro Kondo, began excavating and conserving the West Valley tomb of Amenophis III (WV22: p. 110), in 1993 extending their work to the nearby store-chamber WV A (p. 113) and the wadi between; the Waseda team has, in addition, mapped both valleys anew. 1989 also saw the commencement by John Rose of the clearance of KV39 (p. 89), which was to reveal for the first time its extraordinary plan; and that same year Donald P. Ryan converted into action his long-standing interest in the valley's lesser tombs, with the reinvestigation, over several seasons and with very worthwhile results, of KV60, KV21, KV27, KV28, KV44 and KV45 (pp. 186, 115, 109, 182, 184).

Otto Schaden returned to the valley in 1991 to undertake the clearance of WV24 (p. 182), and the following year he began work in KV10, the tomb of the shadowy Amenmesse (p. 150). In 1992–93, Lyla Pinch Brock embarked on a detailed study of KV55, the Amarna cache (p. 117), demonstrating that a close study of even the emptiest and least-promising of tombs can preserve information of

Recent Archaeology and Epigraphy in the Valley of the Kings

Date	Tomb	Tomb owner	Director
1959–81	KV11	Ramesses III	T. Andrzejewski; M. Marciniak, E
1972	WV23	Ay	Otto J. Schaden, University of Minnesota, A
1972–73	WV25		Otto J. Schaden, University of Minnesota, A
1978–80	KV18	Ramesses X	John Romer, The Brooklyn Museum, subsequently Theban Foundation, E; A, E
	KV4	Ramesses XI	
1982–	KV8	Merenptah	Edwin C. Brock, Canadian Institute in Egypt, A
	KV9	Ramesses VI	
	KV1	Ramesses VII	
1983–87	KV14	Tawosret	Hartwig Altenmüller, University of Hamburg, A, E
1987–	KV5	sons of Ramesses II	Kent R. Weeks, American University in Cairo, A, E
1987–94	KV13	Bay	Hartwig Altenmüller, University of Hamburg, A, E
1989–	WV22	Amenophis III	Sakuji Yoshimura and Jiro Kondo, Waseda University, A, E
1989–	KV39		John Rose, Pacific Western University, A
1989	KV60		Donald P. Ryan, Pacific Lutheran University, A
1990	KV21		Donald P. Ryan, Pacific Lutheran University, A
	KV27		
	KV28		
1991	KV44		Donald P. Ryan, Pacific Lutheran University, A
	KV45		
1991–92	WV24		Otto J. Schaden, University of Arizona, A
1992–	KV10	Amenmesse	Otto J. Schaden, University of Arizona, A
1992–93	KV55	Akhenaten?	Lyla Pinch Brock, ARCE, A
1993–	various		Richard H. Wilkinson, University of Arizona, E
1993–94	WV A		Sakuji Yoshimura and Jiro Kondo, Waseda University, A
1995–	KV7	Ramesses II	Christian Leblanc, CEDAE, A, E

A – archaeological clearance, E – epigraphic documentation

value. And Christian Leblanc, hotfoot from his work in the Valley of the Queens, in 1995 began clearing the repeatedly flooded and badly damaged tomb of Ramesses II (KV7: p. 140) – for a long time written off as a wholly impractical aim.

Agents of destruction

'. . . rest assured, Sir, that one day you will have the pleasure of seeing some of the beautiful bas-reliefs of the tomb of Osirei [Sethos I] in the French Museum. That will be the only way of saving them from imminent destruction and in carrying out this project I shall be acting as a real lover of antiquity, since I shall be taking them away only to preserve and not to sell.'

Jean François Champollion, letter to Joseph Bonomi

Destruction has been endemic in the Valley for

The dual threats of natural and humanly inflicted damage have long affected the royal tombs. This pillar in the tomb of Amenophis III shows destruction caused by water (lower half) and by early antiquities hunters (note the removed face of the king and partially removed face of the goddess).

through their exhaled breath, a problem with which modern conservationists must likewise contend.

The ravaging floods

Quite apart from human threats to the royal monuments, the Valley of the Kings is periodically subject to flash floods, caused by intense rains which run down from the high desert plateau. All but a few of the tombs have been invaded by floodwaters at some time during their history. Until the end of the 19th century, however, the royal valley functioned as a relatively efficient natural drain, allowing floods to pass through the area with little obstruction. But in the present century, archaeological work and the construction of paths and levelled areas for tourists have changed the topography. The entrance to the tomb of Ramesses II, for example, now lies about 2 m (6 ft 6 1/2 in) below the present valley floor, making the tomb more likely to be flooded.

In the region around the Valley of the Kings floods often occur in three-to-four-year clusters every decade or so, usually in early winter, with at least one storm being particularly heavy. This pattern was recognized as early as 1835 by John Gardner Wilkinson and just such heavy storms were witnessed by Howard Carter between 1915 and 1918:

'For three successive Octobers we have had heavy downpours, and this time a peculiar phenomenon occurred. . . . The Valley of the Tombs of the Kings, joined by the Great Western valley, in a few moments became little short of mountain rivers . . . the torrent cutting out wide furows [sic] in the valley bed and rolling before it stones some two feet in diameter.'

The physical effects of such torrents entering the tombs and scouring their walls with particles of rock and sand are compounded by problems of local geology. Beneath the limestone in which most of the tombs are cut lie layers of porous shale which swell as they come in contact with water, cracking and disrupting the overlying limestone. Several tombs near the valley's entrance actually extend through the limestone down into the shale itself, while others, such as the tomb of Ramesses II, reach their lowest point in a transitional stratum of alternating limestone and shale. Such tombs are particularly vulnerable. As well as the structural damage to walls, ceilings and columns from swelling, centuries of alternating flooding and drying have led to the destruction of many decorated surfaces across the royal valley through long-term salt migration.

The preservation of the royal tombs

Today, the Valley of the Kings lies under the care of the Egyptian Supreme Council of Antiquities (SCA) and its designated inspectors, who supervise all conservation, research and excavation.

centuries. Quite apart from the depredations of robbers, officially sanctioned cases of *damnatio* and usurpation resulted in damage to a number of the monuments, such as the tombs of Ay (WV23) and Amenmesse (KV10). During the Greco-Roman, Christian and Islamic periods travellers, monks and hermits carved graffiti and lit fires in tomb entrances, scarring and blackening the walls. What is remarkable is that the Christians who so methodically expunged the images of the old gods from many of the Egyptian temples seem to have ignored or spared these same images in the royal valley.

With the advent of European exploration came new and ever more lamentable losses, Champollion, Rosellini and Lepsius, for example, forcibly removing reliefs from the tomb of Sethos I (KV17). The taking by Belzoni and others of 'squeezes' (mouldings, in wax or wet paper) directly from the walls also severely damaged the delicately painted surfaces of a great number of reliefs. The masses of tourists who flock to the Valley of the Kings today pose no less of a threat. In recent times as many as two million have visited the area each year, and the combined damage done through carelessness or by wandering hands eager to touch the painted reliefs is enormous. Tourists also introduce great quantities of harmful water vapour into the tombs

Conserving paintings in the tomb of Amenophis III. Today Egyptian antiquities staff and foreign specialists are working together to preserve the valley's rich archaeological heritage.

Following extensive flooding in October and November 1994, the SCA reacted quickly by building small protective walls at the entrances to a number of tombs as well as creating drainage channels around the sides of the tombs where possible. In those tombs open to the public, wooden guard rails have been installed to stop visitors jostling and rubbing against the walls, and plexiglass panels have been placed in front of the decorated walls and columns in many tombs to protect the sensitive paint and plaster. By rotating the specific monuments open at any one time, antiquities officials also lighten the pressure on popular tombs – which is so intense that even the construction of tomb replicas outside the valley has been considered.

One commentator has suggested that cracks appearing in the royal tombs may be the result of recent archaeological work in the area; but the royal necropolis is subject to cracking through occasional seismic activity as well as the long-term effects of swelling and contraction of its rock. Recent work in the tomb of Amenmesse has highlighted numerous examples of cracks repaired by ancient workmen who constructed the tombs. Many of these cracks had probably been in the rock for millennia before the tomb was excavated, and others may have appeared during the time it was actually cut. As

any kind of cracking can lead to water infiltration and further destruction of the tombs and their decorations, virtually all Egyptologists see this ongoing process as reason enough for active clearance and conservation. Work in the tomb of Amenmesse has further shown that almost all the decoration on plaster in this tomb – which was cursorily recorded by Lefébure towards the end of the last century – has now disappeared. If not cleared, documented and preserved as soon as possible, the little decoration that remains, in these and other tombs, will be lost forever. Though less publicized than the restoration of the tomb of Nefertari in the Valley of the Queens, proper conservation is at last beginning, with a number of tombs being at least partially restored.

Working with geologists, engineers and hydrologists, Egyptologists are also engaged in many other aspects of preservation: the preparation of detailed maps of the topography – and watersheds – of the royal valley to facilitate the production of hydrological maps; and the monitoring and analysis of rainfall patterns and seismic activity, as well as tourism and other humanly caused problems – to name but a few. A recent grant from the United States Government administered through the American Research Center in Egypt will help with this work, but much remains to be done.

Visiting the Royal Valley

Exploring the Valley of the Kings can be a superlative experience, but it is not one to be accomplished without planning. Even the most seasoned traveller can be overwhelmed by the sheer number of tombs and bewildering variety of images. Although a guided tour as part of a group can be helpful, it is more satisfying to work out one's own individual itinerary.

Tickets to visit all the monuments open on the West Bank (including the mortuary temples) may be purchased at a ticket office at the tourist-ferry landing, and also at a ticket office next to the Antiquities Inspector's office by the Colossi of Memnon. Tickets for individual monuments may sometimes be purchased at the site itself and tickets for the royal tombs are all available at a ticket office at the valley's entrance. The walk to the West Valley tomb of Ay is a fairly long one and visitors should check that this tomb is open and purchase a ticket before attempting to see it. Tickets are currently sold in blocks of three which can be used for any open tombs with the exception of that of Tutankhamun, for which a separate ticket must be purchased.

What to take

A checklist of items to take when exploring the royal valley must be headed by water. Although there is a rest and shade area at the valley's centre, the actual Rest House where food and drinks are available is at the valley's entrance several hundred yards distant, so a reasonably large water bottle is essential. A hat, sunglasses and sun-block are also vital, because just as much time may be spent waiting to enter tombs as within them. A good flashlight is also advisable in preparation for the not infrequent fluctuations in the tombs' lighting. A pen and notebook are often invaluable – if only to write down questions one may want to pursue later. Sturdy shoes are best for visiting the tombs and other monuments, and while relatively few mosquitoes and pests are to be found in the valley and desert areas, a good insect repellent is useful when travelling to and from the valley (especially while waiting for the ferry for Luxor).

Photography is allowed in the tombs (with an additional photography ticket) provided that no flash is used, though the situation with video cameras (often requiring separate tickets) is a little more complicated and travellers may want to enquire through their travel agents as to current regulations. Take lots of film since opportunities to photograph spectacular subjects seem almost endless. Mixed film speeds are needed – the fastest film for within the tombs, and a much slower film for outside shots in the bright desert landscape. A polarizing lens attachment and lens hood can be very useful for these bright outside shots, and also for cutting reflections from the protective plexiglass now installed in many of the tombs. Be sure to take extra batteries if your camera uses them and keep a spare set in your hotel room as the heat can quickly drain battery power if the camera is exposed to the sun.

When to visit the valley

The most pleasant times of year – late autumn, winter and early spring – are of course the busiest times for tourism (average temperatures in Luxor in November range from an 88°F (31°C) high to a 55°F (13°C) low) but waits to visit popular tombs may be considerable at these times. For travellers able to cope with the summer heat, conditions for visiting the tombs are often much better, though even the summer months may now bring large numbers of visitors. An early start to the day is important and the valley is usually much cooler, quieter and filled with softer, photography-enhancing light in the first hours of the morning. The most popular tombs are certainly best seen in the earliest hours and the less popular and remote tombs are often still relatively quiet later in the day. As a rule of thumb, start in the centre of the valley where almost all the most popular tombs are located, and work outwards as the day proceeds.

Some of the tombs are quite steep and enclosed in places, but for the most part these tend to be characteristics of the earlier monuments. If you are somewhat susceptible to feelings of claustrophobia, consider seeing the later Ramessid tombs constructed after the time of Ramesses I, since these are generally larger and brighter, with the entrance still usually visible from the rear sections of the tombs.

Planning your visit

Specific tombs open to the public at any given time are rotated by the Egyptian authorities to minimize damage, so any plan must include alternatives. Probably the best option for the first-time visitor is to see a single tomb from each of the three main phases of tomb design (p. 25) which roughly correspond to the three dynasties (18th, 19th and 20th) represented in the valley. By spending time in one tomb from each group, far more will be learned of the range and diversity of the tombs than in any hurried attempt to examine the whole royal necropolis in one visit.

Recommended first-phase tombs:
KV34 Tuthmosis III
KV35 Amenophis II
KV43 Tuthmosis IV

Recommended second-phase tombs:
KV57 Horemheb
KV17 Sethos I
KV8 Merenptah
KV14 Tawosret/Sethnakhte
KV11 Ramesses III

Recommended third-phase tombs:
KV2 Ramesses IV
KV9 Ramesses VI
KV1 Ramesses VII
KV6 Ramesses IX

Most visitors will also want to see KV62, the tomb of Tutankhamun, if it is open – though it should be remembered that despite its spectacular contents (mostly on display in the Cairo Museum), architecturally this tomb is essentially a modified private sepulchre which does not fit into the developmental scheme of the royal tombs as a whole.

When visiting selected tombs, notice the geological and topographical setting (p. 17) as well as the interior design and decoration. Although none of the smaller undecorated tombs are accessible to the general public, the first-phase and early second-phase tombs which are not completely decorated offer the opportunity to study the stone-cutting and smoothing techniques used in constructing the tombs. Some tombs reveal obstacles which the workmen were unable to overcome (e.g. the large boulder seen projecting from a corridor wall in KV8 (Merenptah)) and others show accidents where nearby tombs were breached (e.g. a corridor in KV11 (Ramesses III) penetrated the ceiling of KV10 (Amenmesse)) and changes of plan had to be hastily implemented.

Using the chart of the major afterlife books on p. 37 in conjunction with the descriptions of the individual tombs in Part III, the visitor can compare the different funerary works employed in the tombs' decoration. Careful observation of the images of the kings and the carving of their cartouches will reveal changes and additions made by the ancient artists when tombs were usurped by later kings (e.g. KV14 (Tawosret/Sethnakhte)), modified to accept additional burials (e.g. KV9 (Ramesses V/VI)), or had decoration removed in order to destroy the memory of kings considered to be heretical or usurpers (e.g. WV23 (Ay)).

For those able to spend longer in the royal valley, it is also often rewarding to examine atypical tombs such as KV16, the tomb of Ramesses I, an excellent example of where construction was cut short and the interior hastily modified for the royal burial.

Further Reading

A vast amount has been written about the Valley of the Kings and its tombs, and the following listing of books and articles on and relevant to the subject, while extensive, is of necessity selective. Many of the publications cited are semi-official in character, and received only limited circulation. The principal surveys are marked with an asterisk, and themselves contain extensive and useful bibliographies which may be consulted with profit. The magazines *Egyptian Archaeology*, *KMT* and *Minerva* regularly contain articles of interest (only a few of which it has been possible to note here) and up-to-date news on discoveries and developments in the field.

Abbreviations

After Tut'ankhamun
    Reeves, C. N. (ed.), *After Tut'ankhamun. Research and Excavation in the Royal Necropolis at Thebes* (London, 1992)
AL   *Amarna Letters*
AMG   *Annales du Musée Guimet*
ASAE   *Annales du Service des Antiquités de l'Égypte*
AsR   *Asiatic Review*
BIÉ   *Bulletin de L'Institut d'Égypte, Cairo*
BIFAO   *Bulletin de l'Institut français d'archéologie orientale*
BiOr   *Bibliotheca Orientalis*
BMMA   *Bulletin of the Metropolitan Museum of Art, New York*
BSEG   *Bulletin de la Société d'Égyptologie, Genève*
BSFE   *Bulletin de la Société française d'égyptologie*
CdE   *Chronique d'Égypte*
DE   *Discussions in Egyptology*
EA   *Egyptian Archaeology*
EEFAR   *Egypt Exploration Fund Archaeological Report*
ET   *Etudes et Travaux*
GM   *Göttinger Miszellen*
JACF   *Journal of the Ancient Chronology Forum*
JARCE   *Journal of the American Research Center in Egypt*
JEA   *Journal of Egyptian Archaeology*
JNES   *Journal of Near Eastern Studies*
KMT   *KMT. A Modern Journal of Ancient Egypt*
MDAIK   *Mitteilungen des Deutschen Archäologischen Instituts, Abteilung Kairo*
NARCE   *Newsletter of the American Research Center in Egypt*
OLZ   *Orientalistische Literaturzeitung*
Or   *Orientalia*
Orient   *Orient. Report of the Society for Near Eastern Studies in Japan*
PSBA   *Proceedings of the Society of Biblical Archaeology*
RdE   *Revue d'Égyptologie*
RdT   *Recueil de travaux relatifs à la philologie et à l'archéologie égyptiennes et assyriennes*
RAs   *Revue asiatique*
RHR   *Revue de l'histoire des religions*
RSO   *Rivista degli studi orientali*
SAK   *Studien zur altägyptischen Kultur*
Sun Kings
    Wilkinson, R. H. (ed.), *Valley of the Sun Kings. New Explorations in the Tombs of the Pharaohs* (Tucson, 1995)
VDI   *Vestnik Drevnej Istorii*
ZÄS   *Zeitschrift für ägyptische Sprache und Altertumskunde*

Abitz, F., 'Der Bauablauf und die Dekorationen des Grabes Ramesses' IX.', *SAK* 17 (1990), pp. 1–40
—*Baugeschichte und Dekoration des Grabes Ramses' VI.* (Freiburg and Göttingen, 1989)
—'Zur Bedeutung der beiden Nebenräume hinter der Sarkophaghalle der Königin Tausert', *SAK* 9 (1981), pp. 1–8
—'Die Entwicklung der Grabachsen in den Königsgräbern im Tal der Könige', *MDAIK* 45 (1989), pp. 1–25
—*König und Gott* (Wiesbaden, 1984)
—*Pharao als Gott in den Unterweltsbüchern des Neuen Reiches* (Freiburg and Göttingen, 1995)
—*Ramses III. in den Gräbern seiner Söhne* (Freiburg and Göttingen, 1986)
—*Die religiöse Bedeutung der sogenannten Grabräuberschächte in den ägyptischen Königsgräbern der 18. bis 20. Dynastie* (Wiesbaden, 1974)
—*Statuetten in Schreinen als Grabbeigaben in den ägyptischen Königsgräbern der 18. und 19. Dynastie* (Wiesbaden, 1979)
—'The structure of the decoration in the tomb of Ramesses IX', *After Tut'ankhamun*, pp. 165–85
—'Die Veränderung von Schreibformen im Königsgrab Ramses' IX', *Miscellanea Aegyptologica. Wolfgang Helck zum 75. Geburtstag* (eds. H. Altenmüller and R. Germer, Hamburg, 1989), pp. 1–5
Aldred, C., 'More light on the Ramesside tomb robberies', in J. Ruffle, G. A. Gaballa and K. A. Kitchen (eds.), *Glimpses of Ancient Egypt. Studies in Honour of H. W. Fairman* (Warminster, 1979), pp. 92–9
—'The parentage of King Siptah', *JEA* 49 (1963), pp. 41–8
—'The tomb of Akhenaten at Thebes', *JEA* 47 (1961), pp. 41–60
—'Two monuments of the reign of Horemheb', *JEA* 54 (1968), pp. 100–06
—'Valley tomb no. 56 at Thebes', *JEA* 49 (1963), pp. 176–8
Altenmüller, H., 'Der Begräbnistag Sethos' II', *SAK* 11 (1984), pp. 37–47
—'Bemerkungen zu den Königsgräbern des Neuen Reiches', *SAK* 10 (1983), pp. 25–61
—'Bemerkungen zu den neu gefunden Daten im Grab der Königin Twosre (KV14) im Tal der Könige von Theben', *After Tut'ankhamun*, pp. 141–64
—'Dritter Vorbericht über die Arbeiten des Archäologischen Instituts der Universität Hamburg am Grab des Bay (KV13) im Tal der Könige von Theben', *SAK* 21 (1994), pp. 1–18
—'Das Grab der Königin Tausret (KV14). Bericht über eine archäologische Unternehmung', *GM* 84 (1985), pp. 7–17
—'Das Grab der Königin Tausret im Tal der Könige von Theben', *SAK* 10 (1983), pp. 1–24
—'Das Graffito 551 aus der thebanischen Nekropole', *SAK* 21 (1994), pp. 19–28
—'Prinz Mentu-her-chopeschef aus der 20. Dynastie', *MDAIK* 50 (1994), pp. 1–12
—'Rolle und Bedeutung des Grabes des Königin Tausret im Königsgräbertal von Theben', *BSEG* 8 (1983), pp. 3–11
—'Tausret und Sethnacht', *JEA* 68 (1982), pp. 107–15
—'La tombe de la reine Taousert', *Dossiers d'archéologie* 149–150 (mai–juin, 1990), pp. 64–7
—'Untersuchungen zum Grab des Bai (KV13) im Tal der Könige von Theben', *GM* 107 (1989), pp. 43–54
—'Zweiter Vorbericht über die Arbeiten des Archäologischen Instituts der Universität Hamburg am Grab des Bay (KV13) im Tal der Könige von Theben', *SAK* 19 (1992), pp. 15–36
Andrews, C. A. R., and S. Quirke, *The Rosetta Stone* (London, 1988)
Andrews, E. B., unpublished diary ('A Journal on the Bedawin, 1899–1912') (Department of Egyptian Art, Metropolitan Museum of Art, New York/American Philosophical Society, Philadelphia)
Arundale, F. and J. Bonomi, *Gallery of Egyptian Antiquities selected from the British Museum* (London, 1843–45)
Assman, J., 'Die Inschrift auf dem äusseren Sarkophagdeckel des Merenptah', *MDAIK* 28 (1972), pp. 47–73
—*Re und Amun. Die Krise des polytheistischen Weltbilds im Ägypten der 18.–20. Dynastie* (Freiburg, 1983)
Aubert, J.-F., and L. Aubert, *Statuettes égyptiennes: chaouabtis, ouchebtis* (Paris, 1974)
Ayrton, E. R., 'Discovery of the tomb of Si-ptah in the Bibân el Molûk, Thebes', *PSBA* 28 (1906), p. 96
—'Recent discoveries in the Bibân el Molûk at Thebes', *PSBA* 30 (1908), pp. 116–17
—'The tomb of Thyi', *PSBA* 29 (1907), pp. 85–6, 277–81
—unpublished papers (Egypt Exploration Society, London; John Romer, Cortona)
Bacchi, E., 'Lo scarabeo del cuore di Thutmôse IV', *RSO* 20 (1943), pp. 211–27
Bacon, E. (ed.), *The Great Archaeologists* (London, 1976)
Baedeker, K. (ed.), *Egypt and the Sudan* (5th edn., Leipzig, 1902; 8th edn., Leipzig, 1929)
Baillet, J., *Inscriptions grecques et latines de tombeaux des rois ou syringes à Thèbes* (Cairo, 1920–26)
Baines, J., and J. Málek, *Atlas of Ancient Egypt* (Oxford and New York, 1980)
Balout, L., B. Roubet, C. Desroches-Noblecourt, *et al.*, *La momie de Ramsès II. Contribution scientifique à l'égyptologie* (Paris, 1985)
Barguet, P., 'L'Am-Douat et les funérailles royales', *RdE* 24 (1972), pp. 7–11
—'Le Livre des Portes et la transmission du pouvoir royal', *RdE* 27 (1975), pp. 30–6
—'Remarques sur quelques scènes de la salle du sarcophage de Ramsès VI', *RdE* 30 (1978), pp. 51–6
Barta, W., 'Die Anbringung der Sonnenlitanei in den Königsgräbern der Ramessidenzeit', *GM* 71 (1984), pp. 7–10
—*Die Bedeutung der Jenseitsbücher für den verstorbenen König* (Munich, 1985)
—'Zur Stundenordnung des Amduat in den ramessidischen Königsgräbern', *BiOr* 31 (1974), pp. 197–201
Bataille, A., *Les Memnonia* (Cairo, 1952)
—'Quelques graffiti grecs de la montagne thébaine', *BIFAO* 38 (1939), pp. 141–79
Beinlich, H., and M. Saleh, *Corpus der hieroglyphischen Inschriften aus dem Grab des Tutanchamun* (Oxford, 1989)
Bell, M., 'An armchair excavation of KV55', *JARCE* 27 (1990), pp. 97–137
Belmore, the Earl of, *Tablets and other Egyptian Monuments from the Collection of the Earl of Belmore, now deposited in the British Museum* (London, 1843)
Belzoni, G. B., *Description of the Egyptian Tomb discovered by G. Belzoni* (London, 1821)
—*Narrative of the Operations and Recent Discoveries within the Pyramids, Temples, Tombs, and Excavations, in Egypt and Nubia* (London, 1820)
—*Plates illustrative of the Researches and Operations of Belzoni in Egypt and Nubia* (London, 1820–22)
[Berkeley] Theban Mapping Project, *Preliminary Reports* (1978–)
Bierbrier, M. L., 'The Salt watercolours', *GM* 61 (1983), pp. 9–12
—*Tomb-Builders of the Pharaohs* (London, 1982)
Birch, S., *Remarks Upon the Cover of the Granite Sarcophagus of Rameses III. in the Fitzwilliam Museum* (Cambridge, 1876)
von Bissing, F. W., *Ein thebanischer Grabfund aus dem Anfang des neuen Reiches* (Berlin, 1900)
Bogoslovsky, E., 'Hundred Egyptian draughtsmen', *ZÄS* 107 (1980), pp. 89–116
Bonomi, J., and S. Sharpe, *The Alabaster Sarcophagus of Oimenepthah I, King of Egypt* (London, 1864)
Botti, G., and T. E. Peet, *Il giornale della necropoli di Tebe* (Turin, 1928)
Bradbury, L., 'Nefer's inscription. On the death date of Queen Ahmose-Nefertary and the deed found pleasing to the king', *JARCE* 22 (1985), pp. 73–95
Breasted, C., *Pioneer to the Past* (London, 1948)
Brier, B., *Egyptian Mummies* (New York, 1994; London,

1996)

Brock, E., 'The clearance of the tomb of Ramesses VII', *Sun Kings*, pp. 47–67
—'Piecing it all together. An ongoing study of later New Kingdom royal sarcophagi', *KMT* 2/1 (spring, 1991), pp. 42–9
—'The tomb of Merenptah and its sarcophagi', *After Tut'ankhamun*, pp. 122–40
—'Sarcophagi in the Valley of the Kings', *Bulletin of the Canadian Mediterranean Institute* 9/2 (April, 1989), pp. 6–7
Brock, L. P., 'Mummy business at the Egyptian Museum', *KMT* 3/4 (winter, 1992–93), pp. 12–18, 84–5
—'Theodore Davis and the rediscovery of Tomb 55', *Sun Kings*, pp. 34–46
—'A walk-through tour of WV22', *AL* 2 (1992), pp. 18–27
Brodrick, M., *Egypt. Papers and Lectures by the late May Brodrick* (London, 1937)
Browne, W. G., *Travels in Africa, Egypt, and Syria, from the Year 1792 to 1798* (London, 1799)
Bruce, J., *Travels to Discover the Source of the Nile* (2nd edn., Edinburgh, 1805)
Brugsch, É. and G. Maspero, *La trouvaille de Deir-el-Bahari* (Cairo, 1881)
Bruyère, B., *Mert Seger à Deir el-Médineh* (Cairo, 1930)
—*Rapport préliminaire sur les fouilles de Deir el Médineh (1931–1932)* (Cairo, 1934)
Bucaille, M., *Mummies of the Pharaohs* (New York, 1990)
Bucher, P., *Les Textes des Tombes de Thoutmosis III et d'Aménophis II* (Cairo, 1932)
Burton, H., 'The late Theodore M. Davis's excavations at Thebes in 1912–13' *BMMA* 11 (1916), pp. 13–18
—unpublished excavation journal, Valley of the Kings. See Jones, E. H.
—and E. Hornung, *The Tomb of Pharaoh Seti I/Das Grab Sethos' I.* (Zurich and Munich, 1991)
Burton, J., unpublished papers (Department of Manuscripts, British Library, London)
Capart, J., A. H. Gardiner and B. van de Walle, 'New light on the Ramesside tomb-robberies', *JEA* 22 (1936), pp. 169–93
Carnarvon, the Earl of, and H. Carter, *Five Years' Explorations at Thebes* (London, 1912)
Carré, J.-M., *Voyageurs et écrivains français en Égypte* (2nd edn., Cairo, 1956)
Carter, H., 'An ostracon depicting a red jungle-fowl (the earliest known drawing of the domestic cock)', *JEA* 9 (1923), pp. 1–4
—'Report of work done in Upper Egypt (1902–1903)', *ASAE* 4 (1903), pp. 171–80
—'Report of work done in Upper Egypt (1903–1904)', *ASAE* 6 (1906), pp. 112–29
—'Report on general work done in the southern inspectorate', *ASAE* 4 (1903), pp. 43–50
—'Report on the robbery of the tomb of Amenothes II, Biban el Moluk', *ASAE* 3 (1902), pp. 115–21
—'Report on the tomb of Zeser-ka-ra Amenhetep I, discovered by the Earl of Carnarvon in 1914', *JEA* 3 (1916), pp. 147–54
—'Report on tomb pit opened on the 26th January 1901, in the Valley of the Tombs of the Kings, between No. 4 and No. 28', *ASAE* 2 (1901), pp. 144–5
—'Report upon the tomb of Sen-nefer found at Biban el-Molouk near that of Thothmes III, No. 34', *ASAE* 2 (1901), pp. 196–200
—'A tomb prepared for Queen Hatshepsuit discovered by the Earl of Carnarvon (October 1916)', *ASAE* 16 (1916), pp. 179–82
—'A tomb prepared for Queen Hatshepsuit and other recent discoveries at Thebes', *JEA* 4 (1917), pp. 107–18
—*The Tomb of Tut.ankh.amen. Statement with Documents, as to the Events which occurred in Egypt in the Winter of 1923–24, leading to the ultimate break with the Egyptian Government* (London, 1924, 'For private circulation only')

—unpublished papers (inc. Department of Egyptian Antiquities, British Museum, London; Griffith Institute, Ashmolean Museum, Oxford; the Earl of Carnarvon, Highclere Castle, Hampshire)
—and A. H. Gardiner, 'The tomb of Ramesses IV and the Turin plan of a royal tomb', *JEA* 4 (1917), pp. 130–58
—and A. C. Mace, *The Tomb of Tut.ankh.Amen* (3 vols., London, 1923–33)
—and P. White, 'The tomb of the bird', *Pearson's Magazine* 56 (July–Dec., 1923), pp. 433–7
Černý, J., *A Community of Workmen at Thebes in the Ramesside Period* (Cairo, 1973)
—*Graffiti hiéroglyphiques et hiératiques de la nécropole thébaine* (Cairo, 1956)
—*Hieratic Inscriptions from the Tomb of Tut'ankhamun* (Oxford, 1965)
—*Late Ramesside Letters* (Brussels, 1939)
—*Ostraca hiératiques* (Cairo, 1930–35)
—'Papyrus Salt 124', *JEA* 15 (1929), pp. 243–58
—'Studies in the chronology of the Twenty-first dynasty', *JEA* 32 (1946), pp. 24–30
—*The Valley of the Kings. Fragments d'un manuscrit inachevé* (Cairo, 1973)
—and A. A. Sadek, *Graffiti de la montagne thébaine* (Cairo, 1969–74)
Champollion, J.-F., *Lettre à M. Dacier … relative à l'alphabet des hiéroglyphes phonétiques employés par les Égyptiens* (Paris, 1822)
—*Lettres écrites d'Égypte et de Nubie en 1828 et 1829* (Paris, 1833)
—*Monuments de l'Égypte et de la Nubie* (Paris, 1835–45); *Notices descriptives* (Paris, 1844)
—*Précis du Système hiéroglyphique des anciens Égyptiens* (Paris, 1824)
Chassinat, É., 'Appendix', *EEFAR* (1905–06), pp. 81–5
—'Un nom de roi nouveau?', *BIFAO* 10 (1912), pp. 165–7
Ciccarello, M., *The Graffito of Pinutem I in the Tomb of Ramesses XI* (San Francisco, 1979)
—*Five Late-Ramesside Lost-Contour Alabaster Ushebties in the Tomb of Ramesses XI* (San Francisco, 1979)
—and J. Romer, *A Preliminary Report of the Recent Work in the Tombs of Ramesses X and XI in the Valley of the Kings* (San Francisco, 1979)
Clair, C., *Strong Man Egyptologist* (London, n.d.)
Clarke, S., and R. Engelbach, *Ancient Egyptian Masonry* (Oxford, 1930)
Clayton, P., 'Royal bronze shawabti figures', *JEA* 58 (1972), pp. 167–75
—*The Rediscovery of Ancient Egypt* (London, 1982)
—'The tomb of sons of Ramesses II discovered?', *Minerva* 6/4 July–August, 1995), pp. 12–15
Cooke, N., 'Burton and KV5', *Minerva* 7/3 (May/June 1996), pp. 7–9
Currelly, C. T., *I Brought the Ages Home* (Toronto, 1956)
Curtis, G. H., 'Deterioration of the royal tombs', *Sun Kings*, pp. 129–33
—*The Geology of the Valley of the Kings, Thebes, Egypt* (San Francisco, 1979)
—and J. Rutherford, 'Expansive shale damage, Theban royal tombs, Egypt', *Proceedings 10th International Congress on Soil Mechanics and Foundation Engineering*, 3 (1981), pp. 71–4
Daressy, G., *Cercueils des cachettes royales* (Cairo, 1909)
—*Fouilles de la Vallée des Rois 1898–1899* (Cairo, 1902)
—*Ostraca* (Cairo, 1901)
—'Rapport sur le déblaiement des tombes 6 et 9 de Biban el Molouk', *ASAE* 18 (1919), pp. 270–74
—'Un plan égyptien d'une tombe royale', *RAs* (sér. 3) 32 (1898), pp. 235–40
D'Auria, S., P. Lacovara and C. H. Roehrig, *Mummies and Magic. The Funerary Arts of Ancient Egypt* (Boston, 1988)
Davis, T. M., *et al.*, *The Tombs of Harmhabi and Touatânkhamanou* (London, 1912)

—*The Tomb of Hâtshopsîtû* (London, 1906)
—*The Tomb of Iouiya and Touiyou* (London, 1907)
—*The Tomb of Siphtah; the Monkey Tomb and the Gold Tomb* (London, 1908)
—*The Tomb of Thoutmôsis IV* (London, 1904)
—*The Tomb of Queen Tîyi* (London, 1910; 2nd edn. [ed. (C.) N. Reeves], San Francisco, 1990. With extensive bibliography)
Dawson, W. R., 'The tombs of the kings at Thebes. A chapter from their ancient history', *AsR* (new ser.) 19 (1923), pp. 319–29
Dawson, W. R., E. P. Uphill and M. L. Bierbrier (eds.), *Who Was Who in Egyptology* (3rd edn., London, 1995)
Denon, V., *Travels in Upper and Lower Egypt* (London, 1803)
Der Manuelian, P., and C. E. Loeben, 'New light on the recarved sarcophagus of Hatshepsut and Thutmose I in the Museum of Fine Arts, Boston', *JEA* 80 (1994), pp. 121–55
Description de l'Égypte: ou recueil des observations et des recherches qui ont été faites en Égypte, pendant l'Expedition de l'Armée Français (Paris, 1809–28)
Dewachter, M., 'Contribution à l'histoire de la cachette royale de Deir el-Bahri', *BSFE* 74 (1975), pp. 19–32
Diodorus Siculus, *Library of History*
Dodson, A. M., 'Amenophis I and Deir el-Bahri', *JACF* 3 (1990), pp. 42–4
—'A canopic jar of Ramesses IV and the royal canopic equipment of the Ramesside period', *GM* 152 (1996), pp. 11–17
—'The canopic chest of Ramesses II', *RdE* 41 (1990), pp. 31–7
—*The Canopic Equipment of the Kings of Egypt* (London, 1994)
—'Death after death in the Valley of the Kings', in S. Orel (ed.), *Death and Taxes in the Ancient Near East* (Lewiston, 1992)
—'A fragment of canopic chest in Sir John Soane's Museum', *JEA* 71 (1985), pp. 177–9
—'Kings' Valley Tomb 55 and the fates of the Amarna kings', *AL* 3 (1994), pp. 92–103
—'A note on the interior decoration of the coffer of the sarcophagus of Ramesses III, Louvre D1=N337', *DE* 5 (1986), p. 35
—'Some additional notes on 'A fragment of canopic chest …', *DE* 4 (1986), pp. 27–8
—'Something old, something new, something borrowed, something … granite', *KMT* 4/3 (fall, 1993), pp. 58–69, 85
—'The sites of the tomb of the kings of the early Eighteenth dynasty', *ZÄS* 116 (1989), p. 181
—'The Takhats and some other royal ladies of the Ramesside period', *JEA* 73 (1987), pp. 224–9
—'The tomb of King Amenmesse. Some observations', *DE* 2 (1985), pp. 7–11
—'The tombs of the kings of the early Eighteenth dynasty at Thebes', *ZÄS* 115 (1988), pp. 110–23
—'A Twenty-first dynasty private reburial at Thebes', *JEA* 77 (1991), pp. 180–82
—'Visceral history', *KMT* 3/4 (winter, 1992–93), pp. 52–63
—'Was the sarcophagus of Ramesses III begun for Sethos II?', *JEA* 72 (1986), pp. 196–8
—and J. J. Janssen, 'A Theban tomb and its tenants', *JEA* 75 (1989), pp. 125–38
—and C. N. Reeves, 'A casket fragment of Ramesses IX in the Museum of Archaeology and Anthropology, Cambridge', *JEA* 74 (1988), pp. 223–6
Dunham, D., 'A fragment from the mummy wrappings of Tuthmosis III', *JEA* 17 (1931), pp. 209–10
Eaton-Krauss, M., 'The sarcophagus in the tomb of Tut'ankhamun', *After Tut'ankhamun*, pp. 85–90
Edgerton, 'The strikes in Ramses III's twenty-ninth year', *JNES* 10 (1951), 137–45
Edwards, A. B., 'The dispersion of antiquities, in connection with certain recent discoveries of ancient cemeteries in Upper-Egypt', *Vienna Weekly News* (9 Nov. 1886), p. 4–5

—'Lying in state in Cairo', *Harper's New Monthly Magazine* 65/386 (1882), pp. 185–204

—'The provincial and private collections of Egyptian antiquities in Great Britain', *RdT* 10 (1888), pp. 121–33

—'Relics from the tomb of the priest-kings at Dayr-el-Baharee', *RdT* 4 (1883), pp. 79–87

—*A Thousand Miles Up the Nile* (2nd edn., London, n.d.)

—*Pharaohs, Fellahs and Explorers* (New York, 1891)

Engelbach, R., *Introduction to Egyptian Archaeology* (Cairo, 1946)

—'Notes of inspection, April 1921', *ASAE* 21 (1921), pp. 188–96

Ertman, E. L., 'Evidence of the alterations to the canopic jar portraits and coffin mask from KV55', *Sun Kings*, pp. 108–19

—'A first report on the preliminary survey of unexcavated KV10', *KMT* 4/2 (summer, 1993), pp. 38–46

Esherick, J., *A Proposal for an Environmental Master Plan for the Valley of the Kings* (San Francisco, 1979)

Fagan, B., *The Rape of the Nile* (New York and London, 1975)

Faulkner, R. O., *The Ancient Egyptian Book of the Dead* (ed. C. A. R. Andrews, London, 1990)

—*The Ancient Egyptian Pyramid Texts* (Oxford, 1969)

Forbes, D. C., 'Cache DB320', 'Cache KV35', *KMT* 3/4 (winter, 1992–93), pp. 22–33, 86

—'Finding Pharaoh's in-laws', *AL* 1 (1991), pp. 5–25

—'Mummy musical chairs', *KMT* 3/4 (winter, 1992–93), pp. 51, 82–3, 87

—'Ritual figures in KV62. Prototypes and correspondences', *AL* 3 (1994), pp. 110–27

Fornari, A., and M. Tosi, *Nella sede della verita* (Milan, 1987)

Frankfort, H., *The Cenotaph of Seti I at Abydos* (London, 1933)

Gabolde, L., 'La chronologie du règne de Thoutmosis II, ses conséquences sur la datation des momies royales et leurs répercussions sur l'histoire du dévelopement de la Vallée des rois', *SAK* 14 (1987), pp. 61–81

—'La montagne thébaine garde encore des secrets', *Dossiers d'archéologie* 149–50 (mai–juin, 1990), pp. 56–9

Gaillard, C., and G. Daressy, *La faune momifiée de l'antique Égypte* (Cairo, 1905)

Gardiner, A. H., *Ramesside Administrative Documents* (London, 1948)

—'The so-called tomb of Queen Tiye', *JEA* 43 (1957), pp. 10–25

—'The tomb of Queen Twosre', *JEA* 40 (1954), pp. 40–44

Germer, R., 'Die angebliche Mumie der Teje', *SAK* 11 (1984), pp. 85–90

Goodman, D., 'Mapping the Valley of the Kings', *Professional Surveyor* (Sept.–Oct., 1988), pp. 6–8

Grapow, H., 'Studien zu den thebanischen Königsgräbern', *ZÄS* 72 (1936), pp. 12–39

Grimal, N., *A History of Ancient Egypt* (tr. I. Shaw, Oxford, 1992)

Greene, H. C., 'A great discovery in Egypt. The tomb of the parents of Tii', *Century Illustrated Monthly Magazine* (Nov., 1905), pp. 60–76

Greener, L., *The Discovery of Egypt* (London, 1966)

Guilmant, F., *Le tombeau de Ramsès IX* (Cairo, 1907)

Halls, J. J., *The Life and Correspondence of Henry Salt, Esq. FRS &c* (London, 1834)

Hamilton, W. R., *Remarks on Several Parts of Turkey*, I. *Ægyptiaca* (London, 1809)

Harlé, D., and J. Lefebvre (eds.), *Sur le Nil avec Champollion. Lettres, journaux et dessins inédits de Nestor L'Hôte* (Orléans-Caen, 1993)

Harris, J. E., 'Who's who in room 52?', *KMT* 1/2 (summer, 1990), 38–42

—and K. R. Weeks, *X-Raying the Pharaohs* (New York, 1973)

—and E. F. Wente *et al.*, 'Mummy of the "Elder Lady"

in the tomb of Amenhotep II: Egyptian Museum Catalog Number 61070', *Science* 200 (9 June 1978), pp. 1149–51

—and E. F. Wente, *An X-Ray Atlas of the Royal Mummies* (Chicago, 1980)

Harris, J. R., 'Akhenaten and Neferneferuaten in the tomb of Tut'ankhamun', *After Tut'ankhamun*, pp. 55–72

Hassan, F. H., review of J. and E. Romer, *The Rape of Tutankhamun*, *Antiquity* 68/260 (1994), pp. 663–4

Hay, R., unpublished papers (Department of Manuscripts, British Library, London)

Hayes, W. C., *Royal Sarcophagi of the XVIII Dynasty* (Princeton, 1935)

—*The Scepter of Egypt*, II (New York, 1959)

Hegazy, el-S. A., 'Le livre des portes', *Dossiers d'archéologie* 149–150 (mai–juin, 1990), p. 53

—'Rescuing the New Kingdom royal tombs', *KMT* 4/2 (summer, 1993), pp. 58–63

Helck, W., and E. Otto (ed.), *Lexikon der Ägyptologie* (Wiesbaden, 1975–92)

Henniker, F., *Notes During a Visit to Egypt, Nubia, the Oasis, Mount Sinai and Jerusalem* (London, 1823)

Hölscher, U., *The Excavation of Medinet Habu*, V. *Post-Ramessid Remains* (Chicago, 1954)

Hornung, E., *Der ägyptische Mythos von der Himmelskuh. Eine Ätiologie des Unvollkommenen* (Freibourg and Göttingen, 1982)

—*Ägyptische Unterweltsbücher* (2nd edn., Zurich and Munich, 1984)

—'Ein aenigmatische Wand im Grabe Ramses' IX', *Form und Mass (Festschrift G. Fecht)* (Wiesbaden, 1987), pp. 226–37

—*Das Amduat. Die Schrift des verborgenen Raumes* (Wiesbaden, 1963–67)

—'Auf den Spuren der Sonne. Gang durch ein ägyptisches Königsgrab', *Eranos Jahrbuch* 50 (1981), pp. 431–75

—'Zur Bedeutung der ägyptischen Dekangestirne', *GM* 17 (1975), pp. 35–7

—*Das Buch der Anbetung des Re im Westen (Sonnenlitanei)* (Geneva, 1974–76)

—*Conceptions of God in Ancient Egypt. The One and the Many* (tr. J. Baines, Ithaca, 1982)

—*Das Grab des Haremhab im Tal der Könige* (Bern, 1971)

—'Das Grab Thutmosis' II', *RdE* 27 (1975), pp. 125–31

—'Zum Grab Ramses' VII.', *SAK* 11 (1984), pp. 419–24

—'Zum Grab Sethos' I. in seinem ursprünglichen Zustand', *After Tut'ankhamun*, pp. 91–8

—*Die Nachfahrt der Sonne. Eine altägyptische Beschreibung des Jenseits* (Zurich and Munich, 1991)

—'Zu den Schlussszenen der Unterweltsbücher', *MDAIK* 37 (1981), pp. 217–26

—*Sethos – ein Pharaonengrab* (Basel, 1991)

—'Struktur und Entwicklung der Gräber im Tal der Konige', *ZÄS* 105 (1978), pp. 59–66

—'Studies on the decoration of the tomb of Seti I', *Sun Kings*, pp. 70–73

—*Das Totenbuch der Ägypter* (Zurich and Munich, 1979)

—'La Vallée des rois', *Dossiers d'archéologie* 149–150 (mai–juin, 1990), pp. 44–52

—The Valley of the Kings. Horizon of Eternity (New York, 1990)

—*Zwei ramessidische Königsgräber: Ramses IV. und Ramses VII.* (Mainz, 1990)

—and A. Brodbeck and A. Staehelin, *Das Buch von den Pforten des Jenseits* (Geneva, 1979–80)

Hoskins, G. A., *A Visit to the Great Oasis of the Libyan Desert* (London, 1837)

—*Travels in Ethiopia above the Second Cataract of the Nile* (London, 1835)

L'Hôte, N., *Lettres écrites d'Égypte en 1838 et 1839* (Paris, 1840)

Hoving, T. *Tutankhamun. The Untold Story* (New York, 1978)

Ikram, S., and D. Forbes, 'KV5. Retrospects and prospects', *KMT* 7/1 (spring, 1996), pp. 38–51

Jacq, C., *La Vallée des Rois* (Paris, 1992)

James, T. G. H., *Howard Carter. The Path to Tutankhamun* (London, 1992)

Jansen-Winkeln, K., 'Das Ende des Neuen Reiches', *ZÄS* 119 (1992), pp. 22–37

—'Die Plünderung der Königsgräber des Neuen Reiches', *ZÄS* 122 (1995), pp. 62–78

—'Die Schreiber Butehamun', *GM* 139 (1994), pp. 35–40

Janssen, J. J., *Commodity Prices from the Ramesid Period* (Leiden, 1975)

Johnson, G. B., '"No one seeing, no one hearing". KV proto-tombs 38 and 20', *KMT* 3/4 (winter, 1992–93), pp. 64–81

—'Tomb 55 today', *AL* 2 (1992), pp. 70–75

Jollois, P., *Journal d'un Ingénieur attaché à l'Expedition d'Égypte* (Paris, 1904)

[Jones, E. H.] *'A Son to Luxor's Sand'* (Carmarthen, 1986)

—unpublished excavation journal, Valley of the Kings (continued by H. Burton) (Department of Egyptian Art, Metropolitan Museum of Art, New York)

—unpublished correspondence (National Library of Wales, Aberystwyth)

de Jong, W. J., 'Het graf van Koning Ramses I', *De Ibis* 9 (1984), pp. 34–76

—*Journal d'Entrée*, unpublished accessions register, Cairo Museum

Keller, C., 'How many draughtsmen named Amenhotep? A study of some Deir el-Medina painters', *JARCE* 21 (1984), pp. 119–29

—'Two painters of the tomb of Ramesses IV', *NARCE* 99/100 (winter/spring, 1977), p. 16

el-Khouli, A. A. R. H., R. Holthoer, C. A. Hope and O. E. Kaper, *Stone Vessels, Pottery and Sealings from the Tomb of Tut'ankhamun* (Oxford, 1993)

Kitchen, K. A., *Ramesside Inscriptions, Historical and Biographical* (Oxford, 1975–)

—*The Third Intermediate Period in Egypt (1100–650 BC)* (2nd rev. edn., Warminster, 1996)

Kondo, J., 'Hieratic inscriptions from the tomb of Amenophis III', *Orient* 26 (1990), pp. 94–104

—'A preliminary report on the re-clearance of the tomb of Amenophis III (WV22)', *After Tut'ankhamun*, pp. 41–54

—'The re-clearance of tombs WV22 and WV A in the western Valley of the Kings', *Sun Kings*, pp. 25–33

Larson, J. A., 'Theodore M. Davis and the so-called tomb of Queen Tiye', *KMT* 1/2 (spring, 1990), pp. 48–53, 60–61; *KMT* 1/3 (summer, 1990), pp. 43–6

Leblanc, C., *Ta set neferou. Une nécropole de Thèbes-ouest et son histoire*, I (Cairo, 1989)

Leclant, J. (and G. Clerc), 'Fouilles et travaux en Égypte et au Soudan', *Or* (annually)

Leek, F. F., *The Human Remains from the Tomb of Tut'ankhamun* (Oxford, 1972)

Lefébure, E., 'Le puits de Deir el Bahari', *AMG* 4 (1882), pp. 1–17

—*Les Hypogées royaux de Thèbes* (Paris, 1886–89)

Legh, T., *Narrative of a Journey in Egypt and the Country Beyond the Cataracts* (London, 1816)

Lemonick, M. D., 'Secrets of the lost tomb', *Time* (29 May 1995), pp. 48–54

Lepsius, C. R. (ed.), *Auswahl der wichtigsten Urkunden ägyptischen Altertums* (Leipzig, 1842)

—*Denkmaeler aus Aegypten und Aethiopien* (Berlin, 1849–59); *Text* (ed. E. Naville) (Leipzig, 1897–1913)

—*Letters from Egypt, Ethiopia, and the Peninsula of Sinai* (London, 1853)

Lesko, L. H. (ed.), *Pharaoh's Workers. The Villagers of Deir el Medina* (Ithaca, 1994)

Lichtheim, M., *Ancient Egyptian Literature*, II (Berkeley, 1978)

Lilyquist, C., *Egyptian Stone Vessels, Khian through Tuthmosis IV* (New York, 1995)

—'Some dynasty 18 canopic jars from royal burials in the Cairo Museum', *JARCE* 30 (1993), pp. 111–16

Littauer, M., and J. H. Crouwel, *Chariots and Related Equipment from the Tomb of Tut'ankhamun* (Oxford, 1985)

Loret, V., 'Le tombeau d'Aménophis II et la cachette royale de Biban el-Molouk', *BIÉ* (3 sér.) 9 (1899), pp. 98–112

—'Le tombeau de Thoutmès III à Biban el-Molouk', *BIÉ* (3 sér.) 9 (1899), pp. 91–7

Lucas, A., *Ancient Egyptian Materials and Industries* (4th edn., rev. and enl. by J. R. Harris, London, 1964)

—'Note on the temperature and humidity of several tombs in the Valley of the Kings', *ASAE* 24 (1924), pp. 12–14

McLeod, W., *Composite Bows from the Tomb of Tut'ankhamun* (Oxford, 1970)

—*Self Bows and Other Archery Tackle from the Tomb of Tut'ankhamun* (Oxford, 1982)

Manley, B., 'Tomb 39 and the Sacred Land', *JACF* 2 (1989), pp. 41–57

Marciniak, M., 'Deux campagnes épigraphiques au tombeau de Ramsès III dans la Vallée des Rois (no. 11)', *ET* 12 (1983), pp. 295–305

Mariette, A., *Itinéraire de la Haute-Égypte* (3rd edn., Paris, 1880)

—*Monuments divers recueillis en Égypte et en Nubie* (Paris, 1872)

Martin, G. T., *The Royal Tomb at El-'Amarna* (London, 1974–89)

Maspero, G., *Ancient Sites and Modern Scenes* (London, 1910)

—*Guide to the Cairo Museum* (4th edn., Cairo, 1908)

—*Guide du visiteur au Musée du Caire* (4th edn., Cairo, 1915)

—'Les hypogées royaux de Thèbes', *RHR* 17 (1888), pp. 251–310; 18 (1889), pp. 1–67

—*Les momies royales de Déir el-Baharî* (Cairo, 1889)

—*New Light on Ancient Egypt* (London, 1908)

—unpublished correspondence with Amelia B. Edwards (Somerville College, Oxford)

Mayes, Stanley, *The Great Belzoni* (London, 1959)

Maystre, C., 'Le tombeau de Ramsès II', *BIFAO* 38 (1939), pp. 183–90

Monaghan, M., *Surficial Geology of the Valley of the Kings, Luxor, Egypt* (San Francisco, 1979)

Montet, P., *La necropole royale de Tanis*, I. *Les constructions et le tombeau de Psousennès à Tanis* (Paris, 1951)

de Morgan, J., 'Compte rendu des travaux archéologiques effectués par le Service des Antiquités de l'Égypte et par les savants étrangers pendant les années 1894–1895', *BIÉ* (3 sér.) 6 (1895), pp. 107–54

Murray, H., and M. Nuttall, *A Handlist to Howard Carter's Catalogue of Objects in the Tomb of Tut'ankhamun* (Oxford, 1963)

Nagel, G., 'Le linceul de Thoutmès III', *ASAE* 49 (1949), pp. 317–35

Naville, É., *The Funeral Papyrus of Iouiya* (London, 1908)

Neugebauer, O., and R. A. Parker, *Egyptian Astronomical Texts* (Providence and London, 1960–69)

Newberry, P. E., 'Discovery of the tomb of Thothmes IV at Bibân el-Mulûk', *PSBA* 25 (1903), pp. 111–12

—'Topographical notes on western Thebes collected in 1830, by Joseph Bonomi', *ASAE* 7 (1906), pp. 78–86

Nims, C., and W. Swaan, *Thebes of the Pharaohs* (London, 1965)

Niwinski, A., 'The Bab el-Gusus tomb and the royal cache in Deir el-Bahri', *JEA* 70 (1984), pp. 73–81

—'Butehamon – Schreiber der Nekropolis', *SAK* 11 (1984), pp. 135–56

Peck, W. H., and J. G. Ross, *Egyptian Drawings* (London, 1978)

Peet, T. E., *The Great Tomb-Robberies of the Twentieth Egyptian Dynasty* (Oxford, 1930)

—*The Mayer Papyri A and B* (London, 1920)

Perepelkin, G., *The Secret of the Gold Coffin* (Moscow, 1978)

Petrie, W. M. F., *A History of Egypt*, II (7th edn., London, 1924); III (London, 1905)

—*Seventy Years in Archaeology* (London, 1933)

—'Forty-five years ago', *Studies Presented to F. Ll. Griffith* (London, 1932), pp. 477–9

Piankoff, A., *Les chapelles de Tout-Ankh-Amon* (Cairo, 1951)

—*La Création du disque solaire* (Cairo, 1953)

—'Les différents "livres" dans les tombes royales du Nouvel Empire', *ASAE* 40 (1940), pp. 283–9

—'Les grandes compositions religieuses du Nouvel Empire et la reforme d'Amarna', *BIFAO* 62 (1964), pp. 207–18

—*The Litany of Re* (New York, 1964)

—*Le livre du jour et de la nuit* (Cairo, 1942)

—*Le Livre des portes* (Cairo, 1939–62)

—*Le Livre des quererts* (Cairo, 1946)

—'Les peintures dans le tombe du roi Aï', *MDAIK* 16 (1958), pp. 247–51

—'La tombe no. 1 (Ramsès VII)', *ASAE* 55 (1958), pp. 145–56

—'La tombe de Ramsès Ier', *BIFAO* 56 (1957), pp. 189–200

—'Les tombeaux de la Vallée des rois avant et après l'hérésie amarnienne', *BSFE* 28–9 (1959), pp. 7–14

—and E. Hornung, 'Das Grab Amenophis' III. im Westtal der Könige', *MDAIK* 17 (1961), pp. 111–27

—and N. Rambova, *The Shrines of Tut-Ankh-Amon* (New York, 1955)

—and N. Rambova, *The Tomb of Ramesses VI* (New York, 1954)

Pococke, R., *A Description of the East, and some other Countries* (London, 1743–45)

Polz, D., 'Bericht über die 4. und 5. Grabungskampagne in der Nekropole von Dra' Abu-el-Naga/Theben-West', *MDAIK* 51 (1995), pp. 207–25

—'The location of the tomb of Amenhotep I. A reconsideration', *Sun Kings*, pp. 8–21

Porter, B., and R. Moss (ed.), *Topographical Bibliography of Ancient Egyptian Hieroglyphic Texts, Reliefs, and Paintings*, I, part 2. *Royal Tombs and smaller cemeteries* (2nd edn., Oxford, 1964); II. *Theban Temples* (2nd edn., Oxford, 1972)

Preston, D., 'All the king's sons', *The New Yorker* (22 January, 1996), pp. 44–59

Quibell, J. E., *The Tomb of Yuaa and Thuiu* (Cairo, 1908)

—'Report on work done in Upper Egypt during the winter 1904–1905', *ASAE* 7 (1906), pp. 8–10

—*EEFAR 1904–1905*, pp. 24–7

Rapports sur la Marche du Service des Antiquités de 1899–1910 (Cairo, 1912), with supplements

Reeves, C. N., 'Akhenaten after all?', *GM* 54 (1982), pp. 61–71

—*Ancient Egypt at Highclere Castle* (Highclere, 1989)

—*The Complete Tutankhamun* (London, 1990). With extensive bibliography.

—'The discovery and clearance of KV 58', *GM* 53 (1982), pp. 33–45

—'[Egyptian varia in the reserve collections of the British Museum]', *VDI* 3 (1991), pp. 220–38 (in Russian)

—'Excavations in the Valley of the Kings, 1905/6: a photographic record', *MDAIK* 40 (1984), pp. 227–35

—'A fragment from the canopic jar of an Amarna queen', *RdE* 45 (1994), pp. 194–6

—'Observations on a model royal sarcophagus in the British Museum', *RdE* 45 (1994), pp. 197–201

—'On the miniature mask from the Tut'ankhamun embalming cache', *BSEG* 8 (1983), pp. 81–3

—'A reappraisal of Tomb 55 in the Valley of the Kings', *JEA* 67 (1981), pp. 48–55

—'A state chariot from the tomb of Ay?', *GM* 46 (1981), pp. 11–19

—'The tomb of Tuthmosis IV: two questionable attributions', *GM* 44 (1981), pp. 49–55

—'Tut'ankhamun and his papyri', *GM* 88, pp. 39–45

—'Two architectural drawings from the Valley of the Kings', *CdE* 61/121 (1986), pp. 43–9

—Valley of the Kings. The Decline of a Royal Necropolis (London, 1990)

—['The Valley of the Kings'], S. Yoshimura (ed.), [The British Museum], II (Tokyo, 1990), pp. 169–70 (in Japanese)

—and J. H. Taylor, *Howard Carter Before Tutankhamun* (London, 1992)

Rhind, A. H., *Thebes: its Tombs and their Tenants* (London, 1862)

Richardson, R. *Travels along the Mediterranean and parts adjacent, in company with the Earl of Belmore, during the years 1816, 1817 and 1818* (London, 1822)

Robins, G., 'Anomalous proportions in the tomb of Haremhab (KV57)', *GM* 65 (1983), pp. 91–6

—'The canon of proportions in the tomb of Ramesses I (KV16)', *GM* 68 (1983), pp. 85–90

—'The value of the estimated ages of the royal mummies at death as historical evidence', *GM* 45 (1981), pp. 63–8

Roehrig, C., 'Gates to the underworld. The appearance of wooden doors in the royal tombs in the Valley of the Kings', *Sun Kings*, pp. 82–107

—review of C. N. Reeves, *Valley of the Kings. The Decline of a Royal Necropolis* (London, 1990), in *JARCE* 29 (1992), pp. 208–09

Romer, J., *Ancient Lives. The Story of the Pharaohs' Tombmakers* (London, 1984)

—*The Brooklyn Museum Theban Expedition. Theban Royal Tomb Project* (San Francisco, 1979)

—*A History of Floods in the Valley of the Kings* (San Francisco, 1979)

—'In the steps of Tutankhamun', *The Sunday Times Magazine* (8 June 1980), pp. 36–47

—'Royal tombs of the early Eighteenth Dynasty', *MDAIK* 32 (1976), pp. 191–206

—'The tomb of Tuthmosis III', *MDAIK* 31 (1975), pp. 315–51

—'Tuthmosis I and the Bibân el-Molûk. Some problems of attribution', *JEA* 60 (1974), pp. 119–33

—Valley of the Kings (London, 1981)

—'The Theban Royal Tomb Project', *NARCE* 109 (summer, 1979), pp. 6–7

—and E. Romer, *The Rape of Tutankhamun* (London, 1993)

—and J. Rutherford and Chekene, *Damage in the Royal Tombs in the Valley of the Kings* (San Francisco, 1977)

Rose, J., 'Excavation of an unidentified tomb in the Valley of the Kings', *AMES Quarterly Journal of the Ancient Middle East Society* 2/1 no. 11 (Dec., 1989), pp. 14–21

—'An interim report on work in KV39, September–October 1989', *After Tut'ankhamun*, pp. 28–40

Rosellini, I., *I Monumenti dell'Egitto e della Nubia* (Pisa, 1832–44)

Rutherford, J., 'KV7, tomb of Rameses II – why save it?', *KMT* 1/3 (fall, 1990), pp. 46–51

—and D. P. Ryan, 'Tentative tomb protection priorities, Valley of the Kings, Egypt', *Sun Kings*, pp. 134–56

Ryan, D. P., 'Exploring the Valley of the Kings', *Archaeology* 47/1 (spring, 1994), pp. 52–9

—'Further observations concerning the Valley of the Kings', *Sun Kings*, pp. 157–61

—'The Pacific Lutheran University Valley of the Kings project. A synopsis of the first (1989) season', *NARCE* 146 (1989), pp. 8–10

—'Return to Wadi Biban el Moluk. The 2nd (1990) season of the Valley of the Kings Project', *KMT* 2/1 (spring, 1991), pp. 26–31

—'Some observations concerning uninscribed tombs in the Valley of the Kings', *After Tut'ankhamun*, pp. 21–7

—'The Valley again', *KMT* 3/1 (spring, 1992), pp. 44–7, 69

—'Who is buried in KV60? A field report', *KMT* 1/1 (spring, 1990), pp. 34–9, 53–4, 58

—and D. H. Hansen, *A Study of Ancient Egyptian Cordage from the British Museum* (London, 1987)

Sadek, A. A. F., 'La tombe de Sêthi Ier', *Dossiers d'archéologie* 149–50 (mai–juin, 1990), pp. 60–63

—'Varia graffitica', *SAK* 6 (1990), pp. 109–20

Schaden, O. J., 'Amenmesse project report', *NARCE* 163 (1993), pp. 1–9

—'Clearance of the tomb of king Ay (WV-23)', *JARCE* 21 (1984), pp. 39–64

—*KV10 at a Glance* 1 (1992–)

—'Preliminary report on clearance of WV24 in an effort to determine its relationship to royal tombs 23 and 25', *KMT* 2/3 (fall, 1991), pp. 53–61

—'Preliminary report on the re-clearance of Tomb 25 in the Western Valley of the Kings (WV-25)', *ASAE* 63 (1979), pp. 161–8

Schmitz, F.-J., *Amenophis I.* (Hildesheim, 1978)

Schott, S., *Die Schrift der verborgenen Kammer in Königsgräbern der 18. Dynastie* (Göttingen, 1958)

—*Zum Weltbild der Jenseitsführer des neuen Reiches* (Göttingen, 1965)

Schweinfurth, G., 'Die neuesten Entdeckungen auf dem Gebiete der ägyptischen Ausgrabungen', *Sphinx* 2 (1898), pp. 14–57

—'Neue thebanische Gräberfunde', *Sphinx* 3 (1900), 103–07

Sethe, K., W. Helck, *Urkunden der 18. Dynastie (Urkunden des ägyptischen Altertums)* (Leipzig and Berlin, 1906–58)

Sicard, C., *Oeuvres* (ed. M. Martin, Cairo, 1982)

Smith, G. E., *The Royal Mummies* (Cairo, 1912)

—and W. R. Dawson, *Egyptian Mummies* (London, 1924)

Smith, J. L., *Tombs, Temples and Ancient Art* (Norman, 1956)

Smith, S. T., 'Intact tombs of the Seventeenth and Eighteenth Dynasties from Thebes and the New Kingdom burial system', *MDAIK* 48 (1992), pp. 193–231

Smith, W. S., *Ancient Egypt as Represented in the Museum of Fine Arts* (6th edn., Boston, 1961)

Spiegelberg, W., *Ägyptische und andere Graffiti (Inschriften und Zeichnungen) aus der thebanischen Nekropolis* (Heidelberg, 1921)

—'Zu dem Grabfunde des Tutenchamun', *OLZ* 28 (1925), cols. 140–44

Steindorff, G., 'Die Grabkammer des Tutanchamun', *ASAE* 38 (1938), pp. 641–67

—'Discovery of the tomb of Thutmosis I' *Biblia* 12 (1900), pp. 425–7

Strabo, *Geography*

Taylor, J. H., 'Aspects of the history of the Valley of the Kings in the Third Intermediate Period', *After Tut'ankhamun*, pp. 186–206

—*Egyptian Coffins* (Princes Risborough, 1989)

—*Unwrapping a Mummy* (London, 1995)

Thomas, E., 'Cairo ostracon J.72460', *Studies in Honor of George R. Hughes* (Chicago, 1976), pp. 209–16

—'The four niches and amuletic figures in Theban royal tombs', *JARCE* 3 (1964), pp. 71–8

—'The *k3y* of Queen Inhapy', *JARCE* 16 (1979), pp. 85–92

—'*p3 hr hnw/n hnw hni*, a designation of the Valley of the Kings', *JEA* 49 (1963), pp. 57–63

—The Royal Necropoleis of Thebes (Princeton, 1966)

—'The tomb of Queen Ahmose(?) Merytamen, Theban tomb 320 [*scil.* 358]', *Serapis* 6 (1980), pp. 171–81

—'The "well" in kings' tombs of Biban el-Molûk', *JEA* 64 (1978), pp. 80–83

Thompson, J., *Sir Gardner Wilkinson and his Circle* (Austin, 1992)

Tillett, S., *Egypt Itself. The Career of Robert Hay, Esquire of Linplum and Nunraw, 1799–1863* (London, 1984)

Trigger, B. G., B. J. Kemp, D. O'Connor and A. B. Lloyd, *Ancient Egypt. A Social History* (Cambridge, 1983)

Tyndale, W., *Below the Cataracts* (London, 1907)

Valbelle, D., *"Les ouvriers de la tombe". Deir el-Médineh à l'époque ramesside* (Cairo, 1985)

Vandersleyen, C., *L'Égypte et la vallée du Nil*, II. *De la fin de l'Ancien Empire à la fin du Nouvel Empire* (Paris, 1995)

—'Royal figures from Tut'ankhamun's tomb. Their historical usefulness', *After Tut'ankhamun*, pp. 73–90

—'Who was the first king in the Valley of the Kings?', *Sun Kings*, pp. 22–4

Vandier d'Abbadie, J. (ed.), *Nestor L'Hôte (1804–42)* (Leiden, 1963)

Ventura, R., 'The largest project for a royal tomb in the Valley of the Kings', *JEA* 74 (1988), pp. 137–56

—*Living in a City of the Dead* (Freiburg and Göttingen, 1986)

de Villiers du Terrage, É., *Journal et Souvenirs sur l'Expedition d'Égypte* (Paris, 1899)

Weeks, K. R., 'Clearing KV5', *Minerva* 6/6 (November–December, 1995), pp. 20–4

—'Protecting the Theban necropolis', *EA* 4 (1994), pp. 23–6

—'A Theban grid network', *MDAIK* 37 (1981), pp. 489–92

—'Theban Mapping Project. Anatomy of a concession', *KMT* 1/1 (spring, 1990), pp. 40–7, 60–3

—'The Theban Mapping Project and work in KV5', *After Tut'ankhamun*, pp. 99–121

—'Tomb KV5 Revealed', *EA* 7 (1995) pp. 26–7

—'The tomb of the sons of Ramesses II – an update', *Minerva* 6/5 (September–October, 1995), pp. 3–4

—'The work of the Theban Mapping Project and the protection of the Valley of the Kings', *Sun Kings*, pp. 122–28

Weigall, A., *The Glory of the Pharaohs* (London, 1936)

—*A Guide to the Antiquities of Upper Egypt from Abydos to the Sudan Frontier* (London, 1910)

—*The Life and Times of Akhnaton, Pharaoh of Egypt* (London, 1923)

—*The Treasury of Ancient Egypt* (Edinburgh and London, 1911)

—*Tutankhamen and Other Essays* (New York, 1924)

—'Miscellaneous notes', *ASAE* 11 (1911), pp. 170–76

—'A new discovery in Egypt. The recent uncovering of the tomb of Queen Thiy', *Century Illustrated Monthly Magazine* (Sept., 1907), pp. 727–38

—unpublished papers of A. Weigall (various sources)

Weinstein, J., *Foundation Deposits in Ancient Egypt* (Ann Arbor, 1973)

Wente, E. F., *Late Ramesside Letters* (Chicago, 1967)

—*Letters from Ancient Egypt* (Atlanta, 1990)

—'A prince's tomb in the Valley of the Kings', *JNES* 32 (1973), pp. 223–34

—and J. E. Harris, 'Royal mummies of the Eighteenth dynasty. A biologic and Egyptological approach', *After Tut'ankhamun*, pp. 2–20

Wilkinson, J. G., *Handbook for Travellers in Egypt* (London, 1847)

—*The Manners and Customs of the Ancient Egyptians* (London, 1837–41; new edn. [ed. S. Birch], London, 1878)

—*Topographical Survey of Thebes, Tâpé, Thaba, or Diospolis Magna* (6 large maps, London, 1830)

—*Topography of Thebes, and General View of Egypt* (London, 1835)

—unpublished papers (Bodleian Library, Oxford)

Wilkinson, R. H., 'The *other* Valley of the Kings. Exploring the western branch of the Theban royal necropolis', *KMT* 2/3 (fall, 1991), pp. 46–52

—'The Paths of Re. Symbolism in the royal tombs of Wadi Biban El Moluk', *KMT* 4/3 (fall, 1993), pp. 43–51

—*Symbol and Magic in Egyptian Art* (London and New York, 1994)

—'Symbolic orientation and alignment in New Kingdom royal tombs', *Sun Kings*, pp. 74–81

—'Symbolic location and alignment in New Kingdom royal tombs and their decoration', *JARCE* 31 (1994), pp. 79–86

Wilson, E. L., 'Finding Pharaoh', *Century Illustrated Monthly Magazine* 34/1(May, 1887), pp 3–10

Winlock, H. E., *Materials Used at the Embalming of King Tut-'ankh-Amun* (New York, 1941)

—'Notes on the reburial of Tuthmosis I', *JEA* 15 (1929), pp. 56–68

—'The tomb of Queen Inhapi', *JEA* 17 (1931), pp. 107–10

—*The Tomb of Queen Meryet-Amun at Thebes* (New York, 1932)

—'The tombs of the kings of the Seventeenth Dynasty at Thebes', *JEA* 10 (1924), pp. 217–77

—*The Treasure of Three Egyptian Princesses* (New York, 1948)

—and W. E. Crum, *The Monastery of Epiphanius at Thebes*, I (New York, 1926)

Winstone, H. V. F., *Howard Carter and the Discovery of the Tomb of Tutankhamun* (London, 1991)

Yoshimura, S. (ed.), *The Egyptian Culture Center, Waseda University. Research in Egypt 1966–1991* (Tokyo, 1991)

—and J. Kondo, Excavations at the tomb of Amenophis III, *EA* 7 (1995), pp. 17–18

Yoyotte, J., *et al.* (eds.), *Tanis, l'or des pharaons* (Paris, 1987)

Acknowledgments

For generously sharing the results of their ongoing work, often in advance of publication, the authors would like to thank those archaeologists currently working in the Valley of the Kings – in particular (in alphabetical order) Prof. Dr H. Altenmüller, Edwin and Lyla Brock, Ian Buckley, Prof. Dr Erik Hornung, Nozomu Kawai, Jiro Kondo, Dr Catharine Roehrig, Dr John Rose, John Rutherford, Dr Donald P. Ryan, Dr Otto J. Schaden, Dr Kent Weeks and Prof. Dr Sakuji Yoshimura. A special debt of gratitude is due to the Egyptian Culture Center, Waseda University, Tokyo, and the Department of Egyptian Antiquities, British Museum, London. The help and cooperation of our Egyptian colleagues is also gratefully acknowledged – Dr Mohammed A. Nur el-Din and the Permanent Committee of the Egyptian Supreme Council of Antiquities, Dr Mohammed el-Saghir, Chief Inspector of Upper Egypt, Sabry Abd el-Aziz Khater, Director of West Bank Antiquities, and Ibrahim Suleiman, Chief Inspector for the Valley of the Kings. For information, comments, observations and much advice, further thanks are due to Dr Morris L. Bierbrier, Peter Clayton, Dr Aidan Dodson, Dr Peter Lacovara, Dr Stephen Quirke, Dr John H. Taylor, Yumiko Ueno and Anna Wilkinson. In addition to the above, Michael Duigan, George Johnson, John Ross, Noelle Soren, Frank Teichmann and Peter Webb were especially helpful in providing illustrations. Without the gentle prodding, tact and extraordinary hard work of the editorial, design and production team at Thames and Hudson, the book would never have appeared at all.

The authors' division of labour was as follows: Nicholas Reeves was responsible for the Introduction; Section II, Agents of Discovery; the historical and archaeological components of Section III, Tombs of the Kings; Section IV, Decline of a Royal Necropolis; the historical and archaeological captions in Sections II, III, and IV; the bulk of the Sources of Quotations and of the Further Reading. Richard Wilkinson contributed Section I, Preparations for the Afterlife; the architectural and iconographic components of Section III, Tombs of the Kings; Visiting the Royal Valley; and the Index. The Epilogue was jointly written by Reeves and Wilkinson. In a number of cases the author with special knowledge of a particular area contributed sections of text for the other author's assigned sections, or helped in other ways.

Sources of Quotations

p. 8 'wonderful things' Carter and Mace, C *Tut.ankh.Amen*, I, p. 96. 'gold – everywhere ... of gold' Carter and Mace, *Tut.ankh.Amen*, I, p. 96. **p. 12** 'My birth ... the west' Litany of Re, after Hornung, *Valley*, p. 89. **p. 14** 'The writings ... Western Horizon' Romer *Valley of the Kings*, p. 166. **p. 16** 'Giving praise ... upon her' Hymn to Meretseger, Turin Stela 102 (=50058), after M. Lichtheim, *Ancient Egyptian Literature*, II, p. 108. **p. 20** 'The hills ... from them' Pococke, *Description*, I, p. 98. **p. 22** '[On that ... come up' ostracon Cairo Museum 25726 and British Museum 50722, after Černý, *Valley*, p. 16. **p. 23** 'One and ... cannot live ...' Romer *Ancient Lives*, p. 116. **p. 25** '[The tombs] ... in parts' Browne, *Travels*, p. 137; 'The architecture ... the dead' Hornung, *Valley*, p. 75. **p. 27** 'drawn in outline', 'engraved with chisels', Carter and Gardiner, *JEA* 4 (1917), p. 142. **p. 28** 'Fourth month ... the gang' ostracon Cairo Museum 25515, after Černý, *Valley*, p. 17. **p. 31** 'The vizier ... [Ramesses IV] ...' ostracon Deir el-Medina 45, after Černý, *Valley*, p. 17. **p. 32** 'Year 1 ... Userkheperre[meryamun]' Altenmüller, *SAK* 11 (1984), pp. 37–8. **p. 33** 'I perceived ... magnificent tomb' Belzoni, *Narrative*, p. 232. **p. 38** 'Hail to ... your mummy-form' Book of the Dead, spell 28, after Faulkner, *Book of the Dead*, pp. 116–17. **p. 44** 'My seat ... every day' Pyramid Texts, spell 698, after R. O. Faulkner, *Pyramid Texts*, p. 131, utterance 402; 'The falcon ... his place' ostracon Cairo 25515, after Černý, *Valley*, p. 15. **p. 48** 'It would ... so deeply' Weigall, *Treasury*, p. 234. **p. 50** 'I, Philastrios ... delightful day' Weigall, *Tutankhamen*, p. 67; 'It appears ... by Diodorus ...' J. G. Wilkinson, *Topography*, pp. 121–2; 'I beseech ... for good' Winlock and Crum, *Epiphanius*, I, p. 19; 'Apa Ammonios, the Martyr' Baedeker (1929), p. 303. **p. 51** 'I have ... to us' Weigall, *Tutankhamen*, p. 67. **p. 52** ''Tis whence ... is gotten ...' V. le Blanc, *Voyages fameux* (Paris, 1658), quoted by Greener, *Discovery*, p. 39; 'the place ... el Melouc' M. de Thévenot, *Receuil de voyages de M. Thevenot* (Paris, 1681), quoted by Greener, *Discovery*, p. 61; 'tunneled in ... astonishing depth', 'Halls, rooms, ...admirable effect ...' C. Sicard, *Lettre à Mgr. le Comte de Toulouse* (Paris, 1717), quoted by Greener, *Discovery*, p. 72. **p. 53** 'signs of ... entered into', Pococke, *Description*, I, p. 98; 'magnificent, stupendous sepulchres', 'a solitary place' Bruce, *Travels*, II, p. 34; 'in fresco, ... an instrument' Bruce, *Travels*, II, p. 36; 'his engraved ... from memory' Browne, *Travels*, II, p. 137; 'within the ... thirty years', 'in expectation ... finding treasure' Browne, *Travels*, p. 137. **p. 54** 'Curiosity and ... for learning' de Thévenot, *Receuil de voyages*, quoted by Greener, *Discovery*, p. 59; 'to seek ... obtain them' Colbert, chief minister to Louis XIV, quoted by Greener, *Discovery*, p. 61; 'by persons ... and adroit' B. de Maillet, *Description de l'Égypte* (Paris, 1735), quoted by Greener, *Discovery*, p. 66; You have ... military venture' Jollois, *Journal*, p. 3. **pp. 54–5** 'I had ... are violated' Denon, *Travels*, II, p. 195. **p. 55** 'How was ... and correctness' Denon, *Travels*, II, p. 197; 'I found ... and fatigue' Denon, *Travels*, II, p. 198. **p. 56** 'Nile-land was ... of Drovetti' R. F. Burton, *Cornhill Magazine* (July, 1880), quoted by Mayes *Belzoni*, p. 225; '... the history ... long *imbroglio*' Rhind, *Thebes*, p. 244; 'a line ... and antiquarians' Henniker, *Notes*, p. 139; '... it is ... sarcophagi unhurt ...' Hamilton, *Remarks*, pp. 154–5; '... there are ... further excavation' Legh, *Narrative*, p. 106; 'Nine or ... lower order' Belzoni, *Narrative*, p. 225. **p. 58** 'The results ... original position' Belzoni, *Narrative*, p. 224; 'females, and ... a little' Belzoni, *Narrative*, p. 228; 'The mechanical ... modern times' *The Times*, 30 April 1821, quoted by Mayes, *Belzoni*, p. 260; 'singular combination ... so striking' *The Times*, 30 April 1821, quoted by Mayes, *Belzoni*, p. 260; 'for the ... at Padua' *The Times*, 11 December 1824, quoted by Mayes, *Belzoni*, p. 287. **p. 59** 'of the ... of it' Belzoni, *Narrative*, p. 236; 'worthy of low shopkeeping' C. Redding, *Past Celebrities Whom I Have Known* (London, 1866), quoted by Mayes, *Belzoni*, p. 264; 'I did ... to be' Belzoni, *Narrative*, p. 231. **p. 60** 'speechless astonishment' Richardson, *Travels*, p. 308; 'Salt was ... on Belzoni ...' Mayes, *Belzoni*, p. 191; 'they turned ... mummy pits' Belzoni, *Narrative*, p. 250; 'It is ... now known' Belzoni, *Narrative*, p. 226; 'Britains farewell ... true Belzoni' Belzoni to John Murray, letter dated 2 September 1822, quoted by Mayes, *Belzoni*, p. 278.; 'Nothing vexes ... with his' Mayes, *Belzoni*, p. 290. **p. 61** 'Sir G. Wilkinson, ... of torches' Rhind, *Thebes*, p. 262; 'I have ... at it' Salt to W. Gell, quoted by H. R. Hall, *JEA* 2 (1915), p. 138. **p. 62** '... and I ... this valley' J. G. Wilkinson, *Handbook* , p. 374; 'owing to ... mephitic air' J. G. Wilkinson, *Topography*, p. 121; 'Mr Hay's ... that country' Hoskins, *Travels*, p. vii.. **p. 63** 'After drawing ... our mirth ...' Hoskins, *Visit*, p. 16. **p. 64** 'The turn ... were expected' Rhind, *Thebes*, pp. 265–6; '... two of ... his displeasure' Bonomi to J. Burton, letter dated 16 August 1829, quoted by Tillett, *Egypt*, p. 47. **p. 65** 'God! Hieroglyphs ... of them!' N. L'Hôte, quoted by Clayton, *Rediscovery*, p. 130. **p. 66** 'This Valley, ... immortalized him' L'Hôte, quoted by Greener, *Discovery*, p. 156; 'only a ... of Tutankhamon' Greener, *Discovery*, p. 156; 'Thebes, the ... be examined' Lepsius, *Letters*, pp. 246–67; 'a decorated ... the chamber' Rhind, *Thebes*, p. 261. **p. 67** '... it has ... been procured' Rhind, *Thebes*, p. vi; 'One after ... by interest' Rhind, *Thebes*, p. 143; '... having dug ... proper limits' Rhind, *Thebes*, p. 145; 'in and ... their place' Rhind, *Thebes*, p. 145; 'The number ... is twenty-five' Mariette, *Itinéraire*, p. 194. **p. 68** 'The interest ... so remote ...' Lefébure, *AMG* 4 (1992), p. 17; 'not physically ...for field-work' Dawson, Uphill and Bierbrier, *Who Was Who*, p. 243; 'In the ... the valley' Griffith, *EEFAR 1897–8*, pp. 16–17; 'but a ... twenty devils' Petrie, *Seventy Years*, p. 168. **p. 70** '... I have ... little obstinate' Maspero to É. Naville, letter dated 5 January 1900, quoted by Reeves and Taylor, *Carter*, p. 56; 'Amenôthes II ... old order ...' Maspero, *Egypt. Ancient Sites*, p. 115; '... always so ... dominant personality' Andrews, diary, 17 January 1902, quoted by Reeves and Taylor, *Carter*, p. 63. **p. 71** '... my agreement ... finder's property' Carter to Lady Amherst, letter dated 19 Dec. 1900, quoted by Reeves and Taylor, *Carter*, pp. 69–70; 'the scribe ... of voice', 'sandstone fragment', 'trial pieces' Carter, *ASAE* 4 (1903), p. 44. **p. 72** 'the pathways ... the season' Carter, *ASAE*, 4 (1903), p. 44; 'preserving ... special monument' Carter to Mrs Goff, letter dated 21 March 1902, quoted by Reeves and Taylor, *Carter*, p. 70; 'It being ... the valley' Carter, *ASAE* 4 (1903), p. 43; 'We entered ... over one' Andrews, diary, 13 January 1903, quoted Reeves and Taylor, *Carter*, p. 71. **p. 73** 'As we ... and forth ...' Breasted, *Pioneer*, p. 155; '... an eccentric, ... he liked ...' J. L. Smith, *Tombs, Temples*, p. 22; '[Davis] often ... Tuthmosis IV ...' Carter, autobiographical sketch, quoted by Reeves and Taylor, *Carter*, p. 71; 'carefully along ... gebel uninvestigated' Carter, *ASAE* 4 (1903), p. 45; 'a third ... of rubbish' Carter, *ASAE* 4 (1903), p. 45. **p. 74** 'This site ... dug out' Carter, *ASAE* 4 (1903), 46; In a ... of Mai-her-pri' Carter, *ASAE* 4 (1903), p. 47; 'fragments of ... Amenophis III' Carter, *ASAE* 4 (1903), p. 46; 'two much ... mumified geese' Carter, *ASAE* 4 (1903), p. 176. **pp. 74–5** 'A few ... of satisfaction' Carter, autobiographical sketch, quoted Reeves and Taylor, *Carter*, p. 73. **p. 75** 'It's really ... out again ...' Jones to his family, letter dated 6 November 1909, National Library of Wales, Aberystwyth; '... Theo said ...the workmen ...' Andrews, diary, 12 February 1904, quoted by Reeves and Taylor, *Carter*, p. 79. **p. 76** 'I have ... more harmonious!' Davis to Weigall, letter dated 20 June 1905, J. Hankey; 'Ayrton ... was ... fluent Chinese ...' J. L. Smith, *Tombs, Temples*, p. 105. **p. 77** 'policy of ... the valley' Davis, *Siphtah*, p. 1; 'I had ... complete clearance' Chassinat, *EEFAR 1905–6*, p. 83; 'difficulties resulting ... the terrain' Chassinat, *EEFAR 1905–6*, p. 83. **p. 78** 'Gold shone ... space [KV55]' Maspero, *New Light*, p. 292; 'in ... a ... the rock', 'several large ... dynasty type' Davis, *Tîyi*, p. 7; 'I am ... particular thing' A. H. Sayce to Weigall, letter dated 20 October 1907, Weigall MSS. **p. 79** 'going underground ... of gods ...' Jones to his family, letter dated 2 March 1908, National Library of Wales, Aberystwyth; 'The disturbing ... be brighter!' Davis to Weigall, 23 November 1908, letter, Weigall MSS; 'As Ayrton ... months' work' Jones to his family, letter dated 31 January 1908, letter, National Library of Wales, Aberystwyth; '... a dark-haired ... young man' J. L. Smith, *Tombs, Temples*, p. 62; 'Dec[embe]r 4th ... in rubbish' Jones, excavation journal, partially quoted by Reeves, *Valley*, p. 309; 'small piece ... gold foil' Jones, excavation journal, 29 November 1908, quoted by Reeves, *Valley*, p. 309; 'The pleasure ... work suffer' Jones to his family, letter dated 30 January 1910, National Library of Wales, Aberystwyth. **p. 80** '... latterly the ... so long' Jones to his family, letter dated 30 January 1910, National Library of Wales, Aberystwyth; 'Harold Jones ... the workmen' Andrews, diary, 11 December 1910; '... [a man] ... railroad ties' quoted by Hoving, *Tutankhamun*, pp. 115–6; 'test trenches ... another tomb' Carter MSS, quoted by Reeves, *Valley*, p. 320; 'I fear ... now exhausted' Davis, *Harmhabi*, p. 3. **p. 81** 'Carnarvon ... was ... with enthusiasm ...' J. L. Smith, *Tombs, Temples*, p. 80; 'We are ... something good' Carter to Carnarvon, letter dated 27 December 1920, now Department of Egyptian Antiquities, British Museum, quoted by Reeves and Taylor, *Carter*, p. 138. **p. 86** 'When we ... prosperous reigns ...' Dawson, *AsR* (new series) 19 (1923), pp. 320–1. **p. 88** 'The eternal ... these inspectors' P. Abbott 2, 2ff., Peet, *Great Tomb-Robberies*, pl. 1, cf. Reeves, *Valley*, p. 3. **p. 89** 'A good ... had expected' D. Rose, *AMES Quarterly. Journal of the Ancient Middle East Society* 2/1 no. 11 (December, 1989), p. 22; 'of at ... nine persons' J. Rose, personal communication through Ian Buckley; 'A calcite ... 18th dynasty' Rose, personal communication through Ian Buckley. **p. 90** 'I believe ... possible doubt' Carter to E. A. W. Budge, letter dated 11 March 1914, quoted by Reeves and Taylor, *Carter*, p. 121; 'bronze eye-brows ... Protective Well' Carter, *JEA* 3 (1916), p. 153. **p. 91** 'I supervised ... no-one hearing' K. Sethe, *Urkunden* IV (Leipzig, 1906), p. 57, 3–5; 'It was ... ever supervised' Carter, autobiographical sketch, quoted by Reeves and Taylor, *Carter*, p. 78; 'which extinguished the lights' J. G. Wilkinson, *Topography*, p. 121. **p. 93** 'some small ... inlay work', 'burnt pieces ... with bitumen' Davis, *Hâtshopsîtû*, p. 80. **p. 94** 'A king ... she shared' Carter and Mace, *Tut.ankh.Amen*, I, p. 82; 'It was ... and departed', Carter and Mace, *Tut.ankh.Amen*, I, p. 80; 'the hereditary ... Lands, Hatshepsut' Carter, *JEA* 4 (1917), p. 115; 'two broken ... by workmen' Carter, *JEA* 4 (1917), p. 115. **p. 96** '1st month ... of] Aakheperkare ...', 'Userhet; ... Iuf[?...]amun' Theban graffito no. 2061, cf. Reeves, *Valley*, p. 236, no. 31; 'No tomb ... Thutmose II' Thomas, *Necropoleis*, p. 75. **pp. 97–8** '... a fitting ... funerary monuments' Hayes, *Royal Sarcophagi*, p. 113; 'even the smallest' Loret, *BIE* (3 sér.), 9 (1898), p. 95; 'One may ... and practicality' Romer, *MDAIK* 31 (1975), p. 346. **p. 99** 'The [presence ... this discovery' Maspero, *Guide* (1908), p. 457; 'late dynastic ... Ptolemaic period' Smith, *Royal Mummies*, p. 116. **p. 100** '... a very important discovery' Carter and Mace, *Tut.ankh.Amen*, I, p. 72; 'between the ... right wall' Loret, *BIE* (3 sér.) 9 (1898), p. 100; 'vases of ... life [*ankh*]' Loret, *BIE* (3 sér.) 9 (1898), p. 103; 'the floor ... other articles' Maspero, *Guide* (1908), p. 457; 'three cadavers ... the door' Loret, *BIE* (3 sér.) 9 (1898), p. 106. **p. 102** 'On entering ... thrown them ...' Carter, *ASAE* 2 (1901), pp. 196–7. **p. 103** 'Absolute silence ... world tremble' Brodrick, *Egypt*, p. 64; 'sledges and coffins', 'some twenty ... earthen jars', some gold ... inlaid rosette' Carter, *ASAE* 2 (1901), p. 198; '3rd month

… the north' Theban graffito no. 714, cf. Jansen-Winkeln, *ZÄS* 122 (1995), p. 70. **p. 105** '… our eyes … Tuthmosis IV' Carter, autobiographical sketch, quoted by Reeves and Taylor, *Carter*, p. 73; 'evidence of … also mud', 'the jackal … nine prisoners', 'originally blocked … painted over' Carter MSS, quoted by Reeves, *Valley*, p. 34; 'practically clean … a boat' Davis, *Thoutmôsis IV*, p. ix; 'partially blocked … and sealed' Davis, *Thoutmôsis IV*, p. ix; 'covered with … with antiquities' Davis, *Thoutmôsis IV*, p. ix. **p. 107** 'Though plunderers … more valuable' A. Lansing, *BMMA* Part II (1931), p. 5. **p. 108** 'Year 8 … [i.e. Thebes]' cf. Reeves, *Valley*, p. 36; 'blue paste', 'yellow plaster' Davis, *Thoutmôsis IV*, CG 46236, 46487; '[Those who … and ingenious' Carter and Mace, *Tut.ankh.Amen*, I, p. 54; '… it is … the well' Weigall, *Guide*, p. 226. **p. 109** 'anciently sealed … mud plaster' Romer, *Valley*, p. 105; 'mummy remains' Lefébure, *Hypogées*, II, p. 187; 'evidence of … the ceiling' Ryan, *KMT* 2/1 (spring, 1991), p. 30; 'This architecturally … rectangular chamber' Ryan, *KMT* 2/1, p. 30; 'red characters … of pit' J. Burton, BL Add. MS 25642, 5 vs. **p. 110** 'It was … preceded us' de Villiers du Terrage, *Journal*, p. 194; 'In the … buried here' Carter and Mace, *Tut.ankh.Amen*, I, p. 79. **p. 112** 'Compared with … and Cairo', I. Shaw, *Daily Telegraph*, 18 June 1990; 'The condition … of restoration …' Kondo, *Daily Telegraph*, 18 June 1990. **p. 113** 'In one … hitherto unknown' Lepsius, *Letters*, p. 262 (25 Feb. 1845). **p. 115** 'Year 3 … day 7' Kondo, *Sun Kings*, p. 30; 'The entry … fragmentary artifacts' Ryan, *KMT* 1/1 (spring, 1990), p. 59; 'at the … forced through', 'a pretty … the centre', 'we found … well preserved …', 'fragments of … of alabaster …', 'with a … of water', 'on the … the staircase' Belzoni, *Narrative*, p. 228; 'a clean … into it' J. Burton, BL Add, MS 25642, 23; 'embalmed in … its side' Ryan, *Sun Kings*, p. 157. **p. 116** 'The following … immediately entered …' Belzoni, *Narrative*, p. 223. **p. 117** '… certainly royal … the wadi' Thomas, *Necropoleis*, p. 82; 'An athletic … Nestor Genakalis' Tyndale, *Below the Cataracts*, p. 192; 'a recess … the rock' Davis, *Tîyi*, p. 7. **p. 119** '… bits of … his handkerchief!' Currelly, *Ages*, p. 142. **p. 120** 'an estate … Amenhotep III', Lyla Brock, personal communication; 'Are you … some mistake' G. Elliot Smith to Weigall, letter, quoted by Weigall, *Glory*, p. 138. **p. 121** 'The body … could be' Weigall, *Akhnaton* (1923), p. 282. **p. 122** 'All next … my feelings!' Carter and White, *Pearson's Magazine* 56 (July–Dec., 1923), p. 437. **p. 124** 'the day of days' Carter and Mace, *Tut.ankh.Amen*, I, p. 94; 'At first … of gold' Carter and Mace, *Tut.ankh.Amen*, I, pp. 95–6. **p. 125** 'Plunderers had … than once' Carter and Mace, *Tut.ankh.Amen*, I, p. 93. **p. 126** 'Originally the … almost intact' Winlock, *Materials*, p. 17. **p. 128** '[WV23] contains … several ages' J. G. Wilkinson, *Topography*, p. 123; 'merely to … after rain' Belzoni, *Narrative*, p. 124; 'I cannot … of distinction' Belzoni, *Narrative*, p. 124. **p. 130** '…here, where … so gloriously!' Weigall, *Treasury*, p. 235; 'The party … elaborate inscriptions' Weigall, *Treasury*, pp. 229–30. **p. 131** 'The whole … Sety I' Ayrton, *PSBA* 30 (1908), p. 117. **p. 133** 'with the … foreign form' Davis, *Harmabi*, p. 100. **p. 134** 'Having proceeded … by east' Belzoni, *Narrative*, pp. 229–30. **p. 137** 'On the … my life' Belzoni, *Narrative*, pp. 230–1; 'a small aperture' Belzoni, *Narrative*, p. 232; 'double staircase with ramp' Berkeley Theban Mapping Project, *Prelim. Report 1979*, p. 19; 'to physically … and rebirth' Berkeley Theban Mapping Project, *Prelim. Report 1979*, p. 20; 'In beauty … at Abydos …' Baedeker, *Egypt* (1902), p. 271; 'On each … of composition' Belzoni, *Narrative*, pp. 235–6. **p. 138** 'a painting … or jar', 'a considerable … the tomb' J. Burton, British Library, Add. MS 25642, 3. **p. 140** 'I have … the sarcophagus …' Lepsius, *Letters*, p. 244 (24 Nov. 1844); 'Sat. 13th … great deal' H. Burton, excavation journal; '… the sarcophagus … the sarcophagus' H. Burton, excavation journal, 28 December 1913. **p. 142** '… cleared the … the door' H. Burton, excavation journal, 14 January 1914; 'a fragment … side, limestone' H. Burton, excavation journal, 18 Dec., 1913; 'of a … superlative workmanship' *EA* 8 (1996), p. 14. **p. 144** 'This is … enormous family' Kitchen, David Keys, personal communication; 'One of … my life' Weeks, British Museum lecture, 16 Jan., 1996; 'Last February … in Egypt …' Weeks, press release, 18 May 1995. **p. 145** '[The tomb … by tentacles' Weeks, quoted by Lemonick, *Time* (29 May 1995), p. 52. **p. 146** 'The objects … adult male' Weeks, *Minerva* 6/6 (November–December, 1995), p. 21; 'New Kingdom … debris itself' Weeks, *Minerva* 6/6 (November–December, 1995), p. 23; 'Now Userhat … great god …' after Edgerton, *JNES* 10 (1951), p. 141. **p. 148** 'placed side … carefully buried' Carter MSS, quoted by Reeves, *Valley*, p. 97. **p. 149** 'Contrary to … burial chamber' Brock, personal communication. **p. 152** '… the [chief] … his place' P. Turin cat. 1949 and 1946, after Černý, *Valley*, p. 15; 'It seems … red lines' J. Burton, BL Add. MS 25642, 6. **p. 153** 'stratum about … square feet' Davis, *Siphtah*, p. 32. **p. 155** 'Ayrton penetrated … its excavation' H. Burton, *BMMA* 11 (1916), p. 14. **p. 157** 'Found a … sarcophagus etc.' J. Burton, BL Add. MS 25642, 6 vo. **p. 159** 'Bones of … took it' J. Burton, BL Add. MS 25642, 9. **p. 160** 'I was … utmost attention …' Bruce, *Travels*, II, pp. 35–6. **p. 161** 'to found … His Majesty' ostracon Berlin P10063, after Wente, *JNES* 32 (1973), p. 224. **p. 162** '[Year 2 … [Ramesses IV] …' ostracon Deir el-Medina 45, 14–17, after Černý, *Valley*, p. 17; 'bodies', 'recesses' J. G. Wilkinson, *Topography*, p. 117; 'encrusted with … with colours', 'up towards … the north', 'debris of … Roman huts' Davis, *Siphtah*, p. 7; 'The first … great entrances …' Thomas, *Necropoleis*, p. 127. **p. 163** 'Upon the … earlier times' Weigall, *Guide*, pp. 197–8. **p. 164** 'I … found … with pitch …' J. Burton, BL Add. MS 25642, 14. **p. 166** 'Until the … since antiquity' Brock, in *Sun Kings*, p. 59; 'two low … of pylons …' Brock, personal communication. **p. 167** 'Other material … tomb robbers', Brock, personal communication;'The tomb … later date' Weigall, *Guide*, p. 196. **p. 168** 'several large … lying together' Davis, *Tîyi*, p. 7; 'The features … offer portraits …' J. G. Wilkinson, *Topography*, p. 116. **p. 170** 'On entering … stood here' Weigall, *Guide*, p. 216. **p. 171** 'The painted … Egyptian taste' Belzoni, *Narrative*, p. 227. **p. 172** 'Ramesses [XI]'s … other chambers?' Romer, *Sunday Times Magazine* (8 June, 1980), p. 38; 'broken pieces … Kingdom pharaohs', 'two fragments … Ramesses II' Ciccarello and Romer, *Preliminary Report*, p. 3. **p. 174** 'Squeezing their … and golden', Greene, quoted by Bacon, *Great Archaeologists*, p. 122; '… so remarkable … become black' Quibell, *EEFAR 1904–5*, p. 25; 'was closed … mud plaster' Davis, *Iouiya and Touiyou*, p. xxvi; 'plastered over … many places' Weigall MSS, quoted by Reeves, *Valley*, p. 148; 'Imagine entering … years ago' Weigall, *Treasury*, pp. 174–5. **p. 176** 'The woman … carved heads' J. L. Smith, *Tombs, Temples*, pp. 41–2; 'One of … the jar' Maspero, *New Light*, p. 247; 'Again Maspero's … over there …' J. L. Smith, *Tombs, Temples*, p. 33. **p. 177** 'a dark red substance' Quibell, *Yuaa and Thuiu*, CG 51106. **p. 178** 'Yuaa was … the round' Quibell, *EEFAR 1904–5*, pp. 25–6. **p. 179** '… on the … a negro' Engelbach, *Introduction*, p. 89. **p. 181** 'tired of … the other' Maspero, *Guide* (1915), p. 394. **p. 182** 'It seemed … Roman wares …' O. J. Schaden, *KMT* 2/3 (fall, 1991), p. 57; 'The tomb … the leftovers' Ryan, *KMT* 2/1 (spring, 1991), p. 30; 'fragments of … Theban necropolis' Ryan, *KMT* 2/1 (spring, 1991), p. 30. **p. 183** 'Their [the … and KV32]' Mayes, *Belzoni*, p. 189; 'It was … not known' Weigall, *Guide*, p. 219; 'probably a … fully explored' Steindorff, in Baedeker, *Egypt* (1902), p. 276; 'a small … of steps' Baedeker, *Egypt* (1902), p. 276. **p. 184** 'This Tomb-pit … of flowers' Carter, *ASAE* 2 (1901), p. 144; 'remains of … funereal furniture' Carter, *ASAE* 2 (1901), p. 144; 'Feb. 25th … rain water' Carter, *ASAE* 4 (1903), p. 46; 'a third … of rubbish', 'scattered remains of wreaths', 'it … impossible … mummy case', 'a small … heart scarab', 'on the … was found' Carter, *ASAE* 4 (1903), p. 46; 'human skeletal-material … forty-four figures' Ryan, *KMT* 3/1 (spring, 1992), p. 47; 'the shaft … the burial' Davis, *Siphtah*, p. 18; 'a man … and well-built', 'had been … one side', 'a rough wooden chair', 'bearing the … good praises"', 'some wooden … of pitch' Davis, *Siphtah*, pp. 18. **p. 185** 'without even … the rock' Davis, *Siphtah*, p. 18; 'The only … further door …' Davis, *Siphtah*, p. 16; 'a dry … white plaster' Romer, *Valley*, p. 208; 'The children … looked alive' J. L. Smith, *Tombs, Temples*, p. 49; 'with bits … mummy coffin' Davis, *Siphtah*, p. 17; 'The most … disc beads' J. L. Smith, *Tombs, Temples*, p. 49. **p. 186** '… next day … his tomb …' Jones to his family, letter dated 14 January 1909, National Library of Wales, Aberystwyth; 'A small … mummified geese' Carter, *ASAE* 4 (1903), p. 176. **p. 187** 'showed every … was found' Jones, excavation journal, 6 January 1910, quoted by Reeves, *Valley*, p. 171; 'potential corridor tomb' Thomas, *Necropoleis*, p. 149; 'unfinished pit … built around', 'workman's house' Jones, excavation journal, 4 February 1909, quoted by Reeves, *Valley*, p. 174. **p. 190** 'Sometimes when … the dead' Weigall, *Tutankhamen*, p. 134; 'Examination. The … will tell"' papyrus British Museum 10052, after Peet, *Great Tomb-Robberies*, pp. 147–8. **p. 191** 'We went … with them …' Papyrus Leopold II-Amherst, after Capart, Gardiner and vand de Walle, *JEA* 22 (1936), p. 171. **p. 192** 'The foreigner … each man] …' adapted from Peet, *Mayer Papyri*, p. 20. **p. 194** 'For the … became certainty …' Edwards, quoted in Bacon, *Great Archaeologists*, pp. 79–80; 'Soon we … own ancestors' Wilson, *Century Illustrated Monthly Magazine* 34/1 (May, 1887), pp. 6–7. **p. 195** 'five thousand … smaller objects' Edwards, quoted in Bacon, *Great Archaeologists*, p. 82. **p. 197** 'The highest … the air' Newberry, *ASAE* 7 (1906), p. 79; 'In this … loved him …' Bataille, *BIFAO* 38 (1939), p. 162. **p. 198** 'The mummies … almost complete' Griffith, *EEFAR 1897–98*, p. 18; 'a thick … left eye', 'shaved except … black hair', 'displayed something … same time' Loret, *BIE* (3 sér.) 9 (1898), pp. 103–4; 'The coffins … everywhere cartouches!' Loret, *BIE* (3 sér.) 9 (1898), pp. 108–9; 'We had … Deir el-Bahari' Loret, *BIE* (3 sér.) 9 (1898), p. 109. **p. 199** 'On the … the cranium' Smith, *Royal Mummies*, p. 68. **p. 202** 'The King's … she live!' Maspero, *Momies royales*, p. 539, cf. Reeves, *Valley*, p. 232; '… the docket … against it …' Winlock, *Meryet-Amun*, p. 58. **p. 203** 'Nebmaatre-Amenophis, life! prosperity! health!' Daressy, *Cercueils*, pl. 61, cf. Reeves, *Valley*, p. 232; 'Year 12 … [by?] … Wennufer(?)' Smith, *Royal Mummies*, pls 32, 100–3, translation after Wente in Thomas, *Necropoleis*, p. 250; 'Linen which … Year 6' Maspero, *Momies royales*, p. 555, cf. Reeves, *Valley*, p. 236. **pp. 204–5** '[To] the … it ready …' papyrus British Museum 10375 cf. Wente, *Late Ramesside Letters*, pp. 59–61 and Jansen-Winkeln, *ZÄS* 122 (1995), pp. 67–8. **p. 205** 'seeing the mountains', Theban graffiti nos. 48, 51, 1001, 1012, 1393, 3492, cf. Jansen-Winkeln, *ZÄS* 122 (1995), p. 70; 'Opener of … the necropolis', 'Opener of … underworld (Rosetjau)', Overseer of … of eternity' coffin Brussels E5288, cf. Jansen-Winkeln, *ZÄS* 122 (1995), p. 73. **p. 206** 'The book … the necropolis' Taylor, *After Tut'ankhamun*, p. 199. **p. 208** 'A new … Egypt itself' Weigall, *Tutankhamun*, p. 30. **p. 209** '… rest assured … to sell' Champollion to Bonomi, letter dated 2 July 1829, quoted by Mayes, *Belzoni*, p. 293. **p. 210** 'For three … in diameter' Carter, letter to his mother dated October 1918, quoted by James, *Howard Carter*.

Illustration Credits